THE BASQUE EXCEPTION

THE BASQUE EXCEPTION

THE HISTORY OF AN IDENTITY IN THE WESTERN PYRENEES

Asier H. Aguirresarobe

BLOOMSBURY ACADEMIC
LONDON • NEW YORK • OXFORD • NEW DELHI • SYDNEY

BLOOMSBURY ACADEMIC
Bloomsbury Publishing Plc, 50 Bedford Square, London, WC1B 3DP, UK
Bloomsbury Publishing Inc, 1359 Broadway, New York, NY 10018, USA
Bloomsbury Publishing Ireland, 29 Earlsfort Terrace, Dublin 2, D02 AY28, Ireland

BLOOMSBURY, BLOOMSBURY ACADEMIC and the Diana logo are trademarks of Bloomsbury Publishing Plc

Cover design by Megan Wilson
Cover image: Close up of Leaves of Red Oak © Nature Picture Library / Alamy

A catalogue record for this book is available from the British Library.

A catalog record for this book is available from the Library of Congress.

ISBN: HB: 978-1-3504-4616-8
PB: 978-1-3504-4617-5
ePDF: 978-1-3504-4618-2
eBook: 978-1-3504-4619-9

Typeset by Deanta Global Publishing Services, Chennai, India
Printed and bound in India

For product safety related questions contact productsafety@bloomsbury.com.

To my father,

who would have loved this book.

CONTENTS

List of Maps and Figures ix
Acknowledgments x
Preface xiii
Author's Note xx

Part I Vascones 1

1 A Little Wildness 3

2 *Vasconum gentilitas* 17

3 *Aracaeli* 29

4 The Vast Emptiness 35

Part II Lineage 51

5 *Princeps Christicola* 53

6 *Dar al-Harb* 69

7 *Rex Ibericus* 77

8 *Manum regis* 87

9 *Aitonen semeak* 97

10 Free and Exempt Forevermore 109

11 Those from Whom We Come 121

12 Worth More 133

13 Erasing Our Names from the Land 145

14 The White Lord 155

Part III Privilege 165

15 ***De Gloria et Nobilitate*** 181

16 Children of the Prophets 193

17 ***Euskal Herria*** 205

18 ***Irurac bat*** 229

19 The Tears of the *vascongados* 255

20 The Basque Jesus 279

Epilogue 305

Bibliography 311
Index 325

MAPS AND FIGURES

Maps

1 The Western Pyrenees: provinces and historical territories xii

Figures

1 Courtyard in The Assembly House in Guernica 167
2 Bronze sculpture of the God Helios from the Roman site of Oiasso, around second–third century AD 167
3 View of the shrine of Saint Michael in Excelsis (twelfth century) with the mountain range of Andia in the background 168
4 *Chronicles of St. Denis*, miniature by Jean Fouquet, Charlemagne discovering Knight Roland's remains at Ronceveaux, fifteenth century, France 168
5 Porta Speciosa from the Monastery of Leyre, eleventh century 169
6 Sculpture of Sancho III the Great on the exterior of the Palacio de Oriente, Madrid 170
7 Sancho IV Garcés, king of Pamplona (1054–76), being pushed into the void from the top of a ravine by his brother Ramón during a hunt in Peñalén 171
8 The tower of Mendoza in Alava, thirteenth century 172
9 View of the city of Mondragón (Guipuzcoa) 172
10 Iron ore mining by Darío de Regoyos y Valdés, *c.* 1900 173
11 Glasswork inside the Assembly House in Guernica 174
12 View of Potosi, engraving from an atlas, Bolivia, seventeenth century 175
13 Portrait of Jeanne d'Albret, queen of Navarre (1528–72), by François Clouet, *c.* 1570 176
14 A gathering of witches 177
15 Monument to the Count of Peñaflorida in Vitoria (Alava) 178
16 Monument to the *fueros* built in 1903 in Pamplona (Navarre) 179
17 Picture of Sabino Arana Goiri in the prison of Larrinaga (Biscay), *c.* 1902 180

ACKNOWLEDGMENTS

While writing this book I have incurred numerous debts of gratitude. First and foremost, I would like to thank my editors, and especially Gabriella Cox and Bella Baillie, who have proven understanding and helpful beyond my wildest dreams. I am also deeply grateful to the personnel from the Department of Contemporary History at the University of the Basque Country, my home institution, and to Santiago de Pablo, Antonio Rivera, and Susana Abad in particular for their unwavering support and supervision of my scholarly activities. Thanks also to my former thesis supervisor, Ludger Mees, for dozens of stimulating conversations and discussions on Basque identity, for his guidance during the hardest moments of this endeavor, and for his careful reading and correction of several sections of the text you now hold in your hands.

Secondly, I wish to extend my sincere gratitude to the Institute of History at Leiden University for receiving me with open arms. I am especially indebted to Professor Raymond Fagel, whose insights about the Early Modern Habsburg monarchy stand among the intellectual highlights of my time in the Netherlands. I am even more grateful to Professor Eric Storm, who, beyond being an illustrious scholar with an almost boundless knowledge of nationalism in all its manifestations, has devoted his valuable time to correcting this text and has shown remarkable patience with a Basque author whose ideas have at times been clearer than his means of expression. I would also like to extend my appreciation to Professor Jonathan Hearn from the University of Edinburgh, whose direction some years ago helped me to conceive the core ideas of this work, and to the Association for Studies on Ethnicity and Nationalism (ASEN) for organizing a summer school where I was reminded of the extent of what I have yet to learn about these subjects.

This book would have never seen the light of day if not for the support provided by the Basque Government's postdoctoral internship program, IKERMUGI, the grant PID2022-138385NB-I00 funded by MCIN/AEI/10.13039/501100011033, and by FEDER, UE, and the Research Group of the University of the Basque Country GIU 23/007.

On a more personal note, I would like to have some words for my mother, Arantxa, and my two brothers, Oscar and Robert. These have been testing years for us as a family, and I have often found solace in their presence and support. I am also profoundly thankful to the many friends whose companionship has sustained me through thick and thin. They are too numerous to name individually, but they know that each one of them has my sincere appreciation. I want to extend special thanks to my partner, Naroa, for her patience and understanding during both my bouts of enthusiasm and those in which I felt that none of this had any meaning at all. I love you, and I hope to have many future opportunities to express my gratitude in acknowledgments, albeit written—I hope—in less complicated times.

I want to take a moment also to remember my father, Manolo, who has recently passed away and from whom I learned more than I would be able to ever remember. The book you hold in your hands is, in large part, a consequence of his love for words.

And finally, I would like to thank you, the reader, for devoting your precious time to exploring the history of this obscure corner of Europe. I hope that you will find the ideas and stories contained in this book to be—if not entirely, then at least in part—worthy of your investment.

Eskerrik asko!

Map 1. The Western Pyrenees: provinces and historical territories.
Source: Asier H. Aguirresarobe

PREFACE

In the spring of 2004, a tree passed away.

The big oak, 146 years old, had for decades suffered an acute disease produced by an infestation of parasitic fungi. The previous August, as temperatures surged in a sweltering summer, its leaves had finally withered and died. It was not until the coming of spring that those who looked closely noticed that new ones had failed to sprout.

Tidings of the tree's passing, as they spread through the nearby town of Guernica, made it clear that it had been much more than a recognizable and venerable landmark. Many lamented its death, long anticipated yet still poignantly painful, and local authorities, aware of the emotional weight of the moment, rushed to address the public and offered them reassurance. As custom dictated, a new sapling of the old ancestor was to be planted in the very spot where the previous one had stood. The carcass, on the other hand, was removed to an appropriate retreat, where it could be admired and honored. Nothing less it deserved, after all, the "symbol of the liberties of the Basque people."[1]

However, and for all that the entire episode was performed under a semblance of routine, fact-of-life practicality, there was to it more than a hint of the ominous. At a time at which the region's politics was dominated by the violent actions of the terrorist group *Euskadi ta Askatasuna* (ETA)—"Basque Homeland and Freedom," whose members carried out over fifteen attacks against those opposed to Basque independence in 2004 alone—the withering and drying of the totemic tree seemed like an all-too-obvious metaphor to miss.

To entertain such ideas, of course, was to walk a well-trodden path. After all, the health of the tree had for decades come to serve as a mirror to the health of the Basque people as a whole. In 1937, after a devastating bombardment by the Luftwaffe, the discovery of its unharmed trunk amid the charred ruins of Guernica had only vindicated those who confided that neither the horrors of the Spanish Civil War nor its dire consequences would succeed in erasing Basque pride. Similarly, once Francisco Franco's dictatorship in Spain collapsed and autonomy was restored to the region, it was under the oak's twisted and bulky branches that Basque public servants had sworn their offices in a ceremony that resembled the restoration of a long-lost spring.

But now, the death of the tree seemed to expose a corruption at the heart of Basque society: one which spoke of violence, extortion, censorship, and silence. A menace that, much like the fungi that had festered on the entrails of the trunk under its bark, threatened to spell doom upon all Basques. "It is said that around a thousand years ago/"—a popular local song declared—"God planted the Tree of Guernica. / Remain in place forever and ever, / [i]f you fall we are lost."[2] The cautionary message, at least for some people's comfort, hit just too close to the mark.

Few today would dispute the standing of the oak of Guernica as one of the most enduring and iconic symbols of the Basque people. At its shadow, as the English Romantic William Wordsworth put it, "[t]hose lofty-minded Lawgivers shall meet / [p]easant and lord, in their appointed seat": a distant evocation of the assemblies that were said to have ruled the Basques at least since medieval times.[3] Moreover, the oak remains the central element of the coat of arms of Biscay, the most populated Basque province, and to this day, Basque authorities continue the tradition of swearing their offices before it, just as their distant predecessors once did.

It is for this reason that it is almost impossible to shake off the sting of sacrilege in pointing out that the picture of the immemorial oak of Guernica as a symbol of Basqueness is, in fact, much more recent than it looks. Records of the Biscayne assemblies meeting under a tree in the Middle Ages exist, and it cannot be refuted that the later General Assemblies—a parliament of sorts—used to meet beside its roots until 1873. And yet, Biscay is merely one of the Basque territories, and others—like Guipuzcoa, Alava, or Navarre—did not enthusiastically share in this veneration of the tree and favored instead their own symbols and traditions. It was not until the late nineteenth century, coinciding with the dismantlement of the edifice of laws and customs that the oak had once embodied, that a broader Basque identity began to gain widespread acceptance and, with it, the idea of the latter as the tree of all Basques. In other words, the age-old reverence for this most prominent emblem of Basqueness can be traced back, at most, for a century and a half.

Not that the case of the oak is either unique or especially noteworthy. In those fateful and pivotal decades surrounding the turn from the nineteenth to the twentieth centuries, numerous symbols, stories, and ingrained traditions from the past were repurposed as essential elements of Basque identity. Often, these included local or regional customs that were—in the case of the tree of Guernica, metaphorically *and* literally—transplanted to the remaining Basque territories. Others, on the contrary, were attempts at homogenization. Calls for the creation, out of its various dialects, of a unified variety of *Euskera*—the Basque language—emerged in the 1910s and would result in the standardization of the language in 1968. Basque cuisine—now globally celebrated for its quality and excellence—only became a distinct culinary tradition during the 1920s. Feasts and celebrations that suggest a continuity with some immemorial Basque pagan traditions, or common Basque first names, either spread widely or were invented in the twentieth century. Even the Basque flag or *ikurriña* dates to 1894, when Sabino Arana, the patriarch of Basque nationalism, designed it to serve—poignantly—as the banner of Biscay.

Does this mean, then, that the Basques are a recent invention? Well, yes, at least in part. Invention only rarely involves creating something from scratch. Most features we associate with the Basques today were already in place long before any nationalist activist, politician, writer, or artist stretched his hand to appropriate them. Some, like the tree of Guernica or the medieval assemblies of the Biscaynes, had deep historical roots. Others, like that Basque flag which so strikingly resembles the British *Union Jack*, were instead born out of pressing contemporary concerns. Ultimately, what emerged from this combination was a version of Basque identity that differed greatly from what had existed before. Like eggs whisked together repeatedly to form an omelet, previous markers of identity were reinterpreted, trimmed, adapted, and repurposed by contemporary Basques, resulting in something familiar but, at the same time, startlingly new.

That this was the case should not come as a surprise. The days when historians regarded nations as homogeneous entities, blooming fully formed from the mists of time, are now long gone. Scholars have become adept at revealing the half-truths, misinterpretations, and outright lies upon which any discourse of nationhood—or, for the record, any other kind of identity—is ultimately reliant, and few today would dispute that nations are not ancient, but relatively new phenomena.* The prevailing consensus establishes that across the world, cultural, religious, and political traditions were transformed during the nineteenth and twentieth centuries to yield a new type of imagined community: one that drew from previous sources, but which in doing so reframed and altered them. From China to Western Europe, and from Africa to South America, the arrival of the world of nations was a revolutionary and, at times, traumatic process. It was also one that, in its wake, did not leave a world populated by some "true" national communities. Rather, it simply furbished a new way of framing social and political existence. A new framework that clothed its naked modernity with odd old ends stolen out of previous traditions and therefore seemed conservative, even when it most played the radical.

See it from this standpoint, and what happened to Basque identity during those crucial decades might appear as only a particular instance within a much broader trend. Just like a mold will come to shape the resulting cake, the conditions of its emergence shaped the contents of Basqueness. Sabino Arana and his followers did not create a new Basque identity out of thin air. Rather, they offered a fresh narrative that cast existing beliefs under a new light. That is, their success lay not in imposing an entirely novel concept on a blank slate, but in crafting a story that resonated with—and evolved from—the values and traditions of their fellow compatriots.

But what were these beliefs, and where did they come from? Finding an answer to these questions is the stated objective of this book. My central argument is that, contrary to what nationalist advocates, institutions of government, or even cultural displays might suggest, the Basques are not—nor ever were—an isolated or homogeneous group easily set apart from their neighbors, and that it was stories and tales, penned both by Basque and non-Basque individuals alike, that created that illusion. It was these accounts, as they were told and retold over the centuries, that instilled in the general public the idea of an "exceptional" Basque people.

*Scholars like Mikel Azurmendi, Xabier Zabaltza, Jon Juaristi, José Ramon Díaz de Durana, José María Lacarra, or Javier Andreu—among many, many others—have furthered our understanding of Western Pyrenean history and have confronted overtly nationalist readings of this past. Over the course of this text, I will cite their works often, but even when not directly acknowledged, due mainly to space constraints, the echo of their voices will resonate in my own arguments.

In this interpretation, and much like layers in a metaphorical lasagna, discourses that singled out the inhabitants of these regions—each one produced to address specific needs and shaped by unique historical conditions—were put on top of one another in a non-stop repetition going on for more than 2,000 years. Therefore, while it might be accurate to say that Sabino Arana largely invented the contemporary concept of the Basques, it is equally important to understand that he was but one—and not even the last—in a long list of individuals who distributed membership cards among the inhabitants of this "very special" spot of Europe.

Throughout this book, I will trace the evolution of notions of identity in the Western Pyrenees from its earliest known origins up until the early twentieth century, the time when the Basque "exception" became widely accepted. I will analyze books, study documents, and critically engage with the general historical record to understand where these crucial markers of identity came from and how they developed over time. At times, the story might appear to take meandering roundabouts, or to delve into matters which appear rather inconsequential or obscure at first glance. Such an approach will force me to make frequent jumps in time and in space, skipping across centuries and leaping across continents, in order to follow the trail of tales and stories that had these Western Pyrenean peoples as their protagonists. I should not apologize for this: For, as I will try to demonstrate, contemporary Basqueness owes as much to traditions cultivated by locals as to the prejudices and bitterness of foreigners. And, even more than to those, it owes its existence to the caprice of happenstance.

Some readers, confronted with these remarks, might reasonably wonder: Is there anything truly distinct about Western Pyrenean peoples, then, that sets them apart from others? The answer is both yes and no. No serious scholar today would agree with Xabier Arzallus, former president of the Basque Nationalist Party (EAJ-PNV), who—in 2000, and echoing questionable genetic studies—declared that the Basques, being "the most ancient inhabitants of Europe," were endowed with a particular blood composition.[4] These were already rather outdated views, even twenty-six years ago. The kind of race-based ideology that was so prevalent in the age of Sabino Arana can hardly, to most people in the West, appear as nothing but dubious pseudoscience. But to deny any biological distinction to the inhabitants of the Western Pyrenees is not to claim that they are simply pretending to be something they are not. Basques today are different largely because they believe themselves to be so, and this is a self-image that stems from a longstanding tradition shaped by two major circumstances: geography and language.

As it happens, the roughness of the Western Pyrenean terrain has usually made it exceedingly difficult to tend roads, bridges, and other communication infrastructure. Even today, constructing highways or train lines across the rugged landscape of Guipuzcoa or Biscay involves digging numerous tunnels and building extensive viaducts. This fact alone has massively limited the chances of the locals creating overarching political institutions and has made communication with the outside costly to establish and hard to maintain, preventing, in turn, extraneous political authorities from gaining a firm foothold in the area. After all, the difficulties of the journey, as it meandered up and down through the rain-swept hills, were ones that could give pause to the tax collector, the general, the messenger, and the sheriff alike.

So why bother then? Why not simply accept that, in this case at least, the juice was not worth the squeeze? As it happens, there were, first, strategic considerations. Given that two of the most important crossings through which the Pyrenees can be negotiated stand in their surroundings, monarchies and nation-states have throughout history felt impelled to supervise what happened in these districts. Second, there is also the fact that, especially from the Middle Ages onward, coastal towns were of key importance as trade hubs in the profitable Atlantic trade. These two circumstances have rendered the Western Pyrenees a highly coveted prize over which to establish direct rule, though one exceedingly difficult to govern for long. Too feeble to stand on its own feet, the region remained equally impervious to assimilation: a perfect breeding ground for tales that cast the locals as a "weird" and "different" people.

Language has similarly contributed to a sense of distinction among Western Pyreneans. *Euskera*, the Basque language, constitutes one of the great mysteries of linguistics. Its origin predates the arrival of Latin on the Iberian Peninsula, and its status as a speech unrelated to the great Indo-European family suggests even older roots. Scholars have long been in the business of searching for *Euskera*'s relatives and predecessors, conducting profound comparisons between it and other languages. Ultimately, the list of proposed candidates—which includes Iberian, Celtic, Latin, Greek, Slavic, Sanskrit, Pictish, Berber, ancient Egyptian, Etruscan, Minoan, and Sumerian, to cite but a few—has been only as impressive in its variety as disappointing in its results.[5] No one today knows where or when ancient *Euskera*—that is, the language that would later evolve to become contemporary Basque—came into existence.

This mystery, unsurprisingly, has allowed Western Pyreneans throughout history to assert their uniqueness with much firmer conviction. Local apologists in the sixteenth century, following the early modern craze with biblical origins stories, would identify Basque as "one of the seventy divinely taught languages" created by God in the tower of Babel.[6] These were absurd fairy tales, twentieth-century folklorists would note, but only moments before claiming, with earnest conviction, that the roots of *Euskera* lay instead in prehistoric cave societies. Some, perhaps being carried a tad too much in their enthusiasm, felt confident enough to describe these primitive hunter-gatherers as nothing short of "the first Basques."[7]

The temporal and intellectual chasm notwithstanding, the conclusion sketched by all these writers is strikingly similar: All other groups have changed but not the Basques. An ahistorical perspective, born from a linguistic enigma whose answer remains shrouded by the absence of evidence, has given wings, over the years, to all kinds of ludicrous reveries. It fuels associations of these Western Pyreneans with pagan rituals and traditions, reinforces the notion that challenging the Basques' purported antiquity is a fool's errand, and conjures vivid images of misty forests, elusive mountain warriors, and altars to nameless deities illuminated by the tingling light of distant stars. In essence, it has made it possible to imagine the Basques as a sort of natural occurrence, a people outside of history.

I have veered away from such arguments. I am not a philologist, and I will spare the reader the embarrassment of witnessing my attempt at divining the origins of *Euskera*, which after all is not the focus of this investigation. My stance, overall, is a more practical one. Suffice it to say that some type of Basque language existed before the arrival of the Romans, as did many other languages in the Western Pyrenees, and that its speakers managed to endure—or avoid—successive waves of acculturation that threatened *Euskera*'s survival.

I do not think that this should be framed as a deliberate decision, but rather a consequence of the historical, geographical, and social conditions of the region. In the final reckoning, the survival of *Euskera* owed more to sheer luck than to any concerted effort of preservation. Nevertheless, once this language reached the early modern period, it was possible for Western Pyrenean intellectuals, eager to assert their distinctiveness, to point to *Euskera*, splendid in its isolation, as a powerful demonstration of their alleged exceptionality. In this way, the mystery of the Basque language quickly became the mystery of the Basque people. And many outsiders, unable or unwilling to provide a valid alternative against this analogy, simply put up with it and accepted that the Western Pyreneans were indeed different. An exceptional people, after all, might do with an exceptional speech.

Yet there is another dispute—one that does not touch the Basques directly—to which *The Basque Exception* aims to contribute, nonetheless. Among scholars, it has become almost an article of faith that nations are, at most, late eighteenth-century inventions.[8] The agreement, however, ends there. To the most radical modernists, the nation represents a clean break, with almost no cross-pollination between it and previous forms of identification. On the contrary, more moderate approaches have sought the faint outlines of national identities in previous eras, even if determining what these were or how they came to be adopted by nationalists is often left in the air.[9] Between these positions, a gulf has opened—a schism that veils our knowledge of this transitional period and which has affected, as a result, our ability to understand how nations came into being.[10] By tracing the long story of identities in the Western Pyrenees, I hope to suggest with this book another possibility: that the discourse of nationhood, for all its undeniable novelty, did not spring forth fully formed by miracle, but rather adopted and transfigured previous patterns of identification whose roots, in some instances, dated back centuries or millennia. Therefore, and though this inquiry concerns but a single case study, I hope that it might serve to inspire others to reconsider where—and when—the foundations of other current national identities might lie.

This book is not an apology for Basqueness. It does not intend to serve as a historical vindication of the political rights of a singular people, but neither does it support the position of those who would see these very rights erased. Having grown up in a society intimidated by routine political violence, premised largely upon vastly different readings of the past, I am familiar with the ways in which history can reinforce power dynamics and lead to radicalization. I am also aware of the risk of some of this book's contents and interpretations being put to tendentious use. I consider these as inescapable hazards of my profession. I can only hope that you, the reader, might share my views: But I cannot—and I wish not to—prevent you from having your own.

What I wanted was to gaze at this story with clearer eyes than has often been possible, to uncover what has been forgotten and to provide nuance to what has been uncritically taken for granted. I wanted to see these Western Pyreneans awoken from the ahistorical slumber imposed upon them by these narratives and to restitute them to their rightful context, one in which their thoughts and actions can make sense, their feats be admired, and their failures be weighed. And I wanted, in addition, to find my own story—that of a migrant's son who considers himself a Basque—amid the incessant buzz of traditions and discourses too often presented in black-and-white terms.

What lies ahead is an account of how, over the centuries, the inhabitants of the Western Pyrenees told and retold stories about themselves and others—about their own origins, their customs, their culture, and their aspirations. Of why some of these stories stuck in the minds of those that heard them, while others vanished, devoured by the opaque fog of history. It explores the emergence and development of everything that unites all Basques today—a common name and the myriad meanings bestowed upon it over time—but it likewise traces the source of the disagreements that, over the past century, have so often ravaged their society. It chronicles, in other words, not so much a people, but the idea of a people.

Izena duen guztia bada—an old saying in *Euskera* goes. "Everything that has a name exists."

This is the tale of how some Western Pyreneans came to be known as Basques.

Notes

1 "Muere el 'Árbol de Gernika' por las altas temperaturas del pasado agosto," *El Mundo*, April 21, 2004, https://www.elmundo.es/elmundo/2004/04/20/ciencia/1082471000.html.

2 José María Iparraguirre, "Gernikako Arbola" (1853).

3 William Wordsworth, "Oak of Guernica" (1810).

4 Lola Galán, "Arzalluz defiende la identidad racial de los vascos y la independencia de Euskadi," *El País*, November 3, 2000, https://elpais.com/diario/2000/11/03/espana/973206020_850215.html.

5 Lakarra, "La Prehistoria de la Lengua Vasca", 77.

6 Poza, *De la Antigua lengua, poblaciones y comarcas de las Españas*, XII, 32–3.

7 Placer, *La religión en Euskal Herria*, 12–13.

8 Some major representatives of this trend are the classical books by Ernest Gellner, Eric Hobsbawm, and Benedict Anderson. See Gellner, *Nations and Nationalism*; Hobsbwam, *Nations and Nationalism since 1780*; Anderson, *Imagined Communities. Reflections on the Origin and Spread of Nationalism*.

9 One of the best-known supporters of this view was Anthony Smith, with others like Caspar Hirschi standing as more contemporary examples. See Smith, *The Ethnic Origin of Nations*; Smith, *Ethno-Symbolism and Nationalism: A Cultural Approach*; Hirschi, *The Origins of Nationalism: An Alternative History from Ancient Rome to Early Modern Germany*.

10 This fact has been denounced, for example, by Storm, *Nationalism: A World History*, 11–13.

AUTHOR'S NOTE

Politically, the land of the Basques is today divided between two states: Spain and France. Spain rules the areas to the south and west of the Pyrenees, while France controls the northern strip. The Spanish-governed regions include, in addition to the Foral Community of Navarre, the provinces of Biscay, Alava, and Guipuzcoa—which together make up the Basque Autonomous Community. In France, on the other hand, the Basque territories of Labourd, Basse-Navarre—to which I will refer across this book as *Ultrapuertos*—and Soule are part of the Department of the Atlantic Pyrenees and do not enjoy the same degree of autonomous governance as their southern counterparts.

This compartmentalized political reality entails a major obstacle for researchers. Simply put, there is no single, accepted name for the land of the Basques, nor any agreement as to what its boundaries are. However, given that anyone working on the topic of Basque history has no escape from the issue, throughout this book I have chosen to refer to this land as the *Western Pyrenees*. While the term may not be geographically precise—as some parts of Biscay, Alava, and even the southern tip of Navarre are all indeed quite distant from the actual mountain range—I hope that the reader can overlook this shortcoming after being presented with its benefits.

Not for nothing, common expressions like *Basque Country*, *Euskadi*, *Euskal Herria*, or *Vasconia*—all of which carry not entirely synonymous meanings—all rely upon a foundational assumption: that a distinct group called "Basques" does, in fact, exist. The claim, which in everyday life prompts no great debate, spells disaster when one tries to trace the evolution of identity. The danger is creating upon the reader the impression of a "fossilized community," a picture of the Basques as a static, unchanging entity. Fail to pay attention to the drift, and the result risks turning into a circular argument that renders the whole attempt useless. What, after all, is the Basque Country if not the territory populated by the Basques? And who are the Basques if not those who live in the Basque Country? By exchanging these terms with the geographical Western Pyrenees I hope to avoid these pitfalls, or at least to mitigate their most pernicious effects. Other names will still be employed in the narration but only to discuss the social, political, and cultural projects that gave birth to them, and never to denote definite geographical realities. In doing so, it is my goal to encourage readers to discover for themselves how successive discourses of identity have shaped this entangled geopolitical situation and to understand how the Western Pyrenees came to be regarded, over time, as the homeland of a unique people.

With regard to the name of provinces, I have generally opted for Spanish and French forms over Basque ones, on the assumption that these would be more familiar to English-speaking audiences. The only exceptions to this are the use of the English Biscay rather than Vizcaya and Navarre instead of Navarra. Crucial terms in Spanish, French, or Basque—like *fueros* or *Euskera*—have been for the most part kept in their original language. Town and city names have been written in Spanish or French for coherence.

Chronological questions echo spatial ones. How far do the roots of Basqueness truly go? If, as I argue, the Basques are not a natural entity but rather the product of countless accounts and narratives told and retold about the inhabitants of a particular space, then it seems reasonable to begin this study by tracing the origins of these discourses. Such an approach, if applied to the earliest periods, can prove exceedingly difficult given the lack of available resources.

Taking these caveats into consideration, I have opted to begin this study around the second century BC, coinciding with the first contacts of the Romans with the region. This is no arbitrary choice, and there are, I think, two main arguments in favor of this decision. First off, a methodological one: It is only with the arrival of Roman armies that historians and intellectuals began to talk about the inhabitants of the Western Pyrenees, their customs, their behaviors, and their towns. Likewise, aside from a few notable exceptions, the first testimonies written by natives date back to around the same time and were likely spurred by their interactions with the invaders. This makes it possible, though still challenging, to convey a picture of these early Western Pyreneans and their beliefs.

The second argument touches on the topic of identity. Mediterranean civilization did not merely bring its armies to the Western Pyrenees: It also brought a particular way of understanding the world. Roman generals and writers were accustomed to comparing themselves to every other group of people they found—and the Western Pyreneans were no exception. Their description of the locals, invariably, was bound to be a prejudiced and tendentious one. We cannot simply take the often negative and barbarous picture that these sources convey as a letter-perfect reflection of reality, but we can be sure that its repetition among the educated and the politically powerful left a lasting mark. It stamped upon the consciousness of foreigners the notion of a wild, untamed ferocity that possessed the natives, and offered the locals a mirror to either embrace or resist. It also provided later activists with an entire cultural repertoire of stories and associations they could repurpose to make sense of their own past, laying the ground for the emergence, in due course, of a discourse of exceptionality. For this reason, it is not far-fetched to affirm that Basque identity is, indeed, a distant child of Roman culture.

PART I
VASCONES

CHAPTER 1
A LITTLE WILDNESS

The legionaries could have easily complained as the freezing winter air blew implacably through their ranks. And yet, while their noses ran and their fingers ached, they all restrained themselves from uttering as much as a single word. Despite the abundant snow, they stood there, unperturbed, contemplating in silence how the heavy plow, carried around by a cow and a bull, pierced the earth and left an unbroken furrow behind. Hours had gone by since the appropriate auspices duly gathered, the animals had been tasked with carving a circle around the little village. However, no one had dared to leave his place. The rituals associated with the foundation of a city were not to be taken lightly, and the Romans knew this better than most. Back in ancient times, Remus, the unfortunate brother of Romulus, the first king of Rome, had learned this lesson the hard way. Mocking the boundary that the latter had piled up in the fresh mud, he had leaped over it with ease. Romulus' response, much like that of an extremely territorial predator, had been to murder his own kin in cold blood. A dreadful episode, of course, and one that, for all its horror, had not been entirely without consequence. For one, it had assured the future glory of Rome, consecrating its soaked, dark soil with streams of royal blood. But it too had served to stamp upon the collective consciousness of the Romans the idea that forces beyond comprehension were at play in the foundation of a new city. To mess up with them—most men and women agreed—was a certain recipe for disaster and damnation.

However, it must have been apparent to all the attendants to the ceremony that this snow-covered backwater, hemmed in by mountains and standing on the edges of the world little resembled a second Rome. Surrounded as it was by strange and barbarous peoples who lived in small huts on the hilltops, it eerily reminded legionaries instead of a time which predated even the birth of their own city. Back in that terrible age, humans had hunted each other as fair game, and the wilderness had extended far and wide, threatening and yet untamed. Thankfully, those times—most intellectuals conceded—were finally a thing of the past. Rome had brought order to the world, and her rule promised peace on a scale never before seen. Or so at least thought the Romans themselves. This new city, stamped upon as remote a place as any that could be imagined, bore testament to their commitment to such an amicable future. A future in which the veil of darkness would be finally lifted for good.

At long last, the two animals completed the furrow that marked the sacrosanct boundaries. For an instant, the young Roman general who overlooked the ceremony waited away, and after a second, he proceeded to make a sign. The combination of the severe gesture and his appearance, dazzling in military garments and surrounded by the eagles and banners of the legions, certainly brooked no argument. Immediately, an official stepped forward and started to read a proclamation. Ironically, it seems unlikely that many among the natives, whose mother tongue was wholly strange to Latin, could pick up so much as a word of what the legate was saying. They might—at most—have been briefed about the essentials. Despite this, and in appearance at least, they all listened with attention.

In reward for the aid provided to the troops of the senate of Rome during these trying times—the official proclaimed—the grateful general would donate to them a Roman city to inhabit. The gesture was not an empty one. To rank as a Roman town meant sharing in the technology, the infrastructure, and the military protection of the mightiest power that had ever existed. Most important, perhaps, was the implication that the city-dwellers would finally be able to step out of barbarism and join the ranks of civilization. The locals were expected to learn by heart an entirely new set of rules, behaviors, and traditions. And these, of course, reeked of Roman cultural practices. It was perhaps to facilitate the satisfactory culmination of this challenging process that the young general had prepared a little surprise. In a display of appreciation that hardly veiled an ostensible attempt at self-promotion, he granted the new *civitas* an invaluable present: the honor of bearing his own name. From that moment on, the Vascones would be ruled from *Pompaelo*—Pamplona—the city of Pompey the Great.

There is no disputing that, for all its later importance, the foundation of Pamplona was not by any stretch of the imagination the first contact between the Romans and the peoples of the Western Pyrenees. Historians, for instance, were quick to point out that during their wars against Rome two centuries before, the Carthaginians had already crossed the outermost passes of the mountain range recruiting many among the locals to wage war on Italy.[1] Fearsome and savage, unrelenting and loyal to the death, these warriors were said to have numbered among the fiercest enemies of Rome.

Extensive dealings, however, would arrive at a much later date. In the wake of Carthage's crushing defeat, Roman magistrates suddenly found themselves free to thrust their claws upon Iberia. From their footholds in the Mediterranean, they headed north following the currents of the Ebro River and, not long after, they had already established a bridgehead among the strange peoples that populated the lands between its shores and the foot of the Pyrenees. Slowly yet steadily, local communities came to recognize—even if reluctantly—the might of their arms. This, in turn, only served to further accelerate the rhythm of the Roman advance.

And yet, despite these unquestionable successes, ruling such far-off territories had proven no smooth sailing for the Roman senate. Generals quickly realized that the further they ventured from their bases, the harder it became to force the locals into complying with Roman demands. Officials arriving at the province soon grew accustomed to being greeted with news of the rebellion of erstwhile pacified populations. Native cities and fortresses, sheltered beyond their tall walls, displayed an annoying tendency to refuse the conditions imposed by the new conquerors. And when this happened, it was the turn for the legions to take center stage. The ungrateful task of vanquishing the rebels and bringing them back to the fold had become so commonplace that at some point the senate had begun to eye it with frustration rather than with anxiety.

Although the pace of expansion was certainly slowed down by these resistances, at around the turn of the second century BC, Hispania—as the Romans called the Iberian Peninsula—had become a favorite playground for ambitious, glory-seeking commanders. The fertile lands of the upper Ebro, a "large and irregular country . . . , for the most part rugged, and watered by rivers," transformed into the stage of numerous military operations.[2] The well-oiled machinery of the legions, seasoned and steeled after the campaigns against Carthage, was simply too overwhelming for any power in the Mediterranean to resist, and the Iberian tribes proved no different. Either in decisive open battles or in sieges that lasted for months, the heirs of Romulus got, almost invariably, the upper hand. The goddess Victory appeared to have so utterly granted her favors to the Romans so as to verge on the unimaginable.

Truth be told, some locals soon sensed the opportunity that lay hidden in this vast imbalance of force. A territory so large and distant from Rome as the Iberian Peninsula was not of a kind that could be pacified simply by the sword. To sustain any measure of long-term control in the inner regions and to make sure that troublesome neighbors were kept at arm's length, the conquerors would sooner or later be driven to rely on local strongmen. And this, in turn, promised to open the door for native oligarchs willing to gain for themselves an attractive, mediatory position.

The deal was a steal. A quick, bloodless submission might not only spare the good-and-mighty the risks of facing the legions but could indeed win them the hearts of those most capable of supporting their cause in the new system. It was a momentous realization, and one whose attractiveness was bound only to intensify with time. As the number of those convinced of the ultimate triumph of Rome in Hispania surged after every battle, the ranks of those in favor of a voluntary compliance with the invader's terms grew in parallel. Was it not, after all, better to be ruled through the metaphorical carrot rather than by the blunt, all-too-real point of the stick?

This was probably what happened in the Western Pyrenees. While the rest of Iberia periodically burst into the flames of revolt and war, tidings from the region waned into the nonexistent. The gaze of their statesmen focused elsewhere, such a scarcity of testimonies should be attributed, first and foremost, to a lack of interest on the part of the Romans. Elsewhere in Hispania, natives compelled to surrender through hunger and thirst were choosing a defiant death over a life of slavery. Others, in the western parts of the peninsula, led a coordinated resistance that threatened to thwart the designs of Roman generals. Cast against such glamorous heroism, brought back to Italy in tales packed to the rafters with drama and charismatic characters, accounts of the lands between the Ebro and the northern ocean could hardly lure even a meager audience. No valiant, fearsome leader here that the Romans could respect; no major settlement whose riches they yearned to plunder. In all, it is not hard to understand why metropolitan writers would often choose to pay little heed to the locals. "I am reluctant," a Greek geographer named Strabo confessed a century after the first appearance of the Romans in the Western Pyrenees, "to fill my page with their names, and would fain escape the disagreeable task of writing them."[3] Marginal savages in the middle of nowhere, the natives were as dull as they were unimportant. A people destined to rule the world had no shortage of pressing affairs to attend to, and, of course, sparing a thought for some nondescript, backward barbarians was not even on the list.

It would be erroneous to conclude that such an unapologetic display of indifference meant that the Romans knew nothing at all about the region. Admittedly, it is mostly thanks to their dispersed and scant descriptions that it is possible to attain a broad—albeit imprecise—picture of the world they encountered as they moved away from the riverbanks of the Ebro. For example, the conquerors found the local custom of building their little settlements on top of large hills and ridges remarkable. Not only that, but they noted that these were often surrounded by massive walls and fortifications.[4] The reason was clear. Roman strategists, ever perceptive to any detail that might give them a military edge, immediately recognized in these the unmistakable features of a politically unstable land. According to their estimates, raids and banditry must have been an endemic recurrence among the natives. That this situation might have been helped by the fact that these towns were of a similar size, without any clear center capable of ruling over the lot, was as good a hypothesis as any. The feeble communities had struggled against one another with frequency or had at one point expected to be forced to do so. In all, the impression conveyed was genuinely bleak. The inhabitants of the Western Pyrenees, for all the contempt and hostility they might have harbored against the Romans, seemed to have been every bit as contentious and belligerent among themselves.

A realization that, while it fitted Roman interests, could hardly have encouraged them to advance further north. Strangers to the lands watered by the Ebro had at least to concede that these were fertile; yet this conclusion was hardly applicable to the entire territory. The deeper one ventured into the countryside, pressing ever north toward the Atlantic and the dark silhouettes of the mountain peaks, the more rapidly the erstwhile fruitful landscape degenerated. Here, cultivated fields and wide skies gave way before a sprawling extension of deep valleys and virgin forests. And not only that, for hidden in them lurked tribes with names so alien and unsettling that few in Rome—even the most distinguished of philosophers—had ever heard about them.

To commanders looking for riches to plunder or native warlords to bully, the occasional rumors that could be gathered about the Western Pyrenees must have left a feeble impression indeed. Not a single one of their little settlements, perched as they stood on barren mountaintops or at the shores of the ever-abating sea, was worthy of ranking as a city. Not only that, for if tales were to be believed, their customs were as savage as they were disturbing. Some claimed that the natives slept on the ground, that their men wore profuse amounts of long hair after the fashion of women, and that they made human sacrifices to Mars.[5] Others brought attention to the odd detail that the northerners washed themselves in stale urine, and that some went as far as to rinse their teeth with it.[6] Whatever the degree of truth behind these unsettling insinuations, the image they furnished was as clear as it was unsurprising. The inhabitants of the Western Pyrenees, a forsaken race isolated on the very edge of the world, were nothing but brutes.

All of which does not mean that these stories were necessarily accurate. Of course, it falls within the realm of possibility that these reports were reliable and that the natives were every bit as unruly and disturbing as Roman ideologues assumed them to be. But there are also reasonable arguments to take these accounts with a grain of salt. After all, stories compiled by conquerors and explorers, charting unknown and outlandish lands, usually tell us more about those who wrote them than about the realities they encountered. View them under this prism, and the sort of hearsay that circulated about the inhabitants of the Western Pyrenees, and which was much later put to paper by geographers and historians, suspiciously resembled deeply ingrained Greek and Roman prejudices. That is, descriptions that wrote the natives off with the tainted stigma of the unsophisticated might owe less to empirical reality than to formulaic xenophobia.

Greeks and Romans alike shared a common disdain for those who spent their lives among wind-lashed peaks. Both took for granted that it was only in a city, in an order founded on the rule of administrative officials and the acknowledgment of one's peers, that humans could hope to conduct a civilized, meaningful existence. Members of the urban elite, especially in crowded metropoles like Rome, might from time to time fantasize about leaving the hustle and bustle for a platonic getaway to "the blessed countryside."[7] But this ideal image of the outside world did not extend so far as to include every kind of landscape. It was an accepted fact—as Greek philosophers reiterated—that different climates and environments bred different kinds of humans. Hippocrates, the father of medicine, would explain that the temperate weather of Asia Minor caused the locals to focus on pleasure but be lacking in courage and industry.[8] On another occasion, he concluded that the dwellers of Pontus had the "deepest voice, because the air they breathe is not clear, but moist and turbid."[9] The underlying assumption behind such argument was as compelling as it was simple to understand: individuals resembled the lands they inhabited. And just much like exposure to "severe heat waves, severe winters, copious rains and then long droughts, and winds" meant that "the physique of Europeans varies more than that of Asiatics," so were the "inhabitants of a region which is mountainous, rugged, high, and watered, . . . likely to be of big physique, with a nature well adapted for endurance and courage, and such possess not a little wildness and ferocity."[10] The wildlands, in short, could only be expected to breed a race of wild men.

This dispassionate method of classification, in carefully coupling spatial attributes with character traits, was, of course, far from innocent, and it should come as no surprise to notice that Greek scholars soon discovered in this procedure an argument for Greek superiority. While other peoples were either too lazy, too fierce, or too compliant with despots, only the mild climate of Greece assured a perfect balance between harshness and commodity. The opposite, of course, was equally true. The more a territory differed from Greece's conditions, the more its inhabitants were doomed to stray off the unflawed equilibrium. Yet again, those unfortunate wild men and women were allotted last position. After all, their only concern was with survival, and under such conditions, what state administration, what orderly way of life, what sophisticated culture could emerge? Nothing of value lurked amid barren rocks and trees: only the brutish primitiveness of humans relegated to the most primordial of biological preoccupations.

It came as a logical conclusion from this assumption that there was simply no being a civilized person outside of Greece. Yet the thought, flattering though it may have been in Hellenic circles, was one that educated Roman audiences could hardly stomach with gusto. It was beyond question for any hard-nosed senator to even entertain that Greek customs could be superior to those of a people who had conquered the Mediterranean. Perhaps for this reason, Romans were generally less keen on the idea of climatic determinism than their Greek counterparts. A people's worth had, in their eyes, nothing to do with something as capricious and unreliable as weather. Rather, the best—the only—yardstick to rank a people was as simple as it was self-evident: to measure how much their society resembled that of the Romans.

To be a proper human, a concept Latin authors called *humanitas*, meant partaking in cultural behaviors that could just barely mask the fragrance of their Roman origins. Chief among these was a project of education that was only believed to be feasible in urban spaces and conducted in respected languages such as Latin or Greek. A framework that utterly oozed Roman chauvinism, yet one that many foreigners, yearning to be accepted as part of the group of the civilized, found paradoxically quite liberating. After all, and regardless of how geographically or climatically removed from Rome their homeland might be, natives could dream of improving their social standing if only they were willing to appropriate Roman customs and language. *Humanitas* implied *Romanitas*: a realization that was rapidly dawning on many indigenous aristocrats under the conqueror's boot. The carefully tended walls of a Roman city, rather than a mere outward symbol of its strength, impressed upon the soil nothing short of a qualitative frontier. On the one side stood a civilized and sacred space. On the other, threatening and perilous wilds, the abode of the nonhuman, the beastly, and the barbarian.

Cast them under the light of these assumptions, and those stories told and retold about Western Pyreneans begin to sketch the silhouette of a cliché. This was especially true of the shameful traditions attributed to the Vascones, which far from being unique to them, were said to be shared by all inhabitants of the northern mountains of Iberia. Reviling these locals, Strabo explained that "they do not lead a civilized life, but pass their days in poverty, only acting on the animal impulse, and living most corruptly." The passage might as well have served as a perfect summary of the views most Greeks and Romans held about mountain-dwellers.[11]

But if there ever was any semblance of truth in this verdict, it was never sufficient to make the Vascones stand apart from their neighbors. Even when scholars, on exceedingly rare occasions, referred to them by name, the resulting picture often lacked focus. The Vascones, a poet once noted, "scorn the protection of a helmet."[12] A curious detail, and one that, had its author been more interested in mapping human diversity, could perhaps have served to peep into the society and beliefs of the inhabitants of the Western Pyrenees. But as it happens, the poet's goals were otherwise. In fact, it was impossible to determine whether the detail was based on firsthand data to begin with or if it was simply added for dramatic effect. Not for nothing, accompanying this passing commentary about the Vascones were references to other Iberian peoples: the Cantabrians "eager beyond others to hire out their swords," or the Concanian "who proves . . . his savagery . . . when he opens a vein of his horse to fill his own belly."[13] Roman audiences, hearkening under the assault of these images of crudeness, must have regarded these savages as suitable companions for a tribe of bare-headed warriors.

While this kind of literary aversion resonated with readers back in the most exclusive circles of Rome, they were of little use on the ground. Any long-term rule rests upon accurate knowledge, and for this reason, Roman soldiers and officials stationed near the Western Pyrenees were content with learning about any local custom, resource, or curiosity that could prove useful in advancing their dominance. For example, they noted that these were not part of a single people, but rather a patchwork of distinct tribes and communities. The Vascones, probably thanks to the story that linked their capital's name to Pompey the Great, might have been the most distinguished of the lot, but there were others: Vardulians, Berones, Iacetanians, Tarbelli, Roman scribes, in an often-thankless task, would duly register their names.

As these testimonies evidence, the Western Pyrenees at the time of their first contact with the invaders was a crossroads. To the west, both peoples and settlements bore Celtic names.[14] To the east and the south, on the other hand, it was Iberian speech that was preferred. In the intermediate zone, that in which ancient geographers most often situated the Vascones, the mosaic was completed by the presence of proto-Basque, which seemed to spill on both sides of the mountain range. The degree to which all of these disparate realities were in contact with each other was manifested in the very word "Vascones," which derived not from a proto-Basque term but from a Celtic word that meant "those who live in the mountains." Similarly, hard-rock evidence to sustain that the Vascones exclusively spoke proto-Basque was simply nonexistent. On the contrary, the image that Roman scholars furnished was one in which all these languages—Celtic, Proto-Basque, Iberian—were in frequent flux and interaction.[15]

Therefore, the most salient feature of the Western Pyrenees in terms of population and cultural influences was their diversity and mixture. But, if that was the case, why would Greek and Roman authors distinguish so starkly between, say, the Vascones and other groups? Criteria could not have been linguistic nor religious—let alone political. Who could say what roster of criteria they based their classifications upon? Unconcerned with recording in detail the customs and cults of the natives, Roman authorities rested content with the bare minimum: ensuring that the collection of tribute was conducted effectively and that any resource of value flowed toward their cities. As far as priorities went, conducting anthropological surveys was never an urgent task for the provincial administration.

However, a discourse of exceptionalism ought to start somewhere, and in the case of the Western Pyreneans, these origins were humble. It had all begun in the decade of the 80s BC when, over the course of a bloody civil war, a Roman aristocrat called Sertorius took refuge in Hispania and rallied many indigenous communities to his side. Many, but not all. The Vascones, as established in the story of the foundation of Pamplona, chose to aid the senate of Rome rather than Sertorius. And so, when in 72 BC the uprising was finally stamped out, and peace was restored to most of Iberia, an up-to-date Roman road, resembling a stream of gravel and stone, was built to connect them to the metropoles of the Mediterranean. The loyalty they had displayed in the campaign had been so staunch, their adherence to the cause of the senate so complete, that no one was able to recall so much as a battle taking place in Vascon territory nor any division within their ranks. Backward though they might appear, they had also proven trustworthy. The Vascones had banked their survival, contrary to other Iberians, in the favor of a distant power over the pressure of a nearby rebel. Needless to say, their bet had reaped them massive benefits.

Or so, leastways, went the familiar account. But the tale, for all that it appeared indisputable at first glance, exhibited, upon closer scrutiny, a pair of clay feet. Its two main pillars were the existence of a Vascon city that sported Pompey's name and the lack of any recorded clash of armies in the area. And yet, while this was a view of events destined to endure, there always lurked beneath it a pervasive alternative. That the whole notion of Vascon support for Pompey was no more than a forgery, and that Western Pyreneans, far from standing as faithful allies of Rome, had instead numbered among her enemies.

Nothing better to illustrate this possibility than the example of nearby Calagurris. This town had been nothing to boast about, a humdrum mid-sized village to the south of the Western Pyrenees and on the riverbanks of the Ebro, and about which little could be said prior to the advent of Sertorius. Strabo, writing a century or so after the events, would identify the Calagurritans with the Vascones.[16] But their story, overall, resembled little the one so often told about other Western Pyreneans. The city's authorities, fierce supporters of the rebel as they had been, chose to pursue the struggle against Pompey to its direst consequences. As was to be expected, they paid a high toll for it.[17]

The siege of the town by the senatorial troops was as systematic as it was brutal, and yet the determination of the local population did not waver. Their defiance continued even as their sources of drinking water were depleted, even as supplies began to run low. Their spirit of resistance—and the dread of what defeat might bring—pushed the Calagurritans to endure the most terrible exertions and to steel themselves for the greatest of sacrifices. And so, one day, after "having devoured all other creatures in their city, [they] fell to feast upon their wives and children."[18] That a city that later Roman sources would associate with the Vascones could fight Pompey to such miserable extents, while news of even the most minor of skirmishes did not exist elsewhere in the region, suggested a tentative conclusion. That the term implied a degree of political unity to the Vascones that was simply far from real.

Be it as it may, Pompey's triumph and the foundation of Pamplona—either as a gift or as a chastisement—would mean the definitive incorporation of most of the Western Pyrenees into the Roman system. Neither those so-called Vascones nor their many neighbors failed to notice that war had only served to accelerate the rate of Roman intrusion in the area. The relentless bustle of legions, especially intense in those lands closer to the Ebro, had resulted in a powerful influx of the conqueror's customs, religion, and language. The trend was only to be expected to continue once many of these veterans retired and were granted plots of land in the surroundings. Roads and paths were opened that fastened the Western Pyrenees tightly to the Mediterranean, and towns like Pamplona grew into hubs of regional importance where Roman and indigenous traditions mixed and mingled in various shapes. The extent of the transformation was mind-boggling; its signs were apparent wherever one might gaze. It was as if, after some tentative and half-hearted beginnings, Roman civilization had finally found a way to take root even in this marginal backwater.

The acquisition and adaptation by the locals of Roman lifestyles, however, was to prove a slow and arduous process, and one that was unlikely to be carried out completely in one or two generations. And yet, the objective was one to which many natives—especially those richest and best-esteemed—appear to have been particularly committed. They changed their names and those of their children in imitation to the three-name structure that was common in Rome. They imported new clothes, new earthenware, and new foodstuffs, and, in doing so, they invariably opted for those goods most likely to pander to Roman tastes.[19] It was, in all, an aggressive program of cultural assimilation, and one carefully designed to flatter Roman aristocratic sensibilities. After all, cooking with olive oil or drinking red wine was, back in ancient times just as ever, every bit a matter of nourishment as it was a display of sophistication.

The overhaul also affected language. Roman authorities, for the most part disinterested in indigenous cultural practices, did not push forward any cohesive or centralized policy to transform how their new subjects spoke or thought. What concern could governors have with the tongue used by distant tribes in an obscure corner of the empire, so long as they gave them no trouble? The terms of the question, as could not have been otherwise, were rather different for the provincials themselves. Under the new system, those willing to advance were hard-pressed to get at least some functional knowledge of Latin, for *humanitas*, after all, was never a concept that could be fully expressed in a barbarous speech. The realization meant nothing short of a death threat to local dialects. Against Latin's overbearing global reach, backed as it was by the dazzling lights of Rome's grandeur, what could languages like Celtic, Iberian, Gallic, or proto-Basque contribute? In a slow yet unopposed process, all were overwhelmed. As the tongue of the newcomers pressed on, they were increasingly pushed back to the private sphere or to marginal zones less touched by the frameworks of Roman society.

But if these tongues were indeed receding, they nonetheless left many traces behind in their withdrawal. Previous languages, as it was only natural, still cast a long shadow over the ways in which Latin was spoken in the Western Pyrenees. A particular accent or a curious way of pronouncing certain words remained, then as ever, key to identifying the geographical or ethnic origins of a given individual. In a sense, these occasional exoticisms amounted to a lingering feeling of continuity. And yet, to those who stuck to the language of their ancestors, they might have appeared a rather insufficient consolation prize.

Not everyone, however, looked back fondly at the legacy of the recent past. For those aristocrats most bent on assimilating into Roman culture, such residues amounted to little more than shameful traces of ignorance that ought to be eradicated without delay. Ashamed of their roots as dwellers of what their overlords took for a flea-bitten backwater, soon they became anxious about their children learning the most pure and prestigious form of Latin to spare their descendants the pangs of such public embarrassment. It was only by leaving the past behind and becoming Roman wholesale, after all, that they would be able to mute any awkward mention of bare-headed, urine-drinking barbarians.

Over the course of the following decades, Roman commanders would continue to campaign in Hispania, especially against the indomitable Cantabrians who lived to the west of the Western Pyrenees. And yet, for all their persistence, these episodes seem to have troubled the Vascones and their neighbors very little. By the first century AD, the ties that bound their lands to Rome had become simply too strong for the defiance of any tribe of mountaineers to disentangle. While Vascon chiefs enthusiastically imitated the latest fashion trends of their conquerors in an evident attempt at upward mobility, their proud warriors were busy taking part in the wars of Rome, be they in distant forests or in foggy islands beyond the ocean.[20]

Imperial bureaucrats and officials, entrusted with the sole task of squeezing the most out of these remote backwaters, were similarly willing to cultivate this relationship. The gathering of the tribute required a costly infrastructure, and maintaining order was essential for avoiding unnecessary—and dangerous—complications. Under such circumstances, to buttress the existing social hierarchies was crucial. Farmers, shepherds, soldiers, merchants, slaves, all had to know their place. For only if the system was crystal clear and if every magistrate in every town knew exactly what was expected of him, could the empire hope to survive.

Embracing such a paradigm, though, bestowed a paradoxical role upon local hubs of Roman administration like Pamplona or the rebuilt Calagurris. As Roman cities, they were part of the oppressive apparatus of government set in place by a foreign empire, isolated amid a sea of indigenous inhabitants that Roman aristocrats despised. Yet, at the same time, they remained regional organizing centers, the only ones, in fact, through which these peripheral populations could communicate with the rest of the empire. Compliance with the Roman way of conducting business was, in other words, an inescapable requirement for engaging with the wider world. And it was through these local branch offices of Roman culture, as a tree spreading its roots deep underground, that *Romanitas*—the proper, civilized way of life—was expected to spread among the native and barbarous peoples of the Western Pyrenees.

And spread it did. Prior to the arrival of the Romans, the main feature of the various communities of the Western Pyrenees had been their diversity and mutual suspicion. Those known as Vascones were in no way a single, homogeneous people; neither were probably any of their neighbors. They all lived in a land that was defined, first and foremost, by its remoteness, its scarce internal organization and, above all else, by a set of prejudices carelessly applied to them by the conquerors. The Romans, in banding together these little hamlets and villages under a single name, had bestowed upon them an identity that they had not possessed beforehand.[21] Now, however, local men and women found themselves forced to conduct their business as Roman provincials, to pay their taxes as Roman provincials, and to organize themselves politically as Roman provincials. They did so regardless of their previous origin, the ties they might have shared with their surrounding groups, the tongue they spoke, or the gods they venerated.

Of course, there were limits to what this imposed uniformity might achieve. In a land for the most part bereft of any indigenous system of writing and whose culture was despised by metropolitan elites, whatever local identity the natives had displayed beforehand soon came to be trampled by the stories that the Romans repeated about them. The process was one familiar all throughout the Roman-conquered world. But whereas in some provinces the locals had chosen to highlight tales that linked them to mythical figures like Herakles or the heroes of Troy, no such prestigious pedigree was available to Western Pyreneans. No stories were told about the distinguished lineage, say, of the Autrigones; not a single valiant episode of dazzling audacity starring the Vardulians.[22] The only accounts about the region that held any degree of brand recognition in the minds of the Roman educated elite—and a tenuous one at that—had invariably the Vascones as their protagonists.

Scarce though they were, these mentions could nonetheless be exploited for several—and not always complementary—goals. The tradition that linked the foundation of Pamplona to an alliance of the Vascones with Rome and Pompey the Great was one upon which Western Pyreneans could take at least a measure of pride, and some natives might have treasured this reassurance long after they had come to see themselves as Roman subjects. Not for nothing, it was a story that spoke of the notion of *humanitas*, of the betterment of former savages, and of the promise of a world in which barbarians could become paladins of civilization. As such, it was one that allowed those willing to embrace Roman customs and traditions to present themselves as worthy of the respect and confidence of the new masters of Hispania.

But at the same time—and for all that the foundation of Pamplona was a powerful association—there was also a very different episode that had the Vascones at its center. *Fames Calagurritana*—"Calagurritan hunger"—was not only a common expression in Latin to denote an urge to eat but also a constant reminder of the terrible fate of a city that had chosen to resort to cannibalism rather than surrender to Roman arms. More subtly, it conjured in the mind of Roman educated audiences an image of the Vascones as individuals capable of taking the most horrifying of actions. Could the patina of civilization—even the all-mighty Roman civilization—reasonably be expected to dispel such unmitigated barbarity? The process promised not merely to be long and ungrateful but also a potentially infructuous one.

Truth be told, some Romans at least fancied the notion that such a man-eating savagery might always be on the brink of reemergence and that only a constant watch could be trusted to keep it at bay. The story of Pamplona's foundation might have given locals an example to which to aspire and a source of hope about their rightful place in the Roman world. But it was these other traditions, populated by barbarians so dull as to not even use helmets in battle, that offered something equally potent: a perennial argument for the conquerors to never let the reins of power slip from their hands.

In the end, the emergence and survival of the term "Vascones" owed more to prejudices, thwarted traditions, and the particular interests of both the native elite and Roman administrators than to any inherent, previously existent self-awareness among the natives. As part of this process, a name, some dramatic episodes, and a set of preconceptions and biases were combined into a literary repertoire that ensured at least some degree of uniqueness for the inhabitants of the Western Pyrenees. In a world advancing at neck-breaking speed toward acculturation into Roman forms, these perks were not to be cast aside as irrelevant. Some of them buttressed the claims of native aristocrats to stand as respectable members of the newly created provincial society. Others manifested the wish of Italian and Greek scholars for the exclusion of these peripheral elites and justified the perpetual necessity of direct Roman control. In both cases, it was in reference to the actions and territories of the Vascones, and not to any other of their various neighbors, that these matters were discussed. And so, over time, this process ensured that their name would become a shorthand for the inhabitants of the Western Pyrenees as a whole.

Notes

1 Polibius, *Historiae,* X, 39. Livy, *Ab Urbe Condita* XXVII, 19 also records the passage. For the recruitment of Vascones and Western Pyreneans by Hasdrubal, see Segura, *Mil años de historia vasca a través de la literatura greco-latina: De Aníbal a Carlomagno*, 15.

2 Strabo, *Geography,* III, 4, 12.

3 Strabo, 3, 7.

4 Martínez, Argandoña and Argandoña, "El campamento romano (castra aestiva) de Gazólaz (Navarra)," 261.

5 Strabo, *Geography,* III, 3, 7.

6 Strabo, 4, 16.

7 Horace, *Epistles*, 1.10.13–14.

8 Hippocrates, *De Aere aquis et locis*, XII.

9 Hippocrates, XV.

10 Hippocrates, XXIII–XXIV.

11 Strabo, *Geography,* III, 4, 16.

12 Silius Italicus, *Punica*, II, vv. 190–200.

13 Silius, vv. 356–61.

14 Blázquez, "Los vascones en las fuentes literarias de la Antigüedad y en la historiografía actual," 112.

15 Gorrochategui, "Onomástica vascónica y aquitana: elementos para el conocimiento de la historia antigua de Navarra," 134. Also, Wulff, "Vascones, autoctonía, continuidad, lengua. Entre la historia y la historiografía," 48. Also, Blázquez, "Los vascones en las fuentes literarias," 121.

16 Strabo, *Geography,* III, 4, 10.

17 Strabo, 4, 10.

18 Valerius Maximus, *Of the Memorable Acts and Sayings*, VII, 6, 3.

19 Larrañaga, *El Hecho Colonial Romano en el Área Circumpirenaica Occidental*, 131–2.

20 There is ample evidence for the stationing of Vascon troops in the Rhine, in Britannia, and in Africa. See Larrañaga, *El Hecho Colonial Romano*, 128–9.

21 Pina, "Sertorio, Pompeyo y el supuesto alineamiento de los Vascones con Roma," 195–214.

22 Mentions of these peoples, such as Pliny's reference in passing in *Naturalis Historia* (Plin. *Nat. Hist.* 3.4), exist but remain obscure geographical annotations that did not make an impact on the public.

CHAPTER 2
VASCONUM GENTILITAS

Western Pyreneans did not like theaters. Evidence of their lack of popularity derives from the fact that not even a single one of them has been found in any of the most important cities and settlements of the region.[1] Not in Calagurris, not in Pamplona, not in nearby Aquae Tarbelli. Perhaps—someone could argue—provisional structures of this kind were built on the occasion of a festivity and were dismantled afterward. Maybe these stages were made from wood and accidentally burned at an indeterminate point in time. Perhaps, local authorities, endemically short on funds, left them to rot, neglected and forgotten. Or it might have been the case that locals simply did not enjoy what was at the end of the day a Greek spectacle; or that they held some kind of deeply ingrained prejudice against those who pretended so ostensibly to impersonate others.

What can be asserted with confidence, though, was that, when compared with other buildings whose purpose was to entertain the public, the absence of theaters was telling in and of itself. After all, the multitudes roared in the grandstand of the circuses of Calagurris and Veleia, while similar crowds gathered regularly in the amphitheater of Aquae Tarbelli to watch executions and gladiatorial combats. Even an unremarkable town like the coastal Oiasso, otherwise a modest seaport populated by obscure traders, artisans, and mariners, could boast its own dedicated complex of bathhouses.[2] Rather than superfluous amenities, it was precisely in such places that business was made, gossip was spread, and alliances were struck. After all, public entertainment, as everyone knew, could be an expression of refinement. And the dwellers of the Western Pyrenees, their dislike of theaters notwithstanding, knew at least how to have a good time.

That this was the case might have come as a surprise to anyone well-schooled in the pools of Greco-Roman literature. Not for nothing, Western Pyreneans had grown accustomed by the early third century to being the subject of far-from-flattering portraits. Strabo's trail of belittlement had been followed by others, leastways when it came to scorning the Vascones. Pliny the Elder, while presenting an overview of these lands in his *Natural History*, did not fail to mention the *Vasconum saltus*, that is, the mountainous and uncultivated woodlands of the Vascones. The historian Tacitus, writing at the turn of the second century AD, still depicted the locals as soldiers eager to charge into battle and spread panic among their enemies.[3] Even on the rare occasion when these books provided new details about these provincials, they only furthered the perceived strangeness and cultural distance that seemed to separate them from true Romans. So happened, for instance, with a passing mention in the late second century, which highlighted the proficiency of the Vascones as augurs and soothsayers.[4] In all, these scattered allusions sketched up a repertoire of associations that would hardly thrill any expert in public relations.

But for all that written sources might perpetuate such an unappealing impression of the region, the reality on the ground was vastly different. Rather than the excesses one might come to expect from a half-cultured and brutish community, the Western Pyrenees were for the most part unremarkable as a Roman-controlled territory. Roads pumped lifeblood to cities, just like anywhere else. Magistrates focused—as was, on the other hand, only expected of them—on the collection of taxes. Altars were raised to the same gods that were venerated in the rest of the empire. To a society like this one, homogenized by Roman lifestyles and patterns of control, what could a few mentions in the best-sellers of the time contribute apart from a tad of homegrown flavor?

At around the year 200 AD, there were, put simply, too many names for anyone to care. Once, in the wake of the conquest, when establishing a functioning governmental structure for the land had been a Roman priority, respect for local peculiarities had been regarded as an endeavor worthy of consideration. Hence why administrators had devoted half-hearted attention to cataloging the locals. Never had this interest, though, gone beyond the limits of actual practicality. When the armies of Caesar arrived in the plains that stretched immediately north from the Pyrenees, for example, contemporary sources accounted for at least twenty-eight distinct communities in the land. After the stamping of Roman power, however, the provincial apparatus would only recognize nine.[5]

Initially, of course, the new divisions were unsurprisingly seen as cumbersome novelties. But once they had proven functional for decades, it was only natural that the small degrees of variance they had originally conveyed were bound to appear increasingly superfluous. Vardulians, Berones, Autrigones: They were provincials all the same. And so, by the end of the first century AD at the latest, most of these ancient terms had disappeared from common speech altogether.

Even the name of Vascones, by far the most recognizable of the lot, had lost much of its former resonance. For starters, local Roman-style epigraphy never mentioned it, thus showcasing the scarce traction the term had among the general population. And if administrative mentions are considered, then it is hard to shake the feeling that the word was in utter decline during the second century AD. A certain *Cohors II Vasconum Civium Romanorum* existed for half a century as a military detachment stationed in Britannia.[6] But how a garrison serving in such a distant land could manage to remain Vascon in any sense other than name was something that is simply impossible to ascertain. Most likely, it did not, and after some brief allusions, the term was not recorded in any imperial document ever again.[7] The memory of the Vascones, that ancient tribe repurposed by the Romans as a geographic and partially pejorative term, died out and faded into oblivion. The same happened to the rest of their neighbors in the Western Pyrenees.[8]

Unlike the latter, however, the Vascones lived on in the stories told about them. And among these, none came near to competing, owing to the stature of its characters, with the momentous confrontation that had pitted Sertorius and Pompey. Schoolboys were encouraged to remember Pompey's city, Pamplona, and most certainly had heard the expression *fames Calagurritana*, a macabre reference to the cannibalism practiced by the besieged population of the riverside town. These episodes, celebrated in the works of famous historians like Sallust or Livy, did not fail in conferring the term a small amount of sophisticated erudition. A meager consolation, perhaps, but one which amounted to vastly more than what either the Vardulians, the Berones, or the Autrigones could ever hope to attain. Sheltered in thick papyri rolls, endlessly copied and copied again to service the libraries of senators, or endowed to the overstrained memory of pupils of aristocratic stock, a certain recollection of the Vascones thus clung on to a ghostly yet enduring existence. It was a paradoxical turn of events. The same homogeneous Roman culture that had done so much to diffuse their sense of distinctiveness was to be responsible, like amber around a trapped mosquito, for preserving their memory for the future.

In any case, it is safe to affirm that by the second half of the third century, when the first Christian preachers established some small communities on both sides of the Western Pyrenees, these populations had already spent decades identifying themselves mostly with the cities in which they lived rather than with any overarching territory.[9] At first, a confrontational attitude with well-established religious practices probably gained Christians no small number of converts. *Gentilitas*, these men and women called their foe: "heathenism." Veneration of other deities, no matter their root, be they native or imported, be they Western Pyrenean or Roman, be they urban or rural: All constituted examples of *gentilitas* all the same. On the other hand, the same radical dynamic ensured that they would enjoy a complex—and potentially lethal—relationship with Roman authorities. The cult of the ancient deities and, most importantly, the veneration owed to the godlike emperor were not merely long-standing traditions that kept the favor of the divine showering upon the empire. They were also a guarantee of the stability and correct functioning of Roman society. In challenging this assumption, Christian hostility could swiftly turn from an annoying nuisance into a very real danger. What could be expected from a group that mocked the gods and those who venerated them?—Roman moralists were quick to point out. Would they not be equally untrustworthy when it came to defending the empire itself? What could their refusal to offer due respect to the emperor and the rest of the gods mean but an overt desire to see the Roman order vanquished and undone?

Especially in times of social and political instability, when the veil of subtlety that generally obscured the brutal contours of Roman domination was stripped bare, the match between Christian opposition and the need for a scapegoat appeared made in heaven. The fatal consequences of this had been proven time and again. Back in the first century AD, the last years of Nero's convulsive reign had witnessed the first persecution of Christians and the martyrdom of the apostles Paul and Peter. Similarly, the tumultuous period of crisis experienced by the Roman state during the third century was reflected again in a disproportionate extension of the maltreatment endured by the followers of Christ. At that time, many Christian communities in the western provinces, which were still comprised in large part of migrants from the eastern Mediterranean, had faced a perfect storm. The anger of traditionalists, the zeal of authorities determined to maintain order at all costs, the looming hatred toward immigrants and dangerous social agitators: All had given wings to those who wished for brutal persecution.

Christians themselves were painfully aware of the consequences of their ambiguous stance with regard to imperial rule, and many among their number judged the situation every bit as worrisome as non-Christians did. In a world in which webs of patronage and influence compounded the crucial machinery of power, to be elected a bishop in a city church with dozens or even hundreds of parishioners was still a position that could merit the respect of even the most arrogant of blue-blooded oligarchs. Yet few of these powerful patrons, even when they were determined enough to take the momentous step of converting, were correspondingly attracted to the idea of giving the world away and abandoning their birthright as members of the provincial elite. Unsurprisingly, most did not, and chose instead to accept the new customs of their faith without entirely surrendering the old ones of their rank.

There is no doubting that many in both camps must have frowned at the outcomes of such an outwardly cynical decision. Was it possible that such a double game could end up resulting in the contamination of the teaching of the apostles by pagan rituals? Or would the empire itself be corrupted by this perilous sect? At the end of the third century, these were questions that an increasing number of Romans, Christian or not, pondered with preoccupation.

As it turns out, many would come to find loyalty to God and loyalty to the empire impossible to reconcile. In the year 285, Diocletian ascended to the throne of Rome. Immediately, he set himself to an extensive and profound reform of the imperial administration. He appointed a colleague, Maximian, to rule the western provinces, as well as two junior emperors to warrant an orderly line of succession. He also set in motion a long list of economic reforms; he tackled the reorganization of the provinces, managing to increase their number to diminish their bid for independence. In parallel, Diocletian pushed for a more ostentatious imperial cult, forcing everyone to prostrate in his presence and styling his power as a direct gift from Jupiter and Hercules. The pace of change, at any rate, was neck-breaking. And, somehow, it all worked. Diocletian's achievements in salvaging the sinking imperial state brooked no argument. After two decades of prolonged and purposeful effort, the entire Roman system had been overhauled from top to bottom.

Predictably, the rebellious and judgmental nature of the Christian Church did not sit well with a man as tenacious and devoted to buttressing Roman hegemony as Diocletian and hence lay perhaps the ultimate cause of his decision to disclose the most terrible of persecutions. It all began when some Christian legionaries refused to offer sacrifices in preparation for a military campaign. Such a blatant exhibition of disrespect to the gods and to Caesar would have been enough to raise the alarms of any general, and of Diocletian in particular. Immediately, he opted to raise the stakes. First off, the legions were purged of Christians. Shortly afterward, in 303, a sequence of imperial letters

> was everywhere promulgated, ordering the razing of the churches to the ground and the destruction by fire of the Scriptures, and proclaiming that those who

> held high positions would lose all civil rights, while those in households, if they persisted in their profession of Christianity, would be deprived of their liberty . . . and then afterwards compelled by every kind of device to sacrifice.[10]

Faced with the prospect of death and torment, many sensible Christians chose either to recant or to keep their faith underground. Others, however, did not.

The memory of Diocletian's persecution was fated to cast a long shadow over the unfolding of Christian history, and not least because Christian apologists seemed obsessed with it. Even a hundred years after the event, in the early fifth century, poets and theologians alike remained enticed with the idea of collecting any accounts of the martyrdoms of those who had wielded their faith against sword and spear.

The Western Pyrenees—yet again—were no different. Prudentius, an aristocrat from Calagurris who had enjoyed a brilliant political career that had led him to holding two provincial governorships, was hardly the kind of figure that one might initially associate with Christian proselytizing. And yet, he proved himself the perfect man for the job. He was aided in this by a close friendship with the local bishop and by a cultural and financial status that made even the haughtiest snobs immediately recognize him as one of their own.[11] Traveling from door to door across luxurious villas, Prudentius would recite his poems in halls brimming with pagan mosaics and illuminated by candlelight. In doing so, he would manage to spread the message of Christ in an environment to which even bishops had only restricted access. And not only that for, unlike many other preachers, Prudentius knew his audience, and he instinctively fathomed that nothing better pumped the blood of a Roman aristocrat, schooled in legends of reckless heroes and careless gods, than an old-fashioned tale of suffering, endurance, and triumph against all odds. A tale, in other words, of glorious self-sacrifice.

Luckily, the ferocious persecution decreed by Diocletian had made available a seemingly endless stream of such stories. One of these, perhaps because it took place in his hometown, spoke particularly to Prudentius' tastes. Emeterius and Chelidonius had been two soldiers stationed in Calagurris who, after being compelled to make sacrifices to the gods, had "abandoned Caesar's standards, choosing instead the ensign of the cross."[12] Their defiance, as was to be expected, had met with a harsh response from the authorities. Tormented with iron and fire, both men had, rather than recanting, chosen "to repay to God all that belongs to God," and after a while, Roman officers, left with no alternative, had carried them outside the city walls and had duly executed them on the spot.

Had not something utterly unexpected then ensued, this should have been the end of the matter. But the Almighty, on a display of his satisfaction with the sacrifice made by his children, had raised to the heavens the golden ring of one of the martyrs and the handkerchief of the other. The judge, the executioner, and all the gathered Calagurritans had been left "motionless, blanching in astonishment."[13]

Needless to say, the mystery begged some introspection on the part of those who had witnessed it. Only a few years on, and Christians in Calagurris had already built a baptistery exactly on top of the execution grounds. The miracle seemed to have settled into their minds the idea that only on the very earth that had borne testimony to the fall of the saints could one be secure of their intercession before God. Just like the legionary who was said to have pierced Jesus' side during his crucifixion, the witnesses of Emeterius' and Chelidonius' fate had been similarly gained for the Christian cause. *Iamne credis, bruta quondam Vasconum gentilitas, quam sacrum crudelis error immolant sanguinem?*—Prudentius reproached in triumph.[14] "Do you now believe, dull paganism of the old Vascones, how holy was the blood which cruel superstition sacrificed?"

The ancient Vascones, of course, were nowhere to be found, and yet the reference was one that the poet knew his fellow aristocrats would certainly appreciate. Not for nothing, Prudentius had a superb talent to adorn the familiar with the supernatural and the banal with the erudite. In addressing the highest tier of Western Pyrenean society as descendants of the old Vascones, he was far from belittling his assembled audience; quite the opposite, he was congratulating them. Mentions of the ancient dullness of their forefathers stood, after all, in direct opposition to the lavishness displayed in their splendid rural estates. Allusions to their paganism stood in stark contrast to the respect that the saints received in their own day. The Vascones, like a distorted reflection in a clouded mirror, offered Prudentius' contemporaries the perfect vantage point from which to measure their own accomplishments.

The plan was deliberate and the message unmistakable. While sinful idolatry might have been suited for the brutish Vascones, Christianity was the worship of the future.[15] Commissioning mosaics that portrayed heathen deities, attending pagan festivities, burying one's relatives under the protection of the *manes*: These were not to be regarded as signs of refinement anymore. Instead, they only served now as marks of boorishness. Christianity was the latest addition to the fashionable Roman way of life, and this made clinging fast to the outdated rites of *gentilitas* both abhorrent to God and inexcusably démodé. The Vascones, like the monster under the bed, like an evil twin, were a cautionary omen of the barbarity that awaited those tempted to abandon the right path to salvation.

Yet on this particular subject, not everyone agreed with Prudentius. Rather than a thing of the past, some regarded the Vascones as a very contemporary threat. In Aquitaine, members of the most exclusive circles of the provincial elite had long been in the business of scorning the customs of others, especially if the latter happened to come from Hispania. Prudentius, who exhibited an illustrious service record and an undeniable gift for wordsmithing, these members of the upper classes might occasionally celebrate as "our lyric poet."[16] But it was one thing to bring attention to the greatness of an exceptional individual, and a completely different one to extend his qualities to the rest of his compatriots. News coming from the south in the early fifth century was, after all, worrisome, speaking of heretical preachers who tricked gullible Christians into retreating to mountain cells, then forced them to practice extreme deprivations like vegetarianism. In light of such tidings, and seen from the comforts of Gaul, the Western Pyrenees—the whole of Hispania even—could therefore not help but appear a land on the fringes of backwardness.

For their part, the qualms of these northern magnates were rather different. The conversion of the empire into an increasingly Christian state over the course of the fourth and fifth centuries had decisively altered the terms of the equation previously confronted by early Christians. That a Caesar, whose forerunners had been drunk with the blood of the saints and the martyrs of Jesus, could cast away "the swelling draperies of the serpents"[17] and take on the standard of the cross seemed the kind of hope that arose from a fever dream. And yet, it was precisely what had happened. The true implications of this momentous conversion, while they would only be discovered over the course of many generations, preyed, more than anywhere else, on the conscience of the super-rich. How was it possible to square, for instance, the equal status that the Gospel granted to all human beings with the existence of slaves? What was the future that awaited the wealthy in the afterlife? Which were the practices that most defined a Christian lifestyle? These, rather than idle questions, were precisely the issues that tormented the uppermost levels of Roman society. It was preoccupation about the health of their souls, after all, that had prompted so many in Hispania to follow those preachers who sought God in austerity and reclusion. And it was this preoccupation as well that would steel Pontius Paulinus—later known as Paulinus of Nola—to abandon his native Aquitaine and settle on the other side of the Pyrenees.

Asceticism was an exacting business. To renounce a promising career and donate one's wealth to pious works was a decision not to be taken lightly, and there existed, in addition, certain associated risks. Anything could happen once one "abandoned their hometown and their native dress and speech."[18] Just as much as in the age of Strabo, it remained an article of faith in late Roman ethnography that civilization could not be sustained in the wilderness, and that falling back into savagery, as Prudentius had cautioned his listeners, was always an insidious possibility. So insidious, in fact, that it was a good friend's duty to prevent it from happening.

Or so, at least, must have thought the poet Ausonius, Paulinus' erstwhile teacher. After sending four back-to-back letters to his former pupil's Spanish retreat and receiving no answer, he began to realize that something was amiss. "Have you, Paulinus, changed your sophisticated manners?"—the old master bemoaned. "Do the woodlands of the Vascones and your lodgings on the snowy Pyrenees and distance from our climate always have this effect?"[19] The flamboyant tone concealed a sinister insinuation. That, in going native, Paulinus might no longer even merit the name of Roman.

Given the severity of such an accusation, it is no surprise that Ausonius, this time at least, did not have to wait long for a response.

> Believe, *pater*, that I am not oblivious of the heavens nor do I live on destitute hills, but abide in a civilized place. . . . And if my life had been led on the borders of Vasconia, why should not the savage folk rather have been molded after my habits, casting aside their barbarous customs to come over to our own?[20]

In other words, Ausonius' fears were unfounded. The asceticism to which Paulinus aspired was not that of a rural preacher, clinging to the rocks of some desolate wasteland.

Rather, it was one that had ornate palaces and magnificent countryside estates as its favorite stages. Not for a single moment did it cross the young man's mind to abandon the mental frameworks his rank entailed, and he did not need to. For, luckily for him, there existed a plethora of places in the peninsula where a blue-blooded aristocrat could give free rein to his most exclusive and courteous instincts.

Regrettably, the Western Pyrenees—which Paulinus for the first time called Vasconia—seemed not to have ranked among these. The pupil did not correct the picture of ferocity and brigandry that his former tutor had conveyed. Quite the opposite, he espoused it wholeheartedly. He did not doubt for a moment that ignorance was the most evident quality that identified the locals, and the root of their disagreement came, instead, from the fact that Paulinus was hopeful that not even these unsophisticated shepherds were out of reach from God's gracious touch. A most optimistic prospect, perhaps, but one that he had nonetheless come to believe sincerely. "If one free of any wickedness spends his life in the woodlands of Vasconia, he draws no infection from the customs of his barbarous host."[21] The wicked, as it turned out, posed no danger to a true Christian. Civilization, once attained, could never be forfeited.

But how wicked were these Vascones exactly? Were one to trust Paulinus' and Ausonius' words, then their abode might appear a den of paganism and crude ignorance. Choose, instead, to heed Prudentius' poems—refined verses meant to be declaimed in the sumptuous halls of a highly cultured elite—and one might get quite a differing impression. What view of the natives, then, was the real one? And, most importantly, who exactly were these Vascones?

In this later point, at least, the apparent contradictions between this pair of sources—the only ones to speak about customs prevalent in the Western Pyrenees during the late empire—stem not from their differences, but rather from their ingrained similarities. Nowhere was this better demonstrated than in the show these individuals made of their erudition. Sprinkled here and there throughout the letters of the Aquitanian aristocrats, for example, episodes from myth and history wove threads that pitted Achilles against Theseus, where Punic Barcelona offered the counterpoint to Tyrrhenian Tarragona, and in which the horses of the god Mars shared a yoke with those that pulled the chariot of the Sun. Prudentius, even if allusions to pagan stories in his poetry were scarcer than references to the Gospels, was hardly to be acquitted from a similar charge: excessive ornamentation. In a literary environment so overcrowded by heroes and gods, in which the archaic mingled seamlessly with the contemporary, mentions of the Vascones did not stand out in the slightest. These were, in a sense, a pastiche of old cliches and venerable utterances. What was, for instance, Ausonius' and Paulinus' mention of the "woodlands"—*saltus*—of the Vascones, if not a loan straight out of Pliny's vocabulary? Just as much as mentions of the Medes or the Arabs could serve as a shorthand for any fierce foe of the Romans, so could the Vascones play the part, should the occasion arise, of the perilous mountain tribe lurking on the edges of barbarism. It was, after all, a metaphor, that ever since the age of Strabo had enjoyed a distinct pedigree of its own.

Thus, a combination of aristocratic haughtiness and contempt for foreigners gave Ausonius and Paulinus reasons aplenty to pile on the Vascones. And yet, in reality, the Western Pyrenees were hardly any entrenched stronghold of paganism. True, ecclesiastical buildings were absent from its landscape until the sixth century,[22] and altars, adorned with pagan motifs such as bull heads, were periodically carved during the early fifth century.[23] Confronted with such evidence, and accompanied by the testimonies of Ausonius and Paulinus, one could be forgiven for believing that the peoples of the Western Pyrenees did not embrace Christianity until very late, and that the veneration of the old gods endured in these parts for longer than in any other province of the empire.[24]

But the evidence that supported such a conclusion was far from unchallengeable. Reference to the alleged paganism of the provincials was too scarce and tendentious, in general, to be taken as anything more than polemic and poetic freedoms. The absence of proof of institutionalized Christianity during the late Roman empire, too, provided no definite proof of its absence. After all, even in Aquitaine—a territory that could brag endlessly about the prominence of its Christian luminaries—the traces left behind by churches and baptisteries were surprisingly rare.[25] No one would go as far as to infer from this that these were areas completely detached from the Christian world. Similarly, the discovery of a fifth or sixth-century Christian church under the cathedral of Pamplona does not confirm any delay on the part of the locals in embracing Christianity. Rather, it is telling of the degree to which the Western Pyrenees took part in the social and religious trends of Hispania, where the construction of churches inside city walls was only undertaken at around the same period.[26] To each altar to the ancient gods to be found in scattered rural villas, it was possible to oppose a similar number of Christian epigraphs and funerary inscriptions. Mosaics depicting the Muses only offered the counterpoint to Prudentius' poems about the triumph of the martyrs.

Of course, not all pagan practices were erased overnight. There were those who preferred instead to preserve their old traditions, sheltered in caves or mountain tops where it was impossible for the condemning eyes of Christian authorities to denounce them. Others proclaimed their outward acceptance of the Gospels while still conducting rituals and ceremonies which bishops and prelates saw as remnants of idolatry. And yet, deep though the residues of the veneration to the old gods ran in the countryside, none of that could single the Western Pyrenees out as an exceptional habitat for *gentilitas*. Prudentius, it is true, regularly admonished his fellow compatriots for their half-hearted embrace of Christianity and for their delight in pagan stories and fine arts: but so too did other fifth- and sixth-century Christian preachers in Gaul, Hispania, and even Rome. Tellingly, no Western Pyrenean that we know of was ever accused of excessive veneration of ancient deities, and that ceremonies of pagan reminiscence were conducted on hilltops and obscure grottoes all while churches were built in the most coveted spaces of the urban fabric ought to be read as obvious demonstrations of the extent of Christianity's victory.[27] The colonization of minds and space over such a rugged and politically unstructured territory was not, of course, an easy task, and it probably took longer than in more Romanized lands. Bishops from Pamplona or Calagurris might have experienced difficulties in keeping these new converts on as short a leash as they thought it was their right to do. But once the process was underway, there seems to have been no stopping it. The encroached paganism of a supposed Vascon community owed, in the final reckoning, more to literature than to reality.

No one can tell the story of the Christianization of the Western Pyrenees in its entirety. When it comes to addressing the battle for the minds and the souls of its inhabitants, the conclusive evidence of one modern scholar is the illusory exception of another. Silence, often, is taken as proof. The discovery of one Christian structure can only serve to highlight, in its splendid isolation, the whole array of possible Christian buildings that might have never been erected. The absence of traces of rural churches is noted, but never is the want of vestiges of rural temples cast under a similar degree of scrutiny. Lacking a consensus on what would constitute definite confirmation, determining the beginning or the end of a process such as Christianization is simply impossible. But it must be wondered why, when focusing this issue on the Western Pyrenees, evidence is hardly ever considered sufficient. Regardless of the amount of supplemental data that we gather—and this is now plenty—there exists always an enduring shadow of doubt. As if that dull paganism of the old Vascones were simply a step away from finally being unearthed.

This conclusion bears witness to the extent to which the accounts of Prudentius, Ausonius, and Paulinus continue to tinge our view of the Vascones and—more broadly—of Western Pyreneans as a whole. The barbarians of the past, through the appropriate Christian makeup provided by these orators, could seamlessly play the role of the pagans of the present. The savage beyond the border was transmuted into the savage within it. Old prejudices, as they often do, made new ones easier to embrace.

But this was a story that lay in the future. In the meantime, the world was shattered beyond repair. Winter's merciless bite had frozen the rivers solid. Violent warriors had overrun the garrisons that stood watch over the mountain passes. Cities, left to their own devices, had been besieged and plundered. And the empire of the Romans, a race of giants that had brought the entire world to its knees, faltered and crumbled beyond repair, never to return.

Notes

1 Blázquez, "Los vascones en las fuentes literarias," 148.

2 Urteaga, "El puerto romano de Irun (Guipuzcoa)," 99.

3 Pliny, *Naturalis Historia*, 4. 46. Tacitus, *Historiae*, 4. 33.

4 *Scriptores Historiae Augustae*, Severus Alexander, XXXVII, 6–7, 231.

5 Pelat, "Les identités ethniques en Novempopulanie, Wasconie et Aquitaine dans l'Antiquité tardive et haut Moyen âge (IIIe-IXe siècle)," 17–18.

6 Blázquez, "Los vascones en las fuentes literarias," 130.

7 Andreu and Lorenzo, "Nuevas reflexiones en torno a las fuentes literarias sobre los vascones en la antigüedad," 247.

8 The last attested mention of the Vardulians, for instance, comes from a garrison at Hadrian's Wall named Cohors I Fida Vardullorum and stationed in Britannia ever since 138 AD. The Caristians' last mention, on the other hand, comes from Ptolemy's *Geography*, which dates from the second century AD. Ptolemy, *Geography*, II, 2. 6. 8.

9 Jimeno, *Orígenes del Cristianismo en la tierra de los vascones*, 61.

10 Eusebius, *Ecclesiastical History*, VIII, II. 4, 259.

11 Hershkowitz, *Prudentius, Spain and Late Antique Christianity: Poetry, Visual Culture, and the Cult of the Martyrs*, 10.

12 Prudentius, "Peristephanon Liber." In Thompson, *Prudentius*, I, 34.

13 Prudentius, I, 90–1.

14 Prudentius, I, 94–5.

15 Sayas, "Algunas consideraciones sobre la cristianización de los vascones," 44–5.

16 "Gallic Chronicle of AD 452." In Hershkowitz, *Prudentius, Spain, and Late Antique Christianity*, 17–18.

17 Prudentius, "Peristephanon Liber." In Thompson, *Prudentius*, I, 34–5.

18 Ausonius, "Letter XXVII to Paulinus of Nola." In Evelyn White, *Ausonius*, 69–71.

19 Ausonius, 50–2.

20 Paulinus of Nola, "Letter to Ausonius." In Evelyn White, *Ausonius*, 195–7, 218–20.

21 Paulinus, 212–15.

22 De Brestian, "Vascones and Visigoths: Creation and Transformation of Identity in Northern Spain in Late Antiquity," 292.

23 See, for instance, the overview of these discoveries made by Hershkowitz, *Prudentius, Spain and Late Antique Christianity*, 58–9.

24 Sayas, "Algunas consideraciones," 56.

25 This is the conclusion of Hershkowitz, *Prudentius, Spain, and Late Antique Christianity*, 67–8.

26 Kulikowski, "Cities and Government in Late Antique Hispania: Recent Advances and Future Research," 63–4.

27 Gaudemet and Basdevant, *Les Canons des Conciles Mérovingiens (VI*e*-VII*e* siècles)*, II, 384–5.

CHAPTER 3

ARACAELI

It had all started back in the year 406. In the remote reaches of Germania, where the chill of the season bit cruelly into the flesh, the mighty Rhine—long the natural boundary of Rome's empire—froze solid. The occurrence transformed the river, so often a barrier against incursion, into an open highway for the restless tribes beyond. Alani, Suevi, Vandals: These groups and others overran the Roman garrisons in one fell swoop and obliterated their defenses. Unhindered by fear of reprisal, they then roamed the fertile lands of Gaul, plundering and indulging in an "orgy of destruction."[1]

Chaos ensued afterward. As news of the devastation spread, it became painfully clear that the imperial center was incapable of coping with the situation. In Britannia, an ambitious general who styled himself Constantine III took the opportunity to make a desperate gamble. Stripping the island of its defenses, he shipped his troops to the continent, abandoning the northern province to its fate. Upon landing in Gaul, he negotiated a truce with the barbarians that still pillaged it. Constantine's eyes were not set, after all, on the quenching of some fires on the frontier. Rather, he had much bigger fish to fry. Appointing his son to command, he sent off a military detachment to Hispania to subjugate the loyalist forces of Honorius, the sitting emperor. The fate of Rome hung precariously in the balance.

The soldiers dispatched by Constantine were probably unafraid of what awaited them as they marched through the Pyrenees. Jagged and unyielding, the shortest route into Hispania carved its way through their western slopes, threading through several cities and towns of the *Tarraconensis* province, but the detachments stationed in fortresses like Pamplona or Veleia were no match for the battle-hardened legions coming from more disputed frontiers. Their usual duties were, after all, pretty mundane: They patrolled the *Iter XXXIV*—the road that connected much of the peninsula with Gaul and the rest of the empire—kept the mountain passes open for travelers, chased brigands and cutthroats, and administered the orderly shipment of goods and taxes to the heartlands of the empire. From a soldier's standpoint, the Western Pyrenees must have offered a relatively quiet and tranquil destination.

Unsurprisingly, the mountain crossings were soon overcome by force, and the local military, which for generations had safeguarded the vital artery of communication, was unceremoniously relieved from its post. The loss was a bitter shock, not only to the soldiers' sense of pride and identity but also to their livelihoods. The outrage in the land, as Constantine's officers took command of cities, towns, and estates, was overwhelming and patent. Yet, infuriating though these vexing circumstances must have appeared to those involved, they were but a prelude. Greater trials, harsher and more devastating, loomed on the horizon.

By 409, a mere two years after Constantine's forces had disembarked in Hispania, a new threat descended from the peaks. The bands of Alani, Suevi, and Vandals, who since the freezing of the Rhine had scourged the countryside of Gaul, arrived in the Pyrenees. Be it because Constantine's men had orders to let the barbarians in or because they were, as a chronicler put it, "tempted by the wealth of the province to let their crimes go all the more unpunished and to have more scope for crime," the road into Hispania opened wide before them.[2] The consequences were nothing short of catastrophic. Defenseless, the inhabitants of the peninsula were soon exposed to the same fate that had befallen the Gauls. The Suevi and the Alani rushed west toward the Atlantic; the Vandals, on the other hand, swept south. Few, if any, settled in the Western Pyrenees. And yet, their eruption in otherwise peaceful and exposed provinces did not fail in irrevocably altering the landscape. Within a few short years, these warlike peoples had already extorted enough payment and carved for themselves a sufficiently strong position so as to claim the rule of western and southern Hispania. By 411, when the legitimate Emperor Honorius finally managed to reassert control over the *Tarraconensis*, the Western Pyrenees had ceased to be an unremarkable stopover on the journey between Gaul and Iberia. Instead, they had become the very edge of the world ruled from Rome.

Unfortunately, the empire of the Romans gave the impression of being utterly unprepared to address the turmoil in its westernmost domains. In no small part, this apparent frailty was the result of years of disgraces and usurpations—Constantine III's among them. The emperor, his attention focused on surviving within his own palace, had become ill-suited to confront any of the large-scale upheavals shaking the empire. The central order tottered and so too did Rome. The ultimate testament to this collapse would come a few years later, in 410, when a people from beyond the Danube to whom the Romans gave the name of Goths seized and stormed the city of Romulus. "And so the city which had been the conqueror of all nations was conquered and overpowered by the triumph of the Goths."[3]

It was tempting, for some, to interpret the succession of calamities visited upon Rome as a symptom of its terminal decline. And yet, even amid the ruin, not everything was lost. The empire, battered though it was, still possessed a potent allure—a gold-lit splendor that could captivate even those who ranked as its enemies. The Goths, who had by no means proved immune to these seductions in the past, could still be drawn to its side if approached with the right blend of well-timed proposals. Treat them with suitable respect, offer them rewards commensurate with their ambitions, and even the plunderers of the city of the Caesars could be made to fight in its defense.

The Goths themselves, naturally, saw affairs rather differently. In an age when internecine wars among the Romans had become the norm, and rival factions vied for supremacy but lacked a strong position to dominate outright, Gothic leaders quickly recognized the unique leverage they possessed as kingmakers. Even when employed by imperial authorities to crush other barbarians—such as the Vandals, Alani, and Suevi in Hispania—they did so with a fixed eye on the reward. In 419, after one such victorious campaign, they extracted from the emperor the right to settle in Aquitaine and saw their status elevated to that of official allies of Rome. So was born the kingdom of Toulouse, and although time would blur the exact details of this arrangement, one fact, at least, stood beyond dispute. The Goths, even while ostensibly acting as agents at the service of the empire, were now a major player in the politics of the western provinces.

A major player, but not the only one. In Hispania, the fractured provincial order that had emerged in the wake of the barbarian incursions of 409 had begun to settle into a grim semblance of stability. While the Western Pyrenees remained tenuously under imperial control, it took only a few days' journey across the *Iter XXXIV* to arrive at the kingdom that the barbarous Suevi had carved for themselves in the westernmost reaches of Iberia. Elsewhere, four decades into the fifth century, the effective dislocation of Roman power in the *Tarraconensis* had become, for all intents and purposes, a fact of life. Communities that had once turned to Saragossa, Tarragona, or even Rome itself for guidance now felt increasingly abandoned to their own devices. The imperial gaze, such as it was, seemed directed elsewhere, focused on balancing out the ambitions of the Goths and the Suevi, rather than on bringing them to compliance.

Especially for those in the periphery, this neglect demanded confronting a series of hard truths. As the prospect of an imperial counterattack faded into impossibility, survival came to depend less on appeals to the court in Ravenna and more on their own ability to adapt to shifting circumstances. To navigate the treacherous waters of a turbulent world was no longer optional, but a matter of life or death. Rome, the lighthouse of civilization, was faltering. And so, an ominous realization took root among the locals: They would have to face the tide on their own.

Such a train of thought must have held particular resonance in the Western Pyrenees. Here, in a territory squeezed between the lands of the Suevi and the Goths, the shadow erstwhile cast by Roman power only arrived in the most diffused of manners. For those tasked with the defense of the frontier, the sensation of being castaways amid a sinking world must have seemed insurmountable. No wonder, then, that those who had reaped the greatest benefits by virtue of their ties with the court and who had prospered thanks to the favor of distant emperors came to suddenly feel the tinge of a threat upon their necks. The class of the *possessores*—landowners and civil servants of whom Prudentius had been a distinguished spokesman—had always felt entitled to look down on the rudeness and brutality of military simpletons. But as the mighty edifice of Roman power crumbled and collapsed all around them, such marks of haughtiness proved to be an increasingly unsustainable luxury. To command a loyal retinue of warriors—small or ragged though it might appear at first glance—was in those times of ever-deepening crisis an asset not even the most presumptuous and well-connected of oligarchs could afford to pass over with arrogance. In such a world, real power lay not in imperial titles or court connections but manifested itself in the ability to control the native troops stationed in the Western Pyrenees. And for the aristocracy, this was no longer a question of pride, but one of survival.

Not everyone, however, must have seemed so concerned with what the future held in store. For those in waiting, the fall of the *possessores* would have presented a prime opportunity to seize their vacant post. Indeed, many were discontent with the current functioning of their society, and the anxieties proper to an age of upheaval formed a perfect breeding ground for opposition against the guardians of tradition to coalesce. Army officers, accustomed to meeting the haughtiness of intellectuals with the martial harshness that came so naturally to men of action, could not let pass the occasion of rubbing the noses of the *possessores* in the fact of their own vulnerability. The few garrisons that dotted the *Iter XXXIV were* firmly under their command, and this meant that they had much to gain were the law of the jungle to be established. Get rid of imperial meddling, and the Western Pyrenees would be theirs—and theirs alone—to rule.

Brewing underground, the opposition had likely been gathering pace and support in the long decades that followed the barbarian invasions. But by the 440s, its reach could no longer be concealed. The first news of the conflict, passed on by a Roman bishop from the neighboring Suevic kingdom, dates the eruption of hostilities to 441—but it is impossible to say how long the tensions had been mounting beneath the surface.[4] One thing, however, was abundantly clear: Large swathes of the Western Pyrenees had become a battlefield.

Back in ancient times, the term *Bacauda* had carried no hint of menace. It simply meant "warrior" in the Celtic tongue—a badge of honor rather than one of shame. But by the fifth century the word had come to bear a far more pernicious connotation. Stained by its association with revolts against Roman authority in Gaul, it had come to signify an outlaw, a rebel against the established order, an enemy to civilization itself.[5] It was likely that the *possessores* of the Western Pyrenees, in their eagerness to depreciate those chieftains who sought to cast off their supervision, might soon have come to refer to the retinues that made up their rivals as *Bacaudae*. And yet, it was equally possible that this label was not merely the invention of embittered members of the traditional elite. In fact, the association might have come from outsiders attempting to apply familiar labels upon the complexities of a local conflict. An option, indeed, that aligns well with the evidence. The Western Pyrenean *Bacaudae*, just like their Gaulish counterparts, was made up of military bands that had been branded the enemies of the emperor: a description that fits to perfection those chieftains who, over the preceding decades, had grown increasingly impatient with the share of power monopolized by the Ravenna-backed aristocracy. The hunch appears further vindicated by the only recorded reference to their stronghold: Aracaeli, a modest surveillance post perched above a particularly narrow stretch of the *Iter XXXIV*.[6] What this suggests is that the eruption of the *Bacaudae*, for all that chroniclers would frame it as the uprise of infuriated peasants or as the anti-imperialistic action of a long-vanished barbarian tribe, represented something different altogether. It was a coup by local warlords determined to shake off the last vestiges of Roman civil authority and to claim power for themselves.

But there is no making an omelet without breaking a few eggs—and in the violent environment of the 440s and 450s, this meant bad news for the locals. Raids and banditry, fires and pillaging: All grew into grimly familiar sights during these years of upheaval, even though the specifics, thanks to the disinterest of the *literati* in what was otherwise an insignificant spot of a diminishing empire, have been lost to time. Military campaigns, too, swept through the region like storms. In 449, the leaders of the *Bacaudae*, after suffering some setbacks at the hands of the imperial forces, turned to the Suevic king for aid in their struggle against the *possessores*. Five years later, it was the landlords' turn to seek salvation—this time from the Goths of Toulouse, who marched into the Pyrenees with the intent of obliterating the rebels.

In all, the destructive capabilities to which native leaders had access could bear no comparison to those wielded by the Suevi or the Goths, but they must have aggravated the scars left by the war all the same. By the time of the last recorded mention of the *Bacaudae* in 454, the entire region had become a wasteland. Of the rosary of thriving towns that had littered the *Iter XXXIV* to serve as havens for weary travelers, less than one in five endured into the second half of the fifth century: Veleia was depopulated; Aracaeli, eradicated.[7] Out of the entire network of settlements that had once constituted the backbone of Roman authority in the region, only Pamplona managed to survive. But now it did so, not as the head of a hierarchically structured district of a Roman province, but rather as a ramshackle boat amid a sea of desolation.

The wreckage, for all that it defied comprehension, also had a further consequence. Ravenna's authority, already faltering across Hispania, had as a result of the civil war receded entirely from the Pyrenees. Under such conditions, what hope could aristocrats harbor about ever restoring all that had been lost? Some, resigning themselves to the inevitable, realized the futility of their resistance and bowed to the winds of change. Others gathered what they could and fled, and any semblance of civil authority departed in their wake. Weakened and diminished, the masters of a ruined and smoldering battlefield, the leaders of the *Bacaudae* had triumphed. Yet their victory, such as it was, was emblematic of the new world dawning around them—a world where the sword, not the law, would reign supreme.

Notes

1 Orosius, *Seven Books of History against Pagans*, VII. 40. 4.

2 Orosius, VII. 40. 9.

3 Isidore of Seville, *History of the Goths, Vandals, and Suevi*, 15.

4 Burgess, *The Chronicle of Hydatius and the Consularia Constantinopolitana: Two Contemporary Accounts of the Final Years of the Roman Empire*.

5 Pozo, *Vasconia tardoantigua. Entre la evolución sociopolítica y la construcción intelectual (400–711)*, 157.

6 Burgess, *The Chronicle of Hydatius*, 120.

7 Pozo, *Vasconia tardoantigua*, 165–9.

CHAPTER 4
THE VAST EMPTINESS

Clovis searched the plain and caught a glimpse of the enemy in the distance: the shining reflection of the sun on their helmets and the tip of their spears, the muted murmur of their footsteps, the plumes of smoke as they rose from their torches. The forces of Alaric, King of the Goths, certainly outnumbered his. Not for a man like Clovis, though, to get scared by unfavorable odds. Since the age of sixteen, when he had inherited his father's position as the leader of a Frankish warband, his life had been defined by struggle—and by victory. After over twenty years of almost constant warring and fighting, he had succeeded in carving out a kingdom for himself in northeastern Gaul at the expense of his rivals: the Alamans, the Armoricans, the Burgundians. Now, in the year 507, the time had come to test his strength against the greatest competitor of the lot.

The Goths were not only the masters of southern Gaul and Hispania, but they had been the most fearsome military power in the Roman west for more than a century. Their treasure hoards in Toulouse overflowed with riches spoiled from cities, villas, and temples which newcomers like Clovis could only dream of. As he traversed the rain-swollen lands that led to the town of Poitiers, the Frankish king must have certainly mulled over these matters, but he had no illusions as to what failing in his attempt to crush the Goths would mean for him. As he dispatched the final orders to his soldiers, set across the field of Vouillé,[1] Clovis realized that this was the moment for which he had been preparing his entire life.

Historians, many years later, would take pains to explain what had happened that bloody day of spring. They would report how Clovis' archers had rained down volley after deadly volley over the Gothic troops; how the Frankish infantry, unyielding in their advance, had surged forward over the muddy plain; the unbearable sound of shields clashing against each other rising above the cries of the embattled armies. More than anything, however, a particular duel amid the carnage would monopolize their attention, for the two kings, Alaric and Clovis, were said to have engaged in single, mortal combat. Blows had been traded, and then, after a brief brawl, Clovis had finally thrust his sword into the neck of the Gothic ruler. No sooner had he done so than two of Alaric's bodyguards "rushed up in the scrum, one on this side and one on that, and struck the Frankish king with their spears."[1]

---

[1]The reference to the *campus Vogladensis* has traditionally been interpreted as directing to this town, although other alternatives—such as Voulon, near Poitiers—have also been suggested.

Saved narrowly from death thanks only to the robustness of his leather corselet, Clovis managed to escape the battle just in time to see the Goths scattering in all directions. The field was indisputably his. In the aftermath of the battle, the treasures of Toulouse, amassed over many decades, were sacked. The city itself was put to the torch. Expelled from most territories north of the Pyrenees, the debilitated Goths retreated southward into Hispania, where they began the painful task of building a new home for themselves. As for Clovis, his triumph in Vouillé would long be remembered. For countless generations, this clash between two rival warlords would be hailed as the precise moment when "France began."[2]

In the Western Pyrenees, news of Alaric's downfall was met with unease. Though half a century had passed since the dark days of chronic unrest, some among the region's elders could still recall the days when the kings of Toulouse had thrown their weight behind their landowning rivals. And yet, no vendettas had been pursued. Quite the contrary. Much like in other territories south of the mountain range, the following period had schooled the heirs of the *Bacaudae* on the benefits of cultivating good relations with the ascendant power of the Goths.

No longer a supplicant at Rome's table, the latter had become, after all, a force capable of dictating the fates of the western provinces. Their dominance, previously shrouded in a veil of nominal submission to the empire, had long before the events of Vouillé been made apparent, and by the time tidings of the deposal of the last Roman emperor reached it in 476, Hispania was already well beyond the grasp of Ravenna's administration. Only a few years prior, an army recruited to crush the last remaining obstacles to Toulouse's ambitions in the *Tarraconensis* had traversed Pamplona unmolested. The passive acquiescence of the city's potentates spoke volumes about the Goths' standing among their neighbors. Fear, after all, was a powerful tool—one that the kings of Toulouse wielded masterfully. Either by parading the decapitated head of a rebel leader across the province, or by dragging their enemies in chains to their capital, there to be sealed in "bronze bulls and burnt alive," the spectacle was one calculated to drive home a single message. That opposing Gothic rule was a fool's errand.[3]

Or so it had been up to this point. The unmitigated setback inflicted by Clovis upon Alaric's Gothic forces threatened to upend this balance. In the process of driving their enemies ever southward, it did not take long for the Franks to establish a tenuous suzerainty over most lands north of the Pyrenees. What lay beyond, on the other hand, seemed to concern them not at all. Occupied as they were with reaping the fruits of their victories and securing the territorial gains these had granted them, the Merovingians—the dynasty to which Clovis belonged—displayed little interest in intervening in Spanish affairs. The heirs of Alaric, in turn, had enough with navigating as best they could the waters of their calamity, and therefore were, at least for the time being, ill-suited to enforce any direct rule over Iberia. The combination of these two factors—Frankish unwillingness and Gothic inability—was to prove most beneficial to the ambitions of peripheral elites. Soon enough, and across the entire expanse of the peninsula, urban governments and regional aristocracies took the reins of power into their own hands.

Much disarticulated though the Western Pyrenees had become in the aftermath of the *Bacaudae*, and perilous though a sojourn through its valleys proved to be due to the disrepair and abandonment of the Roman infrastructure, the military chieftains entrenched in Pamplona and other minor strongholds clung fast to what influence they could muster. Chief among their assets was the control they exerted over one of the crucial roads linking Hispania to the continent, but it was hardly the only ones. Pamplona, modest though it was, was also the seat of a Catholic bishopric. The ties that connected this cleric to the broader structure of the Hispanic church, for all that they remained tenuous and discontinuous, offered the city's elites a fragile window to a larger network of influence and legitimacy. Under the circumstances, it remained the best that their resources could avail. A makeshift order, forged from the remnants of a collapsing world, was better by far than no order whatsoever.

The meteoric rise of the Franks did not fail to affect these petty lords living in their vicinity. On the rare occasions when the chieftains of the Western Pyrenees sought goods of craftsmanship unattainable in their own lands, their gaze would turn instinctively northward. The recurrence of such exchanges had, over time, bestowed upon the warlords of the region a veneer of Frankish glamour. Weapons, belts, rings, the list of luxuries to be found in the tombs of these aristocrats bore witness to a cultural orientation that mirrored the customs of the Franks far more closely than those of the southern Goths.

But this was not merely an act of opportunistic imitation. Rather, these rituals told the story of a society unlike any other that could be encountered anywhere else in the peninsula. One in which, due to the meagerness of its available resources, it was the practice of war, rather than the control of cities or the possession of estates, that mattered most to sustain social hierarchy. Men—and, occasionally, women—marked their rank by interring themselves alongside a spear, or a sword, or a knife that constituted the preeminent symbols of their status. And yet, the availability of such prestigious goods was so dire that each generation had little recourse beyond fighting to garner the wealth and standing needed to reclaim them. Before long, violence became endemic. It was this unswerving devotion to the feats of arms that most singled out these aristocrats from the rest of their counterparts in Hispania. It manifested, for everyone to see, the extent of the transformation that the previous century had wrought upon the higher echelons of Western Pyrenean society. The success of military strongmen to wrest control out of the hands of civil authorities had, over the course of only a couple of generations, enshrined warfare as the ultimate trade of an aristocrat. It had redefined, against the intellectualism so dearly treasured by imperial patricians, what it truly meant to be successful.

A view, naturally, that must have helped in rendering them an object of scorn to their neighbors, who still clung to the estates and attitudes of the late Roman *possessores*. But not only to them. Both the Merovingians and the Visigoths—"west Goths"—had spent the decades after their reckoning in Vouillé solidifying what had initially been the rule of might by inviting provincials in Gaul and Hispania to legitimize their government. Their methods were simple, and they included cloaking the brute fact of their own position in the garments of Roman political tradition. An art that, over the course of the sixth century, the heirs of Clovis and Alaric had come to perfect.

To rule as a Caesar had once demanded a peculiar array of responsibilities, like sponsoring poets and chroniclers, constructing public monuments, promulgating local edicts, or even enforcing an intricate courtly etiquette. Imitators, if they were to be taken seriously, ought to do pretty much the same. Yet a public relations operation on such a scale could not help but produce some unforeseen consequences. By endorsing the foundational precepts of Roman ideology, Frankish and Gothic monarchs could not help but gradually comply with the very traditions they sought to exploit. They increasingly came to adopt a worldview that mirrored the imperial ideal—a vision of a civilized center surrounded by a barbarous periphery. And, in doing so, they subtly redefined their own position, not merely as kings, but as stewards of a civilization they had once sought to conquer.

The view applied especially to the Visigoths. The successors to Alaric's throne, licking their wounds as they were driven south into the Iberian Peninsula, had, against all odds, managed to rebuild a new power base from the ruins of their former strength. Even so, had it not been for the events that followed Leovigild's accession to the Visigothic throne in 568, these would have had little impact on Western Pyrenean history. Nominally, the meager aristocracies of the region were still Visigothic vassals, as they had been before Vouillé, but the ensuing weakness of the new Gothic kingdom had left ample room for those attracted to the idea of commanding their own affairs. Every minor defeat, every miscarriage, every doubtful succession brought the tensions between centripetal and centrifugal forces to the fore. And if that was not enough, the moral stature of the sovereigns themselves, it appears, did not make up for it. Whereas some were remembered for their "bad luck and cowardice"[4] or for being "contemptible in the eyes of all,"[5] others were even accused of having "defiled the marriages of very many powerful men by public prostitution."[6] In such an unsympathetic environment, it was hardly surprising that royal assassinations would rapidly become commonplace. Admittedly, internecine wars and usurpations had become so routine in the nascent kingdom of Toledo that a Frankish historian could playfully refer to the tendency to depose and murder their rulers as the *morbus Gothorum*—the "Gothic disease."[7]

Leovigild's reign, though, was destined to change this situation for good. Almost from the beginning, the new monarch devoted himself wholeheartedly to restoring his people's uncontested dominion over the peninsula. He attacked and conquered the Suevi to the northwest, campaigned against the Byzantines on the Mediterranean coast, and—perhaps most spectacularly—cracked the resistance of the northerners during the early 570s. The leading families of the Western Pyrenees, for all that they opted not to engage in battle and chose instead to renew their pacts of submission, were unlikely to have welcomed this renewed imposition with enthusiasm. After all, from the Atlantic shore to the Straits of Gibraltar, and from the Mediterranean to the slopes of the Pyrenees, no shelter appeared now to lay beyond the reach of Leovigild and his armies. More than a reconquista, his triumphs bespoke a new beginning for the Goths. The creation of a realm that would haunt the imaginations of the dwellers of Iberia for centuries.

Not that Leovigild's victorious campaigns, however, were free from menacing shadows. The king, as part of his attempt to secure the loyalty of the Hispano-Roman potentates, had not hesitated to embrace concepts and attitudes more appropriate to a Caesar than to a successor of Alaric. These signals, for all that they must have been well received by their intended audience, raised suspicions among the Gothic nobility—and not just among them. To many, Leovigild's conciliatory policies only served to underscore an already notable divide. The Goths, though Christian, did not share in the Catholic faith of those they ruled. Instead, they adhered to a doctrine—Arianism—that the orthodox Church had for more than two centuries considered heretical.

Perhaps, had the kingdom of Toledo persisted in its former, tenuous existence, tensions between these two confessions might have taken longer to surface. But Leovigild's triumphs, in ending the effective control exercised by regional authorities, inevitably threatened the dominance that bishops and other Catholic strongmen had erstwhile held over their congregations. The Arian episcopate, though much less numerous, enjoyed royal favor, while Catholics, on the other hand, clamored for the protection of a leader against what they considered a heretical overrun. And so, in 580, when Hermenegild, Leovigild's son, decided to rebel against his father's authority and converted to Catholicism, there was no shortage of malcontents willing to join his cause. The rebellion quickly gained traction, spreading across vast regions of the peninsula. The struggle for the soul of the newly revived Visigothic kingdom threatened, after Leovigild's monumental efforts, to shatter it once again into pieces.

In the Western Pyrenees, Hermenegild's rebellion found considerable endorsement among members of the ruling class, but the reasons behind such a course of action remain unknown. There is no doubting the militant Catholicism of the established elite, but it was impossible to determine whether their support for the rebellion stemmed from religious zeal or rather from an opportunistic attempt to shake off Leovigild's yoke. After all, the affirmation of the Visigothic realm had come at the expense of the autonomy previously enjoyed by these warlords. Whatever the underlying motives, however, the Gothic monarch, in a display of his proverbial determination, acted swiftly and decisively against them. In 581, only a year after the outbreak of the revolt, the unbeatable king invaded the Western Pyrenees.

This time, however, he was not alone. If Hermenegild's actions had put the Visigothic kingdom at risk of fragmentation, a similar fate was already a reality among the heirs of Clovis. The great Frankish kingdom, split over the years among several heirs, had come to resemble in recent decades a chessboard to which recent events in Hispania added yet another layer of play. Supremacy in the peninsula, as both contenders appreciated, could eventually depend on the favor of Frankish kings, and Leovigild, in his effort to chastise his rebellious son, had known exactly where to seek assistance. While his forces marched north from Toledo, a Frankish army prepared to subdue the Western Pyrenees from the opposite end. In a bloody campaign, in which the Frankish commander—a certain Bladastes—was said to have "lost most of his army," the region was occupied.[8] After all, no force the locals could levy could withstand a pincer attack of the magnitude of the one Leovigild had managed to conjure. Hermenegild's supporters, cornered in the mountains, were either defeated or forced to sue for terms. The Western Pyrenees were pacified. Three years later, the rest of Hispania followed suit.

As this rapid succession of events had demonstrated, tending to the delicate web of alliances upon which kingdoms such as that of the Visigoths depended to function could be an arduous and often-thankless task. If the putting out of Hermenegild's uprising could be seen as an unmitigated victory for Leovigild, it was also proof of his failure in attracting key players in Hispania to his side. But now, as swords sheathed again, time was ripe for olive branches. And this, for the aristocrats of the Western Pyrenees, guardians of a sensitive confluence between the Goths and the Franks and therefore valuable players in the frontier, bespoke a promising future. Collaboration with the mighty king might be, in hindsight, a better policy than overt defiance, and both sides had, in the aftermath of the aborted revolt, every motive to seek an uneasy agreement.

Which is why in 587, only a year after the death of the great monarch, his successor had recruited some of these chieftains to launch, in his name, an incursion into the southwestern possessions of the Merovingians. The promise of plunder, as well as the constant need these warlords felt to reaffirm their positions, must have weighed heavily on their decision to participate. So too did, of course, the desire to avoid the wrath of the royal army once again. Sailing with the wind, "the Vascones, descending from the mountains, swept into the plains [of Gaul], devastating vineyards and fields, setting houses ablaze, and taking some captives along with livestock."[9]

Nearly two centuries had passed since Prudentius, Ausonius, and Paulinus of Nola, all of them eager to display their erudition, had last employed the ancient term "Vascones" to describe the inhabitants of the Western Pyrenees. In the meantime, the complete collapse of imperial authority, waves of barbarian invasions, and the long years of civil war had all transformed the region from a quiet, marginal backwater into a contested frontier between two uneasy neighbors. Much had changed. And yet, some things appeared impervious to the touch of time. To Frankish chroniclers—the first to revive the term—the Vascones appeared an unruly, untamable lot, no different in essence from the wild shepherds and bandits who were said to have roamed the hills back in the age of Pompey. The cities built, the roads laid out, the commodities and ideas traded and transported—all, at least on the surface, appeared to have been in vain. Like a sandcastle stranded on a lonesome beach, the frail patina of sophistication that the tenacity of the Romans had poured over the region appeared to have crumbled with the empire's retreat. What remained was the same backwardness that so had disgusted Strabo, the same paganism that had so appalled Ausonius. If the chroniclers' accounts were to be believed, it was as if natural savagery, after a brief respite of hope, had ultimately prevailed in the Western Pyrenees.

If such a description of the region and its surroundings seems an implausibly bleak one, it is because it most certainly was. Later writers may have taken great pleasure in imagining the Vascones as unyielding warriors, tirelessly repelling the efforts of Romans, Visigoths, or Franks to dominate them. But contemporaries knew better. To inhabit a town like Pamplona, and to gaze out from a Roman-built wall over a Roman-laid road, was to confront the undeniable imprint that centuries of integration and assimilation had left on the customs of the locals. Now, the incorporation of the natives as players in the Gothic and Frankish rivalry demonstrated that such dynamics were far from a thing of the past. Ever since the first arrival of the legions, this imbrication—blurry at times, at others painfully concrete—had stamped onto the peoples of the Western Pyrenees a new mental universe. They had navigated this imposed order, at times reluctantly but often with a measure of acceptance. What was, if not an exercise of wishful thinking, to imagine that they had not been transformed by it?

The Vascones among which Pompey had once set up camp were not—could not be—the direct forebears of the warriors defeated by Leovigild. Their clothing, their weapons, and even their ways of thinking had changed far too drastically for such continuity to hold true. And if this conclusion comes so naturally to us, armed with the hindsight of centuries but also the fuzzy myopia of millennia, it likewise raises an intriguing question in turn. Why did so many, in places like Toledo or Paris, persist in believing otherwise?

The answer—as it is often the case—lay in books. The Vascones might have reemerged in 587, yet theirs was a name that had not entirely vanished after the age of Prudentius. More than a century earlier, as the strength of the Romans was faltering, a Spanish chronicler had already made an offhand reference to the "Vasconias."[10] For the first time in recorded history—or leastways as far as we know—the term was applied to the lands that stretched across the southern slopes of the Western Pyrenees. Initially, such a reference might seem to confirm the enduring relevance of the name and the actual existence of the people it described, but a closer scrutiny casts some doubts upon this conclusion. Anyhow, the rest of the chronicle was riddled with outdated and overtly archaic terms. The implication, once again, was that, much like Prudentius and their peers, this mention of the Vascones and other pre-Roman peoples served less as the description of a living, breathing society and more as a convenient shorthand for scholarly erudition. And as was so often the case with such artifacts of literary vanity, the word soon drifted back into oblivion. The silence that followed only underscored how detached this final appearance was from the realities of the time.

Had this been the end of the story, it would have hardly merited a mention. Like so many fragments of Rome's fulgurant past, words too had come, in the aftermath of the empire's collapse, to be treated as relics—either to be neglected or to be stripped of their practical purpose. But now, more than half a century after Alaric's death, winds of change were blowing. As the courts of the Visigoths and the Merovingians gained acceptance in their respective territories, so too did the stakes of maintaining this preponderance become higher than ever. Fail in the effort, and the rule so hardly fought over might fall like a house of cards. While the hostility between Arians and Catholics in Visigothic Hispania might have been the most explosive and dramatic demonstration of what could happen when this delicate balance was upturned, they were hardly the only one.

Winning over the provincial aristocracies meant absorbing their ways of life, their tastes, and their ideologies. After all, for the heirs of Rome, accepting the rule of those whom their ancestors had scorned as savages required just the one, the essential concession: that they masked this yoke in the trappings of the Caesars. Far from being a pastime for idle minds, classical learning was precisely the foundation on which this entire process of social illusionism rested. The Franks offered a case in point. The successors of Clovis—a warrior-king whose lineage, it was claimed, could be traced back to a sea monster—now traded in manuscripts, vied for the services of notorious poets, and surrounded themselves with aristocrats educated in Ravenna or Constantinople. They were living proof of how barbarians—if aided by the self-congratulating cultural handholding of the nobility—could be gained for *Romanitas*.

One such courtier was Venantius Fortunatus. A determined and talented man, Fortunatus had spent his formative years in Ravenna, immersed in the unbroken currents of Eastern imperial influence. There, in a city where antiquity and innovation still walked hand in hand, he had honed his craft. By 566, when his career took him back to Francia, Fortunatus' eloquence and innate boldness rapidly caught the attention of the various Merovingian courts and, shortly after, his poems—loaded as they were with praise for Frankish rulers and brimming with classical references—had already become the talk of anyone eager to project a façade of sophistication. Bishops, noblemen, even members of the royal family—none could resist the allure of having their deeds immortalized by the poet.

Fortunatus' panegyrics were particularly celebrated. Not for nothing, these were texts which bore a potent and intoxicating perfume: of vivid landscapes of antiquity that, in their perfect fusion of the new and the archaic, whispered promises of eternal renown to those they portrayed. Fortunatus, whenever required to perform in front of the *crème de la crème* of Frankish society, had no illusions as to what was expected of him. He knew that creativity, in a poet, was not so much a talent to cultivate as a deficiency to correct. To speak, to think, and to see the world as a Roman had once done: Therein lay the hallmark of a genuinely cultured intellect. A conclusion which rendered him, thanks to his studies and his experiences, the ideal man for the job. A voice from another time, capable of infusing the ambitions of any upstart with the gravitas of antiquity.

Already in 569, a mere three years after his return to Francia, Fortunatus had spoken of the Vascones. That year, on the occasion of the reception of some relics from Constantinople, the courtesan had composed an elaborate tribute to the Eastern emperors in which he had evoked how people from the four corners of the world admired their merits. Batavians, Bretons, Germans, Cantabrians—the poet's inventory of ancient ethnonyms, steeped as it was in classical flourish, was one explicitly designed to appear as exhaustive as it seemed unending. The Vascones, obscure yet faintly resonant to those most acquainted with ancient authors, were only a natural addition to such a catalog.[11]

But a decade later, in 580, Fortunatus once again stirred the ghosts of Rome's past. Addressing this time a Merovingian ruler, he wove a tapestry of grandiloquent praise. "O King, renowned in war and sprung from a noble line of kings, foremost of those of old, commanding the foremost heights," he wrote, "as a leader you inherited honor by birth, but increased it by your wise rule."[12] The portrait, as so often in Roman literary tradition, was an exaggerated one. However, this did not worry the poet one bit. "The Creator decreed that for the sake of your house, your country, and your people, you live, a hero, whom the nations fear."

But what nations was Fortunatus talking about? The ancient enemies of the Romans were a distant memory and, moreover, the Franks had hardly ever fought against any of them. Unbothered by the obvious anachronism, Fortunatus instead seized the moment to dazzle with his erudition and flair for the dramatic. "You inspire fear in the Goth, the Vascon, the Dane, the Jute, the Saxon, and the Briton."[13] The rhetorical display was anything but accidental, for these were the names of the tribes that, back in ancient times, had populated the lands to which the Merovingians now lay claim. Thanks to Fortunatus' words these were now transformed, retrofitted to describe the very elites so recently subdued by the might of Frankish and Visigothic arms. Like the reanimated body of a warrior from a bygone era, forced to rise and fight anew, Fortunatus had salvaged the Vascones from the wreckage of the empire.

An innovation, though, that was not destined to remain confined to his personal use for long. Eagerly recited in the educated circles of the kingdom, the panegyrics and praises produced by Fortunatus soon began to shape how these elites imagined their own world and how they spoke about it, too. And if this could apply to warriors and generals, it certainly was a truth that applied to historians as well.

"Revered eminence, bountiful grace, noblest glory, shepherd delighting in the love of your apostolic see, you whom I will always embrace": This was but a sample of the praises that Fortunatus, so prone to bestowing impossible compliments, had showered upon his benefactor and colleague.[14] Gregory, bishop of Tours and a regular of the highest political and intellectual spheres of Francia, was after all not only a personal friend of the poet but also the greatest historian one could find north of the Pyrenees. Like Fortunatus, Gregory felt it was his duty to preserve and treasure the cultural heritage Rome and—especially—the Church Fathers had bequeathed their successors. Like his friend, too, he bitterly lamented that there was "not one man to be found who [could] write a book about what is happening today."[15] The sentiment, tinged as it was with both admiration for the ancients and reproach for his own era, spoke deep of his anxieties. "To keep alive the memory of those dead and gone; and to bring them to the notice of future generations": This was the crucial calling that had set Gregory on the study of history.

But exhaustive though the author of the *History of the Franks* was when it came to analyzing the actions of the Merovingian ruling classes, he had little time to waste with "minor" peoples like those living in the Western Pyrenees. Not that this made them special by any means. Gregory, despite his meticulousness, appears to have been wholly disinterested in providing any nuanced picture of the societies that surrounded the Franks. In this, paradoxically, he was proving to be but an heir to Rome's intellectual legacy. Just like the ancients, Gregory endorsed a view that portrayed the beneficial touch of civilization as continuously radiating out from a virtuous center and diminishing the further one traveled away from it. It was there precisely, in the outskirts, that one could encounter the "other," the barbarian, the brute. No better vantage point than these fringes, then, to come to terms with the superiority of the kingdom that a succession of Frankish monarchs had managed to build.

Fortunatus' catalog of peoples had nourished this image, and Gregory's historical writings did little to challenge it. By addressing the warrior lineages that in 587 had raided the north of the Pyrenees as Vascones, the bishop of Tours had not only revealed the intellectual debt he owed to his protégé but also the enduring power these age-old labels retained. The Vascones remained the embodiment of the barbarian threat. Was this not clear from the fact that, in their incursions, they were said to have destroyed "the vineyards and the open fields," those most salient markers of a civilized lifestyle? Where ancient Christian polemicists had characterized the Vascones as pagan and restless simpletons, Gregory added a new dimension to their portrayal: brutality. With a single stroke, Gregory had reframed a contemporary event—the involvement of the Western Pyrenean military aristocracies in Visigothic and Merovingian relations—as something very different: the continuation of a timeless conflict. On one side of it stood the Franks, the self-appointed heirs of Rome, guardians of the imperial order and of Christian righteousness. On the other, in direct opposition, were the fierce Vascones. Gregory's vision, profound in its simplicity, was fated to endure long after the events which had inspired it had passed into history.

It might have been in Frankish cultural circles where the connection between the people of the Western Pyrenees and the ancient Vascones was first recovered, but it would be the Goths that would carry this stream of thought to its fullest conclusion. For if there was one thing that was clear at the time—as funerary rituals carried out in Pamplona, with their Frankish flavor, demonstrated—was that the Pyrenees, never a firm boundary, were a porous frontier instead. Soldiers, travelers, and costly goods: All traveled under the shadow of the mighty peaks. So, too, did ideas. Exchanges of letters, books, and relics among the bishops and educated elites of Hispania and Gaul were commonplace and, therefore, it took little time for Gregory's *History* to become well-known in the kingdom of Toledo. Visigothic chroniclers, at any rate, drank profusely from it: sometimes contrasting their available information with that of the *History*; on other occasions, copying Gregory's conclusions outright. Given that, it seemed inevitable that the terminology coined by the bishop of Tours to describe the Vascones would find its way into the Visigothic worldview. Not for nothing, the memory of Leovigild's successful campaigns against the northern aristocracies was still a fresh one, as was the ongoing instability sown by these military elites north of the Ebro.

In fact, the years that had followed Leovigild's own death had significantly complicated the task of those—for the most part devout Catholics—who sought to chronicle his reign. Reccared, his son and the ill-fated Hermenegild's brother, had, unlike the latter, remained loyal to his father's command. And yet, upon ascending to the throne in 587, the new monarch had immediately demonstrated his own independent political intuition. Recognizing the delicate state of the kingdom, torn apart by the religious conflict between Arianism and Catholicism, he quickly understood that reconciliation between the two sides was fundamental to safeguard the Gothic kingdom's survival. For this reason, at a large council held in Toledo in 589, Reccared made a dramatic move: He publicly converted to Catholicism. The Arian clergy, robbed of its most steadfast protector, was dismantled shortly after. The schism was over. Or so, at least, the king was willing to believe.

While Reccared's conversion seemed to signal the end of the religious turmoil in Hispania, it had likewise left a thorny issue in its wake: How to remember Hermenegild and his rebellion? The last thing the Catholic aristocracy needed, after gaining back control of state affairs, was to alienate the newly found support provided by Reccared.

And yet, attaining this goal would require striking a delicate balance. Leovigild's Arianism, the very bedrock upon which the kingdom's foundations rested, could not be ignored if Reccared was to appear as a saintly figure and the corrector of the Goth's erstwhile error. But, likewise, such a framing threatened to cast Hermenegild's hapless rebellion, rooted as it had been in Catholic ambitions and quenched by Reccared and his father, as a direct challenge to the legitimacy of the new sovereign. It was a most sensitive contradiction. And one for which chroniclers would find an almost unanimous solution: the story of the revolt had to be buried; its causes, forgotten. For the stability of the Visigothic kingdom and the health of the Catholic faith, the entire episode had to be consigned to the currents of oblivion.

While this was simple enough to do when it came to Hermenegild himself, the problem grew more complicated when the time came to identify those who had rallied to his cause. With Gregory of Tours' long shadow looming over the debate, scribes found themselves grappling with an answer that, in hindsight, would appear both obvious and convenient. Just like the barbarians that had plundered the Merovingian periphery could be identified with the Vascones, so could those that had previously opposed the founder of the *regnum Gothorum* be similarly damned. To this end, Leovigild's wars were reframed, not as military endeavors within an ongoing intra-Gothic conflict, but rather as a glorious conquest of "part of Vasconia."[16] And so, intellectuals of both Francia and Hispania—both of whom drew inspiration from Gregory's sweeping narratives—began to fashion a new understanding of the Western Pyrenees. What had once been a patchwork of disparate, squabbling communities, born from the chaos of the disintegration of the empire and the wars of the *Bacaudae*, was repurposed as something else entirely: a single ethnic group. The Vascones, for so long a bookish boogeyman, had become a living, breathing reality once again.

And yet, to regard Visigothic historical accounts as mere echoes of the Gregorian masterwork would be a mistake. In fact, one might argue that, when it came to shaping the identity of the Vascones at least, one of these southern voices held a position of even greater prominence than that enjoyed by the bishop of Tours. Isidore, born at the turn of the seventh century, was an impressive man himself. A scion of a wealthy Hispano-Roman family, from his earliest youth he had been steeped in the learning of the ancients. So great was the breadth of his erudition that long after his death, he was still remembered as "the Great Doctor of our times, the newest ornament of the Catholic Church, . . . the most learned man in these latter times, he whom one should name with reverence."[17]

A high praise indeed—and one which would have satisfied the man who received it. After all, and as Isidore had come to believe, wisdom and goodness were indivisible: To be learned was, by definition, to be virtuous. Yet such a conviction, deeply ingrained in his thought though it was, carried a particular social implication. If the knowledge of the ancient past was lost, and if its literary and philosophical treasures were not salvaged and preserved for posterity, the Christian world risked sinking into an unending cycle of darkness and savagery. Urged by such a pressing mandate, Isidore had devoted his life to collecting as many texts, inscriptions, and artifacts from the ancient world as he would come across. Once gathered, these materials would serve as the foundation for a series of works aimed, as he put it, at distilling the vast accomplishments of the Roman world into a coherent summary.

Among Isidore's copious production, two texts would prove pivotal in shaping how later generations would regard Western Pyreneans. The first of these was the *Etymologies*, a vast encyclopedia teeming with numerous classical annotations, in which Isidore painstakingly catalogued the origins of hundreds of words. Here, the Vascones were identified with the dwellers of an ancient town called Vacca and made to occupy "the vast emptiness of the heights of the Pyrenees."[18] A most talented compiler, Isidore took pains to weave together the various strands that half a millennium of discourses of prejudice and otherness had accumulated upon these peoples. Not only that, but as was customary for him, he did not hesitate to mangle these sources in order to create a coherent image. The end result, evidently inspired by the words of the ancients though it most certainly was, stood not so much as a copy as a fusion and interpretation of them.[19] Inhabitants of the mountains, gathered by Pompey in a city, the Vascones of Isidore still bore the indelible stain of barbarism. The margins remained, for him as much as for intellectuals like Fortunatus or Gregory, what they had always been: the home of the savages and the edges of the world.

A second text by Isidore, however, compounded this description. Everything in the *History of the Goths* was carefully designed to provide historical support to the Catholic and Visigothic kingdom inaugurated by Reccared. Throughout its pages, and as in his other works, Isidore had allowed himself the freedom to articulate a strikingly innovative—yet ostentatiously backward-looking—worldview. As he put it, the ancient Romans had been surrounded by indistinct barbarians, against whom the legions were ever triumphant. Now, after their demise, it was none other than the Gothic *regnum* that had inherited their position at the epicenter of civilization. A bold claim that, in elevating once-feared barbarians to a moral stature surpassing even that of the antique Caesars, required of course no small degree of creative invention, given that almost every city and every tribe in Hispania, as befitted a province that had given Rome some of its greatest autocrats, could claim a pedigree far more illustrious than that of Alaric's heirs.

Almost, but not all. The Vascones, whose ancestral roots had barely warranted mention in Roman histories, were the perfect example of a community that even upstarts like the Goths could allow to cast aside with disdain. The portrait painted by Isidore, following as it did in the footsteps of the works of Strabo, Prudentius, and Ausonius, was hardly an innovation. And yet, he reinfused this image with fresh purpose. The more he regarded the Visigothic kings as just, cultured, and devoutly Christian, the more he would cast the Vascones as vicious, rough-edged, and stubbornly pagan. Like the negative of a photograph, hapless Western Pyreneans had come to offer those allured by Isidore's vast erudition a mirror of ignorance and inhumaneness against which to measure their own achievements. In other words, they came to play an essential part in Reccared's realm: that of the barbarians for a race of erstwhile barbarians.

Isidore's blinding influence would go on to sweep across the Christian world, and so, too, would his view of the Vascones. Echoes of this were everywhere to be found. The tomb of the Gothic nobleman Oppila, dating from 642, alternated in its mentions—as the *Etymologies* had themselves done—between the terms "Vaccean" and "Vascon." Other chroniclers, meanwhile, chose to incorporate Isidore's portrayal of the Vascones as a peripheral and unruly people to the harsher depiction coined by Gregory of Tours. "Due to their malice, the fierce Vascones, having descended from the Pyrenees, devastate the land of Iberia with various raids," wrote an influential Gothic bishop named Julian of Toledo in the second half of the seventh century. "The innocent blood of many Christians is spilled; some have their throats cut, others are killed with lances and other diverse weapons; an innumerable multitude of prisoners is captured and a great loot is stolen."[20] An appalling testimony, of course, but unsurprising given that the "fierce tribes of the Vascones" were nothing but conspirators in "gatherings of traitors," agitators in "dens of disloyalty," and participants in "assemblies of the damned."[21] Barbarism, paganism, and rebellion: These became the key markers that, in the eyes of their contemporaries, singled out the inhabitants of the Western Pyrenees.

To reiterate, many in the highest Visigothic and Frankish political and cultural circles had reason to want these tropes to stick for good. The example of the Vascones, deceptive though it was, suited their purposes well and reinforced their own claims to superiority and order. The reality, however, was that contemporary Western Pyreneans, regardless of the occasional similarities they might have shared with the ancient populations of their region, were no less the heirs of the Romans for that. Far from a monolithic group of savages lurking on the periphery, those now labeled as Vascones were the successors of local military chieftains who had wrested power from the hands of the magnates. Their society, fractured and largely dysfunctional, bore little resemblance to the cohesive communities described—or, more accurately, fantasized—by their detractors. While Gothic or Frankish sources may talk endlessly about the actions of a single group, the almost-complete crumbling of any administrative infrastructure in the territory ought to make readers suspicious of their conclusions.

Contrary to these expectations, Western Pyreneans participated, however reluctantly, in the institutional structures of their neighbors. The bishop of Pamplona attended their councils; local families provided refuge to exiles fleeing political upheaval in their kingdoms; their leaders supplied soldiers for Gothic and Frankish armies. Just like their counterparts elsewhere, the supposedly incorrigible elite of the Vascones appeared to have been surprisingly at ease maneuvering the shifting tides of Visigothic and Merovingian power struggles. The ethnic label, which implied some degree of unity and drew a connection between these populations and those who had sheltered Pompey half a millennium earlier, was imposed upon these heterogeneous groups as a pejorative term, and not a descriptive one. Its persistence in historical narratives thus revealed less about the reality of the Western Pyrenees and more about the anxieties and agendas of the kingdoms that surrounded them.

Why, then, if the Vascones were so entangled in the broader currents of their world, were they never able to shake off this deprecative label? A likely answer lies in the fractured and inaccessible nature of their homeland. The crumbling of the towns and villages that had dotted the *Iter XXXIV* had rendered control of the territory effectively impossible. For the heirs of Alaric and Clovis, the region was a land of fleeting victories. Armies could march through, subdue a local warlord in battle, impose their terms, and return home triumphant. The imposition of sustained governance, though, remained a feat beyond their reach. So deprived had the land become of means to exert efficient power that any individual's authority could scarcely extend beyond the confines of a single valley. Even there, it was likely to be exercised through negotiation and continuous contestation. Only in Pamplona, as the seat of a Catholic bishop, could local leaders still dream that they, even if nominally and without much consent beyond their immediate neighborhood, spoke for the Western Pyrenees.

Disunity and fragmentation on such a scale did not fail in inviting both conflict and opportunity. Local disputes escalated, from time to time, into broader struggles. When the so-called Vascones launched the *razzias* that so alarmed Gothic and Frankish chroniclers, or when the armies of the Visigoths and the Franks campaigned in the region, these were not the byproducts of an endless cycle of revolt and repression. Rather, they were but the outward manifestations of much deeper dynamics—disputes exported beyond the mountains as each side sought allies to tip the scales in their favor. The territory, after all, and despite its endemic issues, remained a strategically important one, a frontier between the two great kingdoms to emerge from Rome's ashes. And this—and only this—made its control a prize worth pursuing. Western Pyreneans, for the most part, accepted and endured the consequences. Loyalty and rebellion were not opposites in their political calculus, but tools that could be wielded alternatively, depending on the moment and on what opportunities each one promised to offer.

Not surprising then that, when the Visigothic king died childless in 710 and a new monarch named Rodrigo rose to power in Toledo amid fierce resistance, his opponents knew fully well where to seek support. Some Western Pyrenean aristocrats, enticed by promises and rewards as they had so often been in the past, readily aligned themselves with the discontent. It was, for them, simply business as usual. Equally expected, too, that Rodrigo would respond by marching northward toward Pamplona.

But, as it happens, the king would not manage to capture the town. He had received news that his enemies, desperate for reinforcements, had succeeded in their search for allies across the sea. A sizable contingent, swiftly crossing the straits that connected Europe and Africa, penetrated deep and unopposed in the rearguard of Rodrigo's power base. The king, alarmed, reacted with haste. Abandoning the siege of the northern stronghold, he mustered a formidable force—numbering, as chroniclers proclaimed with more than a touch of hyperbole, "around one hundred thousand" men[22]—and "returned all of a sudden due to the turmoil that was befalling" his lands.[23] Shortly thereafter, Rodrigo would meet his end in battle and, facing the prospect of annihilation, self-centered noblemen, many of whom had up until then been loyal to the monarchs of Toledo, surrendered to the newcomers in exchange for amnesty and concessions.

History appeared to be repeating again. Just like in the aftermath of Vouillé, the death of a king and a catastrophic military defeat spelled doom for a Visigothic kingdom. But this time, it was not the Franks but a new player—the Muslims—that had burst onto the stage of Iberia. What their advent might mean for the peoples of the Western Pyrenees no one could fathom as of yet.

Notes

1 Gregory of Tours, *History of the Franks*, II. 37.

2 So at least proclaims a commemorative plaque located in Vouillé itself.

3 "Consularia Caesaraugustana." In Castellanos, *The Visigothic Kingdom in Iberia: Construction and Invention*, 4.

4 Isidore of Seville, *History of the Goths*, 37.

5 Isidore, 40.

6 Isidore, 44.

7 "Fredegarii Scholastici Chronicum cum suis continuatoribus, sive appendix ad sancti Gregorii Episcopi Turonensis Historiam Francorum," LXXXII. In Fredegarius, *Fredegarii et aliorum chronica. Vitae Sanctorum.*

8 Gregory of Tours, *History of the Franks*, VI, 12.

9 Gregory, IX, 7.

10 Burgess, *The Chronicle of Hydatius*, 99.

11 "Ad Iustinum et Sophiam." In Fortunatus, *Venantii Fortunati opera poetica*, App. II. 28–32.

12 Fortunatus, "Poem 9.1: to King Chilperic on the occasion of the Synod at Berny-Rivière." Quoted in Fortunatus, *Venantius Fortunatus: Personal and Political Poems*, 74.

13 Fortunatus, 76–7.

14 Fortunatus, "Poem 5. 8." Quoted in Fortunatus, *Venantius Fortunatus*, 21.

15 Gregory of Tours, *History of the Franks*, Preface.

16 John of Biclar, "Chronicon." In Fernández, "El 'Chronicon' de Juan de Bíclaro. La crónica del rey Leovigildo y del III Concilio de Toledo. Estudio y traducción," 59.

17 VIII Council of Toledo (653). Quoted in Fear and Woods, *Isidore of Seville and his Reception in the Early Middle Ages*, 11.

18 Isidore of Seville, *Etymologies*, IX, II, 107–8.

19 Pozo, "Vasconia y los vascones de la crisis del imperio romano a la llegada del Islam (siglos V-VIII)," 355–62.

20 Tajon, "Sententiarum Libri Quinque." Quoted in Pozo, "Vasconia y los vascones en la crisis del imperio romano," 364–5.

21 Martínez, *The Story of Wamba: Julian of Toledo's Historia Wambae regis*, 190–1.

22 Lorenzo, *La Vasconia Peninsular en las Fuentes Árabes (años 711–929)*, 17.

23 Lorenzo, 18.

PART II
LINEAGE

CHAPTER 5
PRINCEPS CHRISTICOLA

The anxiety of the man was betrayed by the way in which he moved left and right, unable to find a comfortable spot on his seat. He could not stand this place. The mountain pass was ample enough, and gentle slopes flanked it on both sides. Around him, the hills rolled like the frozen remnants of massive waves, while the distant peaks of the Pyrenees, still clad in snow, loomed against the horizon. All things considered, the scenery itself was not displeasing in the slightest, and yet he could not shake the nagging discomfort gnawing at his thoughts.

The muted sound of a thousand heavy boots treading the way flooded his ears. Nothing else but that slow, rhythmic sound: crunching dirt, munching grass. Even birds appeared to have gone silent as soon as the soldiers had put a foot on the road. The man breathed profoundly. No, it was not the landscape that made him nervous. The reports from outriders had been clear enough—there was no threat ahead, no ambush lurking in the woods. There was no peril. He repeated those words as he felt his senses tingling, telling him to hurry up. The wind that came blowing from the peaks was a refreshing breeze, a fleeting relief from the scorching touch of the sun on his skin. It would not last, he knew. Summer's end was upon them, and the snow that crowned the distant peaks would soon descend, burying the pass in a frozen shroud. The humid breeze was only a warning; a cue not to tarry. Failing to reach the other side of the gorge before the first storms made the crossing impassable, and terrible things would follow.

All was under control, he reminded himself. It would only take the last section of the army—the one that brought the spoils of his war south of the mountain range—to arrive, and all would be right. And yet, what if? The man tried to shake those ideas out of his head. Adjusting his grip on the reins, he stirred his mount into motion. Charlemagne, the most powerful king in Europe, rushed down the road of Roncesvalles.

The retreat of Charlemagne's army through the Pyrenees and the narrow pass in 778 would be remembered in history as the most harrowing defeat of the Frankish conqueror. Much later accounts of the battle, embellished by minstrels and poets, would transform the struggle of the beleaguered rearguard, led by a certain Count Roland, into a tale of almost mythic proportions.

> How many lances were broken and turned red with blood,
> how many pennons, how many ensigns torn,
> how many lives of fine young Franks are lost! . . .
> The pagans die in their hundreds and thousands;
> those who do not flee have no escape from death".[1]

And yet, for all that later generations were prone to appraise these feats of doomed heroism, the accounts penned by contemporaries to the event painted a strikingly different picture. "On the heights of the Pyrenees,"—wrote one sober chronicler—"the Wascones prepared an ambush, attacked the rearguard, and threw the whole army into confusion. . . . In this engagement a great many officers of the palace . . . were killed; the baggage was plundered, and the enemy was able to vanish in all directions because he knew the lay of the land."[2] Rather than a pyrrhic victory, snatched through sheer bravery from the jaws of defeat, the later-to-be-appraised battle of Roncesvalles appeared to have been nothing short of a humiliating rout. The Franks' adversaries were not deadly Muslim warriors, but the Wascones—the inhabitants of the Western Pyrenees.[3] Charlemagne himself might have managed to reach the northern slopes of the Pyrenees unscathed, but the unavenged calamity he had suffered would forever haunt the legacy of his Iberian exploits.

One question that inevitably arose from the few surviving accounts of the battle was the identity of those who carried out the devastating ambush. And yet, for all its intrigue, finding an answer proved to be an arduous task indeed. A difficulty compounded, as ever, by the fact that intellectuals in the Frankish kingdom, striving to make sense of the disaster, instinctively turned to long-standing stereotypes. The portrait of pagan and ferocious savages crafted in the times of Gregory of Tours and Isidore of Seville was, after all, ready at hand. One chronicler, with a single stroke of disdain, dismissed the attackers as *latronum turba nefanda*: an "abominable crowd of robbers."[4] A framing that allowed these authors to slot the ambush neatly into a familiar narrative and to rescue some measure of consolation. The raid, as they saw it, was simply another link in the long chain of defiance that had long characterized the Western Pyreneans' relationship with Frankish authority. Calamitous though the journey back home had proven for Charlemagne and his men, the catastrophe was thus little more than an all-too-predictable annoyance. Just like a child might, from time to time, come to challenge the rules of a stern father, so had Frankish authorities come to regard any occasional upheaval in their southwestern frontier as something to be expected.

It is not hard to see why they would find this thought reassuring. Rather than grapple with the troubling reality—that the ambush had exposed the limits of Frankish power and the vulnerability of their ambitions south of the Pyrenees—these accounts rendered the disaster a minor blemish that could soon be overcome. The Wascones might have acted true to their supposed savagery and unreliability, but the Franks remained firmly in control. All things considered, it was a minor setback.

Unfortunately for those who believed these soothing interpretations, recent events could make it increasingly difficult to uphold the soundness of these inherited tropes. Changes on an enormous scale were in motion in the Western Pyrenees—changes that no Frankish army, no matter how formidable, could hope to reverse. Just as the Visigothic kingdom of Toledo had collapsed beyond restoration, so too were the old certainties of rulers like Leovigild or Rodrigo crumbling into irrelevance. The rules of the political and social game, which had for so long framed the ambitions of Visigothic and Frankish sovereigns in this border region, were being reshaped beyond recognition.

In fact, the self-appointed task of Charlemagne in Iberia had been, largely, to restore and preserve what could be salvaged from that past.

But the shifts underway affected not only the powerful but also the humble. In the countryside, in the huts and cabins where the proud eyes of kings and chroniclers rarely ventured, the extent of these transformations was felt every bit as profoundly. So much so that, in hindsight, the events of 778 could be taken as part of a much larger story indeed: that of the emergence of a people whose destiny would be to carve out a kingdom that, in time, would shape the very future of Iberia. The lifeless silhouettes of the soldiers of Charlemagne, as they lay half-buried in the murky soil of Roncesvalles, marked therefore not the end of a chapter. They were instead the labor pains of a whole new world.

But how could the stain of prejudice—especially of one as insidious and persistent as that leveled against the peoples of the Western Pyrenees—be erased from good? For generations, Roman, Christian, Visigothic, and Frankish intellectuals had ceaselessly produced and reproduced a picture of these peoples—one that had more to do with their own biases and anxieties than with the reality of these lands. Because of this, only a massive mental revolution could hope to render those views inoperable. Yet how could this be achieved? And, perhaps more importantly, why precisely at this very moment?

The answer, as is often the case, was nuanced and tightly connected to the circumstances that surrounded the arrival of the Muslims in Iberia in 711. Broadly speaking, there existed two paths to challenge and eventually dismantle a state-sponsored prejudice like the one that had long been directed at Western Pyreneans. The first one involved foreign intellectuals—in Toledo, Paris, or Aachen—changing their attitudes toward those they had once despised. The second path was even more complex, for it required new voices from within the prejudiced group to arise, gain sufficient strength to be heard, and then go on to present a more positive image of their own people. Both of these processes took place in the Western Pyrenees in these fateful centuries. And both, in the end, were nothing but a result of a great recalibration of power that would see what had up until then been a flea-bitten periphery transformed into the most powerful kingdom in the peninsula.

While all of this lay in the future, it had all begun in defeat. Shortly after dealing with the army summoned by Rodrigo in 711, Muslim forces had pushed further northward. Following the course of the Ebro, they had "attacked the Vascones, penetrating deeply into their country, until the people came to [them], generous as cattle."[5] Local chieftains, unable to muster any significant resistance, were soon overpowered and forced to sign a series of swift capitulations. Several of these captains, following a path well-trodden by their forefathers, took the decision to side with the newcomers in exchange for loyalty and tribute. Others, albeit more reluctantly, followed suit shortly after.

In Pamplona, the native aristocracy made the pragmatic decision and, by 718 at the latest, they struck a deal with the Muslim invaders. The terms of the treaty were not, in essence, very different from those previously enforced by victorious kings like Leovigild. The people of Pamplona would be allowed to retain their properties as well as their religion. Conduct of their internal affairs, other than for the presence of a Muslim-appointed overseer, would remain largely in their own hands.[6] In return, the city would pay tribute and acknowledge the nominal authority of the conquerors. Not that the deserted town or its impoverished surroundings were targets in and of themselves. And yet, their value was not negligible either, for it was possible to use them as perfect stepping-stones for a completely new and appetizing set of conquests. An army marching north from Pamplona, as Muslim generals knew well, would soon reach the shadow of the mountains, and from there set sight on a prize to which the ragtag chieftains of the Western Pyrenees could not hold a candle: the *regnum Francorum*, the kingdom of the Franks.

In fact, while Rodrigo's self-styled heirs exhausted their strength in doomed attempts to resist the advancing tide of Islam, the world to the north of the Pyrenees was undergoing its own transformation. Over the course of several decades, and undermined by the relentless churn of internal strife and the ambitions of regional power brokers, the fragile authority once exerted by the Merovingian dynasty in Francia had steadily withered. The process had proven an almost unstoppable one. Merovingian kings, as their grip on the reins of the realm grew increasingly tenuous, had long relied on a network of officials to enforce their rule in far-flung territories. Yet these agents—entrusted with maintaining the overlordship of the Franks in the peripheral regions—had proven themselves adept instead at turning their mandates into opportunities for personal aggrandizement. By securing powerful local alliances, they gradually transitioned from stewards of royal authority to the latter's most vigorous and determined opponents.

Under the shadow of the Pyrenees, straddling the precarious boundary with the fragmented domains of the Vascon chieftains, one such Frankish duchy had existed ever since 602. The duke tasked with defending the rugged passes from the occasional incursions had initially been a royal appointee. However, over time, the office of duke had slowly shifted away from the hands of distant monarchs and into the grip of these local potentates. Absorbed though these were into the machinery of royal administration, they began to wield this power with an eye set on regional affairs rather than in Merovingian interest.

Unlike in the south, where Roman infrastructure had been shattered by the twin blows of the *Bacaudae* and the ceaseless skirmishes between Visigoths and Merovingians, the northern side of the Pyrenees had withstood the crumbling of the empire remarkably unscathed. Here, provincial aristocracies—descended from late antique *possessores*—had endured, and so had their ability to maintain effective command over the land. The Merovingians, upon finding these well-articulated patronage networks, had relied on them to assert their dominion in the periphery. Yet this reliance was a double-edged sword. The same imbrication between crown officials and native elites which secured Frankish nominal authority had proven, by putting too much responsibility upon these intermediaries, to erode the monarch's ability to rule directly. By the late seventh century, with Merovingian authority in decline, this fragile equilibrium had entirely unraveled. Freed from the constraints of royal oversight, it did not take long for the dukes to shed any pretense of obedience to the distant court.

Invariably, as the frontier march drifted further and further from the gravitational pull exerted by the Merovingians, intellectuals too came to pay closer attention to their leaders. After all, now more than ever, their actions and allegiances played a pivotal role in the internecine struggles that continued to plague the Frankish world. But the problem, as ever, was one of vocabulary. How best to describe the dominion these figures commanded over a region sprawling from the banks of the Garonne to the foothills of the Pyrenees? In the absence of better alternatives, pragmatism prevailed. The duke charged with guarding the southern frontier against the Vascones came to be known, simply, as duke *in* Wasconia. The title, though one born of convenience, carried profound associations. It not only marked the geographical reach of its holder's responsibilities; it also appeared to ascribe a distinct identity to the lands and peoples under his sway. Before long, the potentates of the northern Pyrenees, the very magnates who upheld the government of the dukes, began to be called in Frankish documents "lords of the Wascones."[7]

Initially, of course, these locals held no illusions about what the designation implied. The connotations were all too clear, steeped as they were in a legacy of disdain that Merovingian propaganda ever since Fortunatus' poems and Gregory's histories had only deepened. For this reason, while a Frankish duke might begrudgingly accept the designation of duke *in* Wasconia—a geographical descriptor, after all—he would never tolerate being addressed as a Wascon duke. The pejorative weight of the term was evident in narratives about the frequent insurrections that marked the breakup of Merovingian dominion. When the population of the region between Bordeaux and the Pyrenees dared to assert their autonomy, they were invariably cast in a familiar mold. Rebels, brigands, and feeble adversaries whose defiance served only to highlight the stature of sovereigns: Such was the portrait endlessly rehearsed in Frankish propaganda. Isidore's mighty authority, just as much as Gregory's, cast a long shadow over these accounts. The parallels drawn with their southern neighbors—the Vascones—were no accident. Instead, they served to reinforce an enduring trope.

The arrival of the Muslims only served to further complicate this already unstable and volatile landscape. Whether surging from Pamplona or crossing from the Mediterranean, the generals of Al-Andalus—as Arabs called the lands they had come to rule in Iberia—marched their armies in tentative incursions that grew bolder and fiercer the deeper they ventured into Frankish territory. The fate of the Visigoths, their kingdom torn asunder and their surviving remnants wasting away in inhospitable redoubts, must have been ever-present in the minds of the Franks. A recollection, perhaps, that ignited their resolve to brave the enemy onslaught. In 721, only a few years after Pamplona's capitulation, Eudes, the duke in Wasconia, inflicted a grievous defeat on a Muslim army besieging Toulouse.[8] A decade later, a far larger expeditionary force was crushed further north. The two victories accomplished their goal and, in their wake, the regularity and scale of Muslim military operations in Francia began to ebb. Never again would the forces of Islam threaten the villages and sanctuaries that dotted the landscape of Tours. With internal unrest now sowing discord in Al-Andalus, the triumphs of the Franks had afforded the latter a much-needed respite.

Unfortunately for the Merovingians, even these hard-won victories and the fragile peace they had produced could not prevent centrifugal forces from tearing their realm apart. In 751, after decades of dim, ineffective rule, a coup ousted the last of Clovis' heirs, whose descent from a sea monster proved insufficient to keep him on the throne. The new ruling dynasty—the Carolingians—ascended to power with a clear goal in mind: to reunite the fractured kingdom of the Franks under a single, strong authority. A lofty ideal, of course—yet one with which counts and dukes, well-accustomed by now to doing largely as they pleased and increasingly indifferent to the commands of a distant court, found it difficult to comply.

Hard though the pill was, the Carolingians were resolute in making the nobility swallow it. In 768, after a long series of virulent struggles, they subdued and fully annexed the territory of Aquitaine, on the shores of the Garonne. The very next year, Duke Lupo in Wasconia, confronted with the looming possibility of military invasion, opted to give up the fight and he too surrendered to the king.[9] What this voluntary submission truly entailed, however, remained a thorny issue to disentangle. After all, Lupo would continue to hold sway in the duchy, and the impression was that, aside from offering support for a few Carolingian campaigns, little in his conduct had actually changed. Whatever the precise terms of his capitulation, it seemed to have amounted to little more than a renewal of the vassalage once paid to the Merovingians, calculated to placate Lupo's powerful neighbor. The duke's strategy, ostensibly, was a tried and tested one in the Western Pyrenees: to feign loyalty when the enemy was strong and, at the first hint of weakness, seize the opportunity to throw off the yoke.

But weakness, unfortunately for Lupo's hopes, was hardly an attribute one might use to refer to the man he had surrendered to. Charlemagne was not simply a monarch endowed with an unshakable sense of mission. He was also possessed by a strength and determination that more than matched his ambitions. From the moment he was raised to the throne, the young Charlemagne had embarked on a brutal line of policy: to visit "widespread devastation with both iron and fire" upon the northern and eastern nations, raiding their villages and plundering their towns, all in the name of spreading the Christian faith by force.[10] The effectiveness of his approach had proven as terrifying as it was uncontestable. By 777, Charlemagne had secured the northern frontier. And now, with his campaigns concluded, the monarch was already seeking out new targets to satisfy his insatiable drive. He would not have to look far. The following spring, at the head of a massive army, the unbeaten Charlemagne, king of the Franks, crossed the Pyrenees and entered Iberia. His target: the Muslim city of Saragossa.

Pamplona, as an unavoidable station along the way, fell to the invaders not long after their army had arrived in the peninsula. The small, dilapidated town held little allure for a monarch of Charlemagne's stature. Like Muslim generals before him, the sovereign showed no inclination whatsoever to spare even the most meager thought for the locals. He left a modest garrison behind to secure the rearguard of the army before rushing southward toward the large metropolis in the middle course of the Ebro. For months, only the occasional, fleeting rumor from Charlemagne reached Pamplona. Then, in August, the Franks returned. Though they had failed in capturing the city, Charlemagne could at least contemplate the results of his foray in Saragossa with satisfaction. Not only had a good number of valuable hostages and a considerable amount of plunder been captured, but he had also sent a message. Muslim authorities, who had so often regarded the Franks as a people on the defensive, had suddenly found themselves having to come to terms with an unsettling realization. Charlemagne's armies could hit back and—if given the chance—they could do so with strength.

Only one potential inconvenience could darken the prospects of the successful campaign, and the king, of course, was aware of it. Hostile peoples now surrounded him in a land cut off from his bases north of the Pyrenees, and the summer was coming to an end. Acknowledging the peril head-on, the Frankish sovereign chose to withdraw without delay to the safety of his kingdom. Before doing so, however, he would make sure to take a cautionary provision. The imposing late Roman walls of Pamplona, which had withstood assaults from Visigothic, Merovingian, and Muslim armies, were to be razed to the ground. It was a move that displayed strategic foresight. Dismantling the fortifications would make any subsequent Frankish incursions easier while depriving the Muslims of a harbor of security on their route northward. With astonishing effectiveness and speed, the command was executed under the livid gaze of the town's beleaguered inhabitants, who witnessed powerlessly as hammers smote the mighty stones and as the imposing towers crumbled into heaps of rubble. Soon enough, even the last rampart and parapet lay flattened. Only then, content that he had offset a potential thorn in his side, did Charlemagne feel secure enough to embark on the long road back home. A road that led to the Pyrenees, and to the narrow gorge of Roncesvalles.

While the tradition of the *Chanson de Roland* would much later blame Muslim forces for the attack in the mountain pass, all surviving sources concur in identifying the assailants as Wascones. An apparent contradiction, however, need not be one at all. One plausible explanation is that the attackers were made up of the retinues of one or more local warlords, possibly indebted to the Muslim powers of the Ebro basin, who took the opportunity to strike back at the seemingly invincible Charlemagne and his retreating forces.[11] Another option is that these Wascones were acting under the orders of, or in alliance with, Lupo, duke in Wasconia. Resentful of the king's interference in his once-autonomous domain, Lupo might have, in doing this, sought to reclaim some of the political leverage lost in his capitulation of 769. The fragmented dynamics of the region, where local rivalries frequently embroiled external backers, could thus help explain the calamity at Roncesvalles. And yet, these are all but guesses, for the vagueness and opacity of Frankish chronicles, in trying to downplay the scale of Charlemagne's defeat, make determining the exact nature of the forces that brought disaster upon his soldiers a frustratingly hopeless endeavor.

But it is paradoxically this very confusion that best suggests a revealing side effect of the Carolingian campaign to consolidate royal power: the imprint it left upon ethnonyms. Frankish authors, marinated in a venerable tradition of writing, frequently allowed their biases to shape the very vocabulary they employed. Consider for example the people of Aquitaine, the region immediately north of the duchy of Wasconia. Prior to the Carolingian annexation of this land, its inhabitants had often been referred to as "Wascones."[12] In want of a better explanation, some scholars took these puzzling mentions as proof of a mass migration of mountain peoples from the Western Pyrenees.

Yet this interpretation, which appears reasonable on the surface, becomes less convincing if one notices the sudden disappearance of the term after 768, the year of Aquitaine's formal surrender to Charlemagne. Almost overnight, "Wascones" gave way to "Aquitani," a term far less charged with condescension. Did the former simply vanish without a trace once the Carolingians seized the territory? An unlikely explanation. Far more plausible to consider that "Wascones," rather than an ethnic descriptor, was indeed a term instrumentalized to brand as savages and rebels those who resisted the authority of the new rulers of Francia.[13] In all, the example demonstrates how cautious one ought to be when dealing with references to the "Wascones," particularly when these focused on key episodes such as the ambush at Roncesvalles. Not for nothing, to Frankish chroniclers the word was far from neutral and it still carried the weight of centuries of scorn and disdain.

Certainly, this explanation might succeed in shedding some light upon the dynamics at play in Aquitaine. But the more one traveled south, the more the picture dissolved into a shapeless fog. Lupo and his predecessors, keeping watch over a frontier long removed from the meddling of Merovingian kings, had spent decades consolidating a sizable authority in Wasconia. This meant that their loyalty, bereft of the threat of reprisal for breaking it, could hardly be taken as a given. This precarious balance could explain why the Carolingians, contrary to the policy they had followed in Aquitaine, had chosen not to abandon the potent propaganda tool that centuries of prejudice against the Wascones had provided them with. Western Pyreneans, in the mental universe of most Frankish intellectuals, remained as unruly a people as ever, as untrustworthy a people as ever—and their periodic uprisings only confirmed them in their suspicions. Even though the duke in Wasconia might have ostensibly pledged his allegiance to Charlemagne, and even if the land and its inhabitants could nominally be considered part of the Frankish dominions, a profound distrust lingered on. Wasconia continued to be, in many ways, beyond the pale—and to fail to acknowledge this self-evident fact risked proving extremely naive.

But if the ephemeral control that Charlemagne had wrested over the territory was to be a lasting one, then even here the savage features so often attached to the Wascones almost by default—rebellion, paganism, ferocity—would need to be gradually softened. True, depictions of these men and women as dangerous brigands retained their utility, particularly when recounting events like the disaster at Roncesvalles. But, at the same time, one could perceive the emergence, among Frankish writers, of a subtle yet significant shift in tone. In a land in which the king's control continued to be so contested, after all, it was a most unwise line of policy to hurt unprovoked sensibilities. For this reason, the dwellers of the Western Pyrenees should not always be written off as some faceless enemy, condemned to an irredeemable state of barbarity. Rather, they began to be acknowledged as the inhabitants—carefully monitored yet no less respectable for that—of a particular territory: that of the duchy itself. The region's rulers, including the dukes, knew better than to see in this an end to the gazes of suspicion that had so often turned toward them. And yet, increasingly, these were paired with concessions and privileges as part of a calibrated political strategy.[14] The Carolingians had recognized, as the Merovingians and the Visigoths had never done, that to tame the unruly Pyrenean frontier was as much a battle of ideas as it was one of arms. And if they had any hope of attaining their self-appointed goal of reuniting the kingdom of the Franks, then they could not afford to perpetuate a trope that was unmistakably onerous to those it branded.

Wascones rabidos domuit pius arte magistra, / Deque lupis torvis progeneravit oves.[15] These artful lines—playing on the double meaning of "Lupus" as both the name of the duke and the Latin word for "wolf"—distilled the essence of the project that the dynasty strove to carry out in Wasconia. Were they to prove up to the task of disentangling the ancient ethnonym from its associations with violence and rebellion, perhaps the Carolingians might yet win the loyalty of the region's ruling class. In fact, even the locals could assume it, granted that the taint of barbarity was erased for good. Bit by bit, as the rabid Wascones were tamed through pious skill, the process was one which promised to allow Charlemagne and his successors to beget sheep out of the fierce wolves of yesterday.

For Frankish intellectuals, however, the very project implied facing a new dilemma. How to distinguish between those they sought to seduce—the subjects of the duke in Wasconia—and the unruly communities, also known as Vascones, that lived beyond even the most nominal reach of Frankish authority? If Wascones was the term applied to the population in the north, how then should one describe those ruffians roaming in the hills south of the Pyrenees?

A problem, of course, with several possible solutions. The simplest and least demanding was to retain the name Wascones and rely on context to solve the issue. An approach that, while appealing in its simplicity, entailed obvious drawbacks nonetheless—most notably that it made it exceedingly difficult to discern whether the Wascones of an author lived on the northern or southern skirts of the mountain chain. At best, chroniclers perceptive enough to acknowledge the problem might slide a geographical qualifier, dubbing the latter, for example, as *Hispani Wascones.*[16] But this strategy, too, soon died out. Its inherent capacity for fostering confusion—blurring distinctions between subjects of the Frankish crown and the untamed denizens of the Iberian highlands—proved, in the end, an insurmountable flaw.

But just as the term *Hispani Wascones* was beginning to fade from the Carolingian lexicon, a second pair of designations emerged in its stead. The first of these new terms was *Pampilonenses*, a word obviously derived from the city of Pamplona itself. The origins of the second, *Nabarri*, remained considerably more obscure. Some suggested that this was the name given to the inhabitants of the southern plains,[17] or that it originated in the archaic Euskeric term *nabar*, meaning "plow."[18] Yet beyond such speculative etymologies, there was little doubt that chroniclers sought to draw a distinction between the two: *Hispani Wascones* and *Pampiloneses*, on the one hand, and *Nabarri*, on the other.[19]

To decipher what these distinctions entailed in reality, however, was almost impossible. Did these groups occupy different areas, perhaps a reluctant concession to the fragmented nature of social life in the Western Pyrenees? Were, perhaps, their languages different—some using a broken Latin, and the rest speaking a kind of proto-*Euskera*? Or did these labels, instead, point toward a stark social stratification, one distinguishing between lordly elites and those who labored under their dominion? Sources, scant and brief as they were, only responded with a deafening silence.

Few contemporaries would have accepted that the parting of fates between the southern lands and their Wascon neighbors to the north owed everything to the influence of Frankish chroniclers. After all, circumstances on both sides of the Pyrenees were markedly different. To the south, amid the disturbance of the age, the politically fragmented territory was brooding a quiet revolution. In the plains and valleys where forests once loomed unbroken, and on the rocky coast, beleaguered by the waves, new settlements had recently begun to emerge. The change brought by these signs of growth, in a landscape depressed ever since the end of the empire, was one that its few inhabitants must have welcomed with enthusiasm. Clearings in the woods were opened to plant crops and provide pastures for cattle; the remains of mighty oaks used to build huts and shelters. Villagers seeking spiritual connection with their forebears raised small cemeteries and modest churches and tended them with care. Not that the process of expansion was an easy one by any means. Peasants, spurred by hunger for land, often found their ambitions at odds with the entrenched interests of petty magnates. The sparks of their tensions would be of a kind that later testimonies would memorialize in vivid detail.[20]

But the emergence of a dense tapestry of hamlets and villages, woven together by improvised trails, did not necessarily signal the ruin of those who had up until this moment held power in the region. The expansion, for all that might have originated in peasant communities, offered after all tantalizing opportunities for the region's warring aristocracies. After the collapse of the Visigothic kingdom of Toledo, which had dismantled the uppermost rungs of the old hierarchy, some well-connected families had found themselves in a position to freely pursue their supremacy over nearby districts. Roles once designated for communal service—judges settling disputes, captains leading their neighbors into battle: all could be transformed into a measure of authority that was unwise to sniff at. The ascent of at least some of these individuals was encouraged by the tacit approval of the new Muslim overlords, eager to avoid unnecessary unrest in such a distant region. Others, perhaps less fortunate in gaining endorsement, sought instead alternative paths and alliances to maintain their influence. And so, year after year, the informal gatherings where members of these families convened to discuss the allocation of grazing rights, the management of forest resources, or the ownership of monasteries and arable land soon became the primary arenas where ambitions were put to the test. Prosperity, far from bringing the struggle for social primacy to an end, had only sharpened its edge.

Nowhere in the Western Pyrenees did these tensions blaze more fiercely than in Pamplona.[21] The town itself had long since faded into insignificance, and Charlemagne's expedition and the tearing down of its mighty walls was only the last nail in a coffin that had been rotting at least since the sixth century. Yet for all its dilapidation, the city's carcass still possessed an invaluable advantage over any other settlement in its direct neighborhood. While many other prelates, like those of Calagurris, had been expelled from their seats by the Muslims, the pact struck by the Pamplonese with the conquerors had preserved their bishop in place.[22] Paradoxically, the arrangement had not weakened the position of the bishopric; quite the contrary: It had strengthened it. Entrusted with the collection of the tribute owed to Al-Andalus, the small number of families that controlled it had added this critical role to the already important prerogatives wielded by any bishop. Prerogatives that, in a world in which the death rattles of old structures could still be heard, would prove far from trivial.

The lineages that held the reins of Pamplona's destiny would make extensive use of these instruments to shape a regional power that could talk face-to-face to their mighty neighbors. But this did not alter the fact that the boundaries of their authority remained as fuzzy as they had ever been. Alliances and pacts between local magnates, or between them and foreign backers, were frequent, not because their power was entrenched, but precisely because it was so petty that new supporters were always in short supply. Divisions, too, undoubtedly existed. And among these, none was more politically significant than the split between those who leaned toward Frankish dominance and those favorable to Muslim suzerainty. Looking back at the marriage of a daughter of Lupo, duke in Wasconia, and a Pamplonese chieftain named Jimeno, conspiracy theorists who held that the famed ambush at Roncesvalles had been a collaborative effort to resist Frankish meddling were bound to frown with suspicion.[23] Moreover, the fact that some Pamplonese families regularly supported Wascon magnates in their attempts at throwing off the burdensome yoke of Carolingian rule also compounded this hunch. So happened, for instance, during a particularly virulent uprising that was brutally suppressed by Louis the Pious, Charlemagne's eldest son, in 812. It is no great jump in logic to imagine that it could have also happened in earlier times.

At least initially, Muslim agents in the area, seeing that these fractious dynamics greatly undermined Frankish rule, were more than happy to see them continued. Yet pretty soon, Cordoba too came to recognize the double-edged consequences of encouraging these tendencies. In 799, the Pamplonese—perhaps at the instigation of a pro-Carolingian clique—orchestrated the assassination of a leading Muslim figure dispatched to the city to ensure that locals behaved according to appropriate directives.[24] Such an overt act of rebellion, of course, was not one that the emir in Cordoba could calmly stomach, and only a year later, after a quick campaign, the uprising had already been aborted in its cradle and the untrustworthy Pamplonese population had been forced to offer "the tribute and the compromise of obedience."[25] Order was duly reestablished. The faction most favorable to Muslim control was restored to its position at the helm of the city.

For all the speed and ruthlessness with which Muslim troops had put out the fires of discontent, the eruption itself carried with it the unmistakable aroma that so often permeates deeper tides of change. Signs were manifold. The Pamplonese powerbrokers, tottering precariously in the buffer zone between mighty empires, held a card that neither the Carolingians nor Cordoba could easily trump: the option to resort, if need be, to the dukes in Wasconia. These allies, operating beyond the direct control of either sovereign, provided a source of leverage that those in charge of the small town could deploy to keep their autonomy alive. Not even the semblance of normality reestablished by the emirate could entirely conceal the fact that the treaty itself bore the hallmarks, not of a master dealing with a vassal, but of an agreement between two independent powers. The creation in 802 of the town of Tudela, perched securely on the shores of the

Ebro and commanding a strategic artery leading north to Francia, was only a material manifestation of the lack of confidence the emir had in the locals. A recognition that Pamplona, a land far off from the Muslim heartlands and allied to a foreign duke, ought to be dealt with caution.

Truth be told, the threat posed by the tiny district ebbed and flowed constantly. In 812, following the suppression of the Wascon rebellion, Louis the Pious had not hesitated in setting out to punish those who had had a hand in the uprising. In a move that echoed the exploits of his distinguished father, he crossed the mountain passes to bring Pamplona to heel. As residents of the city soon found out, resistance was futile, and Louis "stayed in that area for as long as it seemed there were things to arrange that would lead to the public or private good."[26] Which, in other words, meant that he expelled the supporters of both Cordoba and the duke in Wasconia from the city, reshuffled its governance to suit his interests, and reinstated pro-Carolingian families to the most prominent echelons of power. Only once these endeavors were completed did he return to his realm. But this time he was cautious enough to avoid falling into the same trap that Charlemagne had so sourly tasted in 778. The Franks had learned from their mistakes. Roncesvalles would not happen again.

Louis' victories, in the wake of his crushing of Wascon autonomy in the north, threatened to bind the country around Pamplona to the orbit of the Carolingians once and for all. Had he succeeded in consolidating his gains, then today we might still refer to the Basques as Gascons. But fate, as ever, had its own mysterious designs. As was crystal clear to all observers, the superficial preeminence of Carolingian appointees in Pamplona rested on rather delicate foundations. For as long as the threat of a Frankish counterattack remained a certainty, members of the pro-Muslim faction had indeed no other choice but to bow their heads and abide by the new situation. Yet this compliance was always conditional, and dependent upon a balance that the successors of Charlemagne found increasingly difficult to uphold. What would happen—some wondered—once the attention of the Carolingians was focused elsewhere on their vast kingdom?

The opportunity to test this scenario would come sooner than expected. In 816, the lords of the northern Wascones, "on account of their ingrained fickleness," seized a weakening of Carolingian grip to take up arms once again.[27] Events then unfolded quickly. Realizing that the Frankish monarch had his hands tied, the pro-Carolingian officials who ruled Pamplona braced themselves for what was to come. The ominous news arrived shortly after: The forces of the emirate were marching upon the city. "[T]he Muslims attacked them openly, impelling them towards gorges and rough paths with no way out, where they were hacked with swords and by the thrusts of the spears or they drowned in the waters."[28] The troops of Velasco the Wascon—Louis' appointee as his man in Pamplona—were utterly crushed. A more compliant local chief, willing to serve as Al-Andalus' instrument in the north, was immediately placed at the head of Pamplona.

Many centuries later, Enneco Arista would be enshrined as the first king of Pamplona, dubious though this title truly was.[29] What was indisputable, however, was that his biography provided a compelling window into the labyrinthine politics that during his lifetime had come to shape the Western Pyrenees. For starters, and even though a contemporary priest—a saint no less—would applaud Enneco as *princeps Christicola*—"ruler who worships Christ"[30]—it is all but certain that Enneco was the leader of the pro-Muslim faction within Pamplona's nobility. His political stance, at any rate, had little to do with religion. As he knew well, to govern a scarcely structured patchwork territory demanded not just internal authority but external support, and prestige and resources, as Western Pyreneans had come to learn, depended largely on foreign patronage. Holding sway in a small district theoretically subjected to the emir, Enneco could at least use this position to elevate himself over his squabbling peers.

In this, he had two advantages. Years of foreign intervention had left the local elite battered and diminished. Repeated purges and shifts in leadership had drained their resources, scattered their alliances, and skimmed their capacity to mount any significant opposition. Such instability produced a vacuum that a shrewd leader like Enneco could exploit to his benefit. But the new ruler of Pamplona also held the upper hand when it came to family networks. Enneco's grandparent was none other than Lupo, the duke in Wasconia: a personal connection to the northern duchy that had cast a large shadow upon the events leading to his accession. No clearer testimony exists than the blood that ran through his veins of the alliance that the ruling elites on both sides of the Pyrenees had sealed over the preceding decades.

And blood, in such a world, was a valuable asset indeed. After the death of his first husband, Enneco's mother had married again. The identity of the new groom, however, might have initially proven shocking to many. Musà ibn Fortún, the Muslim who ruled the margins of the Ebro in Cordoba's name, was not, despite appearances to the contrary, a foreigner. His family, descended as it was from a certain Cassius—probably a small Visigothic official—had early on embraced Islam and thrown their lot with the conquerors. Time had vindicated their decision. Within a few generations, Cassius' descendants, well-established in the lands around the Ebro, had already managed to secure for themselves key posts in the emirate. It is thus perhaps trivial to say that members of the family treasured the memory of their common ancestor dearly. So dearly, in fact, that the lineage into which Enneco's mother had married was better known across Al-Andalus simply as the *Banu Qasi*: the children of Cassius.

To claim that the partnership between Enneco Arista and his in-laws was merely fueled by ties of kinship would be misguided. For, at its core, it was equally driven by political ambition. Although both the Aristas and the Banu Qasi were, in their respective domains, influential and respected figures, they were also keenly aware of the ambiguity of their respective positions. Their territories, straddling the dividing line between various competing powers, afforded them a sizable degree of autonomy from their superiors. And yet, it was an autonomy that was constantly flirting with disaster. The urgency of setting the foundations of their respective regimes upon firmer grounds must have weighed equally upon the two families. Factor these elements in, and it becomes easy to see why it was only logical for both of them to acknowledge their common goals and to recognize who stood in their way. Before long, the Aristas and the Banu Qasi made an agreement: one which involved an ambitious plan to become the chief power brokers between the Pyrenees and the Ebro. But, for this to happen, a single—yet truly enormous—hindrance had to be overcome. The Carolingians had to be pushed back to the north of the mountain range, once and for all.

The plan, all things considered, was sound. By 820, Enneco and his Banu Qasi allies had attracted some regional aristocrats to their side and had managed to isolate and intimidate those who remained loyal to Louis. The son of Charlemagne, though, was not one to let his southern holdings slip away without resistance. Determined to restore his authority, the hosts of the Franks trod the familiar road that led them directly toward Pamplona. Enneco, as tidings of the impending march reached him, fled the city. The campaign, yet again, was an overwhelming success for the Franks. Like in a déjà vu, Louis' triumph in the southern Pyrenees appeared to be repeating itself.

The delight of their victory, though, would prove a short-lived one for the Franks. Whereas the king, almost a decade prior, had acknowledged the dangers posed by the abrupt cliff-faces of the Pyrenees, he appeared to have failed to instill that same caution in his commanders. As they rushed north back to Francia, the unlucky generals got to experience "the customary treachery and innate deceit of the inhabitants of the region."[31] Ambushed by an enemy that descended upon them in the narrow mountain corridor, their soldiers were scattered, taken captive, or outright massacred. Louis the Pious, hearing news of the debacle, must have felt himself trapped inside a recurring nightmare. Could it be that Roncesvalles, that resounding humiliation that had forever scarred his august father's legacy, had been so painfully re-enacted?

"[S]urrounded by local people, and after having lost their supplies," his men had fallen "into the hands of the enemy."[32] This time there could be no visiting immediate retribution, for any attempt at returning the blow, with the Frankish sovereign embroiled in the endless list of internal troubles consuming his empire—which included, invariably, rebellions in the duchy of Wasconia—was simply beyond discussion. The idea of punishing the Pamplonese and their Muslim allies, a campaign that promised to be costly beyond his available resources, was therefore put off indefinitely.

Pamplona had, unexpectedly, slipped from the grasp of the Franks. Enneco Arista—with the aid of the Banu Qasi—had prevailed.

Notes

1 "The Song of Roland," 1399–401 and 1417–18, 74.

2 "Royal Frankish Annals, 778." In Scholz and Rogers, *Carolingian Chronicles: Royal Frankish Annals and Nithard's Histories*, 56.

3 Ever since the age of Gregory of Tours, Frankish authors had usually written *UUascones* in place of *Uascones*. This process would result in the application of the name Wasconia to the northern Western Pyrenean region.

4 *Poetae Saxonis Annalium de Gestis Caroli Magni Imperatoris Libri Quinque*, I, 778. Indict. 15.

5 Lorenzo, *La Vasconia Peninsular*, 44.

6 This is at least the impression given by later Andalusian sources. See Lorenzo, *La Vasconia Peninsular*, 45.

7 "Fredegarii Scholastici Chronicum." In Fredegarius, *Fredegarii*, 78.

8 "Mozarab Chronicon" (754), X. In López, *Crónica Mozárabe de 754. Edición Crítica y traducción*, 69.

9 *Annales Einhardi* (769), 1, 147.

10 *Poetae Saxonis Annalium de Gestis Caroli Magni Imperatoris Libri Quinque*, 772, Indict.9.

11 Letteron, "Échanges transpyrénnnéens dans les textes navarrais du Codex de Roda (VIIIe-Xe siècles)," 324.

12 Wood, *The Merovingian Kingdoms, 450–751*, 175–6.

13 Pelat, "Les identifications ethniques en Novempopulanie, Wasconie et Aquitaine dans l'Antiquité tardive et au haut Moyen Age (IIIe-IXe siècle)," 202.

14 Pelat, "Les identités ethniques en Novempopulanie, Wasconie et Aquitaine," 120.

15 "In Honorem Hludowici Christianissimi Caesaris Augusti Ermoldi Nigelli Exulis, Elegiaci Carminis Liber Incipit Primus," 57–8. In Dümmler, *Poetae Latini Aevi Carolini*, II, 6.

16 *Annales Laurissenses* (778), 1, 158.

17 Oihenart, *Notitia utriusque Vasconiae tum Ibericae, tum Aquitanicae*, 62.

18 Martín, *Sancho III el Mayor de Pamplona. El rey y su reino*, 132.

19 An exception to this trend could be found in the *Annales Einhardi* (778): "[. . .] congregato exercitu, profectus est, superatoque in regione Wasconum Pyrinei iugo, primo Pompelonem Navarrorum oppidum adgressus . . ." And yet, the same source claims: "[. . .] Pampilona destructa, Hispani Wascones subiugatos, etiam et Nabarros . . ." (1,159). The distinction, then, remains unclear.

20 Larrea, *La Navarre du IVe au XIIe siècle. Peuplement et sociéte*, 196–7.

21 Pavón, *Poblamiento altomedieval navarro. Base socioeconómica del espacio monárquico*, 336.

22 Orella, "Relaciones medievales entre Gascuña y Guipúzcoa: la diócesis de Pamplona y de Bayona," 128.

23 Letteron, "Échanges transpyrénnéens dans les textes navarrais du Codex de Roda (VIIIe—Xe siècles)," 319–34.

24 Lorenzo, *La Vasconia peninsular*, 59. The identity of the victim, Mutarrif ibn Musá, remains contested. See Lorenzo, *La Dawla de los Banu Qasi. Origen, auge y caída de una dinastía muladí en la frontera superior de Al-Andalus*, 2010, 120–1.

25 Lorenzo, *La Vasconia peninsular*, 53.

26 Astronomus, "Vita Hludowici imperatoris." In Noble, *Charlemagne and Louis the Pious: the lives of Einhard, Notker, Ermoldus, Thegan, and the Astronomer*, 242.

27 *Annales Einhardi* (816), 203.

28 Astronomus, "Vita Hludowici imperatoris." In Noble, *Charlemagne and Louis the Pious*, 242.

29 Martín, "Vasconia en la Alta Edad Media. Somera aproximación histórica," 875.

30 Eulogius of Cordoba, "Letter to the bishop Wilesindus." In Monreal and Jimeno, *Textos Histórico-Jurídicos Navarros I: Historia Antigua y Medieval*, 106.

31 Astronomus, "Vita Hludowici imperatoris." In Noble, *Charlemagne and Louis the Pious*, 266–7.

32 Astronomus, 266–7.

CHAPTER 6
DAR AL-HARB

The death of the last king of the Visigoths back in 711 had marked the beginning of a tidal wave, as the invaders swept across Iberia like an unstoppable flood. But, as it turns out, not everyone had been willing to submit without resistance. Much later, histories would proudly recall the name of a certain Pelayo, who during the tumult of the conquest had managed to flee to the far north, there to command a ragtag band of soldiers with whom to fight back the Muslims. His audacious act did not go unnoticed for long. An army of "one hundred and eighty-seven thousand men, with all kinds of weapons and impedimenta" was said to have crossed the borders of Asturias, determined to crush Pelayo and his followers as the latter took shelter at a mountain grotto known as Covadonga.[1] The odds were, by any measure, stacked against them, and there is little doubt that Pelayo and all his men would have been wiped out had they not received, on the edge of time, a most unexpected aid.

The Mother of Jesus herself, moved by pity for the beleaguered remnants of Pelayo's forces, had manifested at the slopes of Covadonga and had cast her mantle of protection over the Christians to miraculously reflect the missiles of the Muslim artillery. The chaos brought by the supernatural intervention had been colossal. Many were struck down by the wrath of the redirected bombardment, but for those who managed to escape the carnage, any hope of survival proved a fleeting one. For, "by an evident disposition of God, a part of the mountain crumbled from its base" and collapsed upon the fugitives, "throwing them into the river and burying them all." Pelayo's surprising triumph was accompanied, in the aftermath of the battle, by his proclamation as king. And so, "with the aid of the Divine Providence, it was born the realm of the Asturians."[2]

Implausible though these stories might appear at first glance, it remained undeniable that their God seemed particularly fond of these northerners. What began as a desperate redoubt had, over the course of a generation, grown into a leadership whose influence reached the very edges of the Western Pyrenees. Meanwhile, the rulers of Al-Andalus, more interested in plundering the lands of the Franks than in fighting a costly war of attrition in the highlands, had increasingly taken the sensible approach and had opted to avoid the region altogether. By 737, when Pelayo was succeeded by Alfonso I, these promising circumstances had improved even more, and the new ruler had managed to push forward the reconquest of the northernmost settlements occupied by the emir. Towns like Salamanca, Segovia, Leon, and a host of others fell to Alfonso's forces. So too, further east, did Veleia.[3]

By the eighth century, little remained of the once-mighty fortress overlooking the *Iter XXXIV*, except some small, scattered hamlets and overgrown piles of rubble. Over the course of the long years that had gone by since the end of the empire, the city had been drained of any semblance of order. Unlike in Pamplona, where the infrastructure laid by the Romans—fragile and battered though it was—had managed to preserve a shadowy hierarchy, no such continuity existed to the west. Here, the land was governed by a mishmash of local warlords and small assemblies, their reach limited and their power often reliant on short-range trade or outright brigandage.

These groups, in a pattern that might have seemed all too familiar to individuals like Enneco Arista, had learned to navigate a precarious course between the poles of placating distant patrons and the desire to conduct their own affairs. Yet, barring that, differences were stark. Whereas in Pamplona the authority of the bishop offered at least a focal point for power, there existed in the district around Veleia no such prize to which to aspire. Periodic gatherings to resolve disputes or coordinate military efforts might occasionally see an outstanding chieftain raised to prominence. But, at any rate, these displays of patronage and influence, while meaningful, were hardly sufficient as a basis for sustained command.

Or so it was, leastways, up until Alfonso's arrival. The Asturians, locked in their pitted struggle against the might of the Muslim emirate, had quickly recognized the strategic importance of these territories. Their own bases, nestled securely within the rugged peaks that formed the northern crust of Iberia, were almost unassailable. A stronghold, nevertheless, that as any Muslim general would have noted, had but a single weak point. The river Ebro, winding its way in an ample diagonal from its sources near the Atlantic, cut through the mountains in its upper course, carving out in doing so a perfect stepping stone for an attack. A whim of nature, indeed, and one that made tending to the affairs of the region a crucial priority for the survival of Alfonso's young kingdom. *Alaba*—Muslims called this strip of land. A name that, soon enough, the Asturians adopted as well.[4]

Pelayo's successors, keenly aware of the stakes as they were, tended for this reason to be especially thoughtful in their dealings with the inhabitants of these lands. Asturian chronicles, for instance, never delved into the meager status of its many petty chieftains and strongmen nor questioned their shadowy origins. Rather, they described the territory as having always been "possessed by their dwellers" and as having never suffered any foreign control.[5] A curious claim to make; yet one that in its ambiguity sidestepped a more prosaic reality: that there was precious little here to tempt any conqueror.

But propaganda, for all that could help in softening up these peripheral nobodies, was nothing if not paired with more tactile efforts. It was for this reason that King Fruela, Alfonso's brother and heir, had chosen to marry, not an Asturian, but a noblewoman of local stock. Far from an idle gesture, it was one deliberately calculated to demonstrate to the region's inhabitants the esteem in which the monarch held their opinions and their alliance.[6]

Which is not to say that relations between these two communities were easy. In fact, and regardless of all these conciliatory policies, the specter of danger was never far from view. The strategic value of Alava made its control an imperative for the Asturians, and this was a goal that could be achieved either through the carrot or the stick. Local rivalries, a perennial feature of the region's social landscape, might on occasion erupt into open conflict. And such disputes, rather than a simple nuisance for Asturian administrators, opened the door for the penetration of more insidious foreign meddling. Muslim agents, whose reach lay only a few miles to the south, were after all always attentive at such breaches of trust, and there were doubtless many who would rather support the emir than endure the consequences of opposing him.

Thus, when persuasion failed, the Asturians displayed no qualms in resorting to arms. The chronicles praising King Fruela's decision to marry a Western Pyrenean, after all, also made a point of recording a very different achievement of the king. *Vascones rebellantes superauit atque edomuit*: "He overcame and subdued the rebellious Vascones."[7] Could it be that the bride, rather than a queen chosen to gain the natives' approval, might have first been her new husband's hostage? A startling thought, but not *too* startling. In their framing of the Western Pyrenees at least, the Asturian kings, who styled themselves elsewhere the recipients of the Gothic legacy, had proven a chip off the old block. The confrontational contours of their dominion over Alava were of a kind that would have made a man like Leovigild proud.

Without a hint of doubt, what this example demonstrated was that the association of the Vascones with rebellion—an image that had grown inescapable ever since the times of Isidore—was a trope that Asturian mouthpieces had inherited and were always keen to dig up for profit. But even these scribes, much like their Frankish counterparts, would in time come to recognize the limitations posed by such a Manichean formula. To be labeled a Vascon was, after all, to be blacklisted as a barbarian, a pagan, and a rebel. As such, it was a description that only befitted a foe—and this, under the current circumstances, created some complications. How could the Asturian sovereigns expect to win the loyalty of the inhabitants of Alava, upon whose collaboration so much hinged, if at the same time they branded them with such scornful terms? For their realm to endure—intellectuals must have reflected—the struggle for the narrative might prove as important a battlefield as any physical one, and just like writers on the other side of the Pyrenees, they too arrived at an astonishing conclusion. That in order to win over the Western Pyreneans to their cause, the pejorative connotations entangled with the word "Vascon" had to vanish for good. Not an easy undertaking, by any means, but one that offered a far simpler alternative right at hand. For if the term could not be rehabilitated, then it at least could be abandoned altogether. Before long, Asturian accounts began to be punctuated with mentions of the *Alavensium*: the dwellers of Alava.

In hindsight, few things captured the shifting political conditions of the Western Pyrenees more vividly than this terminological evolution. The region's destitute aristocracy, caught between the competing demands of distant powers, thrived in a delicate equilibrium that oscillated between nominal allegiance and de facto independence. Bound on paper to the monarchs of Asturias, the various groups and cliques that made up the people of Alava must have understood all too well the dangers that a stiff approach to loyalty could involve. To pledge obedience to one overlord, no matter how ambiguously, was to risk retribution from another.

Which might explain why Muslim armies began to campaign against Alava from 767 onward, in the immediate aftermath of Fruela's incursion and his polemic marriage. Just as much as the Asturian sovereigns, the emirs in Cordoba were hardly men prone to surrender a strategic territory without a fight. What followed was an age of unrelenting combats, with Islamic forces striking deep into the north and chasing their enemies to their shelters and strongholds. For the Alavese, resistance was a costly undertaking, and not always a successful one at that. Little by little, like a cloth disfigured by innumerable rips and rends, Alava came to be engulfed in a seemingly perpetual spiral of conflict, violence, and plunder. *Dār al-ḥarb*, Arabs called such places: the "abodes of war."

So it came to pass that, in the first decades of the ninth century, relative temperatures in the political climate of the Western Pyrenees shifted: While tensions in Alava grew hotter, those in Pamplona cooled off. With the Franks out of the way, the nascent domain of Enneco Arista had gravitated decisively to the orbit of Muslim and—more specifically—Banu Qasi influence. Of course, these political allegiances had not erased the deeply rooted Christian identity of the country's inhabitants. The authority of the metropolitan bishop and of venerable monasteries like San Salvador of Leyre was one intensely intertwined with the rhythms of everyday peasant life. Christian travelers, arriving in Leyre from territories governed by the appointees of Allah, marveled at the prosperity and devotion these northern monks displayed. "In this association and blessed congregation"—a future martyr and saint would write—"all glowed like the stars in the sky with different merits and virtues."[8] Such an aura of dazzling holiness as the one emanating from Leyre and other monasteries was, quite literally, a blessing—and Enneco Arista was cautious to tend it with care. He lavished donations and favors upon the community and granted its abbots plots of land and even the tribute of nearby villages. In return, the monks prayed for the health and salvation of the Pamplonese ruler, thus tacitly recognizing his right to tower above his peers with the acquiescence of the Almighty.

A powerful endorsement. And yet, for all that the divine support garnered by the brothers of Leyre was undoubtedly essential, Enneco must have been painfully aware of the fact that the true foundations of his rule lay elsewhere. Which is why, on occasion, he acted decisively to strengthen the ties that connected his house to that of the Banu Qasi. The policy of rubbing down prominent non-believers, while effective in cementing alliances, was invariably frowned upon by clergymen, but even the most devout clerics must have recognized that little could be done to stop them from taking place. The monks laboring tirelessly on the windswept terraces of Leyre may well entertain, from time to time, the dream of an Iberia restored to the veneration of Christ. But Enneco Arista was a man bound by harsher realities. Lofty ambitions for the reconquest of the peninsula, if they ever crossed his mind, were far beyond his reach. He might present himself before his subjects as a Christian king—a patron of monasteries and a defender of the faith—but, despite this, to the emir in far-off Cordoba he was something different altogether: simply "one of the polytheist rulers of Al-Andalus."[9]

Peace prevailed, therefore, as long as both the Aristas and the Banu Qasi recognized the overarching authority of the emirate. For nearly two decades, while Muslim raids wreaked havoc in Alava, not a single document recorded any attack upon Pamplona. But prosperity, as it often does, ultimately bred ambition and envy. The prominence of the Banu Qasi, entrenched as the latter was in the support of the Aristas, appeared to many Muslims to have grown too conspicuous, too vital to the emir's interests in the Western Pyrenees. Poisonous whisperings noted that it was as if it was the lineage of Cassius, rather than Cordoba's authority, that ruled the northern frontier. Anyone would have quickly recognized the sense of peril that lurked behind such rumors. And so, determined to make an example out of the Banu Qasi, the Andalusian emir prepared a breathtaking show of force. In 839, their leader, Musà ibn Musà, after having assisted Enneco Arista in fending off an incursion personally sanctioned by the emir, found himself denounced as a rebel. An army was dispatched against him, and Musà was forced to yield. Enneco Arista, ever the pragmatic, followed suit shortly after. The emir's message had been delivered with resounding clarity. No family, however influential, could ever hope to eclipse his authority.

The war might have been an unmitigated disaster for the Arista and Banu Qasi alliance, but, for all its severity, it did not spell the end of their ascendancy. The emir, despite his might, could not dream of controlling the institutionally dislodged northern frontier without the cooperation of local magnates, and he readily understood that his power relied not in the eradication of these middlemen, but rather on their subordination. The privileges and autonomy that had allowed the rise of the Aristas and the Banu Qasi were, in such a view, the counterpart for unflinching loyalty to Cordoba, and the events of 839, in turn, a brutal reminder calculated to make these upstarts remember the terms of the agreement. Once the lesson was crystal clear, pragmatism prevailed. Both lineages, their recent chastisement notwithstanding, were almost immediately reinstated to their original positions.

The inhabitants of Pamplona and its surrounding lands would grow accustomed to bearing the brunt of such balancing acts on the part of the emir. When Muslim factions, eager to alienate the Aristas from Musà, periodically swept northward, they would torch their farms and raid their hamlets. Each year brought its own unpredictability, whether in the form of a new invasion, a fresh rebellion, or the collapse of an old alliance. And as if that were not enough, to the north, too, rumor spread of ominous ships with black sails teeming to the brink with demonic creatures. These "Vikings," bypassing the feeble Wascon stronghold of Lapurdum, had sailed up the Adour River and laid waste to the hinterland of Wasconia, and had even managed to murder the duke.[10] The northern coast of Iberia, too, suffered their attacks. Along the stretch between Alava and the ocean, an impoverished region that the Asturians had only recently begun to call Biscay, fishing towns were hastily abandoned in fear of Viking longships.[11] Panic spread like wildfire among the fleeing populations, and yet, not even distance from the coast was a guarantee of safety. In 859, a Viking force disembarked off the coast and made a sudden appearance at the very gates of Pamplona. García, the son of Enneco Arista and the lord of the land, was captured in an operation as daring as it was astonishing, only to be freed after an enormous ransom had been extorted from his subjects.[12]

Consolation from these calamities, hard though it was to find, was in any case not impossible to come by. Hard times, so the saying goes, create hard men. And in the Western Pyrenees, this verdict was etched on fact. The Viking onslaught, swift and unexpected as it had been, had coincided with a general—and improbable—strengthening of the Asturian monarchy. The latter's forces had managed to weather the Muslim assaults during those decades in which the Aristas had been allied to the Banu Qasi, and, against all odds, their kingdom had survived. Alava and its surroundings had been patrolled, garrisons had held the line, and fortresses had been erected on top of inaccessible outcrops. Such was the proliferation of fortifications that Muslim chroniclers came to know the entire frontier as *al-Qila*: "the castles." An embattled territory in a state of almost perpetual warfare and responsibility of which, therefore, soon became a matter of the highest priority.

Evidence of this importance was displayed in the symbiosis between the crown and local power brokers. The steady backing some influential Western Pyrenean families received from the Asturians had allowed them to become more adept at exercising control over both land and people. Much like Enneco Arista had risen to prominence in Pamplona under the wing of Al-Andalus, so too did a new cadre of leaders begin to take shape in these war-torn territories. These so-called counts, charismatic and respected by their fellow inhabitants, did not hesitate in presenting their authority as an extension of that wielded by the Asturian kings. In 860, a certain Rodrigo surfaced in the annals as the count in Castella, "Castile."[13] Twenty years later, the stewardship of Alava was put in the hands of a certain Vela Jiménez, a local magnate with close ties to the Asturian court. In all, nothing better than the presence of such figures to illustrate both the revival of political structures in the land, as well as their imbrication with the dominion carved out by Pelayo's successors. The unruly Vascones of yesterday had come to uphold, in a capricious twist of fate, the rule of the heirs of the Goths.

But while the Asturian position grew stronger, conditions around Pamplona were rapidly deteriorating. In 880, Fortún One-eyed, a descendant of Enneco Arista who had been captured by the emirate and had spent twenty years of his life as a prisoner in Cordoba, ascended to power. Perhaps due to such a traumatic experience, Fortún was said to have come to abhor conflict with a passion. A distaste for war, however, that and much to his discredit, soon transformed him into little more than a puppet for Banu Qasi interests. Slowly, his seeming lack of martial vigor, paired with his dubious position vis-á-vis the Muslim, alienated his Christian neighbors. Among Pamplona's leading families, too, frustration intensified. Previously overshadowed by the supremacy of the Aristas, their discontent with the lack of bounty and the frequent devastation of their lands had made them unruly and defiant. They yearned for a king who could drive off raiders, who would prevent invaders from setting fire to their farms and forests, and who could—most importantly—deliver them the spoils of war. As none of these longings came to fulfillment, their patience with Fortún grew thinner by the day.

Therefore, when in 905 the aged and faint-hearted monarch was invited by some aristocrats to retire to the isolated monastery of Leyre, few voices were raised to utter the slightest objection. "So it was raised in Pamplona a king named Sancho Garcés, a pious and compassionate man with all the faithful and oppressed Catholics."[14] The new leader, closely associated with the Asturian court, immediately revoked the compliant attitude of his predecessor and cast away even the nominal vassalage to the emir. And so, the kingdom of Pamplona was born.

The laconic mention of Sancho Garcés' ascension, however, begs a major question: Who was this man? The new king, despite being married to a member of the Arista lineage, was at best a scion of a minor offshoot of Enneco's family tree. In his alliances, too, he was hardly a continuator. While Sancho rose to the throne with the explicit backing of the Asturian court, his circle of friends displayed a telling absence: that of the Banu Qasi. Indeed, one of his earliest recorded acts was the setting up of an ambush that had led to the death of the leading "children of Cassius." A message that could hardly have been more poignant. The Aristas had ruled by walking a tightrope, playing a perilous double game with the Andalusian power; Sancho, by contrast, rejected this approach outright. Inspired possibly by the combative ideology of the embattled Asturians, he declared Pamplona free from the guiding hand of Muslim officials. In the great geopolitical contest between the emirate and the Asturian kings, a major player had, thus, switched sides.

The stars could hardly have aligned more perfectly for this momentous recalibration. In Al-Andalus, internal tensions and rivalries had ever since the time of the conquest been a fact of life. Now, however, not even the central authority entrusted with the task of appeasing them could prevent them from tearing the whole emirate apart. Rebellions flared across its heartlands, and soon the situation spiraled out of control. Even the quarters of the prince, the neuralgic fulcrum of the power of Cordoba, had devolved into a fatal pit of snakes. In the shadowy corridors of the palace, talk of assassination and schemes to engineer a favorable succession filled the air. The frontiers of the emirate, too, became battlefields in which old grudges between competing factions were redeemed in blood. And what of the emir? Incapable of acting, and reduced to a powerless figurehead, he stood as a helpless spectator to the implosion of his realm.

The faltering of the strong grip did not go unnoticed in the north. Sensing the tide beginning to turn, Pamplonese and Asturian rulers moved immediately to capitalize on the opportunity. In June 918, their combined forces marched southward, crossed the Ebro, conquered Calahorra—former Calagurris—and Nájera, and then struck at Tudela. The fertile plains beyond the river—Rioja—were captured by the Christians in a momentous expansion. For Sancho Garcés, once an upstart encumbered by Pamplonese party politics, these exploits were much more than a vindication of his rule. Thanks to his victories, he amassed more than enough wealth and land to secure a towering position over his peers—not through intrigue, as the Aristas had once done, but through conquest. The kingdom of Pamplona stood now, it seemed, upon firm ground, and the dream of reconquering Iberia, some might have enthusiastically believed, stood within the grasp of Christian kings.

The two centuries following the arrival of the Muslims in Iberia marked the demise of an entire mental world. Visigoths and Franks had sought to carve kingdoms out of previously Roman provinces, and to this end had appropriated the ideologies of those they subdued. By 711, however, the social and political world of the Western Pyrenees had grown much more complex.

In Wasconia—a land destined to be known in time as Gascony—the Carolingians found themselves constrained by the realities of local power to accept the existence of energetic dukes and entrenched regional authorities. So too, in Alava, did their Asturian counterparts come to regard native potentates as decisive power brokers. In both cases, dependence upon the collaboration of these chieftains had compelled royal officers to rely more and more upon seduction rather than oppression. In Pamplona, magnates navigated similarly precarious waters, but over the decades of subjugation to Cordoba's oversight they had managed to exploit an unexpected advantage. The inchoate stereotypes that had so often colored views of the Vascones in the Roman world were, on the whole, alien to their new overlords.

In all, the consequences were profound. The ancient label "Vascones," improbably preserved through the centuries, finally met its doom. Simultaneously abandoned by the Franks, the Muslims, and the Asturians, it soon sank into obscurity. In its place, new names and new notions emerged—realities previously concealed by the dense clouds of foreign prejudice and political interest. For the first time in history, people long burdened with the weight of scorn found themselves free to speak with their own voices.

But what these would say, as of yet, no one could fathom.

Notes

1 "Chronicon Rotense." In Ubieto, *Crónica de Alfonso III*, 33.

2 Chronicon Rotense, 35.

3 Martínez, *El condado de Castilla (711–1038). La historia frente a la leyenda*, 73.

4 Lorenzo and Pastor, "Al-Andalus, ¿en la periferia de Vasconia? Sistemas de dominación de bilad Banbaluna y Alaba wa-l-Qila en la octava centuria," 65.

5 "Chronicon Rotense." In Ubieto, *Crónica de Alfonso III*, 36.

6 "Chronicon Ovetense." In Ubieto, *Crónica de Alfonso III*, 38.

7 Chronicon Ovetense, 38.

8 Eulogius of Cordoba, "Letter to the bishop Wilesindus." In Monreal and Jimeno, *Textos Histórico-Jurídicos Navarros I: Historia Antigua y Medieval*, 104.

9 Lorenzo, *La Vasconia Peninsular*, 85.

10 Besga, *Astures et Vascones*, 63–4.

11 Martín, "Vasconia en la Alta Edad Media. Somera aproximación histórica," 898–901.

12 Lorenzo, *La Vasconia Peninsular*, 93–4.

13 Martínez, *El condado de Castilla (711–1038). La historia frente a la leyenda*, 192.

14 *Additio de regibus Pampilonensibus of the Chronicon Albeldense*, XX. 1–2.

CHAPTER 7
REX IBERICUS

The marriage in 1010 between Sancho Garcés III of Pamplona—destined to be remembered as Sancho the Great—and Munia of Castile would, in hindsight, mark a momentous juncture in the history of the Iberian kingdoms. That, of course, was something that few could have anticipated. To their contemporaries, it likely seemed little more than another knot in a long tradition of matrimonial diplomacy, a strategy that had entangled the ruling families of the northern peninsula for more than a century. For example, Sancho the Great's grandfather, Sancho Garcés II, had married the widow of two Leonese kings—lords, at least nominally, of the counts of Castile. One of his sisters had likewise been betrothed to Fernán González, Count of Castile—himself the widower of Sancho Garcés II's aunt. Such a family tree, crisscrossed and twisted as it was, constantly branching in and out, was one that resisted any attempt at simplification. Over the decades, the intricate web of alliances had ended up resulting in close relatives controlling the nascent political spaces of Leon, Pamplona, and Castile. Now, the impending union between Sancho and Munia promised to continue this tradition.

Yet, as time would soon reveal, there was nothing secure about the future. The newlyweds were stepping into a world far less stable than it appeared, and by the end of their lives, even the unshakable customs and hierarchies that had underpinned the political order of the Christian kingdoms for over a hundred years would find themselves upended.

Family affairs—especially those that embroiled the ruling elites—were essential to the organization and perpetuation of medieval society. Dowries and endowments, a key aspect of marriage policies, were the subject of painstaking negotiation to ensure that the interests of both the bride and the groom's families were equitably balanced. These arrangements were far more than mere formalities. Given that most loyalties were markedly personal, exchanges of areas of influence or administrative control, along with economic benefits or even outright payments, were a frequent feature of such dealings. Plunder lost to the enemy on the battlefield could later be won over again at the negotiation table, and crafty diplomacy could allow an otherwise obscure figure to ascend rapidly to prominence. But social mobility of this kind was not entirely free from entailing certain risks. Just as the birth of an heir could secure the status of a dynasty, untimely deaths, miscarriages, or a barren union could result in meticulously planned arrangements going to waste, leaving inheritances fragmented and households vulnerable to rivals eager to exploit their weakness.

To avoid such fate, prosperous families usually sought to strike a balance between the allure of expanding their reach and the safety provided by endogamous marriages. After all, it would otherwise take little more than a few missteps, some weak link in the chain to snap, and entire territories could slip irretrievably from a dynasty's patrimony. The descendants of Sancho Garcés on the throne of Pamplona, who had seen their kingdom regularly harassed by the troops of the caliphate in the decades following their illustrious ancestor's reign, were no strangers to this conclusion. For them, strengthening ties with the kings of Leon was not merely an advantageous line of policy: It was an essential one. The very survival of their kingdom hinged upon their ability to keep these partners close at hand.

Luckily for them, few contemporaries had matched the diplomatic brilliance of Sancho Garcés' wife, Queen Toda. Her remarkable ability to negotiate with an array of powerbrokers—kings, counts, and even the caliph in Cordoba himself—seemed almost miraculous in retrospect. On the western threshold of the realm, in the advanced outposts carved out by the Leonese in Alava and, to a lesser degree, Biscay, traces of the insidious influence deployed by the queen were unmistakable. Even after her husband's death, she had still managed to orchestrate the marriages of two of her daughters to the lords of these strategically significant counties, drawing them deftly to her side. Bit by bit, like a hard-working spider carefully tending to her web, the queen had ensnared the ruling Christian families into an intricate grid of cooperation that had kept them tightly united against Al-Andalus. Yet, in doing so, Toda's mastermind had also granted her descendants something much more valuable: ready access to the most coveted positions of power in the neighboring realms.

This was no minor accomplishment, especially considering how close the Pamplonese had stood to the brink of collapse. In 992, following a series of disastrous defeats against Muslim troops, the then-sovereign of Pamplona—a grandchild of Sancho Garcés I—had been forced to travel all the way to Cordoba to publicly declare his submission to the Muslim ruler. Only five years later, the city of Pamplona had been yet again overrun, sacked, and set ablaze.[1] The kingdom, like overripe fruit, seemed to hang low precariously moments away from falling to the ground.

But it still fought on. Chronicles written in Pyrenean monasteries, the earliest preserved expressions of the ideological underpinnings of the Pamplonese monarchy, ostensibly captured the combative spirit of the age.[2] Nowhere to be found in them was any memory of past alliances with the Banu Qasi, or with the Carolingians, or with the Wascones. Rather, the Pamplonese kings had come to cast themselves as the rightful heirs of the Visigothic kings, and fully appropriated the ideal of their Asturian counterparts of reclaiming Iberia from Islam. Any chance of attaining this goal, of course, now that the star of Cordoba was yet again ascendant, was nothing short of a wild dream. But the aspiration, in and of itself, exposed better than anything the crucible of ideas in which the monarchy of Pamplona had matured and developed.

These documents, like the famous *Codex Rotense*, were actually not only telling for what they said but also for what they did not. Among the most glaring omissions was any mention of the Vascones. For centuries, the label had been a constant presence in the written records, and compilers like Isidore of Seville and Gregory of Tours had accorded the term both prominence and a certain mystique. Therefore, it was significant that the first political institution from the Western Pyrenees ever to produce its own propaganda should so clearly have avoided it. Either the Pamplonese monarchs did not want to showcase this connection or, perhaps more intriguingly, they felt no attachment to it whatsoever.

And why should they? "Vascon" summoned images of lawlessness—of raiders haunting the passes and brigands preying upon travelers. Pamplona, by contrast, offered its rulers a far more honorable lineage. Through its bishopric, the city could claim, nebulous though it was, a direct connection to the sanctified realms of Christianity, the shattered glories of the Visigothic kingdom, and ultimately, the eternal authority of Rome. Even as the derelict urban landscape crumbled and its streets grew silent, it was this enduring memory, more than anything else, which allowed their rulers to proclaim their right over the surrounding lands. These families had long taken for granted that it was from Pamplona that the Western Pyrenees should be governed. And these magnates, just as much as their Asturian counterparts, readily understood what symbols defined dominion and the legitimacy to exercise it; for these were, precisely, those against which the image of the Vascones had been outlined: the use of the Latin language, the veneration due to Christ's teachings, the loyalty to the Visigothic monarchy. Fail to recognize them, and the frailty of the entire edifice of Pamplonese kingship would immediately stand revealed. Pamplona, as in the times of Pompey, was envisioned as a haven of civilization amid a sea of darkness. A vision, therefore, that left no space for its kings to cast themselves as Vascones.

A second and perhaps more pragmatic reason for the rejection of Vascon identity lay in the transformed geography and ambitions of the Pamplonese kingdom itself. The city alongside its neighboring district, for all that it treasured the ideological capital of the monarchy, had become ever since the times of Sancho Garcés just a part—and not even the most vital—of a realm stretching from the sunlit plains of Rioja to the rugged feet of the Pyrenees. Here, deep valleys that had long ago accepted the distant authority of the Carolingians had gradually become a playground for the ambitions of the Pamplonese dynasty. Far from their original properties around the city, Sancho Garcés' successors had carved for themselves a sizable territory. An embattled and besieged dominion, to be sure, but a politically stable one; part of a dense web of defensive alliances that granted it a chance of sustaining the continuous onslaughts from Al-Andalus. Such a diverse organization required careful governance to sustain itself. To manage the ambitions of fiercely independent mountain princelings while simultaneously securing aid and recognition from powerful neighbors like the sovereigns of Leon demanded a unifying vision. And in this, a political discourse founded upon the defense of Christianity promised to be far more effective than any appeal to a parochial and fraught Vascon past.

The prospects for contemporary Pamplonese of rendering such protection an effective one were, as expected, quite grim. But these were soon to be favored by a most unexpected occurrence. In 1009, the mighty caliphate of Cordoba—born out of the troubles that had engulfed the emirate in the age of Sancho Garcés I and long the bane of Christian Iberia—was once again torn apart by internal strife. The caliph himself was assassinated, and a civil war of titanic proportions soon raged throughout the land. Shortly after, the once-unified Islamic polity splintered into a mosaic of tiny principalities and independent warlords.

It was precisely as these violent events were unfolding to the south that Sancho the Great and Munia of Castile celebrated their engagement. Sancho was the heir to the throne of Pamplona. Munia, on the other hand, was the daughter of the Count of Castile, a man who, though not a king, wielded unmatched influence among the Christian rulers of Iberia. Recently, Munia's father had begotten a son to succeed him as count, and this meant that the match, valuable though it remained, brought little immediate promise of inheritance to her new husband. For the time being at least, the marriage bore the perfume of the dynastic strategies inaugurated back in the times of Sancho Garcés and Queen Toda. But very soon, things would take an unexpected turn, and all previous calculations would be rendered obsolete.

While many celebrated the newlywed, not everyone did, as not every Christian had welcomed the steady rise of Pamplona to prominence. The heirs of Sancho Garcés, bolstered by their alliance with the Leonese kings, had swiftly sought to extend their reach into Alava and Biscay. In these fractious territories, their promises of Andalusian booty must have been greeted positively by a sizable portion of the "lords of the land and people."[3] Before long, and as some of the most distinguished clans and families in Alava increasingly aligned themselves with the Pamplonese monarchy, two opposing factions began to take shape.

In all, the situation bespoke peril for the counts of Castile, the nominal agents of the Leonese in the region. While they admitted that some portion of the local population would always remain dissatisfied with how affairs were run in Alava, the thought of these discontented families being funded by a foreign monarch was an entirely different beast altogether. For this reason—and hoping to take advantage of the confusion that followed Sancho Garcés I's death—they had moved decisively to oust that local count who had married a daughter of their rival. The coup, in all, was one calculated to keep Alava under Leonese suzerainty, but it was also one that could not but muddle the political waters in the county. The dispossessed count's lineage, who must have managed to retain the loyalty of no small part of their erstwhile supporters, opted for taking a momentary step back.[4] The king of Pamplona, suddenly faced with a potentially volatile situation, likewise chose agreement over confrontation. His realm, when all was said and done, could not be expected to survive without Castilian collaboration, and this was a necessity that Alava, important though it might have been to the ambitions of the Pamplonese, could not ever hope to outweigh.

But these setbacks notwithstanding, the unraveling of Al-Andalus had opened new paths for the Pamplonese to extend their reach. At around 1010, the Pyrenean counties of Ribagorza and Sobrarbe were incorporated into the realm. Similarly, Sancho the Great did not fail in making his power felt to the north of the mountain range. Here, the duchy in Wasconia, which stretched from the Garonne to the Pyrenees and included, since 977, the district around Bordeaux, had become an independent entity in the wake of the Carolingian empire's collapse in the late ninth century. It was, perhaps, a stroke of fate that the current holder of the title, Sancho Guillaume, was not only a descendant of the Wasconian ducal dynasty but also a scion of Pamplona's royal house. Having spent a long portion of his life in the Iberian court, ties of sympathy as well as of descent connected the rulers of the two territories. In 1010, when the head of John the Baptist was miraculously discovered in Saint-Jean-d'Angely and the duke organized a grand festival to celebrate its finding, Sancho the Great made sure to attend it. He was the first Christian ruler from Iberia to travel north of the Pyrenees ever since 711. The visit had marked the beginning of a flourishing alliance between the two Sanchos and, over the ensuing decades, the ties between the rulers of Pamplona and Wasconia would only grow deeper. So much so, in fact, that the duke in Wasconia would come to ostensibly brand himself a vassal of his Pamplonese neighbor.[5]

This close connection then renders understandable that when Sancho Guillaume passed away without direct heirs in 1032, Sancho the Great would immediately step forward to proclaim his "reign in all of Wasconia."[6] Considering the absence of male descendants from the Wasconian, the wondrous title might have come from an agreement between the Pamplonese king and the late Sancho Guillaume.[7] But if this was the case, and Sancho harbored the hope of stamping his rule as far as the Garonne, his dreams were soon to be dashed. Although he could arrogate to himself the legitimate rule of the duchy based on his agreement with the deceased duke, the actual government of the territory had already passed, in the meantime, into the hands of Eudes, heir to the duke of Aquitaine and Poitiers. This had not only secured the inheritance of Wasconia for the Aquitanian family, but would mark something more momentous: the definitive parting of ways between Wasconia and Pamplona. Some small enclaves north of the Pyrenees, it is true, would eventually be incorporated into the kingdom by Sancho the Great's successors, but never again would the entire duchy come close to accepting the authority of his descendants. Wasconia, after all was said and done, had firmly turned away from the Pyrenees.

Momentous though the tremor of these events would prove in the following decades, the most striking episode in Sancho the Great's reign had little to do with Wasconia. Instead, it played out in the heart of Castile. Here, after the death of Munia's father in 1017, his Pamplonese brother-in-law had taken the responsibility of guiding the steps of the infant count, García. This was not simply a selfless act of familial compassion. In assuming the role of the count's tutor, Sancho had seen an opportunity to reinforce the alliance between the monarchies of Pamplona and Leon with a series of high-flying marriages. García, Count of Castile, was betrothed to Sancha, the daughter of the king of Leon. The Leonese king, in turn, would marry Urraca, Sancho's sister. Gazing down from the heavens, Queen Toda would have smirked approvingly.

But, as is often the case, what had initially appeared a stroke of diplomatic genius quickly spiraled into chaos. In 1028, as García, Count of Castile, traveled to Leon to take Sancha's hand,

> the count Vela . . . , godfather of the groom and his sons, impelled by hatred, while King Vermudo with almost all the Leonese and Castilian knights was taking part in tournaments, entered the city and, murdering as many Castilians as they could

find in it, stormed the palace where the infant García Sánchez stayed, and killed the innocent man.[8]

The tragedy immediately blew up the cautiously placed pieces of the Iberian dynastic chessboard. The Velas, the aristocratic clan from Alava displaced from power by the murdered García's predecessors, certainly lacked no motives for undertaking such a terrible course of action. But even if that proved to be the case, the consequences of the assassination far surpassed the traditional bounds of internecine rivalries in Alava. With García now dead, the county of Castile passed into the hands of his sister, Munia. In other words, rather than merely consolidating the Pamplonese-Leonese alliance, Sancho the Great's marriage had inadvertently secured for him the richest Christian territory in all of Iberia.

An unforeseen inheritance—and one that, compounded by the weakened state of the caliphate and the political fragility of the infant king of Leon, immediately propelled Sancho the Great to an unrivaled dominance on the peninsula. Superiority comes by chance, however, ought to be wielded with care. For starters, the king of Pamplona was cautious enough not to take the title of Count of Castile for himself, but to give it to his son, Ferdinand, thus easing the minds of any Castilian noble that harbored suspicions about this sudden dynasty swap. Despite the gesture, few were fooled. Many noted that, while conducting these public relations maneuvers, Sancho had at once set out to raise pro-Pamplonese cliques to the ruling heights of Alava and Biscay. In the span of just a few years, his kingdom, once relegated to the modest foothills of the Pyrenees, had managed to develop its influence into a tacit preeminence over much of Iberia.

But human destinies are fragile, and oftentimes those of kings can prove even more so. In October 1035, the forty-year-old monarch of Pamplona abruptly fell ill and passed away. So surprising and swift was his end that his firstborn and heir, García, was not even present when his father breathed his last. But if there had ever been a moment to measure the staggering accomplishments of Sancho's reign, it was this very one: the moment of his death. The monarch that now enjoyed eternal rest had controlled the kingdom of Pamplona—with its southern and eastern appendages in Rioja, Aragon, Sobrarbe, and Ribagorza—and had secured dominance over Castile. During his final years, he had even styled himself—albeit with a touch of wishful thinking—the master of the country that lay north of the mountains as far as the Garonne. Although with varying degrees of effectiveness and under different legal and customary conditions, Sancho had succeeded in something truly unprecedented. In his heyday, he had laid claim to an authority that covered all the lands that, ever since Visigothic and Merovingian times, had been described at one point or another as the home of the unruly Vascones. Now, after his passing, it was this unity, however tenuous, that made up his most lasting legacy.

But did this mean that Sancho's was a Vascon kingdom? No source endorses such a verdict, and despite the doubtless grandeur of his accomplishments, the reality was far more banal—and far less romantic. In early medieval times, it was usually circumstances bred from intricate and complex dynastic arrangements—and not any sense of historical trajectory or common ethnic identity—that ultimately determined who ruled what territory. In Sancho's case, his incorporation of Alava and Biscay had little to do with any shared Vascon identity, if such a thing had even existed in the first place. Instead, it was a consequence of a series of opportunities that the assassination of the Castilian count by the Vela family had left wide open. Not that this pattern of territorial acquisition was in any way unique to these western districts. In Ribagorza, Wasconia, and Castile—the latter pretty much devoid of any previous association to the Vascones—Sancho's control had likewise been one bred of a mixture of chance and compromise. A dominion that owed less to the will of a single people than to his ability to navigate the political and dynastic complexities of the age.

Royal titles reinforced this argument. Throughout his reign, Sancho almost invariably signed his documents with the simple title of *rex*, and at most he would name-check the vast possessions—Pamplona, Aragon, Ribagorza, Sobrarbe, Castile, Wasconia—over which he claimed different measures of power. Interestingly, it was foreigners who, occasionally, might employ different labels to refer to him. Rodulfus Glaber, a Burgundian chronicler, called the Pamplonese monarch *Sancto rege Nauarriae Hispaniarum*, echoing a terminology familiar to the Frankish world ever since the reign of Charlemagne.[9] Closer associates of the sovereign, too, sporadically celebrated him as *rex ibericus*.[10] But nowhere, in the vast list that made up his surviving documentation, was it possible to encounter anything resembling *rex Vasconum*. A significant absence given that some outsiders, overwhelmingly Leonese, used Vascones to describe the Pamplonese every now and then. On these rare occasions, mentions were invariably accompanied by unsavory—and recurring—examples of "destruction of churches, . . . mean depredations, . . . and murders, and robberies."[11] Unsurprisingly, no ruler, not to say a Christian one, would tolerate such associations.

The haphazard nature of Sancho's territorial achievements was similarly evident in the division of his inheritance. The kingdom of Pamplona, now enlarged with the counties of the Pyrenees, Rioja, and the easternmost reaches of Castile, was bequeathed in its entirety to García, his firstborn.[12] However, and as true Pamplonese fashion dictated, the day-to-day government of some of these districts was entrusted to his brothers, who exercised authority as princelings under García's command. This was what happened in Aragon, which passed to Ramiro, one of Sancho's illegitimate children. In Castile, on the other hand, the death of the great monarch only meant that Ferdinand, who had taken the title of count ever since his uncle's assassination back in 1028, could now assume direct control upon a much-diminished set of territories.

Shortly after Sancho's passing, this delicate equilibrium came undone. Hostilities broke out almost immediately between the king of Leon and Ferdinand, Count of Castile. Whether driven by an ambition to recover the lands that had fallen to the kings of Pamplona, or stemming instead from the opportunity of striking at Ferdinand now that his resources had been severely diminished, Vermudo III launched an offensive in 1037 against the combined forces of Pamplona and Castile. However, fortune did not favor the Leonese monarch. In the ensuing battle, fought at Tamarón, Vermudo was struck down and fell dead on the field.[13]

The irony of Vermudo's death was profound. With no heirs to inherit his kingdom, the throne of Leon passed to his sister, who, in a twist of fate, was married to none other than Ferdinand, the very man whose forces had slain her brother. The Castilian count immediately took the magnificent opportunity he was presented with and crowned himself king of Leon. In an outcome that must have appeared almost extraordinary mere years before, the children of Sancho the Great now reigned over the most powerful Christian kingdoms in the peninsula. The labors of the Pamplonese monarch had, upon the blood-soaked field of Tamarón, come to a fructiferous end.

All in all, to retell the story of Sancho's dynasty and that of his kingdom up to this point was to undertake an almost unbelievable challenge that defied, in its utter implausibility, any attempt at rationalization. How could it be explained that a family that could trace its lineage from the wolf-like and barbarous rebels of Vasconia had succeeded in ruling, as indisputable arbiters, over the destinies of Iberia? How to square this with the fact that the Western Pyrenees, with the sole exception of the lands which belonged to the dukes of Aquitaine, were now for the first time since the fall of Rome united under a single rule? To speak of such feats was to confront a story that resisted any simple narrative.

Under the surface, however, matters were hardly as settled as they appeared. Extending one's power without attending to the needs of local aristocracies, as the example of García's assassination by the Velas had demonstrated, was a short-sighted policy—and one with which Sancho's successors would have to deal in the long run. Many among the displaced noble families of Biscay and Alava, who scorned the new masters set in place by the Pamplonese, might have regarded recent events with equal amounts of resentment and quiet defiance.

But, for the moment, the verdict of Sancho's reign was impressive. The Western Pyrenean periphery—once a chaotic, fragmented region—had slowly but surely given birth to a cohesive political center. During the harsher, most calamitous of times, the kingdom of Pamplona had, like a sturdy twig perched on a cliff, managed to blossom and bloom against all odds. Now, at long last, its future seemed bright.

Notes

1 Martín, "Vasconia en la Alta Edad Media," 878.

2 Miranda, "Sacralización de la guerra en el siglo X. La perspectiva pamplonesa," 225–43.

3 *Becerro Galicano Digital*, doc. 221.

4 Larrea, "La herencia vasca: acción política y arquitectura social en Vizcaya y Álava antes de su incorporación al reino de Alfonso VI," 76.

5 Orella, "Relaciones medievales entre Gascuña y Guipúzcoa: la diócesis de Pamplona y de Bayona," 162.

6 Jimeno and Pescador, *Colección documental de Sancho Garcés III, el Mayor, rey de Pamplona (1004–1035)*, docs. 36 and 63, 164–5; 231–4.

7 Martínez, *Sancho III el Mayor. Rey de Pamplona, Rex Ibericus*, 113.

8 "Chronica Naiarense." In Ubieto, *Crónica Najerense*, 89.

9 "Historiarum sui temporis libri quinque." In Glaber, *Rodvlfi Glabri Historiarum libri quinque*, 110.

10 Jimeno and Pescador, *Colección documental de Sancho Garcés III*, doc. 67, 240–1.

11 "Veremundus III. Castrum, quod de Lapio dicebatur, Sedi Lucensi, ejusque Episcopo Petro Donat. Anno 1032." In Risco, *España sagrada. Tomo XL: antigüedades de la ciudad y Sta. Iglesia de Lugo*, 410–12.

12 Martínez, *Sancho III el Mayor*, 191–7.

13 "Lucae Tudensis Chronicon Mundi." In Falque, *Lucae Tudensis Chronicon Mundi*, 280–1.

CHAPTER 8
MANUM REGIS

Murders in the eleventh century were, for the most part, byproducts of hot blood and personal closeness. Even though one of God's commandments identified homicide as one of the most condemnable of sins, a hunting accident or an argument between neighbors could rapidly get out of hand and result in the victim's death. All of which led medieval authorities, for the most part, to tread with care over the subject. In fact, given the right conditions—self-defense, for example—most scholars agreed in affirming that it was possible to atone for the killing not only of pagans but also of fellow Christians.

These progressive views applied to crimes committed against commoners, but they never did extend to those who murdered a king. To assassinate a lawful monarch, especially one that had undergone the mysterious sacrament of anointment, was to commit a hideous act that went directly against every foundation of both human and divine order—and thus one that merited no mercy. Tyrants might in time be expected to receive their punishment from God, naturally, but until that came to pass, no one recognized their subjects on earth any other alternative than patiently putting up with them. Therefore, nothing but the most imperious reasons could push an individual to undertake such a deed, and the infante Ramón must have been ceaselessly dancing around his own motives in the weeks that had led to this fateful moment. Then, on June 4, 1076, he finally set out to kill Sancho Garcés IV—grandson of Sancho the Great, king of Pamplona, and his own brother.

Later chroniclers, no doubt appalled by the sheer horror of the event, painstakingly labored to compile every little detail of the episode. How Ramón and his supporters invited the oblivious king to a hunting party. How they took him to a place called Peñalén, near the village of Funes where, amid a landscape of forests populated by deer and boars, stood a crag of great altitude. How they convinced Sancho to climb it on the pretense that it made for a splendid spot from which to scrutinize the riverside and the long miles of the plains below. Some authors, perhaps pushed by an insatiable thirst for explanations that could shed light upon the terrible occurrence, added dramatic points of their own making: improper love affairs, uncontrolled jealousies, deluded husbands.[1]

And yet, for all that, the skeleton of the story remained invariably the same. The unsuspecting monarch had been lured to the lookout with the excuse of enjoying a better view. He had covered his eyes and had looked ahead at the distance. Then, coming under the impression of hearing something—and encouraged by the infante—he had even dared to take a few steps forward until he could see the faint line of silver of the river below. And then, as he stood on the brink of the precipice, the conspirators, "coming to him from behind, at a sign of the evil infante given amid horrors of nature and instigations of infernal fury, had shoved the king with great force."[2] Sancho, tumbling on the rocks and unable to keep his balance, fell off the cliff to the certain death that awaited him at the bottomless pit. The regicides caught the noise of stone clattering, of bones breaking, of howls rending the air. Then only that of gravel sliding down. Gasping from his vantage point on the top of the peak, Ramón must have then anxiously scoured the forest for any sign of his brother. He saw none. To kill his king was to become an enemy of both men and God: a great punishment indeed. And yet it was one that, as long as it gained him a crown, he was willing to endure.

At first, though, few could have predicted such a course of events. García, the firstborn of Sancho the Great and his successor on the throne of Pamplona, not only had governed an enlarged kingdom but also a stable and powerful one. Unlike the Leonese monarchy, which tended to periodically find itself engulfed in internecine confrontations, not once had the Pamplonese, ever since the times of Sancho Garcés I, been plagued by civil wars or struggles between claimants from within the royal household.

This unheard-of stability stemmed, in large part, from the fact that the power that the king enjoyed was simply unparalleled. His territorial possessions and domains were vast, and equally exceptional were the rights he enjoyed over the use of pastures, rivers, mills, furnaces, and any lands gained back from his Muslim rivals. Jewels, coins, expensive clothes—all flowed out from the disparate mosaic of the erstwhile caliphate and directly into his personal coffers. However, none of these was more impressive—nor lucrative—than the monarch's commandeering resources in a very different trade: that of human beings. A plethora of serfs labored on his lands, paid him tribute, and served him in his host. Under such circumstances, how could anyone in the kingdom stand comparison to the sovereign, the ultimate judicial authority in any lawsuit, the chief leader of the army, the defender of all Christians? Simply put, no one could.

The imbalance of forces that separated the king from even the haughtiest of Pamplonese noblemen was nowhere more overtly displayed than in the system employed to assign official posts. After all, strongholds had to be manned and defended, justice had to be dispensed, rent from the peasants had to be collected, and the king, for all his great attributes and properties, could not expect to do all that on his own. A seeming dependence on others, though, did not necessarily mean that the sovereign had to resign himself to letting aristocrats go without supervision. If anything, it forced him to tread upon the subject even more carefully. First off, the entrusted concessions were—with few notable exceptions—small and included at most a lonely fortress and the surrounding hamlets and homesteads. Such meager resources rendered them ineffectual as stepping-stones for ambitious underlings tempted to use them against their sovereign. Second, and most importantly, the king did not renounce his Lordship over the granted lands in any way. The title holders received these positions *per manum regis*, that is, by hand of the king; which meant, in turn, that the monarch was always free to alter the terms of the deal at his convenience. At a single gesture, they could be relocated from one district to another, and this fact alone eschewed for the most part the possibility of carving for themselves an all-too-comfortable position. The king of Pamplona might be forced by circumstance to share with his nobility the burdens of government, but he was equally adamant in making sure that this reliance would not siphon off his power. Barons, at any rate, reluctantly nodded.

But why? Why would these families comply with a system that seemed so evidently partial toward the interests of kings and against their own? The answer was short: because they had no alternative. The wealth of their own domains, split and split again over the course of the generations, was so scarce that most of them found that the only way of sustaining themselves was to garner the favor of the monarch. To be appointed a tenant, despite the obvious caveats and constraints, remained still their best opportunity of extracting a worthy enough payment. And, to gain access to it, putting up with the king's every wish was a crucial, inescapable requisite.

Sancho of Peñalén's father had inherited intact from his mighty predecessor all these sources of power, both material and immaterial. In the wake of the battle of Tamarón, in fact, García's hold on power had been increased even further with the incorporation of fresh domains in formerly Castilian territories. Initially meant as payment for the help he had granted his brother Ferdinand in the latter's rebellion against the Leonese, these concessions constituted an open display of the influence and superiority that the dynasty was capable of exerting even beyond its borders. Pamplona, which his father had found a beleaguered and shaken kingdom, had thus come to offer, under his son's guidance, a very different facet: that of the most powerful kingdom in all of Iberia.

Not everything, though, could be cast as a net positive for García. For all that new lands could bring new tributes, they equally entailed new obligations: obligations that might, in turn, tinge with a shadow of suspicion the royal mind. Ferdinand, it was true, owed his brother the crown of Castile and Leon. But how long would it take him to buttress a stable position in this new kingdom—the largest in all of the peninsula—and dare to entertain the ambition of surpassing his elder sibling? The two brothers, after all, had inherited not only two thrones but also opposite power dynamics, clienteles, and interests in places like Alava or Biscay. For the time being, respect for family ties might be trusted to keep these tendencies under control. And yet, to burden these with forever reining in the imperatives of geopolitics was a tough ask indeed.

And tougher, perhaps, considering recent precedent. Only a few years after inheriting Pamplona, García had already been schooled on how fickle familiar allegiances could be. In 1045, a minor rebellion had erupted in Aragon led by none other than his half-brother Ramiro, Sancho the Great's illegitimate son. Encouraged by a local nobility that looked in apathy at the distant rule of the Pamplonese, and aided by the Moorish kinglets of the Ebro, Ramiro had tested his luck in a pitched battle near Tafalla.[3] García, even if initially caught by surprise, had confronted the situation with merciless resolve. In the event, the setback for Aragonese plans of independent rule had ultimately been complete. And yet, and this unequal result notwithstanding, concord between the two relatives had almost immediately been restored. After all, just as with his other clients, the king of Pamplona was deeply aware of the fact that he depended on the loyalty of men like Ramiro—mouthpieces for the local aristocracies as they were—to keep his vast dominions under control. He also knew, of course, that had the battle gone differently, he would have been incapable of holding for long any presence in Aragon. The more the kingdom expanded, the less it was possible for the sovereign to keep a perennial watch over the barons' actions: This was the foremost conclusion that García had extracted from the rebellion. Coincidentally, it was one not far from Ramiro's own calculations. Better to remain nominally loyal to the Pamplonese monarchy and thus hold effective power than to claim independence and risk losing everything. Their struggle, when put into these terms, had served both siblings as a cautionary tale.

A tale whose lesson García had made sure to learn by heart. After all, who could anticipate where the next spark of insurrection might kindle? Who was to be the next nobleman to entertain dreams of toppling his rule? His unassailable position in Pamplona rested upon an overarching economic and military superiority; on the superposition of his rights over churches, villages, and rivers; on his undisputed mastery of hundreds of serfs and vassals, each one bound to him through a variety of services, honorable or obsequious, military or otherwise. In contrast, to the west and the north, in lands the reach of his predecessors had never managed to scratch and only recently incorporated into his domains, García's authority appeared to be rather frail and spectral. Local communities might be content, for the time being, with acknowledging Pamplonese oversight in hopes of personal advantages or in fear of punishment, but they otherwise kept lands, churches, pastures, and dependents firmly in their own hands. Many aristocrats—even more threateningly—had inherited personal interests on both sides of the Castilian-Pamplonese border, and this caused them to be unreliable and untrustworthy. If his rule was meant to be a lasting one, then García would have to correct these situations. Only once they acknowledged his undisputed authority would these regions truly become part of his kingdom.

Coincidentally, he had at his disposal a perfect solution to this problem. It was a time-honored policy among empire-builders to settle territorial disputes by bringing the most distinguished families of a region to their side, and the king of Pamplona had an impeachable candidate at hand. Iñigo López's lineage had its roots in Biscay, where it possessed a vast array of estates and privileges. Back in Sancho the Great's time, Iñigo's father had taken the momentous decision of supporting the Pamplonese western expansion and, only a few years later, this choice had already gained him and his household a relevant position in the court, marriages with the foremost aristocracy of the kingdom, and important tenancies in Alava and Rioja.[4] Already esteemed, powerful, and rich, it seemed that few things could tempt a man like Iñigo López.

The king, however, knew better. Possession of lands might make up the basis of the pyramid of medieval power, but it was hardly enough to satisfy ambitious landlords. Many profitable revenues and privileges, such as those received in exchange for dispatching justice or for gathering the royal tribute in a determinate land, stemmed instead from public attributions that only a king could award. Endowed with the backing of a monarch, Iñigo López could very well dream of using these powers to enlarge his lineage's possessions, not only in Biscay but all across the kingdom of Pamplona.

García, instead of putting such ambitions out, made sure to spur them. What did it matter if Iñigo kept for himself a sizable chunk of the tributes collected in Biscay as long as it did so in García's name? Better by far to have a trustworthy vassal who felt it was in his best interest to furbish Pamplonese authority than for the king to deal with myriads of petty barons and village communities in a distant land he knew little about. Similar deals were struck in Alava.[5] For all that he allowed not his authority to be disputed, García's power, just as it was in Pamplona a result of the brute facts of wealth and strength, could equally be elsewhere a spectacle of smoke and mirrors.

In all, his calculations would prove accurate. As many contemporaries had predicted, tensions between the king of Castile and Leon and that of Pamplona mounted up and up over the course of the 1040s and 1050s. The cause, according to Castilian sources at least, was none other than the envy García felt about "the opulence and happiness of King Ferdinand"—and who could have doubted that there was more than a grain of truth to it?[6] Ever since Sancho the Great's decision to grant Ferdinand the throne of Castile, and having witnessed the consequences of the struggle at Tamarón, many had been dumbfounded by what they saw as a reversal of the natural order of things. For where—they must have wondered—had ever been seen that the second brother might enjoy a larger estate than that of the firstborn? García, standing as he was as the main injured party, might as well have shared in these mumblings.

But there were limits to what a king might be willing to do out of jealousy. Castilian chroniclers, by emphasizing García's ill disposition toward his brother, might have tried to conceal more mundane justifications. In 1045, the same year which had witnessed Ramiro's defeat, García had also conquered Calahorra for good. Control of the ancient homeland of Prudentius, in addition to boosting the monarch's prestige among those eager to restore the saint's relics to their rightful abode, spelled a direct threat to Muslim populations down the Ebro. And where there was Muslim fear, there was payment to be exacted. This García knew and so too, in turn, did Ferdinand. Both sovereigns, staring avidly beyond their borders, concurred in regarding the prize that flowed north from the disentangled patchwork of what had once been the mighty caliphate as being worthy of any effort made to secure it. An already tense situation, and one that the conquest of Calahorra could not help but tighten. Mutual rivalry, tucked away behind talks of García's jealousy and Ferdinand's lack of fraternal propriety, deepened and deepened. Local power brokers, in frontier regions such as Alava or Biscay, began to ponder their allegiances.

So it was that when war finally broke out, few thought that it could have ever been prevented. On September 1st, 1054, the armies of García—king of Pamplona and son of Sancho the Great and Munia—and Ferdinand—king of Castile and Leon and son of Sancho the Great and Munia—clashed in the rugged fields of Atapuerca. For hours the battle lines pushed and pulled, forward and backward, under the scorching sun. But in the event, it would be the Pamplonese soldiers that would give way, and their retreat, as Castilian knights pursued them, soon transformed into a total rout. It was at this moment that "a cohort of vigorous riders . . . , plunging from the heights and cutting amid the ranks with their lances, in their impetus charged against the King García, and after sinking their blades on him, struck him down from his horse, lifeless."[7] The king's death certified the extent of his defeat. On the very battlefield where his father lay dead, butchered at the hands of the troops of his uncle, a bunch of battered warriors proclaimed the fourteen-year-old Sancho—the future Sancho of Peñalén—as king of Pamplona.

The position of the new monarch, from the beginning, was excruciatingly difficult. In addition to the snake pit that had been the war with Leon, the debacle had also brought the loss of most of the Castilian territories owned by his father west of Biscay and Alava. No sooner had these peripheral lords—who had once pledged their loyalty to the ill-fated García in the times of his predominance—sensed the turning of the tide than they had hitched their wagon to Ferdinand's rising star. Of those that might have proven loyal even in defeat, many had carried this allegiance to their utmost consequences and now lay lifeless in Atapuerca alongside their king.[8] Iñigo López, it is true, did not betray the hopes placed upon him by his lord and had managed to keep Biscay under Sancho's control. And yet, even there, the fall of García precluded a situation that the new king's forebears had never had to face.

Men like Iñigo, though initially enriched thanks to their collaboration with the Pamplonese, had suddenly found themselves capable of taking a more independent stance, appropriating royal rights and extending their networks of patronage even to the Castilian side of the border.[9] A strong ruler like his father, perhaps, might have reined these barons in. But Sancho, a teenager, was hardly the kind of figure ambitious landlords, schooled in an age of warfare and conquest, were instinctively prone to respect. His own temperament—immature, arbitrary, militarily incapable—did little to change their minds.[10] Before long, many aristocrats began to entertain a notion that to their predecessors might as well have appeared unimaginable. That the king of Pamplona, instead of ranking as their overlord, might prove indeed nothing but an equal.

For the time being, though, these whisperings were kept in private. The vast resources available to the monarchy had not, after all, disappeared with García's death, and the same could be said about Sancho's ability to extort wealth out of the pockets of the southern kinglets. However, as the new king would soon come to discover, it was one thing to drain the incommensurable riches of the Muslims as they stood at their weakest, and a very different one to actually protect them from what seemed, to many, the rightful claims of Christian noblemen. Ramiro, lord of Aragon and that erstwhile rebel to his father, had only been prevented from campaigning in Muslim territories under Pamplonese protection with a large bribe in lands, strongholds, and privileges.[11] New tenancies, too, were created to keep the barons content.[12]

But these were short-sighted solutions. The Pamplonese aristocracy, as eager as their Aragonese counterparts to partake in deeds of glory that promised plentiful bounty, faced under Sancho's rule an unsolvable dilemma. What could they do when it was precisely the lord to whom they owed lawful allegiance that most opposed their legitimate interests? What action to take when the wealth of Al-Andalus, rather than being shared among the nobility as it was their birthright, was instead being skimped by a greedy tyrant?[13] Even to the north, in Biscay and in the lands that bordered Wasconia, the push for expansion seemed to have halted altogether.[14] Increasingly, more and more heads of lineage came to deem action—collaborative, decisive action—unavoidable to right these wrongs.

Soon enough, problems for the sovereign started to mount. Already in 1061, a royal document acknowledged a certain "tribulation" between the barons and Sancho.[15] A decade later, in 1072, so great had the chasm between the king and the aristocracy grown that the former was forced to sign a humiliating capitulation simply to be able to keep the throne. Members of the upper class, the document established, were to be treated honorably. Among other things, this meant that they would no longer tolerate the king disposing of their offices at will. In the absence of proven treachery or conspiracy, noblemen would not be sacked from their posts and would retain their tenancies.[16] No longer a sign of royal favor and caprice, appointments were to be conceived, from now on, as rewards for loyal service, binding both for sovereign and aristocrats alike. Sancho's surrender, in all, was nothing short of complete.

If the threat of losing their offices had always loomed large over the barons, constraining their independence and forcing them to cater to the monarch's every wish, the new *status quo* established after 1072 was to prove transformative and far-reaching. Noblemen suddenly found their hands free to extend their networks of patronage in their dominions, carving a semi-autonomous basis of power for themselves, and all without the anxiety of the sovereign ever meddling in their affairs. Of course, the king of Pamplona was still the mightiest of the barons, the richest, the most authoritative among their number. But he was now a baron nonetheless, and one, at that, obliged to collaborate with those that not so long ago he had commanded without any limitation. The tables had turned. In the aftermath of the struggle between Sancho's commanding monarchy and the interests of the Pamplonese aristocracy, everyone could perceive that it was not the sovereign who had succeeded in gaining the upper hand.

Massive and unheard of though they were, not even these concessions could save Sancho in the long run. When merely three years later, he was toppled—quite literally—by his brother Ramón and other conspirators, no member of the high nobility of the kingdom flinched as much as a finger to prevent the assassination from happening. By then, the true power brokers had realized that it was they, and not the heirs of the lineage of Sancho the Great, who now controlled the realm. Being as they were in full command of their tenancies and presented with the option of either supporting a regicide or a child, aristocrats opted for the time-honored strategy of shrugging their shoulders and looking out for new patrons. Sancho's son was sidelined; so too, in turn, was Ramón. The lords of Castile and Aragon, who had probably encouraged the infante to commit the dreadful act to begin with, proved now equally swift in abandoning him to his fate and branding him a traitor. Instead of being hailed as king, Ramón found himself, all of a sudden, without allies and persecuted. He was dutifully sent into exile.

As for the barons, their decision seems to have been made beforehand. The heads of the most formidable western families, such as that of Iñigo López, swore their allegiance to the king of Castile.[17] In Pamplona and in its eastern swathes, in contrast, most barons were tempted by the bounty promised by Ramiro's son, Sancho Ramírez.[18] The kingdom, as a result, was split into two. Rioja, Biscay, and Alava became Castilian domains; all the rest went to Sancho Ramírez, who also took for himself the title of king of the Pamplonese. The northern frontier with Wasconia—a land which chroniclers were only then beginning to call Guipuzcoa—so distant from the centers of power and for this very reason unappealing for the new overlords, was nominally demanded by both and was practically secured by none.[19]

So it happened that the kingdom of Pamplona, as a political entity, simply vanished overnight. The primary branch of the lineage of Sancho the Great and Munia, the most impressive dynasty ever to rule the fates of the peninsula, was deprived of its rights. Some might rightfully wonder, reflecting on recent events and pondering that their debacle had come after two successive fratricides, if it had not, in fact, torn itself to pieces.

Notes

1 Esteban de Garibay, in his *Compendio Historial* (1571), rejects these later traditions as unreliable. See Garibay, *Los XL libros del Compendio Historial de las Chronicas y universal Historia de todos los reynos de España*, II, XXXIV–XXXVII, 112–23.

2 Moret, *Annales del Reyno de Navarra*, II, 110.

3 Larrea, "El reinado de García de Nájera, entre el viejo y el nuevo orden: rey, barones e infanzones entre la monarquía isidoriana y la feudal," 154–5.

4 Mañaricua, *Vizcaya, siglos VIII al XI: los orígenes del Señorío*, 285.

5 Pescador, "Tenentes y tenencias del Reino de Pamplona en Álava, Vizcaya, Guipúzcoa, La Rioja y Castilla (1004–1076)," 109–12.

6 "Chronica naiarensis," III, 20. In Ubieto, *Crónica Najerense*, 95. Also, "Lucae Tudensis Chronicon Mundi." In Falque, *Lucae Tudensis Chronicon Mundi*, 282.

7 "Chronica naiarensis," III, 20. In Ubieto, *Crónica Najerense*, 96.

8 Pescador, "Tenentes y tenencias del Reino de Pamplona," 123.

9 Larrea, "La herencia vasca: acción política y arquitectura social en Vizcaya y Álava antes de su incorporación al reino de Alfonso VI," 108.

10 Martín, *Sancho III el Mayor de Pamplona. El rey y su reino*, 352.

11 See, for instance, the gift of the towns of Sangüesa, Lerda and Undués to Ramiro by Sancho in 1063–4. In Ubieto, *Cartulario de San Juan de la Peña*, 219–21.

12 Pavón, *Poblamiento altomedieval navarro. Base socioeconómica del espacio monárquico*, 268–9. Also, Pescador, "Tenentes y tenencias del Reino de Pamplona," 123–4.

13 Larrea, "El reinado de García de Nájera, entre el viejo y el nuevo orden: rey, barones e infanzones entre la monarquía isidoriana y la feudal," 162.

14 Pescador, "Tenentes y tenencias del Reino de Pamplona," 112.

15 Martín, *Documentación medieval de Leire (siglos IX a XII)*, 63, 101.

16 Larrea, "El reinado de García de Nájera, entre el viejo y el nuevo orden: rey, barones e infanzones entre la monarquía isidoriana y la feudal," 158–9. Also, Lema, "Un obscuro pasado: Guipuzcoa y Navarra (siglos X-XII)," 19. Also, Ubieto, *Cartulario de San Juan de la Peña*, 219–21.

17 Larrea, "La herencia vasca: acción política y arquitectura social en Vizcaya y Álava antes de su incorporación al reino de Alfonso VI," 110–1.

18 Martín, "Vasconia en la Alta Edad Media," 882.

19 "Doña Galga de Guipúzcoa da el monasterio de Santiago de Luquedeng a San Juan de la Peña" (1048). In Ubieto, *Cartulario de San Juan de la Peña*, 78–9.

CHAPTER 9
AITONEN SEMEAK

To the medieval mind, the distinction between noble and peasant was not merely one of property. It was a deeper, more elemental one—a difference that seemed to pulse beneath the skin itself. Most scholars self-evidently assumed that nothing better than blood, passed down from parent to child across countless generations, could determine a man's or woman's worth. In the age of the Merovingians, for example, only members of the royal clan were considered to possess the talents necessary for government. And even before that, in the distant years before the ultimate triumph of Christianity, Roman citizens had revered the kind of potency that was only manifest in the members of the imperial household. Such a power-bearing pedigree, it went without saying, was one that had to be earnestly preserved. For it was it, and nothing else, that branded its holder as capable of command.

Yet this theoretical insight, at least in the buffer zone between Leon and Pamplona, was one that had long been contested. Here, in a frontier region battered by centuries of military incursions and yet peripheral to all major centers of power, men had grown accustomed to taking care of their own affairs. Assemblies of locally respected householders were commonplace. After all, who better than them could mediate disputes over land, safeguard communal resources, or uphold the ancient rhythms of village life? In Castile, documents routinely accounted for the actions of these *maiores* or "principal settlers," who acted zealously to preserve what they considered their hard-earned liberties.[1] Elsewhere in Leon and Pamplona, too, members of the upper crust of valley or village communities were likewise celebrated as *filii bonorum patres*.[2] And all across the Western Pyrenees, treasured in the oral language most peasants spoke, the appellation would give rise, over time, to a particular yet synonymous expression: *aitonen semeak*, "sons of good fathers,"[3]

Little is known about these individuals and their gatherings. Much like in the times of the Visigoths, or at the arrival of the Muslims, their decisions were at most glimpsed in the responses these produced in neighboring, more powerful statesmen. Held beneath the sprawling canopies of ancient trees or in valleys hemmed by steep slopes, they left behind no jurisprudence, no charters, and no records. Every aspect of these meetings—their frequency, their functioning, their internal hierarchies—eludes the gaze of the historian. Yet these assemblies, for all that, were a vital thread in the tapestry of local order, for decisions agreed on them were widely considered to be binding to all those present. Passed down orally, their verdicts acquired a weight that often transcended the moment and constituted, in this sense at least, the true law of the land. Therefore, what began as pragmatic solutions to immediate concerns, reinforced by the acquiescence of the most prominent inhabitants of the territory, could, over time, come to seem to their descendants something ancient and immutable: a truly immemorial commandment.

Over the course of the tenth and eleventh centuries, as the apparatus of government and the pull of the Pamplonese and Leonese monarchies grew more and more intense, many of these self-governing institutions, which had long thrived on the fringes of their power, were gradually drawn into their orbit. So happened in much of Castile. So, too, in the kingdom of Pamplona. Yet, in Alava and Biscay, too distant and peripheral to the great courtesan centers, the story unfolded along different lines. The deeper the ambitions of neighboring kingdoms in these territories ran, the more local worthies were put in a position to take advantage of the situation. The most respected and distinguished families must have found it relatively easy to negotiate terms with Leonese emissaries, first, and with Pamplonese ones, later. The deal they offered was as straightforward as it was sketchy on its application. In return for the gifts, privileges, and perks of legitimacy that only a monarch could bestow, these petty oligarchs promised to put their own clienteles and relatives at the service of foreign sovereigns.

Thus, and thanks largely to the mediation of such powerful families, the assemblies that had once stood as symbols of communal independence were gradually compelled to accept and obey the newcomers. So it had emerged the first counts of Alava and Biscay, under Asturian aegis, over the course of the ninth and tenth centuries. So it was, too, that the Pamplonese had ruled the territory. Occasional mentions of "the soldiers of the Alavese" or "all the lords of Biscay" stood witness to agreements that were far from mere gestures of polite inclusion. On the contrary, they were a subtle yet pointed reminder of the authority these associations wielded and also of their readiness to rent it for profit—so long as the price was right.[4]

But the frequent contacts between the upper echelons of these householder gatherings and distant courts—notably intensified during the reign of Sancho the Great—did not fail to bring about a remarkable alteration in the inner workings of these frontier societies. The array of powers, rights, and concessions extracted by these aristocrats from their royal patrons did more than simply enrich them: They also armed them with the necessary means to widen their connections. Their networks, extended thanks to marriage alliances, strategic gifts, and generous bribes to influential landowners, now encompassed not only their native communities but also their surrounding villages and valleys. It was a deliberate policy, of course. The larger the number of supporters an aristocrat could summon to steer the decisions of a local assembly, the firmer his position as the bigger fish in the pond. Influence begot more influence. In Alava and in Biscay, the power wielded by the counts, once fluid and nominal, soon came to be recognized as the patrimony of a handful of families.

Yet such a transformation, for all that it helped in making the leading families exceedingly rich and powerful in comparison to their peers, was not bereft of dangers. The very success of these aristocratic lineages, amplified as it was by their participation in Christian victories on the frontiers of Al-Andalus, only exacerbated the rancor felt by those sidelined by their rise. It became common for emerging, ambitious families, or for those who had banked on the wrong kind of foreign allies, to come to be regarded as natural poles of opposition. The result was a dangerous paradox. The institutionalization of these territories under the oversight of the Christian monarchies, initially intended as a way of stabilizing the countryside, now risked plunging its inhabitants into civil conflict. The example set by the Vela family who, back in 1028, had felt so desperate after losing the post of counts of Alava so as to decide to murder their main rival at his own wedding was only a most salient case of this dynamic. These blood-chilling episodes underscored the delicate balance that monarchs like King García had sought to maintain. To endorse a candidate was not merely a matter of administration but also a high-stakes gamble. And any misstep, an affront to the wrong lineage, could threaten to send the fragile web of Pamplonese influence spiraling into chaos.

Fortunately for Pamplonese ambitions, King García had proven a masterful tailor of compromises. This was demonstrated not only in the meteoric rise of figures like Iñigo López but also in the establishment in Alava of a loyal dynasty of agents, with Munio González and his son, Munio Muñoz, at their head. Thanks to the mediation and the endless oversight of these men, a delicate equilibrium had been achieved, one in which both the sovereign, the assemblies, and the magnates themselves could feel that their interests were safeguarded. The project of consolidating Alava and Biscay into the orbit of Pamplonese control was, or so it seemed, off to a flying start.

And yet, the consequences of García's demise in Atapuerca had changed everything. His passing did not merely rob the kingdom of its ruler, leaving as successor a rather ineffectual teenager. It had also marked the end of Munio's lineage, a family that had served as the lynchpin of Pamplonese rule over Alava for nearly four decades.[5] Though Iñigo López, still firmly entrenched in his sanctioned dominion over Biscay, had remained outwardly loyal to Sancho of Peñalén's cause, the price paid for García's fall was unmistakable. The strong reins with which the kings of Pamplona had previously checked his ambitions were now gone, and as royal power waned from Biscay in the years that followed, the leash on Iñigo loosened too at a similar rate. He was, after all, a respected middleman on a particularly hot frontier, and this meant that there was little that the new sovereign could do but put up with him. Even when Iñigo married into the family of a Castilian magnate—a move that openly signaled the broadening of his loyalties—no disciplinary measure was undertaken.[6] Cautiously scouting from within his domains, Iñigo had learned to keep his options open, balancing efforts to strengthen his independence with timid gestures of submission that did not fool Sancho in the slightest. And, as the situation had persisted and no attempt to reinstate direct royal authority had been set in motion, Biscay's upper classes had increasingly found a clear incentive to support Iñigo's expanding influence. They had come to realize that it was his guidance which provided a much clearer path to privileges and rewards than any his opponents could offer. And so, as Sancho of Peñalén's struggles with his rowdy barons deepened and deepened, so too did Biscay begin to slip further from Pamplonese supervision.

In Alava, on the other hand, the political landscape was marked by considerable turmoil. The new king of Pamplona and his aides, confronting the very real possibility that their control over the district might disappear alongside its dynasty of counts, avidly searched for a substitute. This was not a concern limited to the royal court, but one that reached the very heart of Alava's elite. With the death of the second Munio, the power vacuum left in his wake had rendered many without patrons, cut off from the levers of authority that had once guaranteed them a preeminent place in Pamplonese politics. Thus, for both the monarchy and the local oligarchies, the absence of natural leadership threatened to spell disaster.

Which is why, when Sancho of Peñalén appointed a Pamplonese baron named Don Marcelo as his man in Alava, those who had once supported the Munios made sure to immediately rally to the side of the newcomer. Only this massive wave of local support could explain that a man with little to no property in the territory, an outsider supported by outsiders, could hold sway over such a contested frontier for almost twenty years. Alavese chieftains, much like their Biscayne counterparts, had come to instinctively understand that, in a convulsive age like that in which they lived, their best bet was to uphold the power of their own leaders. The stability brought by Marcelo's rule, though less overtly calculated than Iñigo's feigned deference to Sancho, bore witness to the same reality nonetheless: that those living in the margins of the realm were increasingly capable of making their own decisions.

But in a land riven by the ambitions of two rising monarchies, maintaining unity was no easy task. Whereas in Biscay the might of Iñigo López's position had allowed him to steer the course of public opinion and to silence those who opposed him, Don Marcelo's standing in Alava rested on altogether less solid foundations. It was a testimony to his great political ability that he had even managed to keep the land at peace for so long. However, upon his death around 1072, the forces that up until then he had held at bay erupted in full. Household heads and soldiers, prosperous peasants and even lowly priests, all split along lines of allegiance that had been drawn more than a century prior. Either to endorse the Castilian-Leonese realm, lured by the wealth from the tribute of Al-Andalus, or to stand loyal to Sancho of Peñalén, their rightful lord: alternatives, both of them, that in the absence of a direct successor to Don Marcelo's unifying authority had come to be embodied in two particular individuals. On the one hand, representing Sancho's legitimate position, was a member of the Vela family, who had managed to overcome the murderous legacy of their forebears and now claimed dominion over the land of Guipuzcoa.[7] On the opposite camp, increasingly detached from the Pamplonese strings that had impaired him, stood Iñigo López.

The rivalry between the pro-Pamplonese Velas and the Castilian-backed lineage of Iñigo López would prove a pivotal one in shaping the destinies of the Western Pyrenees. The Biscayne magnate, in surrendering his castles to the king of Castile and Leon in 1076, had grasped the stakes with clarity. He had understood that, just as the tide of power was shifting westward, so too was the reach of those acting as agents for the Castilian sovereigns bound to grow as well. Events seemed to have proven him right for, by 1082, after Iñigo's death, his son had been recognized as the most important nobleman in Biscay, Alava, and Guipuzcoa.[8]

But far from only boosting their position, the settlement of 1076, which had carved the Pamplonese kingdom into pieces to be shared between Castile and Aragon, had likewise emboldened Iñigo's and his family's rivals. True, the position of the lineage in Biscay appeared unassailable, but the same could not be said about their authority over Alava and Guipuzcoa. The calculation was only exacerbated by the fact that the family's eager gaze was fixed southwards, where the true prizes for an ambitious nobleman truly lay. Confronted with the decision of either stabilizing their position or expanding their influence beyond Biscay, Iñigo's heirs had devised a strategy that promised to bring a solution to both problems: to display an unwavering loyalty to the crown of Castile. Only thus, by channeling the flow of riches and privileges down the webs of well-oiled client networks, could they hope to safeguard their overlordship in the Western Pyrenees.

Diego López, a grandson of Iñigo López, was said to have married a creature "very beautiful and good-looking in all her body, except for her feet, which were twisted like those of a goat."[9] More importantly, perhaps, was the fact that he had succeeded in elevating his family as one of the most prominent in all of Castile. By 1110, Diego's steadfast fidelity to the sitting queen had already earned him a very special recognition. By the terms of the concession, no royal nor ecclesiastical official was allowed to enter his territories or to collect tribute in them without his explicit permission. In practice, the grant made Diego the sole arbiter of power within his domains, for responsibility over justice, taxation, and military recruitment, albeit executed in the monarch's name, was entrusted to him alone.[10] Naturally, these privileges did not apply to any tenancy nor honorary holding. Diego's appointments as custodian of Nájera, Buradón, Haro, and Grañón—all of them formidable bulwarks watching over the profitable pilgrim road to Compostella—or his role as representative of the Alavese and Biscayne nobility, all remained under Castilian monarchs' nominal control. And it was precisely these holdings, strategically dotted along the foremost trade and military routes of the age, that most mattered to Diego. So much so, in fact, that when he sought to project his standing and authority, the magnate would spare any mention of his meager Western Pyrenean dominions. Rather, he thought that it was as Diego López de Haro that the scale of his importance got through best.

Political prominence of such an order, so often a prize to be coveted, could just as easily become a double-edged sword. While keeping an influential magnate on board was a necessity of medieval government, it took only an ambitious sovereign to realize that perhaps there was a limit to what any vassal could receive before it became a vassal in name only. As it happens, Alfonso I of Aragon and Pamplona—nicknamed "the Battler"—was every bit as determined as his epithet suggested. Indomitable in both spirit and ambition, the consort ruler of Castile and future conqueror of Saragossa was not one to suffer any encroachments upon his authority.

Qualities, all of them, that made him a hard sell among barons like Diego López, and to which the ruler reciprocated. Although bound by his marriage agreements to preserve intact the domains of his Castilian wife, Alfonso held dearly to the claims of his Pamplonese predecessors. And this, in what concerned Western Pyrenean affairs at any rate, meant directly opposing the *status quo* that had seen Diego López's lineage rise to prominence. Over the course of the following years, at the same pace at which the marriage between Alfonso and his Castilian bride soured, the same two alternatives—

east and west—that had been lurking in the shadows ever since the times of Don Marcelo resurfaced yet again. The battle for Alava, Biscay, and Guipuzcoa was, indeed, far from over.

A change of perspective that was well received by the pro-Pamplonese faction. Already by 1110, gathered in solemn assembly at the town of Argote, several "Alavese men" had pledged their fidelity to the Battler, acknowledging his sovereignty in explicit defiance of Castilian interests.[11] In Biscay, where the looming dominance of Diego López had not failed in breeding some resentment, the king's cause likewise found ready recruits. But these internal supports, valuable though they certainly were, remained in and of themselves largely insufficient to uproot the entrenched position of local barons. Which is why Alfonso, while making sure to pander to those natives most opposed to Diego and his clique, had decided to set in motion a decisive policy of land grants and privileges to lure fresh waves of knights from beyond the Pyrenees. Then, once the balance of forces had already tilted in his favor, Alfonso finally struck.

Between 1113 and 1124, Diego López was stripped of all his tenancies in Rioja and Alava. The baron resisted as best he could, plotting in the shadows, fostering uprisings, forging desperate alliances—but in vain. Even Haro, that jewel of the lineage's possessions, had ended up falling to the king's troops. Embittered and humiliated, Diego chose to surrender his arms, sue for pardon, and take the road into a self-imposed exile at the court. His fall brought to an end the position that his lineage had built as the indisputable trendsetters of the frontier. The tenancies they had amassed were divided among those whose loyalty to the Battler was beyond question. Any excessive accumulation of wealth and property was carefully avoided. A member of the Vela family, Count Ladrón, was appointed—as could not be otherwise—at the head of Alava and Biscay.

Had events unfolded differently, then this might have settled the border for a long time to come. For good, even. A domineering ruler and an enemy of any underling too prone to go his own way, Alfonso had understood well what it took to command the respect of the nobility while containing their more predatory and destabilizing instincts. Unlike Sancho of Peñalén, he had offered them something in exchange for their submission. But, despite all his military triumphs, Alfonso had proven inept at perhaps the most crucial stage that any medieval sovereign could face: marriage. His tumultuous union with the queen of Castile had produced no heirs and had ended in open hostility. And so, in 1134, when death found him a sixty-year-old man, it did so without any readily available successor. His will, when it was finally made public, proved a shocking one. The kingdom he had more than doubled in size and which he had controlled with an iron hand was to be passed on, not to a kinsman, but to the military orders: the Templars, the Hospitallers, and the knights of the Holy Sepulcher of Jerusalem.

To say that this was a doomed project from the get-go would be a massive underestimation. The leading men of the realm, tired after decades of putting up with Alfonso's unyielding dominion, and faced with the prospect of obeying a bunch of strangers, agreed almost immediately not to comply with what they saw as a bout of royal delirium. Making their move, they got ready to elevate their own candidates to the throne. In Aragon, the great lords plucked one of Alfonso's brothers from his monastic seclusion and crowned him king. But to the nobility in the west, the Battler's untimely death presented an opportunity of an altogether different kind. An opportunity to restore the kingdom of Pamplona.

The man they elected to lead them could hardly have been more fitting to the role. García Ramírez "the Restorer" was not only descended from the eldest son of Sancho the Great through an illegitimate branch, but he had also been a reliable servant of the Battler, entrusted with key tenancies along the Ebro. Pedigree and past service, though, had come to count for little in the new order of things. The nobility, brought low by the rule of an overbearing monarch, had no intention of enduring yet another master. No coronation whatsoever awaited García Ramírez, nor the sacred anointment of the kings of old. Instead, before he could ascend, he would be made to kneel. In a ritual as theatrical as it was unprecedented, García was compelled first to grant sweeping privileges to his noblemen, and then—and only then—was he allowed to stand upon a shield and be raised as a king. "[H]e would swear to them, before they raised him, on the cross and the holy gospels that he would hold them rightly, and always improve their laws, and not worsen them, and that he would undo injustices . . . and upon rising he ascends his shield, held by the rich men, all shouting three times 'King!, King!, King!"[12] The symbolism of such a ceremony, staggering in its presentation and revolutionary in its implications, could have hardly escaped all those who took part in it. Yet García, if he wished to keep his throne, would need to learn to stomach such compromises. Whatever the cost to pay for his crown, he had little option but to afford it.

Not for nothing, his current circumstances were unpromising for sure. Hemmed in by Aragonese hostility, the new regime in Pamplona had no alternative but to secure what little stability it could in his western domains—even at the cost of the most humiliating of concessions. "I, García Ramírez, King of Pamplona, do homage to you, Emperor of Spain, for Pamplona and for all the land that I hold today, . . . in good faith and without evil deceit."[13] The submission to the Castilian ruler that, albeit positively shameful, guaranteed that García's kingdom would not simply become an international pariah. But one which, at the same time, inspired little confidence among his servants. Some of these vassals, seeing no point in obeying a puppet king, quickly opted for rallying to the service of their lord's lord and, among them, taking his dominion of Alava alongside him, was none other than Count Ladrón.[14]

The wave of desertions, of course, did not please the Pamplonese ruler. García the Restorer, for all that he had no other choice but to put up with its terms, could feel the weight of his homage to the king of Castile as a colossal burden upon his shoulders. So did his son, Sancho—later to be dubbed "the Wise"—who was raised to the throne in 1150. Barely a teenager when he first took up the rule of the realm, no sooner had Sancho ascended the throne than he had witnessed several of the most important among his father's aides abandon him. A blow that, for a recently established dynasty of kinglets, was not merely a bad omen, but an existential threat. The early years of his reign had been spent in precarity and weakness. And during these trying times, Sancho the Wise had grasped a bitter truth. If the destinies of Pamplona were allowed to remain dictated by the whims of fickle barons or foreign overlords, then neither his father's legacy nor his own would ever be safe. If both his dynasty and his realm were to survive, then he could no longer afford to be a king in name only. The Pamplonese had to get matters back into their own hands.

Sancho's first real opportunity to do so came in 1159. In a move as pragmatic as necessary, the sovereigns of Pamplona and Aragon finally agreed, after a quarter of a century of tense coexistence, to set their differences aside and formally recognize each other. With his eastern flank thus locked, Sancho was at last free to push forward his attempt at independence from Castile. Leading his troops across the Ebro, he struck deep into Rioja, occupying castles and towns. Only Nájera, Haro, and Calahorra—held fast by a descendant of Diego López de Haro—managed to resist his offensive.

The campaign, in all, served as much more than simply a declaration of the end of Sancho's homage. It doubled as an ultimatum directed at his own nobility. Families that had thrived in the game of twin allegiances that had come to define the political landscape of the frontier now suddenly found themselves, in the wake of Sancho's reckless attacks, commanded to pick sides. Nowhere was this more certain than in Alava, where the Vela family had time and again showcased that their loyalties were as unreliable as they were shifting. Sancho, at last, had had enough. As his forces pressed south, he did so with a new determination: to finally see for himself who was with him—and who was his enemy.

These ambitions, however, were not confined to the battlefield alone. The same year in which he had invaded Rioja, Sancho had dropped the title "King of the Pamplonese" in favor of that of "King of Navarre," and he had made sure that the connotations of the change were adequately comprehended. The old name had carried some contractual notions, a sort of imagined partnership between the ruler and his barons. The new title, by contrast, not only swept away the stigma of the recent homage paid to Castile, but likewise proclaimed the right of the sovereign to singular dominion over his realm. By 1167, when a ten-year truce with Castile was finally agreed, Sancho could afford at last to take stock of his achievements. The work of his father had been vindicated; the independence of the kingdom, restored. For the first time in almost a century, Pamplona was the seat of a true monarchy. Sovereign, undisputed, and beholden to no one.

But what, exactly, was this *Navarre* that Sancho now claimed as his own fief? The surroundings of Pamplona and the banks of the Ebro—which included the city of Tudela, conquered by Alfonso the Battler—stood firmly under his vassal's grasp. The same, however, could not be said of Alava, Biscay, or Guipuzcoa. In these regions, Sancho's policy of defining clear-cut allegiances had suffused local leaders, previously comfortable in a veiled autonomy, in a state of existential crisis. Forced to choose between Castile and Navarre, noble lineages like the Velas had immediately discovered the seeds of future confrontations. The stakes of such a gamble, at a time when the resources and aspirations of monarchs were growing larger and larger, appeared to them impossibly high. Back the wrong ruler, and even the most exalted lineage could rapidly collapse into obscurity. Pick the right side, though, and the rewards might be equally unmatched. Frantic calculations began to flood the Western Pyrenees. And so, as the twelfth century neared its final decades, many must have realized that the moment of reckoning, so long delayed, was approaching at last.

The uneasy truce shattered, its terms jettisoned, when the Castilians, taking revenge for the events of 1162, occupied most of Biscay and large chunks of Alava in 1175. Yet, the campaign, though fierce, yielded no decisive victor. After a series of inconclusive skirmishes—and brought to the negotiating table by the urgency to fight back the Muslims—the two monarchs opted for an agreement. According to its terms, Guipuzcoa, most of Alava, and the lands around Durango were to remain under Sancho the Wise's sovereignty. Biscay, Rioja, and western Alava, on the other hand, were now recognized as part of Castile. A stark line was drawn: "and from the boundaries set up to Navarre, everything shall belong to the King of Navarre . . . and from the aforementioned designated boundaries up to Castile, everything shall belong to the King of Castile."[15] Notably absent from the text—to Sancho's credit—was the suggestion that he owed any homage to Castile, or any hint that the monarch of Navarre was in any way inferior to his rival. Whereas the cost of the war had been grievous both in land and men, at least in dignity, the court of Pamplona had secured something priceless: recognition of its right to exist.

The signed agreement soon became the guiding reference point for Navarre's policy in the Western Pyrenees. In a sense, in accepting two differentiated spheres of power, their monarchs further demonstrated that they did not regard the entire region as a coherent whole, bound either by shared kinship or tradition. In the unlikely scenario that they had ever treasured such an idea of a "Vascon" world, then memory of it, by the time of Sancho the Wise, had completely faded into insignificance. But the treaty, while it had imposed limits upon the ambitions of Navarrese monarchs, also conferred on them a measure of authority. The sovereignty of the king was now acknowledged all throughout his territories. Where once the loyalty of magnates had sufficed to maintain order, now a stronger, more centralized administration was imposed. Across Alava, Guipuzcoa, and Durango, the system of tenancies was set in place. Command over these districts was entrusted not, as had traditionally been the case, to the heads of local families, but rather to Navarrese men whose loyalty to the king was beyond question.

Sancho the Wise, determined though he was to wrestle back these marginal, disputed areas from the hands of the barons and their assemblies, did not merely seek to curb the influence of the great lords—he sought to bypass it altogether. From the late 1170s, Sancho started to found free cities in the newly acquired territories, settlements that would only recognize the authority of the crown. The most important of these, San Sebastian and Vitoria—founded in 1180 and 1181, respectively—were, from their inception, intended to serve as counterweights to contain the grievances of discontented noblemen. In this, they proved their worth. Even as the local population resented the displacement of their traditional representatives, its citizens thrived and held watch over the kingdom's border. Had the future been otherwise, perhaps, and given enough time, then Alava and Guipuzcoa, much like the lands along the banks of the Ebro, would have come to be regarded as seamless parts of Navarre.

However, this was not their destiny. For all that the court of Pamplona might feel its future secure in 1179, the Castilian monarch regarded the current situation as little more than a convenience to be upheld only for as long as it suited his interests. And by the late

1190s, this was no longer the case. In the summer of 1199, a Castilian army advanced into Alava, laid siege to Vitoria, and then pressed onward to secure Durango. The king of Navarre, busy abroad with negotiations to open a second front against the Castilians, could do little to oppose them. By the end of the year, he received a missive from Vitoria asking for permission to surrender. In January 1200, the city—and with it the entirety of Alava, Guipuzcoa, and Biscay—had already capitulated.

The swiftness with which the Navarrese administration, after two decades of apparent consolidation, had suddenly crumbled down in the west probably startled contemporaries. To later chroniclers, however, it seemed barely worth remarking upon. "King Alfonso had a war with the king of Navarre and won twenty-five very good castles. Of these, he returned fourteen, but he kept eleven for himself."[16] The laconism of the entry betrayed the want of interest the entire episode sparked among Castilian audiences. Not a single pitched battle, not a victory against insurmountable odds, not even the slightest twist of fate had ever threatened the chances of victory of their troops. In Navarre, as was to be expected, the mood was altogether darker, and the search for scapegoats was immediate. The blame for the kingdom's humiliation was laid squarely at the feet of those title holders entrusted with its defense. "People of inconstant heart, in whom [King Sancho] trusted; though if he had them hanged high, he would do very well."[17]

A damning verdict indeed—but not a terribly unjust one. Only Vitoria and a handful of other cities had, after all, shown even the faintest inclination to resist, while the nobility, far from coming to their aid, had almost unanimously thrown their lot in with the enemy. Their motives, and the exact terms under which they had reached an understanding with King Alfonso VIII of Castile, would in time become pressing questions for the inhabitants of the Western Pyrenees. But for the time being, what these talks evidenced was one inescapable truth: that the native inhabitants of Alava, Guipuzcoa, and the surroundings of Durango much preferred to live under the rule of Castile than to do so under that of Navarre. Why, otherwise, had there been no popular revolt at the crossing of the Castilians through Alava? Why was there no news about any fighting in the rugged hills of Guipuzcoa? Why had no one come to the relief of the siege of Vitoria? Sancho the Wise might have sought to transform the frontier, to mold these peripheral regions into a full-fledged part of Navarre. But, in doing so, he had upended the traditional order, and had thus alienated the very factions which had previously sustained his rule. The dream of a firmly Navarrese west had not simply failed—it had collapsed under the weight of his own overreach. With that, the centuries-old tug-of-war between Castile and Pamplona for dominion over the Western Pyrenees was, at last, settled. Castile had triumphed. Shortly after, Alfonso VIII bestowed upon Diego López de Haro II and his descendants the title of Lords of Biscay.

That winter of 1199, as the siege of Vitoria drew to its inevitable close, a small retinue made its way through the snows of Alava. Their march was slow, not only for the biting cold and the thick fog but also because at their head rode an elderly, 78-year-old woman. In what would prove one of the final episodes in a life packed with memorable events, the twice-Queen Eleanor of Aquitaine had agreed to travel to Castile and escort her granddaughter—the princess—back to France. Neither age nor the inclement weather would deter her. Nor would, remarkably, any local warlord. There could have been no clearer testament to the power Alfonso VIII now wielded than the simple fact that he could guarantee his mother-in-law's safety as she rode through an active warzone.

The days when the ambitions of unruly barons could outmatch the resources of kings and when the whims of local lords could dictate the course of events seemed, at last, to be fading into history. The age of the nobility was passing. Dawning upon the Western Pyrenees was an age of kings.

Notes

1 Escalona, "Unidades territoriales supralocales: una propuesta sobre los orígenes del señorío de behetría," 41.

2 See, for instance, the mention of the "bonorum hominum" in a document from Leire from 938. In Martín, *Documentación Medieval de Leire (siglos IX a XII)*, 7, 20–1.

3 Larrea, *La Navarre du IVe au XIIe siècle: Peuplement et sociète*, 328–9.

4 Lacarra, *Colección Diplomática de Irache. Vol. 1. (958–1222)*, 8, 11–13. Also, Ubieto, *Cartulario de San Juan de la Peña*, 107, 98–100.

5 It remains unclear whether Munio Muñoz died in the battle of Atapuerca. The last document in which he is mentioned dates from 1053, and by 1056 an unrelated tenant appears as governing Alava. See Pescador, "Tenentes y tenencias del Reino de Pamplona," 111–12.

6 Larrea, "La herencia vasca: acción política y arquitectura social en Vizcaya y Álava antes de su incorporación al reino de Alfonso VI," 108.

7 Pescador, "Tenentes y tenencias del Reino de Pamplona," 114, 119.

8 Ledesma, *Cartulario de San Millán de la Cogolla (1076–1200)*, 48, 44–5.

9 "Livro de linhagens do conde D. Pedro" (*c.*1344). In Prieto, "Las leyendas de los Señores de Vizcaya y la tradición melusiniana," 66.

10 Lacarra, "El Señorío de Vizcaya y el Reino de Navarra en el siglo XII," 40M.

11 Martín, *Documentación medieval de Leire (siglos IX a XII)*, 238, 325.

12 "Fuero General de Navarra." In Jimeno, *Los fueros de Navarra*, 30.

13 Grassotti, "Homenaje de García Ramírez a Alfonso VII," 65.

14 Fortún, "La quiebra de la soberanía navarra en Álava, Guipúzcoa y el Duranguesado (1199–1200)," 445.

15 Fortún, 456.

16 De la Campa, *La Estoria de España de Alfonso X: Estudio y Edición de la Versión Crítica desde Fruela II hasta la muerte de Fernando II*, 587.

17 Anelier de Tolosa, *La Guerra de Navarra. Edición trilingüe: occitano, castellano, vasco*, 88, 224.

CHAPTER 10
FREE AND EXEMPT FOREVERMORE

Not every traveler could enjoy as safe a passage through the Western Pyrenees as Eleanor did. A guide written for pilgrims in the mid-twelfth century warned those making the long and arduous journey to the tomb of Saint James about the many hurdles an imprudent voyager was expected to face in the region. For those coming north from Bordeaux, the desolation began well before catching sight of the mountains. Beyond the deserted plains of Gascony stretched a land unlike any other, "barbarous due to its language, full of forests, rugged, [and] desolate from bread, wine and every nourishment for the body, save the consolation of apples, cider, and milk."[1] *Tellus Basclorum*—the guide called it—the land of the Bascles. The most peripheral of all the peripheries of Gascony, a barren country such as this, it went without saying, was one that ought to be traversed with exceeding caution. Not only were the locals habituated to "collect[ing] unjust tributes" from passing pilgrims, often with the tacit approval of local noblemen, but "if any traveler refuses to give them the money they have demanded, they strike him with their darts and take the tribute, insulting and searching him down to his breeches."[2] The author's judgment was as clear as it was disapproving. "They are fierce, and the land they inhabit is fierce, wild, and barbarous: the ferocity of their faces and the grunts of their barbaric tongue terrify the hearts of those who see them."[3]

The hypothetical traveler's fortune improved somewhat upon crossing the Pyrenees and descending into Navarre—at least in terms of landscape. Here, the soil was richer and its fruits more abundant. But the Navarrese, pretty much like the Bascles, were hardly the kind of people a Frankish writer, schooled in the wisdom of the ancients, would allow himself to admire. "If you saw them eat, you would mistake them for dogs or pigs eating. And if you heard them speak, they would remind you of the barking of dogs, for their language is completely barbaric."[4] Like their northern neighbors, they were "depraved, perverse, perfidious, disloyal, and deceitful." Like them, they were naturally hostile to all outsiders. Yet it was when the time came to reflect upon their origins that the author's disdain reached its full expression. The very name of *Navarrus*—he declared—did not derive from the word locals used for an agricultural implement, or from their term to refer to a flat landscape. Rather, it was a mutation of a Latin expression: *non verus*—"untrue." The conclusion, to his mind, was inescapable: for these were a people "born of an untrue lineage or illegitimate ancestry."[5] In other words, the Navarrese, just as much as the Bascles, were a race of bastards.

The pilgrim's condemnation of the inhabitants of the Western Pyrenees, for all its undeniable vehemence, was hardly a novelty. Rather, it was but the latest entry in a long tradition of contempt that stretched back to the times of the Romans—Strabo, Paulinus,

Prudentius, Isidore, all had partaken in it. But there were also much more recent examples. Only a few decades earlier, a bishop and a papal emissary had been forced to journey along the region's coastline. Their impressions were similarly unflattering. "In those mountainous, remote, and isolated lands, wild men live who speak an incomprehensible language and are ready for any wickedness, for it is no wonder that inhuman and unrestrained beings must dwell in rugged and frightening places."[6] Barbarous lands bred barbarous people: There was a tale as old as time. In echoing these familiar tropes of savage tribes haunting inhospitable mountaintops, the pilgrim's guide had positioned itself within a tradition that had endured for over a millennium. A tradition whose main axiom stated that, at least as far as the Western Pyrenees were concerned, things always remained the same.

But things, for all that the authors of these accounts failed to perceive it, were changing indeed—and doing so fast. That kings and princes in Navarre, Castile, and beyond all were willing to risk war to subdue the so-called Bascles and *Navarri* was more than a mere coincidence or a show of irrepressible bravado. Rather, it served as a reminder of the new opportunities that the Western Pyrenees, long dismissed as a backwater of savagery, had come to promise to those who could master them.

Nowhere were the effects of these profound transformations more readily detectable than in the disaster that had befallen Navarrese interests in 1200. The swift and near-unanimous capitulation of the leaders of Alava, Guipuzcoa, and Biscay, though undoubtedly spurred by the rising might of Castile, was almost impossible to understand without reckoning with another factor: the deep unease that Navarrese policies had sown among the region's governing elites. Among these grievances, one particularly stood out. Sancho the Wise, in granting the inhabitants of new towns such as San Sebastian or Vitoria their charters—or *fueros*, as they were also known—had done much more than simply lay down the laws and principles that would frame their settlers' lives. Rather, he had sought to strike at the very power structures that had upheld the influence of the aristocracy.

Over the course of the centuries, after all, particularly influential members had come to put the local and regional assemblies that had once regulated the affairs of Alava and Biscay in their shadow. The Haros and the Velas had long been the main players in the ample territory that extended from the Ebro to the ocean, but they were not the only ones. Many other householders, less resourceful yet equally resolute, had followed their trail in dozens of low-scale gatherings. The webs of alliance, woven with ties of blood, carefully placed bribes, and the dispensation of favors, had all ended up structuring these territories into a great arterial system of influence, one that linked the mighty to the lowly, the village to the court, and the nobleman to the serf.

These associations played out in the assemblies. The ancient laws and customs of the land, ever adjusted to circumstance yet preserved orally down the generations, had long been safeguarded thanks to the relative independence of local governance. But these were not, by any means, rulings of impossibly old origin, nor commandments handed down from time immemorial to single out those who followed them from their neighbors. Instead, they had been forged by necessity, as products of a poorly hierarchized, economically depressed, politically peripheral backwater.

Once, these same conditions had fed enduring tropes about the unruly Vascones. But now, in an age when monarchs and their bureaucracies were steadily quenching similar traditions elsewhere, they enabled these legal particularities to pose as survivors of an older world. Just as the power of counts and lords had hardened into something more permanent, so too had the rulings come to embody the true, undeniable law of the land. In turn, those who upheld them had increasingly found their authority legitimized as guardians and protectors. "Should the Lord perceive that in certain matters the law is lacking, then the Lord, having gathered together all the land, . . . may amend alongside them these laws, remove one, and put a better one in its place."[7] The prominence of some was always premised, under such a system, on the acquiescence of the rest.

It was precisely this imbrication between a magnate's position and the laws of the householders he claimed to represent that had provided the backbone for the game of complicated allegiances that had characterized the region throughout the eleventh and twelfth centuries. Monarchs, incapable of asserting long-term rule over these districts, had been hard-pressed to grant privileges and gifts to those who held local power. Yet in so doing, they had unwittingly acknowledged the distinct character of these lands and the necessity of yielding, at least in part, to their customs. In an ironic twist of fate, the very efforts by foreign kings to secure a foothold in places like Alava or Biscay had ended up rendering their full assimilation all the more elusive.

Contrary to expectations, none of these developments had anything to do with language. The peasants and householders, as had been the case since the collapse of Rome's Latin-speaking settlements, no doubt spoke some form of *Euskera*. But among the magnates—men accustomed from childhood to dealings with foreign courts and noble families—this was of little consequence. What truly set them apart from their Castilian and Navarrese counterparts was not their tongue, but rather the set of regulations and privileges to which they felt entitled. And it was this cycle of identification between aristocrats and local laws—virtuous or vicious, depending on perspective—that Sancho the Wise, once he had secured a temporary dominion over these lands, had been determined to crush.

By 1180–1, when San Sebastian and Vitoria received their charters, cities had already been a familiar presence in the Western Pyrenees for more than a century. Their origins lay with the great pilgrimage road to Compostela, which, in the late eleventh century, had drawn small groups of settlers from the north to try their fortune in the lands of Navarre. At first, these newcomers had clustered in ghettos, physically detached from already existing towns. Here, they had built their own mills, their own houses, and their own churches. Meager in size, they had survived, for the most part, by catering to the needs of pilgrims and the occasional passing traveler.

Yet, in these seemingly fragile settlements, royal authorities had seen an opportunity. These ambiguous social spaces, which escaped the well-established division of freemen and serfs, had been lavished with privileges and exemptions. Like noblemen, urban settlers were given the right to own land and property. Like noblemen, they were freed from the burdens of servile tribute and placed under a legal system of their own. However, these *fueros* were not grants of nobility; instead, they sought to spawn an entirely novel social class. New cities were granted tracts of land and rights over rivers, forests, and pastures. They received a monopoly to hold markets and control trade in their surroundings. And over all these concessions it was the authority of the city council, elected annually by the townspeople, that was to reign supreme. In return, the monarch demanded only one thing: a collective tax, to be paid by all.

A minor imposition, and one which did little to dampen the town's magnetic pull on new settlers. Spurred by a feverish legislative activity, the new chartered towns flourished. So much so, that before long they began to look upon their non-chartered neighbors with a certain haughtiness. *Burgos de Francos*, the new cities were called in Navarre—"Frankish bourgs." An ethnic label that soon, as the full implications of these privileges manifested in earnest, would become synonymous with freedom.

But a freedom that was to be carefully policed. While the foundation of places like Sangüesa or Estella could serve as a release valve that promised much-needed resources to a monarchy beleaguered by its barons, no one—not even the king—was foolish enough to entertain the prospect of every town becoming a Frankish bourg. Migrants from beyond the kingdom's borders, particularly artisans, weavers, and shoemakers, might bring undeniable value to these new urban centers. But Navarrese serfs, if given the chance to cast off their bondage simply by stepping inside the bounds of a chartered city, could before long nourish the hopes of others to do the same. This was a deeply unsettling thought indeed. For without serfs to stand beneath them, what meaning would the status of freeman hold? A social upheaval of such an order did not appeal to the interests of the nobility; nor—for that matter—to that of the sovereign.

To prevent such things from happening, the *fueros* explicitly prohibited any Navarrese from living within a bourg. In the earliest Frankish settlements, this policy was staunchly enforced. In Estella, for instance, the original inhabitants—dwellers of a village known as Lizarrara—not only remained physically apart, but even the city itself, so as to mark a clear separation between those who lived under privilege and those who did not, was granted a different name. Liberty, if it was meant to last, had to be kept from spreading too far.

Not that a charter was always a response to an existing reality—it could just as easily be a means of creating one. Once it became clear that to sponsor the foundation of a bourg could yield tangible rewards, competition to attract settlers was always bound to arise. Pamplona offered a perfect example. In 1083, the appointment of a man from Toulouse to the city's episcopal see had triggered a flood of monks and clerics from beyond the Pyrenees. Entrusted with extensive powers by the king, the new prelate had embarked on an ambitious project: the creation, from scratch, of a Frankish bourg dedicated to none other than the patron saint of his homeland—Saint Saturnin. The local Navarrese population, while drawn to the new town's market and the attractive goods it offered, was strictly forbidden from putting down roots within its limits. Meanwhile, the newcomers energetically propagated their own cultural preferences, among them the worship of markedly Tolosan saints—not only Saint Saturnin but also Saint Fermin. In all, the bishop's project succeeded in revitalizing the old capital. But, for all his efforts, he could have hardly done it alone. No one but the king, not even the most blue-blooded of aristocrats, was authorized to grant the bundle of privileges and exemptions that had come to be associated with a Frankish bourg. Which meant that only after tense negotiations between the episcopate and the sovereign about the rights each of them was to enjoy over the new city was Saint Saturnin finally granted its *fuero* in 1129, "so that it will always belong to the bishop and Saint Mary."[8]

The compromise reached in Pamplona, though, stood as an exception. Elsewhere, cities signaled an undisputable expansion of royal power and intervention. Both fiscal revenues and taxation over local markets were collected there and went, without further stops, straight into the king's coffers. Moreover, disputes between townspeople and their rural neighbors, rather than settled according to the ancient customs of the land, were now resolved in accordance with the kingly endorsed *fuero* of the bourg. Councils—elected by the citizens but sanctioned by the sovereign's will—increasingly pressed their claims to holding sole jurisdiction over their districts. Economic control, legislative primacy, and political domination: These were promises that any king, if presented with the opportunity, would find it hard to resist.

Not everyone, however, was happy to see such transformations go forward. When Sancho the Wise, seeking to export this new instrument of royal authority to his possessions beyond Navarre, created the first cities in Guipuzcoa and Alava, few among the local aristocracy greeted the development with enthusiasm. In Guipuzcoa, truth be told, resistance was unlikely to crystallize. The region's landowners were petty householders with little chance of opposing the king's commands, and the city founded there was a successor in spirit to the tradition of Frankish bourgs. Families of Gascon merchants, fleeing the endemic unrest that plagued their homeland, had established some years prior a minor trading and fishing hub at the mouth of the Urumea River. As in Estella, the outsiders had lived geographically isolated from the local population, whose own community—named Izurun—had housed an ancient monastery to Saint Sebastian.[9] And, as in Estella, King Sancho had wasted no time in rewarding the newcomers with a *fuero*.

Similarities, though, ended right there. History would not preserve—as it did with Lizarrara—the name of Izurun. Its people, placed under the controlling oversight of their Gascon neighbors, were implacably absorbed into the jurisdiction of the new city. And yet, perhaps in a flash of his proverbial wisdom, Sancho had come to realize in his foundation that a lasting peace between the two communities would require at least a token effort to get the peoples of Izurun on board. Breaking the Estellan precedent, he decreed that the new bourg and the old village were to share a single name. So it was that the city that was intended to serve as Navarre's main port was called, just like the ancient monastery of Izurun at the shores of the sea, San Sebastian.[10]

The scene was very different in Alava. Here, oligarchs could lay claim to a legacy of effective self-rule which dated back, with ebbs and flows, to the time of the Asturians. Local legal particularities, reaffirmed time and again in periodic assemblies of notables and preserved thanks to the ambiguous position of the territory between Castile and Navarre, had come to seem, by the late twelfth century, a very real source of legitimacy. Little wonder, then, that King Sancho's decision to grant the hamlet of Gasteiz—the future Vitoria—privileges that placed it directly under royal authority was met with nothing but unease.

The great houses, such as those of Haro and Vela, had exerted their dominance in Alava not through rigid law, but by the tacit acceptance of a superiority that the rest of the population upheld. An acquiescence that had allowed them to wield an influence that could float upon very different types of communities, and whose limits were always waxing and waning according to the might and the interests of those it touched. A *fuero* like that of Vitoria, on the other hand, in putting in rigid terms the rules by which the townsfolk were to conduct their affairs, completely undermined this fluid system of power. In Vitoria, it was space, and not fealty paid to a commanding patron, that ensured both status and enrichment. Perched upon a promontory not far from ancient Veleia from which it was possible to survey the widest plains of Alava, it embodied an authority built on documents, foreign legal notions, and economic supremacy that was wholly strange to the assumptions that had governed Alavese society for generations. Which is why, when in 1199 the chance finally came to shake off Navarrese control, the retinues of the great lineages and the urban officials of Vitoria would stand on opposite camps.

Perhaps, once negotiations for surrender to Alfonso VIII of Castile were concluded, the principal householders had found solace in the assurances of their new monarch. No further chartered cities, they had been promised, would be imposed upon them. Strategically relevant and with a tendency to switch sides as they were, the new king had rapidly understood that, when it came to the Alavese at least, the surest course was to tread with care. No such constraints, however, applied in Guipuzcoa. The most remote of his recent acquisitions, this was a land that, until now, had remained largely on the margins of Castile's grinding struggle with Navarre. Mountainous and isolated, it was a prize that for centuries had not been worth the squeeze.

But that, too, was changing now. All along the coastline of the Atlantic, from Flanders to San Sebastian, new opportunities were opening to those ready to take advantage. Trade and fishing, as maritime routes were increasingly patrolled by powerful princes and towns, bloomed as never before. An ocean that Western Pyreneans had long learned to fear as a hunting ground for marauders and a graveyard of ships was proving, thanks to the emergence of important hubs of commerce in France, England, and beyond, to be something else indeed: a source of unknown wealth. It was for this reason that Alfonso's representatives, after assuming control over the Navarrese administration in Guipuzcoa, had seen little merit in reversing the policy of their immediate predecessors. Unlike in Alava, the arrival of the Castilians was to be marked there by an unapologetic display of urban planning. Only three years on from the annexation and the same privileges enjoyed by the inhabitants of San Sebastian had already been granted to the nearby port of Fuenterrabia. In 1209, similar charters were conferred to Guetaria and Motrico. In all, just as they had done in Alava, these settlements had meant the introduction of a foreign element into the land's existing social fabric.

A risk whose benefits, for Alfonso and his realm, promised to far outweigh any grievances among the locals. Not only were cities, here as elsewhere, pockets of royal power, bastions from which royal norms and influence could penetrate deep into the countryside. That only coastal ports had been elevated in Guipuzcoa to the rank of chartered towns suggested an additional—and purposeful—policy. Were these privileges intended to push their inhabitants into the burgeoning trade networks of the north? Were their vessels seen as potential assets that could be put to use in Alfonso's military campaigns? Or was the overarching intention of these foundations to counterbalance the influence of San Sebastian, whose pro-Navarrese leanings might still be in question? Perhaps all these possibilities held some truth at once. What was certain was that, by the mid-thirteenth century, a whole constellation of coastal bourgs had come to reshape the landscape of Guipuzcoa.

These charters, once granted, proved to be outstanding instruments of social transformation. They drew in migrants, who in turn became new citizens with needs to satisfy; new needs sparked fresh economic opportunities that, in turn, attracted yet more settlers. The cycle was a virtuous one. So virtuous, in fact, that rulers soon came to throw away any hesitation they might have initially harbored. Ever since the foundation of San Sebastian, the trend had been increasingly to allow local peoples—and not only outsiders—to become citizens. In Guipuzcoa, this was a decision imposed by practical limitations. Unlike other regions along the most well-trodden routes of pilgrimage, it lacked a steady influx of Frankish migrants and, outside of San Sebastian and a handful of nearby harbors, outsiders were almost nonexistent. But, despite not sharing in these conditions, that of integrating native peasants into the bourgs was becoming a fashionable custom all across the Western Pyrenees. Even in Navarre, once it became clear that the amount of travelers willing to settle in its cities was gradually dwindling, it came the turn for local inhabitants to be drawn into urban life. No better example of this than Pamplona. Although the Navarrese remained barred from settling in the bourg of Saint Saturnin, the old town had gained, sixty years after the foundation of its Frankish counterpart, a *fuero* of its own. The name of *Navarreria* given to the city—an evident homage to the indigenous origins of its dwellers—clearly displayed the extent of the transformation that had ensued in less than a century. Perhaps, in the end, it was not necessary for a Frankish bourg to be Frankish in order to be free.

Not that the widening of citizenship rights did much to dispel rivalries—if anything, its effect was the exact opposite. As variations in legal status between Frankish and native bourgs gradually faded, mental barriers constructed around a particular sense of cultural identity were heightened at a similar rate. In 1180, a few years before the creation of the Navarreria, the inhabitants of Saint Saturnin had taken a drastic measure to stage their preeminence, expelling all peoples of Navarrese origin from their quarters. Not only that, for residents were made to swear that they would never again admit any *vilains peyter*—"servile peasants"—on their houses.[11]

A radical, yet not necessarily unpopular, pledge to make. Speakers of Occitan and Gascon, conscious of their numerical inferiority, had always been aware of their position as a battered island in a vast ocean of peoples with whom they shared little. Under such conditions, rather than risk assimilation, they had opted to cling to a time-honored strategy: to deal mostly among themselves. The approach, at least as far as the survival of their culture was concerned, would prove a successful one. In the seventeenth century, a document from San Sebastian still attested that Gascon "was spoken at present vulgarly in the city."[12] A persistence that could hardly be attributed merely to sheer luck, especially considering that Gascons had initially numbered but a few hundred at most. It bore testimony, instead, to a deliberate choice, a communal effort to remain distinct.

Not that San Sebastian's case was wholly abnormal, for almost every city in the Western Pyrenees bespoke a similar enough story. Whereas in rural villages it was varieties of *Euskera* that continued to dominate, those tasked with the government of chartered cities only rarely employed this language in public life. Instead, when it was time for them to conduct their administrative or commercial tasks, these men and women turned to Occitan, to Gascon, or increasingly to Castilian. Reasons to do so varied. In some places, as in the Frankish bourgs, this was a somewhat natural consequence of their demographic makeup. In others, it was a decision enforced by the authority of kings and princes. Whatever the cause, the effect was a process of acculturation that would prove momentous. *Euskera* would remain the language of the rural world, but now it found itself increasingly excluded from the most dynamic social entities in medieval society. Those in the spheres of power, of learning, of commerce, all pushed it to the side. And so, to the fractures that already divided the privileged from the unprivileged, and the new order from the old, another chasm was added. A wall made up entirely of words.

All things considered, there was little need to resort to the topic of language to realize that coexistence between bourgs and their rural neighborhoods was far from smooth. As the case of Izurun and San Sebastian had made clear, villagers living under the dominion of a town were seldom allowed to voice their opinions in its council. More often than not, citizens preferred to leave these communities to their own devices, free to manage their affairs as they had always done. Often, but not always. When the interests of the bourg were at stake, councilors could be as uncompromising and ruthless as the most iron-fisted of lords. Peasants who lived close to Vitoria, for instance, repeatedly protested against a practice known as *urundiru*—"flour money"—a levy that required them to weigh their flour in the city and give away a fraction of the product in return. Understandably, they saw in this a grievous burden that obliged them to undertake unnecessary journeys and, moreover, pay for the privilege of doing so.[13] Similar impositions were enforced elsewhere. In Bayonne and San Sebastian, officers defended what they claimed as their rightful due: the first whale harpooned every year in the nearby towns of Biarritz and Guetaria.[14] Even forests, due to their importance to key urban economic activities like shipbuilding, barrel-making, or construction, could become a source of bitter contention and one in which violence was not off the table. In all, these measures, apart from securing immediate economic gains, displayed the council's undeterred purpose to reinforce the town's dominance over its hinterland. To those who suffered these exertions, indeed, it must have seemed as if the much-proclaimed freedom of the city stopped right in the shadow of their walls.

A slightly paradoxical conclusion given that, more and more, it was the locals themselves who petitioned for the creation of a bourg. This held particularly true in those regions where the monarchy's direct holdings were sparse. There, it was often well-established landowners who willingly would give up portions of their estates to build a city, obtaining in return the remission of taxation. It was a sweet deal. The tribute that these householders had once owed was then redistributed across the entire community of the bourg and, moreover, it granted these lands an undisputed monopoly over the trade in their surroundings. Meanwhile, the monarchy obtained a secure spearhead in a region where its presence had previously been weak. Everyone had something to gain.

And yet, for all the seemingly undeniable benefits, not everyone was persuaded about the advantages of the trade-off. In those places where the consuetudinary attributions and networks of domination of local magnates had been most entrenched, the emergence of these urban enclaves was delayed and always looked upon with suspicion. In Biscay, for instance, no city was founded before Bermeo in 1236. Perhaps, as oral tradition would much later enshrine, such an apparent reluctance stemmed from the intricate internal politics that had to be navigated before a city could be created. Biscaynes, after all, "had as law and usage and custom that the lord of Biscay could not order the creation of any city in Biscay, except . . . with all Biscaynes giving their consent."[15]

But why would they do so? To settle in a town meant, by definition, to surrender the old privileges in favor of a new communal order, and this was an evident downgrade for those who had flourished under the previous system of personal patronage. Forced now by the city council to contribute to the mutual welfare of the commonwealth, they might look back in regret at what they had lost. And it was not only those of lesser condition who balked at the transformation. The members of the Haro lineage themselves had every reason to fear the introduction of such foreign legislation into their lands, regardless of any economic opportunities it might bring. In Alava, too, once the kings of Castile, treading back on their previous promises, renewed the push for urbanization in the 1240s, tensions between the law of the land and the law of the bourgs escalated yet again. But these were resistances that, however fierce, could only hold back the tide for so long. As the benefits that trade could yield were ever more widely acknowledged, so were the kings of Castile and the lords of Biscay less likely to pay heed to the complaints of exasperated householders. Unsurprisingly, dissenters saw their qualms put to the side. More cities were founded. The new system took root.

The Frankish monk who, in the 1140s, had cautioned pilgrims about the perils that awaited them in the Western Pyrenees had encountered a world still divided in two. On one side stood those subjected to serfdom, prostrated by law and custom, the most wretched and wicked of all humans. On the other, like a reflection on a mirror, were those who could boast the liberty that was so earnestly denied the rest. Service—that equalizing term that yet made so much difference in practice—had been the defining notion of this society. It was service, after all, that bound a serf to his master; that tethered a householder to his lineage; that secured a baron's loyalty to his lord. It was not a nobleman's fate to suffer the ardent touch of the summer sun on his neck as he plowed the king's lands. Rather, it was on the battlefield, as he stood clad in mail, sword in hand, ready to meet without hesitation his sovereign's foes, that his worth as a vassal was best put into evidence. Those on the honorable side of the widening social chasm were thus defined, above all, by the terms of their service.

Fast forward a century and a half, and what had erstwhile been a twofold division had undergone a revolutionary transformation. The social tapestry of the Western Pyrenees, caught for so long between the ambitions of landowners and the penuries of peasants, had come to harbor a new kind of community that, like a sickness growing from a single defective cell, threatened to overturn the entire body. What had first arisen as a makeshift response to strengthen royal power had evolved, over the course of the decades, into the basis of an entirely new model of social and political life. Citizens, unlike serfs, recognized no law save that contained in their town's *fuero*. No lord could force them to prostrate or demand from them a shameful tribute. None but the king could lay claim to their service. And yet, unlike the great magnates, they knew that their liberties had not always existed. Rather than immemorial, they owed everything to a particular time and to a particular place.

"I grant to you . . . that you shall be free and exempt forevermore, both you and your descendants, from all taxes and dues, as well as from military levies and repairs and from other obligations and duties of any kind."[16] Contained in declarations such as this one were the foundations of a worldview in which a franchise marked, simultaneously, the birth of a community and the ultimate validation of its right to exist. This was because a charter served both to nurture loyalty toward those who upheld it, and, at the same time, to inspire opposition toward those that threatened it.

And challenged it was—frequently and from many quarters. At times, hostility came from peasants, unhappy with what they took as abuses from haughty urban authorities. On other occasions, and especially in those places where the powers of the nobility were more entrenched, it was householders that took on the offensive, seeing the stature of their privileges diminished by the concessions made to others. And there were some times, too, when it was cities themselves that fought fiercely against each other over resources and jurisdiction.

Tensions that, from the land of the Bascles to Alava and from Biscay to Navarre, were slowly building up. For now, as the tide of newfound prosperity bathed the region, most of these were appeased and cooled down. Yet, like a sword, there was a limit to the times a blade could be tempered before it would finally snap. The question remained to know who—peasants, noblemen, burgers—would be the ones with their hands on its handle when the time came and the heat of conflict could no longer be contained.

Notes

1 Klaus and Santos, *Liber Sancti Jacobi Codex Calixtinus*, V, 7, 239.
2 Klaus and Santos, V, 7, 239.
3 Klaus and Santos, V, 7, 239.
4 Klaus and Santos, V, 7, 240.
5 Klaus and Santos, V, 7, 240–1.

6 Quoted in García de Cortázar, "La sociedad guipuzcoana antes del Fuero de San Sebastián," 106–7.

7 "Fueros de la M. N. Tierra de Ayala, recopilados por Don Fernán Pérez de Ayala, señor de ella antes del año de 1373 y aumentados en el de 1469 por el mariscal Lopez de Ayala su bisnieto." In De Uriarte, *El Fuero de Ayala*, 123.

8 Quoted in Jimeno, *Los fueros de Navarra*, 224–6.

9 Lema, "Un obscuro pasado: Guipuzcoa y Navarra (siglos X-XII)," 21. Also, Tena, *La sociedad urbana en la Guipúzcoa costera medieval: San Sebastián, Rentería y Fuenterrabía (1200–1500)*, 261–2. Also, Etxezarraga, "La organización del territorio de San Sebastián y su entorno durante la Alta Edad Media: Una visión panorámica de su evolución," 72–3.

10 Donostia seems to have evolved as a contraction of the Basque term for Saint Sebastian, "Done Sebastian."

11 Lacarra, "Las villas navarras y la colonización urbana," 179–80. Also, Anelier de Tolosa, *La Guerra de Navarra. Edición trilingüe: occitano, castellano, vasco*, 75.

12 Orella, "La gasconización medieval occidental del Reino de Navarra," 181. Also, Goyheneche, *Bayonne et la région Bayonnaise du XIIe au XVe siècle*, 351.

13 Fernández de Larrea and Díaz de Durana, "El discurso político de los protagonistas de las luchas sociales en el País Vasco al final de la Edad Media," 332.

14 Pontet, *Histoire de Bayonne*, 42. Also, Ciriquiain, *Los vascos y la pesca de la ballena*, 43–5.

15 Monreal, *The Old Law of Bizkaia (1452). Introductory study and critical edition*, 176.

16 "Charter of Bilbao" (1300). In Monreal, *Fuentes del Derecho Histórico de Bizkaia*, 53.

CHAPTER 11
THOSE FROM WHOM WE COME

Little, at present, betrays the pedigree once enjoyed by the hamlet of Arriaga. Few would guess, upon seeing it, that what is now a nondescript neighborhood of Vitoria, crisscrossed by tram lines and squeezed between a football field and a repository of old tires, could once have been the beating heart of the political life of Alava. For centuries—perhaps even before the region's incorporation into Castile—its modest church had stood as the stage upon which the weightiest affairs of the land were settled. Alliances, punishments, marriages, reconciliations, all had been solemnly performed, under a public scrutiny which certified their validity, in Arriaga. Here, too, magnates and householders had chosen representatives to speak on their behalf before the monarch. "And at times, they took as their Lord one of the sons of the Kings; and at times, the Lord of Biscay; and at times, the Lord of Lara; and at times, the Lord of the Cameros. And in all past times, no king ever had lordship over this land, nor did he appoint officials there to administer justice."[1]

One should know better than to mistake this post of lord for a grant of true dominion. The appointment conferred no mastery nor immunity, but instead the fleeting honors of widely recognized prestige. The elected leader, tasked with military and executive duties and receiving in exchange for his trouble a testimonial payment known as the "oxen of March," understood fully well that he was little more than a *primus inter pares*.[2] True power lay elsewhere. It was the assembly known as the Confraternity, where the great men of the land, flanked by their clients and retainers, convened to settle affairs as their forebears had done, that best embodied the immemorial tradition of Alavese self-government. No other similar gatherings held in Biscay, Guipuzcoa, or in any other nearby circumscription could match it in importance. Be it in reach of jurisdiction, in the stature and grandeur of those in attendance, or in the sheer gravity of its proceedings, the assembly of Arriaga stood unmatched. It was, as far as governance was concerned, the indisputable heart of the Western Pyrenees.

Yet time is an unrelenting tide, and the long decades that followed Alava's submission to Castilian overlordship had witnessed the waning of the once unchallenged assembly of Arriaga. What had once been a thriving, lively gathering, in which all imaginable dilemmas and disputes had been thrashed out, now found itself under attack. Not any longer did everyone, as had long been customary, take for granted the Confraternity's right to decide the destinies of Alava. Chartered towns, Vitoria chief among them, had after all no need to pay reverence to any old-fashioned code of conduct. Intricate and exhaustive, the *fueros* of these bourgs, sanctioned by the king, left little space for the unwritten norms that had long sustained the region's traditional order. And this, in turn, left them outside the jurisdiction of the Confraternity and overall bespoke ill news for the wardens of the old ways. Not for nothing, bourgs were the most economically dynamic elements in the entire country: a success which now threatened to relegate Arriaga to irrelevance. The self-government which generations of Alavese chieftains had banked on was, as it now confronted the intromission of the monarch's underlings, at risk of being eroded for good.

Which is why magnates, now more than ever, clung to these traditions with ever greater determination. The lords of Biscay, scions of the illustrious lineage of Haro, had thanks to their might and influence long enjoyed a preeminent place within the Confraternity. Yet even they, for all their ability to muster the allegiance and resources of their many estates across Castile, also regarded the encroaching tide of urbanization with suspicion. True, the monarchy still acknowledged their ascendancy in Biscay, just as much as it continued to recognize the authority of the assembly of Arriaga. But there was no denying that the officials appointed by the king to oversee them had grown increasingly dismissive of these nobiliary jurisdictions.[3]

A push and pull that the policy of creating new bourgs, pursued with renewed vigor in Alava and Guipuzcoa from the mid-thirteenth century onward, could only exacerbate even further. When in 1272 the lord of Biscay, alongside the rest of the great houses of the realm, revolted in spectacular fashion against the reigning sovereign, high among their listed demands was one that proved how invested they were in preventing any modification of the *status quo*. "The towns that he had ordered to be built in Castile"—the rebels demanded—"he should order them to be undone."[4]

An impossible ask, of course—but one that struck a chord among the freemen of Alava. For these individuals, the threat posed by the chartered towns was not merely an affront against the reach and applicability of the ancient laws of the land. What they feared most was that the new *fueros*, in giving serfs a goal toward which to aspire, might gradually place landlords under mounting pressure to apply conditions and wages that matched those in the city.[5] They kept in mind the many known cases of serfs who had slipped away from their manors and had sought new lives in the chartered towns, far from the justice of the magnates. A bad enough prospect on its own; yet one which, at a time when the previous economic acceleration was starting to display signs of stagnation, was nothing short of calamitous. For those most powerful barons, whose wealth depended on the labor of dozens or hundreds of serfs scattered across the countryside, the burden of policing these breakouts promised to be backbreaking. Yet even the most irrelevant of householders could comprehend that, were the rigid distinctions between free and unfree to be dissolved, their own position might be far from assured.

The lord of Biscay—no doubt with his own selfish interest in mind—had therefore known precisely what he was doing when he presented himself as the chief spokesman of nobiliary discontent. With calculating defiance, he garrisoned in the Western Pyrenees, prevented the king's officers from entering Alava and Guipuzcoa, and even led a few *razzias* against bourgs that remained loyal to the crown.[6] In all of this, the magnates followed him. Why not, if all they were doing was to act as the true guardians of the ageless customs? If they thought there was a destabilizer, it was indeed none other than the monarch himself. So when the king, brought to the negotiating table, surrendered to the demands of the lord of Haro and granted him Biscay as a *mayorazgo*—an indivisible inheritance to be passed down from father to son in perpetuity—many saw in this much more than just a personal triumph for Iñigo López's successors. Their request to revoke the charters might not have been heeded, true, and yet the confreres of Arriaga could still take satisfaction in the outcome of their defiance. A sign that the old ways, perhaps, could be salvaged after all.

A sign, but far from a guarantee. Over the course of the following decades, city councils continued to press ever harder, albeit undercover, against the old jurisdictions. Village by village, hamlet by hamlet, they sought to draw as many properties and peoples as possible under their exclusive control. By 1310, the Confraternity had once again raised the alarm. The council of Vitoria, they denounced, was trying to absorb forty-five villages in their surroundings that had long been under the magnate's control. Fast forward twenty years, and the situation, rather than improving, had worsened to the point of crisis. Municipal authorities, claiming that they had lawfully purchased those lands from the confreres, now asserted the right to impose their *fuero* upon them. The barons, on the other hand, had a very different perspective. "[T]hat the Council of Vitoria has seized these [villages] from us, and that these . . . and all the land of Alava, are and must be ours, just as they were of those from whom we come."[7]

The dispute soon resulted in a stalemate, but a bloodstained one. Officials on both sides, when they sought to stamp their authority on the ground, were often beaten and ambushed; gangs of brigands and hired thugs plundered the properties of those that stood in their patron's way. A sad state of affairs that, unfortunately, was not unusual in the Western Pyrenees. Only a few years earlier, what had begun as a dispute over the rights to exploit pastures and forests between the inhabitants of the Guipuzcoan bourg of Mondragón and a neighboring noble house had descended into an uncontrollable spiral of challenges and vendettas.[8] In the border region between Guipuzcoa and Navarre, too, cutthroats had grown accustomed to preying upon unsuspecting travelers and stealing livestock, and cities had come to fear the violent backlash of the landowning elite. Little by little, in the surroundings of Vitoria just as elsewhere, "many deaths, wounds, captures, and other things that should have been avoided arose."[9]

To the respite of those involved at least, the bitter litigation between Vitoria and the Confraternity of Arriaga seemed, by 1331, at last to be nearing its conclusion. Weary of the instability their feud had provoked in the land, both the council and the assembly had agreed to submit their case to the arbitration of the Castilian king. Holding their breath, the two sides awaited what promised to be a decisive event in their struggle for supremacy in the land of Alava. Their respective representatives at court, in turn, made sure to remind the monarch of their past services to the crown, but also to hint, with calculated delicacy, at the dangers of an ill-advised ruling.

Therefore, when on February 8, 1332, the official appointed by Alfonso XI of Castile read aloud the king's verdict in the open fields of Arriaga, grunts of consternation were no doubt heard among the attendees. In what seemed a deliberate assertion of his authority, the sovereign had unconditionally endorsed the pretensions of the bourg. Of the forty-five contested villages, the city council was granted undisputed jurisdiction over forty-one, so "that they be exempt, free, and frank, according to the charter, usage, and custom of the said Council of Vitoria."[10]

The decision struck like a depth charge, sending shockwaves through each and every web of patronage that sustained the Confraternity. It was as if the very foundations of Alava's ancient government had cracked in unison. From the most momentous lawsuit of the century, in which everything hung at stake, it was not the treasured customs of the land, but instead the law of the chartered towns that had emerged victorious. Not even the mediation of those powerful noble houses, which had once secured the king's acquiescence to the Confraternity's rule, had managed to extract so much as a fair deal from the monarchy. The traditional way of things, it seemed, had been tested—and it had been found wanting.

To no one's surprise, whispers began to circulate. What—some confreres wondered—was the point of enforcing the antique rulings of Alava if the king, inevitably, would side with the chartered towns to diminish their reach? What use was the tribute paid to a great magnate like the lord of Biscay if his much-vaunted influence at court was insufficient to protect their interests? Of course, such mutterings were far from innocent. The king himself, thanks to his deft handling of the arbitration, had done much to sow doubt in the minds of the Confraternity's members. He had made their authority seem obsolete. And now his agents—members of unimportant Alavese lineages with tenuous links to the leading families—only needed to deepen this ongoing split, whispering in the ears of the small, struggling landowners damning verdicts against the richest barons. Was it not the king that could ensure that fugitive peasants were returned to their fields? Who, if not the king, could check the relentless expansion of the cities? The fear of being left behind, pariahs in a world that no longer moved at the pace of the old gatherings of Arriaga, must have weighed heavily on the mood of those who listened to these questions. A paradoxical idea, a thought that went against centuries of self-governing tradition in Alava was gaining momentum: that to better resist the gnawing power of the monarchy, the best course of action was in fact to surrender to it.[11]

The dissolution of the Confraternity of Arriaga on April 2, 1332—barely a year after the publication of the resolution of the Victorian lawsuit—was a patent demonstration of the rapid transformations in governance that were taking place across the Western Pyrenees. The final settlement was a momentous and complete victory for the monarchy. For

> [t]hey granted us the land of Alava so that we might have lordship over it, and it became royal land, placing it under the Crown of our kingdoms and for us and those who would reign after us in Castile and Leon. And they renounced and withdrew from ever having a Confraternity or assembly in the field of Arriaga or in any other place in the name of a Confraternity, nor would they call themselves confreres. And they renounced any charter, usage, and custom forever.[12]

No stipulation, no condition had been placed upon the sovereign in return for such a coveted trophy. Yet Alfonso XI, of course, understood well what was expected of him. Without delay, he issued a privilege directed at the erstwhile members of the

Confraternity. The decree ordered that all peasants in Alava were to remain bound to the land. Fugitives ought to be hunted down, apprehended, and returned to their rightful lords. It was, for all intents and purposes, a populist move, but to those most grievously wronged by the events of the previous year it was a welcome consolation prize nonetheless. A consolation, however, that came at a heavy cost. Alfonso's officers quickly took control of the gears of power across Alava. The "oxen of March," once an offering to the Confraternity's leader, became a direct contribution to the royal coffers. The old rulings of the land, upheld by generations of resolute and zealous householders, were erased in favor of the king's law, never to return.

The obliteration without resistance of Alava's ancient self-government cast an ominous shadow over that of its neighbors. Bereft of the leading model of Arriaga, there was little hope left for the majority of localized, small-reach assemblies. The only exception was Biscay. Shielded from direct royal intervention thanks to the privileges enjoyed by the Haro family, this territory owed its autonomy not to communal resistance but to the shrewd maneuvering of its ruling dynasty. The lineage of the lords had long mastered the art of walking the tightrope that separated self-interested faithfulness and ambitious self-preservation. As lords of Biscay, they had carved for themselves a domain impervious to the kind of legislative and urbanizing onslaught that the monarchy had elsewhere unleashed. For some time, even, their blackmail might have rendered their position stronger than that of the king himself.[13]

But by the early fourteenth century, a series of ill-fated political gambles, coupled with some untimely deaths, had compromised their standing. With the male line extinguished, a woman—María Díaz de Haro—ascended as Lady of Biscay in 1289. Yet her rule, endlessly challenged and usurped by minor male relatives, was all but secure, and, by 1326, the Haros' star was seemingly declining for good. Alerted to fresh conspiracies plotted by María's own son, the self-styled lord of Biscay, and no doubt schooled in the consequences of past nobiliary insurrections, Alfonso XI acted without hesitation. The head of the Haro lineage was murdered in cold blood. Greeted by the news of her son's death, María, by then almost sixty, was called again to the forefront of Biscayne affairs. The burden she shouldered with reluctance but also with unyielding dignity. When the king tried to buy off her family's titles over the Lordship, María did not waver. As she saw it, she was the daughter, sister, and mother of lords of Biscay, and she was determined not to be the one to dilapidate the legacy of her forebears. It proved a stance that, admirable though it certainly was, did not necessarily strengthen her position. When in 1334, after having found a suitable successor in her granddaughter—also called María—she finally stepped aside, the king wasted no time. The Lordship he had failed to secure by negotiation, he would now take by force.

As Alfonso marched northward with his army, the fates seemed to smile upon his campaign. The lord of Ayala—who ruled a minor dominion on Biscay's southern frontier that the monarch had managed to place in the hands of one of his loyal agents—came to surrender his lands to the king. Just like Alava, Ayala was immediately incorporated into the Castilian apparatus of government. Yet here, unlike in Alava, the local laws and customs enforced by its assembly were left untouched.[14] In a calculated move, Alfonso XI was offering clemency and continuity to those who voluntarily bent the knee: a maneuver by which he sought to chip away at the lingering influence that the lords of Biscay could still possess. Sweeten the deal, make submission palatable, and soon even these proudly autonomous lands would come to acknowledge the king's supreme authority.

Biscayne magnates, however, would prove far less pliant to these terms than their Alavese and Ayalese counterparts. For starters, many still held fast to their ties with the house of Haro, while others, whatever their true allegiances, balked at the notion of submitting to what was, in essence, the crude law of conquest. Determined to press his claim, Alfonso paid little heed to his opponents and summoned a mock-up assembly at Guernica, the customary spot where such gatherings were held in Biscay. His agents, extorting and bribing their way out of the stalemate, then forced his declaration as lord.

The oath of allegiance he received at Guernica, for all it echoed the surrender of the Confraternity of Arriaga only two years prior, could not help but ring somewhat hollow. After all, one key figure had been conspicuously absent from the gathering. The fourteen-year-old María, who many still regarded as the true holder of the lordly title, had been smuggled away by loyalists and carried by sea to Bayonne. Moreover, there she had married Juan Núñez de Lara, one of the most powerful noblemen in all of Castile. This was all really bad news for Alfonso. Pitted against the alliance between two of the greatest noble houses in the realm, confronted with the refusal of Biscaynes to cooperate, and with his presence required by a plethora of other affairs across his kingdom, he had little alternative but to back down. Sometime later, the fugitive Lords were permitted to return to their domain. The Haros' legacy, though diminished, had managed to endure. So too had the laws of Biscay.

The constant dance of rulers, paired with the foreign origins of most of them, could hardly have inspired confidence among the freemen of Biscay. Alfonso XI, it was true, had attempted to subdue the Lordship by force, but it was no less correct to point out that Juan Núñez de Lara, the new consort ruler of the land, was an outsider all the same. Neither of them, in the eyes of many in the Lordship, could be expected to be familiar with the ancestral legacy of laws and customs so cherished by Biscaynes. This immediately prompted some fears. How could such a man be entrusted with the task of upholding these ordinances? Would he not, in ignorance or indifference, fail to enforce them properly? Worse still, would he import his own foreign ways into the country? All of which seemed, given the circumstances, foreboding prospects. With the turmoil and instability bred by the recent war still unanswered, many in Biscay still longed for clear guidance.[15]

An insecurity that those on the commanding side of things also shared. For, without knowing the precise nature of the laws and obligations that governed his post, how could a lord be sure that his own prerogatives were not being quietly undermined by all-too-knowledgeable underlings? Perhaps it was these anxieties, as they preyed upon Juan Núñez's mind, that led him to seek illumination. Beneath the tree of Guernica, where King Alfonso had recently staged his coup, he made a request. He wished for a document that would serve him as a guide to imparting justice and punishing crimes in his new dominions. Shortly after, he was presented with a little codex: the first partial version of the *fuero* of Biscay ever to be written.

And then, the plague came. The disease swept the Western Pyrenees like a wind shakes the branches of a tree. Striking from the north via the crossings of the mountain range, it had already made its presence felt in Pamplona by mid-June 1348. In short order, the humid valleys to the north were devastated, as entire villages disappeared in a matter of days either due to the death toll of the sick or the flight of the still healthy. The population of the Navarrese capital and its surroundings, enfeebled by a succession of insufficient harvests, braced themselves for what seemed to many a punishment of divine origin. First to suffer its excruciating touch were those who lived outside the walls and in the vicinity of markets, for the sickness appeared to have a particular fixation on those more prone to social intermingling. Before long, the lethal pathogen had already found its way into the city itself, hopping from host to host, from street to street, from north to south and from east to west.

Entire households were wiped out in a matter of weeks; others had to live instead in the permanent fear of infection, forced to reduce their contact with the outside world to an indispensable minimum. After all, who was to doubt that the plague had been directly conjured up from the darkest nightmares of mankind, to take advantage of their fears and instill dread in their hearts? Even its infallible virulence bore the resemblance of a reaper's unerring strike. Within days of contagion, the symptoms of the malady were already manifest: fevers, chills, malaise, delirium, and finally, amid unbearable agony, death. So gruesome was this affliction that it has been calculated that only one in three survived its course.[16]

Contemporaries found it difficult to rationalize the true scale of the destruction. In Navarre, data from the royal administration suggested that in some parts of the kingdom as many as eight out of ten of the inhabitants perished in the wake of the disease, be it due to contagion or the ensuing starvation caused by the loss of the harvest. In the outskirts of Estella, the first wave of the epidemic wiped out two-thirds of the population.[17] Further afield, dozens of small villages and hamlets were abandoned by the scant survivors and were never reoccupied. Regions like the corridor of the Araquil River—the ancient abode of the late antique *Bacaudae* and which probably lost a third of its dwellers—could be regarded, against the bleak background offered by the rest of Navarre, as relatively fortunate. In all, more than half of the population of the kingdom died between 1347 and 1349. Figures were similarly appalling in nearby regions.[18]

So, by the time the plague came back a decade later and killed another third of those that remained, the region was already on its knees. A troubadour in the court of Navarre wrote in despair that the plague

> . . . so many did it slay and devour
> That every day, in great heaps,
> One found ladies, youths,
> Adolescents and old of every kind,
> Lying dead inside the churches;
> And they were cast into great pits,
> All together, all dead from the buboes.[19]

Its devastating toll on the population notwithstanding, the epidemic also triggered massive social and political consequences. In Navarre, this manifested in the brutal enforcement of a rising taxation, aimed at making up for the rents lost as serfs and tenants either perished or fled.[20] In Castile, Alfonso XI paired a similar economic policy with an ambitious military program against Al-Andalus that brought him as far as the mighty walls of Gibraltar. Knights and their retinues, impoverished by the ensuing crisis and attracted by the prospect of loot, thronged in anticipation.

Yet Gibraltar, far from being the stage for his conquering of the crisis, would mark Alfonso's demise. Shortly after the beginning of the siege, his soldiers began to fall sick, pierced by a contagious malady that passed from one tent to the next in a matter of hours. The physicians tasked with tending to the victims immediately recognized the signs of the plague. The king, blinded by the prospect of capturing a city that dominated the entrance to the Mediterranean, chose to ignore the counsel of those who advised a retreat. Rather, he put his destiny and that of his army in God's hands. "And so, by God's will, he contracted the plague, and died on the third day."[21]

As his campaigns in Alava and Biscay had demonstrated, Alfonso XI had been a domineering figure, a ruler determined to extend the reach of his power at the expense of the entrenched networks of clients and supporters maintained by his grandees. But his death, abrupt as it had been, heralded the end of such a line of policy. His heir, the sixteen-year-old Pedro, for all that he was a chip off the old block when it came to his conception of royal power, lacked the same firm grip on the throne. Besides a realm ravaged by the plague and a high nobility alienated from the monarchy, Alfonso had likewise left Pedro, by the time of his departure from this world, a brood of illegitimate stepsiblings. One of them, Enrique Trastámara, was coincidentally a youth of the same age as the new king. And so, when Pedro, following his father's example, sought to tighten royal oversight and to curb aristocratic privileges, great magnates in search of alternatives had not to look very far. By 1352, violence between Enrique's and Pedro's supporters was already raging all over Castile.

The civil war would be a long and many-sided one, shifting between different theaters and lasting until 1369. Biscay, as a fief held by members of two of Castile's greatest noble houses—the Laras and the Haros—found itself unsurprisingly entangled in it. Twice did Pedro march upon the Lordship, and twice his enemies caved in before him. On the second occasion, in 1358, he—just like his father—managed to secure his proclamation as lord by "ten thousand" Biscaynes, who demanded to "have no other Lord in Biscay save the king of Castile."[22] Such election, no doubt, owed in large part to the battle-hardened troops accompanying the monarch, but it was also prompted by the discontent that many had started to harbor against the consequences of the rebellious line of policy so favored by their lords. Sadly for members of this faction, the shifting tides of the war made compromises weak. Going back on his word given at Guernica a decade later, King Pedro would promise Edward, the Black Prince of England, the Lordship of Biscay in return for his help against Enrique's forces, backed in turn by the French. In April 1367, Enrique was decisively defeated in pitched battle and forced to flee for his life. The legitimate king seemed at last, after fifteen years of discontinuous rule, secure on his throne.

Or was he? Finally free to act, Pedro moved swiftly to exact vengeance on those who had for so long defied him. This proved to be a murderous course indeed. Even his staunch supporters, terrified by the fury with which the monarch seemed to exercise his justice, increasingly distanced themselves from a regime that had, in appearance, cast aside any façade of moderation. However, it is also possible that, beyond morbid cruelty, Pedro's behavior was spurred by an ever more momentous reason: a preoccupying lack of funds. Amid the greatest economic and demographic crisis of the century, with his mandate tottering due to the ambitions of uncontrollable aristocrats, what choice did the king have but to appropriate the domains and resources of his erstwhile enemies?

The results rendered by such an approach, however, were pitiful. For all that he might have laid hands on the properties of some powerful lineages, Pedro was still incapable of paying off the enormous debts he had contracted. As the flow of coin that oiled up the machinery of government dried up, problems for the king and those who had helped him get the throne mounted up and up. The Black Prince, unable to face the cost of the many knights he had commanded in his Castilian campaign, retreated ignominiously back to his domains with creditors on his heels. Pedro's Castilian endorsers, unsatisfied with the rewards received in exchange for their services, abandoned his side as well. So many did so, in fact, that when Enrique, encouraged by tidings of the hardships of his rival, came back and declared himself once more the legitimate ruler of Castile, he encountered many followers in those who had grown discontent with their former candidate. Two years later, after a terrible battle, Pedro was finally captured and, under the pretense of a negotiation, struck down by Enrique in cold blood. The war was over. With the aid of France and the sponsoring of fortune, the house of Trastámara had finally gained the throne of Castile.

Though the conflict had concluded, there remained of course some loose ends in need of tidying up. The confrontation, after all, had been much more than simply a dynastic struggle between two competing branches of the royal family. Soldiers on both sides, as they spilled their blood on dozens of skirmishes and battlefields, had known they were fighting for much more than that. Pedro's authoritative leadership embodied the hopes of a whole class of clerks, jurists, and lesser nobles who were more likely to benefit from posts of responsibility in a stable royal administration. Enrique's approach, on the other hand, pandered to the mightiest individuals of the realm. Victory in the civil war was as much the triumph of the magnates' aspirations as it was his own. And for this reason, the end of the struggle would witness a wave of donations to the great nobiliary houses without parallel in Castile's long history. Lordships, estates, cities, official posts—all were gifted to his aides. Enrique, the king who had seized power on the shoulders of the aristocracy, now reigned as their debtor.

This was especially true in Alava. Here, the great families that had once monopolized the principal seats in the assemblies of Arriaga had seen their endorsement of the new sovereign generously rewarded. The Mendozas, for instance, got dominion over sixty villages, and would eventually manage to marry into the royal family.[23] The Guevaras, heirs to the ancient lineage of the Velas, were granted the Lordship of the Guipuzcoan valley of Leniz.[24] The chartered town of Villarreal was gifted to the Avendaños.[25] Examples were plentiful. Handsome sums of money were lavished upon the victors; new lands and lordships in distant regions saw them elevated to the ranks of the highest nobility. Entire cities—Balmaseda, Orduña, Labastida, Salvatierra—were handed by Enrique to his most loyal supporters in the Western Pyrenees. By the end of this process, the transformation was complete. Three-quarters of Alava lay firmly in the hands of the magnates—an astonishing reversal for a class that, only thirty years earlier, had been so uncertain of its fate that it had dissolved its own Confraternity and entrusted its lands to the king for protection.[26] Only Vitoria, a lone island of urban independence, now braved the waves in a sea ruled by the lords.

It was only fitting, then, that the task of justifying the new king's rebellion—and condoning him from the hideous crime of fratricide—should befall an Alavese nobleman, and a turncoat at that. King Pedro, in what soon became the new official stance, was said to have "killed many in the kingdom, and it was for that that he received all the harm that you have heard."[27] The toppled monarch, rather than the legitimate ruler to whom all his subjects had owed obedience, had been quite the contrary: a bloodthirsty tyrant. Such a reframing of the causes of the civil war could not but pander to the new dynasty. The Trastámaras, pitted against a despicable despot like Pedro, were not—could not—be usurpers: Their triumph, rather, was indeed the triumph of liberty. Enrique, naturally, was only too happy to espouse such a description of events.

The example of Alava, scavenged by aristocratic lineages, did not bode well for Biscaynes. Their sole saving grace was that they already were the inhabitants of a lordship and thus were protected from being cast as part of one of Enrique's bribes to the magnates. But the long civil war had left deep scars in the internal functioning of the territory. For forty years, ever since María Díaz de Haro's escape to Bayonne, Biscay's relationship to Castile had been in flux: a connection that recent events had only further complicated. Nowhere was this ambiguity more starkly revealed than in the fact that the current holder of the title of lord, who was none other than Enrique's own brother, Tello, had been unseated by the Biscaynes when their assembly had accepted Pedro. That fact alone was proof enough of the half-hearted endorsement that the new dynasty could expect from the dwellers of the Lordship. The recent past was similarly rife with embarrassing—and potentially lethal—memories.

But if the people of Biscay might have every wish of forgetting their wavering loyalties, so too did the new masters of Castile harbor their own motives for encouraging amnesia. The territory remained strategically important and embedded in the trade circuits of the north, and Enrique was currently in no mood, or position, to agitate what could rapidly become a nest of angry bees. Because of this, the new regime set out to trumpet that the assembly's decision to recognize Pedro had been void. Not only had the rightful lord, Tello, still been alive at the time but their choice had obviously been made under duress. No evidence, naturally, was offered to sustain these affirmations—for none existed. And yet, no one protested. No one objected. A willful forgetfulness settled over the land. By 1370, when the childless Tello passed away and the Lordship fell into the hands of his nephew Juan, King Enrique's son, few dared to question his entitlement to it. "And from then on the lords of Biscay and Lara all became part of the royal crown of Castile, forever and ever."[28] The ambiguity upon which generations of northern rulers had thrived was, finally, dissolved for good.

The Castilian civil war, along with the turbulent decades that preceded it, had irreversibly altered the balance of power in the Western Pyrenees. Biscay and Alava, which had previously ranked as vulnerable spots in the Castilian political tapestry, had over the course of these momentous years witnessed their structures of command incorporated into the monarchy's machinery in an unprecedented manner. The paths taken in each case might have been different, but not so the outcomes. Aristocrats in both regions now recognized the sole authority of Enrique and his lineage, and treasured feudal ties that linked them directly to the king.

The old order, by contrast, had been exhaustively dismantled. The Haros were gone; so, too, was the Confraternity of Arriaga. Yet the king's authority, weakened by the overarching crises, the long wars, and the overreliance on the high nobility, had nonetheless also been compromised. The overcentralizing ambitions of Alfonso XI and Pedro had, at best, yielded mixed results. In Biscay, local law still endured. In Alava, although their assembly had been abolished, it was once again the magnates that ran the show. Guipuzcoa barely counted at all.

In all, a dangerous vacuum had filled the Western Pyrenees. The retreat of royal authority, in a land battered by epidemics, pestered by economic recession, and riven by military strife, left a prize that would not go unclaimed for long.

The seeds of an uncertain future had been sown.

Notes

1 Cerdá y Rico, *Crónica de Alfonso el Onceno*, I, 177.
2 Ojeda, "El Señorío de Ayala durante el reinado de Alfonso XI," 58.
3 Ojeda, 54.
4 González, *Crónica de Alfonso X*, XXV, 87.
5 González, XXIII, 78.
6 Baury, "Los ricoshombres y el rey en Castilla: el linaje Haro (1076–1322)," 66–7.
7 Landazuri, *Suplemento a los Quatro Tomos de la Historia de la M.N. y M. L. Provincia de Alava*, VI, 105–6.
8 Ayerbe, *Historia del condado de Oñate y Señorío de los Guevara (s.XI-XVI)*, 280–1.
9 Landazuri, *Suplemento*, VI, 106.
10 Landazuri, VI, 116.
11 Ojeda,"El Señorío de Ayala durante el reinado de Alfonso XI," 59–61.
12 Landazuri, *Suplemento*, VII, 125.
13 Baury, "Los ricoshombres y el rey en Castilla: el linaje Haro (1076–1322)," 72.
14 Ojeda,"El Señorío de Ayala durante el reinado de Alfonso XI," 79–80.
15 Monreal, *Fuentes del Derecho Histórico de Bizkaia*, 83.

16 Harper, *Plagues Upon the Earth. Disease and the Course of Human History*, 204.

17 Salaberri, "El Euskera en la Edad Media," 312.

18 Fernández de Larrea, *Guerra y sociedad en Navarra durante la Edad Media*, 48. Also, Monteano, *La ira de Dios. Los navarros en la Era de la Peste (1348–1723)*, 42. For figures in Gascony, see Wade, *Gascony, England's first colony, 1204–1453*, 206. For an approximation to the data of Biscay, Guipuzcoa and Alava, see Tena García, *La sociedad urbana en la Guipúzcoa costera medieval: San Sebastián, Rentería y Fuenterrabía (1200–1500)*, 249–51.

19 Guillaume de Machaut, *Le Jugement dou Roy de Navarre contre le Jugement dou Roy de Behaingne*, vv. 368–73. Based upon the text by Hoepffner, *Oeuvres de Guillaume de Machaut*, 150.

20 Larrañaga, *Campesinado y conflictividad social en la Navarra bajomedieval*, 165.

21 García de Salazar, *Libro de las Buenas Andanças e Fortunas que fizo Lope García de Salazar*, 595.

22 López de Ayala, *Crónicas de los reyes de Castilla*, I, Año Noveno, Pedro I, V, 244–5.

23 Sánchez, *La casa de Mendoza hasta el tercer duque del infantado (1350–1531). El ejercicio y alcance del poder señorial en la Castilla bajomedieval*, 33–4, 302–3.

24 Minguito, "Los Guevara (siglo VIII-siglo XVI). Morir antes que ser deshonrado: proceso de consolidación de un linaje en su paso de la Edad Media a la Edad Moderna," 31–2.

25 García, "El linaje Avendaño: causas y consecuencias de su ascenso social en la baja Edad Media," 527–61.

26 García de Cortázar, "Álava, Guipúzcoa y Vizcaya en los siglos XIII a XV: de los valles a las provincias," 222–3; Tena, *La sociedad urbana en la Guipúzcoa costera medieval*, 113.

27 López de Ayala, *Crónicas de los reyes de Castilla*, I, Año Veinte, Pedro I, VIII, 557.

28 "Crónica de Vizcaya." In Aguirre, *Las dos primeras crónicas de Vizcaya*, 48–9.

CHAPTER 12
WORTH MORE

The deep valley of Leniz, like most of Guipuzcoa, stood on the brink of war. Biscay and Alava might have witnessed, during the long years of the struggle between Pedro and Enrique, their political standing as territories under Castile's control ebbing and flowing. But to the east, the mid-century crisis had had very different consequences. Rather than settling its relationship with the Castilian crown, the situation had uncovered social cleavages that prosperity had previously concealed. Now, as recession tightened its grip, these stood revealed in all their mighty dimensions. A chasm that, if it was not quickly patched up, threatened to engulf the whole of Guipuzcoa in an endless cycle of blood and vengeance.

In Mondragón and its surroundings, as it happens, the rope stood at its tensest. For nearly a century the city had grown prosperous thanks to the steady and supportive hand of a succession of monarchs. In 1262, shortly after the bourg's foundation, its council had been granted a monopoly over all the mineral wealth of their surroundings. A few years later, residents were discharged from paying tolls in most Castilian cities. Key advantages, indeed, which suggested the great interests that the location arose. For here they

> forge steel . . . , being the strongest that is known to be made anywhere, to such a degree that even if a sword or any other weapon made from this metal is reforged five or six times, with each time returning to the fire, it never loses its rigidity and strength, which . . . other steels would not do.[1]

This was the precious source from which the town's prosperity ultimately sprang, and the Mondragonese, if given the chance, were not shy about flaunting these concessions. In fact, so proud were the city bigwigs of them that it was easy to forget that some of these freedoms had been initially meant as responses to particularly terrible calamities. In 1316, for instance, a sudden fire had left the urban landscape little more than a mound of ashes and charring ruins. The following year, trying to prevent the site from being abandoned altogether, the king of Castile had been generous enough to concede an extraordinary exemption from tributes and rents for a period of fifteen years. The gamble actually paid off. Within a few short decades, Mondragón had been entirely rebuilt, including a brand-new set of walls that dwarfed the ones the fire had brought down.

However, what could, at first sight, be taken as a symbol of the vitality and accomplishments of a city could, if examined from a different standpoint, hint at the shadows that threatened it. The monarchs of Castile, in granting Mondragón its liberties and immunities, had never lost sight of the fact that—apart from steel—there had been other interests at play in its foundation: "for it is located on the border with Biscay and Oñate and Navarre, which are under other lords."[2] Protecting the frontier from the ambitions of foreign contenders had been a time-honored occupation for those living in Western Pyrenean cities, and privileges constituted the calculated counterpoint that ensured this loyalty. The population of Tolosa, in 1326, had seen most of their payments redeemed for their city "to better be guarded against the Navarrese."[3] In Fuenterrabia, on the westernmost tip of Guipuzcoa, a similar bargain had been struck. Mondragón was no exception. Its walls, a black silhouette that dominated the valley from a verdant and steep slope, stood as a magnificent reminder of the might and splendor of the monarchy that sponsored the city and safeguarded its liberties. And yet, at the same time, the fortified bulwarks told a very different story: that perhaps, for all that the Mondragonese had come to take them for granted, these freedoms might not be as secure as they assumed them to be.

As it happens, attacks from neighboring realms had grown, in the first decades of the fourteenth century, a somewhat common recurrence, with the southern border with Navarre a particularly hot spot. Yet important though these incursions certainly were, there existed other reasons for the protection granted by a wall to remain relevant. The diminishing yields and the economic hardship that had heralded the coming of the crisis had driven many, in Guipuzcoa as elsewhere, to seek their fortune in more profitable—even if illegal—means of subsistence. Bandits and brigands infested the roads. Robbers, taking full advantage of the rugged terrain, emerged from the hills, captured the grazing cattle, and then proceeded to disappear without a trace.[4] Particularly violent groups of wrongdoers, emboldened by impunity, did not wimp out and tended to respond to persecution with brutal beatings and other abuses. Dread silenced the victims. As one of them lamented, "know, that whatever thing we lose in this our county, we do not dare to say nor to denounce, for fear of having our houses burnt, and of having worse that we currently have."[5]

These, in all, were day-to-day realities in the Western Pyrenees. And yet, nowhere was the recurrence of banditry more damning for farmers and citizens alike than in borderlands like Mondragón. Here, where the authority of one lord diffused into that of another, raiders and their retinues could act with near-total impunity. And it was here, too, that theft and pillage could acquire, on occasion, a curious sheen of legitimacy. Robbers, as they crept across the border in the dead of night, looting whatever they could carry, might indeed have fashioned to cast their unlawful activities in loftier terms. To plunder an enemy, in their eyes, was no crime: It was part of the honorable service they owed their sovereign.

The victims, of course, found such an interpretation exceedingly difficult to abide by. But what choice did they have? However much they longed for the stealing of their scarce properties and the chopping down of their trees to cease, they also knew about the futility of entrusting the task to royal officers. Their jurisdictions, after all, had limits: a constraint that cutthroats understood and exploited to the full. In some places, like in the valleys straddling Guipuzcoa and Navarre, attempts had been made to concoct a response. Here, city and village councils had managed to create an international institution with authority on both sides of the frontier to bring the outlaws to their knees. But this, too, had been a short-lived solution. While the alliance had initially worked wonders in containing abuses, it had taken only the bound-to-come ramping up of hostilities between Navarre and Castile for the idea of a cooperative, overarching framework to be put aside indefinitely.[6] The crisis that engulfed the century, productive as it could be of all kinds of violence, could not be solved in the absence of mutual confidence. And in the Western Pyrenees that was a commodity in perilous short supply.

Perhaps this was the reason why so many turned to a different strategy: sheltering behind thick walls. As brigandage became more and more usual, so too did the number of petitions to create new cities surge at a similar rate. Renteria was founded in 1320; Elorrio in 1330, Marquina in 1355. All were conceived as refuges. Some peasant communities, taking matters into their own hands, opted instead for surrendering their lands to the protection of a nearby urban settlement: a sense of urgency that had justified the council of Mondragón's absorption, in 1353, of seven once-independent villages.[7] The petitioner's arguments tended to be remarkably similar, and often mentioned how they could not otherwise "defend themselves from the woes, and grievances, and robberies that they suffered" ceaselessly at the hands of "evil peoples."[8] And what did it matter whether these wrongdoers hailed from Guipuzcoa, Navarre, or beyond? Borders were a concern of kings. And banditry, when all was said and done, was banditry all the same.

Or was it? For all that law-enforcing officials might have wished to put an end to these criminal activities, there were some in the land who, rather than eye their perpetrators with reproach, contemplated them as valuable assets instead. It had long been assumed, in the Western Pyrenees as in much of Europe, that it was the duty of noblemen to protect society from its enemies—a task, of course, that required both an unwavering moral compass and an exceptional ability to exert brute force if need be. No justice could be upheld, after all, if the shadow cast by a sword did not, at times, flash menacingly over those that infringed its commandments. Seen through this lens, tempered violence might even be considered a force for good. Bandits, if placed at the disposal of an honorable lord, might indeed be redeemed.

No one better than the *Parientes Mayores*—literally, "major relatives"—to preach about the benefits that could be reaped from defending others. Their forebears had lived in a world in which family connections meant everything. Gathered in assembly, these groups of freemen had decided over all kinds of subjects affecting their lives, from inheritance laws to common defense. Yet for all that the entire community had a say in these affairs, there were of course matters which were far above anyone lacking specialized knowledge, and which only the wisest, the most trained, or the most respected could be expected to deal with satisfactorily. It was for this reason that such functions had been bestowed upon certain preeminent households, who in exchange had received a salary from the tithes collected in the local church.[9]

On a scale that would have seemed negligible to the mighty, these humble institutions followed a trajectory similar to that which had seen families like the Haros become the spokespersons of the gatherings of Guernica or the Confraternity of Arriaga. What had begun as modest payments for a service soon evolved, as contacts with neighboring monarchies and distinguished noblemen intensified, into a source of social status and distinction. Members of these families increasingly found themselves engrossing the clienteles of the great magnates, marrying their relatives, and exchanging loyalty for resources and patronage. It was they, in practice, who had ensured the territorial control that had allowed barons to play their political games and to even blackmail kings. Now, with the great noblemen of the realm far away, prowling like vultures around Enrique's court, it was also they that began to entertain ambitions far greater than simply speaking on behalf of their neighbors. They began to dream of ruling them.[10]

Half a gang boss, half an entrepreneur, the ultimate goal of a Pariente was nothing short of absolute social superiority. After all, to be the leader of a lineage meant, first and foremost, to be conscious of one's right to stand at the top of the chain. However, unlike the greatest families of the land, most of these upstarts lacked the kind of immaculate pedigree that would allow their claims to be accepted without discussion. Perhaps it was these anxieties, prompted by the lack of aristocratic extraction, that drove them to play dirty to secure every inch of recognition from their neighbors. While the property of a mill by the river might be attractive for the charges and levies that peasants were forced to pay to use it, it also had value as a means to control the water supply of those further downstream. A forge, similarly, was as much a profitable enterprise as it was a bargaining tool vis-à-vis the coastal cities, whose very survival rested on iron trade. Bridges and mountain crossings were perfect spots for toll gates; collecting timber or fruits from a Pariente's forest meant, invariably, being charged with an onerous compensation. Examples such as these, which many took for unsufferable abuses, were manifold. And as they spread further, every juncture that kept Western Pyrenean society functioning—from grain production to trade routes—was pressed, at some point, to pass through the eye of a lineage's proverbial needle.

But how had this come to pass? After all, when compared to the nobility of kingdoms like France or Castile, most Parientes could not fail but to appear as little more than parvenues. Their resources and patrimony extended little beyond their immediate geographical surroundings, and they could never dream of having a say in the highest spheres of decision-making. Theirs was hardly an impressive basis of power—nor a sufficient one. But a Pariente, like any other freeman, had more at his disposal than mere economic leverage. Principal among his assets was an ability to provide the king with soldiers for his retinues, either for peacekeeping functions in the land or as spearheads in the brutal wars of Al-Andalus or France. In such instances, monarchs would reward these services with rents and properties from the royal coffers, with the greatest prize being—as Alavese magnates knew fully well—a title over a jurisdictional lordship. Prospects, all of these, that led the Parientes, at the same time, toward a wholesale military specialization and to displays of unbreakable loyalty to the monarchy.

But as most peasants knew, a far darker alternative lurked at the bottom of a lineage's bag of tricks: to use their armed bodyguards, not to defend, but to take advantage of the locals. It was a common occurrence that groups of henchmen under the protection of a Pariente, descending without warning on the pastures of neighboring villages, would steal grazing livestock. At other times, it was the peasants themselves who were kidnapped, only later to be ransomed. Extortion proved equally profitable. Even though most freemen were not legally obliged to make use of a Pariente's mill or to cross his private bridge—and therefore to pay for it—the leader of the lineage and his armed gangs were an encouraging factor nonetheless. The threat of physical abuse could see a farmer, a family, or even an entire village entering a "truce"—in other words, an agreement to give out an assigned payment or service in exchange for military protection—aimed at bribing, precisely, those acting under the Pariente's command.[11] At any rate, this protection was not something to sniff at, and the majority would, if put to the test, rather stand on the good end of a bully's sword than risk the consequences. Perhaps, and only perhaps, steadfast loyalty to the local Pariente might be someday repaid with a fixed salary or a plot of land from the local monastery. Security and oppression were but two sides of a single coin. One which the heads of the lineages, incidentally, safely stored in their pockets.

Nowhere was the paradoxical nature of the Pariente as simultaneously a benefactor and an exploiter better showcased than in his residence. A block-shaped building garnished with the family's coat of arms, the dwelling of a head of lineage was in equal proportion a management headquarters and a stronghold. These towers, initially crafted from timber and only later expanded into stone,[12] were usually surrounded by an entire system of warehouses, stables, minor residences, and forges that provided all the assets required to conduct both economic and military activities. The largest ones, which exhibited massive walls and fortified ramparts on their summits, could harbor as many as 700 people and resembled a castle more than anything else.[13] That these facilities could either be used to grant asylum to those under a Pariente's protection in case of attack or to store away the fruits of a local gang's pillage expeditions was precisely the point. A tower was an emblem of authority: a reassuring image for those cast under its custody and a vision of dread for those who stood against it. Humid and poorly lit though it might be as a consequence of prioritizing defensive capabilities over habitability, its solid outlines nonetheless demonstrated in space the social ambitions of the lineage that raised them. Gazing upward from a road that wound through the feet of one of these constructions, the metaphor of the Parientes towering over their countrymen was hardly a metaphor at all.

Naturally, the handsome profits generated by a Pariente's endeavors only served to further cement his claim to primacy. And yet, the real standing of these characters was hardly as secure as their massive residences seemed to imply. They did not, unlike noblemen in other parts of Europe, possess a legal right over vast numbers of serfs, but this does not mean that they did not aspire to achieve something similar.[14] After all, in a world as attentive to the position of an individual in the web of service and retribution as that of medieval Europe, certain behaviors could not help but carry an entire array of social connotations. For peasants, the act of bringing their grain to a Pariente's mill and paying tribute there—whether coerced by force or lack of alternative—must have felt uncomfortably reminiscent of the feudal duties serfs owed their lord. Similarly, privileges that enshrined the right of the head of a lineage to receive seasonal gifts, like cheese in May or butter at Christmas, were less relevant for their economic impact than for what they meant to those involved. To be required to perform these gestures, so often associated with dependent status, was it not eerily similar to admitting that such status existed in the first place? Symbolic though they might have been initially, these exchanges, if repeated with regularity, could soon come to constitute something else: proof of a Pariente's de facto superiority. Insofar as legal documentation was scarce or even nonexistent in the Western Pyrenean world, it was these rituals, in their repetition, that constituted the true benchmarks of hierarchy. A hierarchy the Parientes would later seek the monarchy to validate, as "proven by the continuous reception [of these services . . . from time immemorial to this day, by just and rightful titles."[15]

Mills, roads, woods, piers: These were, for the medieval mentality at any rate, as much the vital hubs of trade and commerce as the perfect stages to display the kind of order the Parientes wanted to uphold. However, the ultimate prize—both socially and financially—was to become the patron of the local church. Be it with the compliance of their neighbors or thanks to royal concessions of privilege, many lineages had already gained the ability to collect at least a fraction of the revenue from these shrines. These rights, early on at any rate, had been considered a way of sustaining their position as a specialized class of defenders. More recently, though, the heads of the lineages had started to appropriate most of the rents and tithes for themselves, to place their sons or other relatives as priests, and to manage these places of worship as if they were their own.[16]

Uncomfortable with the idea of lay men and women having authority over religious affairs and sensing a direct attack against its sources of income, the high echelons of the church had more than once complained to the king about the situation. They had denounced that "in many churches, the Lord of Biscay, and many other knights and freemen, collected the tithe: and that . . . this was against all reason and all right because no tithe could be taken by a layman." An accusation to which the Parientes invariably retorted by invoking immemorial privileges for which, as usual, they could provide no written evidence. Their entitlement to these sanctuaries, they said, came

> from when the Moors won and conquered Spain, and the freemen, escaping from that debacle, set to establish in the mountains, which were barren and strong and hardly populated at all, and there they defended themselves from the Moors. . . . And to better defend themselves, they decided to have some leaders in their counties to lead them in the wars they had with the Moors. And to sustaining that chief or chiefs, . . . they agreed upon giving a tithe of all they labored to him.[17]

The Parientes—or so the moral of the story implied—had always protected the Western Pyrenees, and it was only natural for their descendants to rank as the most prominent among their inhabitants. The argument, simple as it was, aligned seamlessly to these families' pretensions of dominance. The monarchy, unwilling to alienate a class of warriors that commanded the adherence of many in a distant frontier, was quick to endorse these views. The bishops' pleas were ignored, the patronages stood in place, and the Parientes moved one tile closer to their objective of becoming titled lords.

Most individuals abided by these terms, but there surfaced, from time to time, occasional acts of resistance. In 1388, for example, the freemen of Oñate had had more than enough. Oñate, a chartered bourg near Mondragón, had been the only one in all Guipuzcoa forced to recognize a nobleman as its lord after King Enrique had sought to pay back the Guevara family for their service. Reproving the Pariente for trampling down their exemptions and imposing over them a grievous taxation "by force and against our will, without reason nor right," the locals now threatened to abandon the land altogether if their conditions were not met.[18] The situation was certainly exceptional. So much so that many observers suspected that the wronged dwellers of Oñate must have had some external support before undertaking such a drastic endeavor. To guess who might be plotting behind the scenes, however, was far from a difficult question.

There were many reasons for the natural antagonism between city councils and Parientes; almost as many as occasions for it to transpire. At any rate, the causes behind these confrontations were as varied as they were banal. Sometimes they had to do with property rights. In other instances, with irregularities in the appointments to juries or border patrols. At especially tense times, even the fact that a Pariente's mausoleum in the local church did not comply with previously agreed dimensions could lead to years of lawsuits and embittered disputes.[19] In the end, and for all that these matters might carry weight for those involved, they were little more than excuses that offered the chance for deep-seated differences to surface.

The reality was that the *fuero* of a city and the structure of lineage fidelity were unworkable together. Not only that, but they were almost the opposite. Whereas the town council toyed with the idea of becoming the sole authority within a given set of boundaries listed in its charter, the rule of a Pariente, manifested instead in webs of patronage and customary uses, knew not of such constraints. His main strongholds might be located in the same valley, or around a single river or monastery, but this did not mean that a Pariente understood himself as the head of a territory. In fact, he did not recognize the existence of any. As the Parientes saw it, every single one of their rights over people and resources stemmed either from custom or from royal benefits, and these were always different in each case. No single status tied together all the clients nor all possessions of a Pariente—except, of course, their direct submission to him.

How different this was in towns, where a clear-cut division was made between those who lived within and without the walls! Either one was a citizen, and therefore entitled to a series of privileges, or he was not. Physical space, more than anything else, defined belonging: A notion which in turn entailed that, within those sanctioned limits, urban authorities could not, and would not, accept any other rule but their own. Parientes might perhaps rest content with applying pressure on key points of the social and productive chain, expecting time and ingrained tradition to take their course. But cities, on the contrary, aspired to nothing short of absolute territorial dominion.

Few contemporaries, if asked, might have dared to frame the situation in such radical terms. Although the inflexible application of an urban charter might be at odds with the traditional, unwritten customs that the Parientes aspired to uphold, it was no less true that there existed many in-betweens. If competition for status and power was intense outside the walls, it was no less feverish within them. From the times of the earliest foundations, freemen and enriched individuals had sought to rule the destinies of their communities. Across the coastal towns, the slow consolidation of their power had increasingly pushed commoners away from the levers of governance.[20] But supremacy, once attained, demanded constant vigilance. Just like the Parientes in the rural areas, the preeminence of urban families depended on their ability to secure posts and revenues for their supporters, and these were especially scarce in a city. In some places, like San Sebastian, the hegemony of a particularly rich and esteemed family allowed for the distribution of honors to be conducted in relative concord. More common, however, was for rival factions to jostle for rank, each determined to advance along the greasy pole of achievement.[21] Competition, just like it did in the countryside, could on such occasions rapidly degenerate in the emergence of opposing alliances. These, in turn, rarified the political climate of the town and threatened its correct functioning.

A tried and tested solution to the perils occasioned by these strains was to double the number of offices and then to divide them evenly between the two most dominant factions in a city. On the surface, this seemed an elegant compromise: It kept the urban government firmly in the hands of the elite while, at the same time, it minimized the chances of violent conflagration. But in the final reckoning, the entire agreement hinged upon the maintenance of an exquisitely delicate balance. It took only a faction's fortune to falter—be it due to internal disagreements, ruinous businesses, or any other cause—before its members would look beyond the city walls for assistance from a powerful Pariente to buttress their position. It was so, in ways that no charter could have entirely anticipated, that many cities had come to appear yet another playground for the competition between Parientes to be staged. The old ways, despite their institutional sidelining, might indeed still be capable of trampling the *fuero* of a bourg.

Which was why, in the search for those behind the rebellion of Oñate, eyes had immediately turned to Mondragón. The suspicion was well merited. For decades, a succession of mayors had waged a shadow war against the master of the nearby Lordship, and this despite the fact that one of the most important families of the city, the Báñez de Artazubiaga, was declared allies of the latter.[22] The Mondragonese had, with deliberate intent, welcomed enemies of the Guevaras into their midst, and villages vulnerable to this family's influence had been sheltered under the city's charitable wing.[23] The lords of Oñate had answered to these provocations with force, issuing challenges against members of the council and cautioning public officials about the consequences of their actions. For both sides, it was fear—of losing privileges and property, of coming to be ruled by the designs of others—that fueled their hardly veiled hostility. Now, the episode of 1388 threatened yet another outburst of strife in an already tension-packed relationship.

But if cities and peasants could, on occasion, menace to thwart a Pariente's hopes, these were hardly the only obstacles on the path that led to social domination. Just as two suns could not share the sky, nor two territorial predators the same forest, so too was a nobleman ill-disposed to suffer the presence of anyone who could cast his accomplishments in the shade. Competition—over resources, over status—was, in the final reckoning, the principle upon which a Pariente's entire existence was founded. Insofar as honor was compromised, no issue was so banal, no means so vile, no victory so pyrrhic, that it could make withdrawing from conflict an acceptable course of action. To be "worth more" than their compatriots: Therein lay, summarized, the doctrine by which the aspiring lords of the Western Pyrenees had always lived—and for which they were ready to die.

A declared refusal to endure comparison with others was a creed that tied both the mighty and the insignificant, and this in turn rendered the careful calculation of one's standing in society the most crucial of matters. The greatest Parientes would commission stories, poems, and songs that narrated the lives of the mighty founders of their lineages and their households. The Guevaras themselves, with particular immodesty, boasted the existence of records that demonstrated that their house had been "counts in Guevara before there were kings in Castile."[24] Other lineages, the precise circumstances of their rise to prominence either lost or purposefully forgotten, simply insisted that their origins dated back to time immemorial.[25] Put it in this way, and for all that the fog of history might have erased their memory, both their own ancestry and that of the rights over which they claimed possession could very well have seemed as old as time itself.

Memory and history could thus readily become, when one's prestige was on the line, a sort of battlefield. Yet no metaphorical battlefield was ever more decisive than the real thing. When the benefits to be reaped from conflict justified it, Parientes could exhibit little qualm in turning what had initially been a dispute over economic or social matters into outright violence. Pitched battles, raids against the properties of an enemy's supporters, the siege or the burning of a fortified tower: These were events that had become, in recent decades, the stuff of life in the Western Pyrenees. Here, just like elsewhere in Europe, the crisis of the century had raised the stakes. The Parientes, watching their resources dwindle, saw more clearly than ever the importance of holding tightly the grip of power. A trade route, a forge, a monastery—any of these could, in such troubled times, mark the difference between supremacy and utter annihilation. And if securing them meant violence, then they would not be afraid to make use of it.

Never did it occur to the Parientes, though, that they stood not on the side of angels. For all that war might be framed as a necessary evil, these individuals always strived to frame their exploits as legitimate. One of them, reflecting upon an entire career of bloodshed and coercion, could still find solace in the fact that he had "never carried out a war against anyone in the world . . . for arrogance's sake but to maintain his and his lineage's honor, nor had he ever broken truces with his adversaries," nor slain any man who had not willed his own death first.[26] These were not alibis. They established that payback and retribution, rather than being stimulated by greed, were instead imperatives imposed by a scrupulous code of conduct. One that took for granted that to be "worth more," in the end, was justification enough.

This code not only applied to the Parientes themselves. To claim that only the heads of the great households lived by such maxims would be to misrepresent truth, for many among the rural population looked favorably upon their actions. When, on the occasion of the death of a member of the lineage, brides and widows would set to chant lamentations in front of the victim, scratching their faces with their fingernails and caressing the hair of the deceased, these soon would find an echo among the common folk. When one of these women declared that she would take a dart in one hand and a torch in the other and would set an entire valley on fire to avenge the murder of her husband, no one doubted her sincerity.[27] Few, similarly, felt that she was not entitled to her vendetta. Solidarity and protection were, after all, as much what the Parientes offered as what they expected from their dependents. To serve a powerful patron resolutely, to fight his skirmishes, or to tend his cattle were, in their own way, a means of survival, of belonging, and of feeling honored. Perhaps, even, a path for the whole community to be "worth more."

Naturally, as overt military action became increasingly the norm, the Parientes began to seek allies to back their claims with force. So it was that *bandos* were born. A great network of allegiances that often divided all the Parientes within a territory into two opposing sides, a *bando* was less a formal coalition than a sort of reiterative collaboration prompted by fear of being overwhelmed by enemies.[28] Collaborations, however, had a tendency to harden. The more abuses were exchanged, the deeper the wounds; the deeper the wounds, the greater the impossibility of reconciliation. In time, the gulf between competing *bandos* could yawn so wide that it could even mean taking different sides in a civil war, as proven by the case in Biscay, where one side had supported King Pedro while the other had pledged itself to the house of Trastámara.[29]

No amount of common suffering, though, was ever enough to maintain the loyalty of so many local potentates. A *bando*, like the lineage it mirrored, functioned not just through mutual protection, but through well-oiled patronage too. The greatest Parientes lavished rewards, secured positions, dispensed justice, and in return received what mattered most: recognition of their supremacy. That expectations in this regard were often met is evidenced by the fact that it was never necessary to go beyond these informal structures.[30] Indetermination of this kind, it is true, rendered *bandos* contradictory and prone to jealousies and betrayals by unsatisfied members.[31] But for all their instability, to be the leader of a *bando*—be they those of Gamboa and Oñaz in Guipuzcoa and Alava, Butrón and Avendaño in Biscay, or Agramont and Beaumont in Navarre—meant to stand at the apex of the political and social ladder of the land. It was to be, beyond dispute, the greatest Pariente Mayor of them all.

To reiterate, social superiority was everything for a Pariente: the basis of his power, the foundation of his status, the justification of his self-image. It was too, crucially, what the freemen of Oñate had challenged directly in 1388 with their rebellion. By framing the actions of their lord as illegal abuses, they had tried to question the right of the house of Guevara to treat them as resources to be exploited. But, at the same time, in threatening these prerogatives, they had left themselves open to the wrath of a nobleman for whom this mattered more than life. With the honor and renown of his house called into question, who was to doubt that the lord of Oñate would act decisively? The ensuing repression, as it happens, vindicated these predictions. Rather than putting an end to the oppressions denounced by the leaders of the uprising, the aftermath of the rebellion served only to exacerbate them. The soldiers of the lineage and his allies, making use of the same violence that the freemen had so vehemently complained about, forced them back to their lands. Sentences of exile and expropriations ensued. Any talk of improving living conditions was silenced.

The lord of Oñate, having thus prevailed in the face of those who had made "gatherings and gangs and conspirations" against him, could rest satisfied.[32] In successfully defending his privileges, he had demonstrated his entitlement to them just as much as his mutinous vassals, as their claims came to naught, had failed in safeguarding their liberties. Freedom, in the medieval world, was never an abstraction, but a mirror pointing directly at the subjection of others. That, by standing atop the social chain, anyone was meant, invariably, to cast others into shadow was, by the late fourteenth century, what had always been: a self-evident truth. No society, it was believed, could function without a clear-cut distinction between superiors and inferiors. The starker the division, the clearer the boundaries, the more society would necessarily stand in order. That a farmer in a pitiful plot of land or an artisan working in a city would dare to rank as an equal to a Pariente was simply a subversion of all the laws, both human and natural. A person's worth, just as it could surge upward to touch the skies, could as easily decline so as to barely rise from the mud.

Only fools—or so the Parientes believed—could think otherwise.

Notes

1 Garibay, *Los XL libros del Compendio Historial de las Chronicas y universal Historia de todos los reynos de España*, XV, XV, 971.

2 Crespo et al., *Colección documental del Archivo Municipal de Mondragón (1260–1400)*, 16.

3 Roldán, *Colección Diplomática el Archivo Municipal de Tolosa (1256–1407)*, 11.

4 Azkarate and García, "Las casas-torre bajomedievales. Análisis sistémico de un proceso de reestructuración espacial/territorial," 17.

5 Zabalo, "Una encuesta de 1349 sobre bandoleros navarros y guipuzcoanos," 494.

6 García, *Gobernar la ciudad en la Edad Media: Oligarquías y élites urbanas en el País Vasco*, 296. Also, Tena, *La sociedad urbana en la Guipúzcoa costera medieval*, 224–5. Also, Díaz de Durana and Fernández de Larrea, "La frontera de los malhechores: Bandidos, linajes y villas entre Álava, Guipúzcoa y Navarra durante la Baja Edad Media," 186.

7 Crespo et al., *Colección documental del Archivo Municipal de Mondragón (1260–1400)*, 25.

8 Martínez, "Poblamiento y Ordenamiento Jurídico en el País Vasco. El Estatuto Jurídico de la población rural y urbana," 154.

9 Díaz de Durana, *La otra nobleza: escuderos e hidalgos sin nombre y sin historia. Hidalgos e hidalguía universal en el País Vasco al final de la Edad Media (1250–1525)*, 124–5. Also, Marín, "¿Qué es un Pariente Mayor? El ejemplo de los señores de Oñaz y Loyola," 224. Also, Marín, *"Semejante Pariente Mayor." Parentesco, solar, comunidad y linaje en la institución de un pariente Mayor en Guipuzcoa: los señores del solar de Oñaz y Loyola (siglos XIV-XVI)*, 86–8, 89.

10 Marín, "Semejante Pariente Mayor," 137–8. Also, Achón, "Los Parientes Mayores," 228–9.

11 Tena, *La sociedad urbana en la Guipúzcoa costera medieval*, 180–2.

12 Azkarate and García, "Las casas-torre bajomedievales," 20.

13 Aguirre, *Lope García de Salazar. El primer historiador de Bizkaia (1399–1476)*, 58.

14 Aguirre, 138.

15 The text comes from a lawsuit between the inhabitants of Berástegui and Elduayen and the lord of Berástegui (1536). In Díaz de Durana, *La otra nobleza*, 151.

16 Marín, "¿Qué es un Pariente Mayor?" 224. Also, Díaz de Durana, *La otra nobleza*, 158. Also, Martínez, *Casa, Provincia, Rey. Para una historia de la cultura del poder en el País Vasco*, 238.

17 López de Ayala, *Crónicas de los reyes de Castilla*, II, XI, 326–33.

18 Ayerbe, *Historia del condado de Oñate y Señorío de los Guevara (s. XI-XVI)*, App., 11, 40.

19 Ayerbe, *Documentación medieval del Archivo Municipal de Azcoitia (m.s. XIII-1500)*, 77.

20 Díaz de Durana, *La otra nobleza*, 99.

21 Díaz de Durana, 101.

22 Aragon, "Linajes urbanos y Parientes Mayores en Guipúzcoa a finales de la Edad Media (1450–1520)," 272.

23 Ayerbe, *Historia del condado de Oñate*, 280–1, 293.

24 García de Salazar, *Libro de las Buenas Andanças*, 705.

25 Fernández de Larrea and Díaz de Durana, "La construcción de la memoria: de los linajes a las corporaciones provinciales en Álava, Guipúzcoa y Vizcaya," 145.

26 García de Salazar, *Libro de las Buenas Andanças*, 888–9.

27 Garibay, *Los siete libros de la progenie y parentela de los hijos de Estevan de Garibay*, I, 9, 174–5.

28 Orella, "Territorio y sociedad en la Guipuzcoa medieval: Los parientes mayores," 68–9.

29 Laborda, *El Señorío de Vizcaya. Nobles y fueros (c.1452–1727)*, 103–4.

30 Achón, "Los Parientes Mayores," 230.

31 Dacosta, *Los linajes de Bizkaia en la Baja Edad Media: Poder, parentesco y conflicto*, 337–8. Also, Díaz de Durana and Dacosta, "La dimensión social del liderazgo del linaje: solidaridad, poder y violencia (País Vasco, siglo XV)," 99.

32 Ayerbe, *Historia del condado de Oñate*, App., 12, 50–1.

CHAPTER 13
ERASING OUR NAMES FROM THE LAND

Mondragón, 1448. The city was in flames. Spires of smoke floated over the narrow valley and the dense fragrance of charred wood permeated the ambience. Days earlier, urban factions, in support of the interests of the lord of Oñate or against them, had vied for control of the city. One of these factions had turned for aid to Gómez González de Butrón, a powerful Pariente, and had thus granted him an excuse to burst inside the walls. Going "with as many as he could gather," his forces had easily dispatched the makeshift resistance mounted by the city's authorities.[1] Yet lineage alliances being what they were, and competition over resources and status as fierce as it was, such exceptional situation was not to last. The Guevaras and their allies, rushing to relieve their own clique, had made their presence felt, and a bloody skirmish had raged over the city.

However, Gómez González de Butrón had not given up; what is more, he had set a trap. He knew that if he could hold Mondragón against an enemy that vastly outnumbered his troops, reinforcements would soon arrive. The enemy would be left with only two choices—withdrawing or being annihilated. Two days later, the tidings that the head of the Butrón lineage had been waiting for reached the besieged defenders. The Parientes of his *bando* were on their way to their rescue. The lord of Oñate, albeit reluctantly, would have to retreat.

But the hopes of Gómez González were to be tragically thwarted. His foes, upon learning of the reinforcements and "seeing that they could not take it by force, set fire to the town." The strategy was as ruthless as it was effective. Like a pest control patrol waiting patiently outside a nest for the desperate animals to emerge, so the head of the Guevaras awaited the moment the Pariente of Butrón would realize the futility of his defiance. Unfortunately for those involved, he had misjudged his foe. Butrón would not yield. Instead, he dispatched the Pariente of Unzueta to fortify a nearby forge just beyond the city walls in preparation for a final stand. Meanwhile, he would try to put out the fires that devoured the buildings and rooftops of Mondragón.

Beyond the walls, the situation was no less fraught. Not only was the besieging army nervous at the prospect of approaching reinforcements: There were also moral dilemmas of a more personal order. As it happens, one of the main leaders on the side of the Guevaras was Martin de Olaso, who, by a twist of fate, happened to be the son-in-law of the encircled Gómez González. The close family relationship, naturally, pulled in a very different direction than did the logic of lineage ideology. Torn between duty and kinship, Martin faced an agonizing decision, but at last came up with a solution. After writing a hasty safe-conduct, he entrusted it to a servant to carry the missive to the burning city. As the servant made its way toward the smoky silhouette of the walls, Martin was certain of having had a stroke of genius. His plan promised to spare the life of his relative and yet not threaten the capture of the city by the head of his *bando*.

A compromise which, in light of what followed, only served to make matters worse. The servant, approaching the walls, found himself intercepted by the scouting party of the Pariente of Unzueta. "I bring a letter for Gómez González de Butrón"—the man explained—"from Martin de Olaso, his son-in-law." It was at this precise moment, amid the asphyxiating clouds of ash that ceaselessly elevated from the burning houses, that one of the most perfidious and treacherous deeds in the annals of lineage memory was to take place. For the Pariente of Unzueta, making himself pass for Gómez González, claimed the letter of safe conduct for himself and vanished from the battlefield. Having received no tidings of the entire affair, Gómez González finally set out for the forge where he had expected to make a stand. He found it, to his surprise and his calamity, unfortified and unmanned. Then the enemy—among them Martin of Olaso, by now assured by his servant that his father-in-law had safely escaped—rushed to the attack. Gómez González was butchered, alongside many of his supporters. For the first time in history, a Pariente Mayor, the head of one of the great lineages of Guipuzcoa, was killed in pitched battle. And of the mighty city of Mondragón nothing remained but a black silhouette at the bottom of the valley.

By 1448, when the Parientes staged their duel over Mondragón, more than a century had passed since the beginning of the wars between *bandos*. Social unrest, although not always erupting in direct confrontation, remained barely over the flotation line. Now, once again, this line appeared to have been crossed.

Violence touched every sphere of society, and even among popular classes, honor remained a delicate thing. A servant, for instance, might be murdered for no greater crime than asking a group of mariners to lower their voices.[2] Weddings, funerals, and other festivities that brought emotions to the surface were particularly prone to ending up coming to fists or daggers. A feuding that was not only spontaneous but also systematic. When in 1480 a Pariente was denounced for having "corrupted and deflowered one hundred and fifty maidens, young girls, as the oldest would have been fourteen or fifteen years old," this served as a reminder that where law was no stronger than the alliances of kin, brutality flourished unchecked.[3] Not even the most sacred occasions offered a respite from violence. In 1320, on Christmas Eve, a Pariente's tower was put to the torch. The magnate, jumping "out of bed in his nightshirt through a window into the river that flow[ed] beneath the house," had barely managed to escape. Others were not so fortunate. Among those who perished was his twelve-year-old brother—slain in the arms of his mother.[4] Needless to say, these were not the kind of vendettas that were ever put to rest.

And yet, for all that violence had long been the order of the day, the mid-fifteenth century had witnessed a fever pitch of private wars and criminal activities. In Mondragón, for example, a public challenge issued by one of the city's leading lineages had plunged the community into a vicious domestic confrontation that had only ceased in 1447.[5] The town's convulsions, at least partially, mirrored a general trend. The very same year of the burning of the city, another chartered bourg in Guipuzcoa—Segura—had also been illegally occupied by a Pariente Mayor who saw it as his right to rule over its townsfolk.[6]

A chronicler, surveying in hindsight the appalling state of the realm, admitted that "there were more wars, civil seditions, and upheavals in [this] time than ever before in the kingdoms of Castile and Leon."[7]

The *bandos* thrived under such conditions. The absence of a firm royal hand to restrain them was, after all, a prerequisite of their own existence. It was that which allowed them to poise as the king's soldiers and to reap handsome benefits for doing so; it was that which ensured that their raids and oppressions would go unpunished; it was that which rendered their potential rivals—particularly city councils—fragile and vulnerable. A bitter irony, then, that these decades, which otherwise coincided with the moment when the region was finally coming out of the economic crisis of the previous century, were paradoxically the most unstable. Prosperity had brought new incentives for conflict. Competition had become more acute. The opportunity to gain a lordship, for the Parientes, must have seemed tantalizingly within reach.

Of course, more than a century of unbridled violence had forced their opponents to step up their resistance. The move for the creation of *Hermandades*—"Brotherhoods"—emerged in full force after the Trastámaras' rise to the throne of Castile, but their origins could be traced back even further.[8] Back then, they had probably been little more than alliances of towns, villages, and local authorities united in a single purpose: ensuring justice and persecution against bandits. It was under the guise of an *Hermandad*, for example, that the short-lived effort to stop violent incursions between Guipuzcoa and Navarre had been born. Some of these collaborations could be large-scale, as was the formidable Brotherhood of the Seas, founded in 1296 and which included Vitoria plus every coastal city from Santander to Fuenterrabia. Others, on the contrary, were small, limited to a handful of neighboring settlements.

And yet, there tended to be more to these alliances than simply their stated purpose of apprehending criminals. When the Brotherhood of the Seas was created, it was not merely to keep vessels safe in a dangerous, conflict-riven ocean but also to serve as a political weapon. In uniting their strength, these towns had sought to balance the influence of the nobility, always plotting to erode urban franchises. With their own officials, budgets, and regulations, the largest Brotherhoods aspired, from their inception, to much more than being assemblies of preoccupied weaklings. Rather, they wanted to become valid players in the highest spheres.

In a sense, this made the *Hermandades* the heirs of a venerable tradition. The notion that those with a stake on the decisions of government were entitled to have a say in their development was a time-honored one in the Western Pyrenees. The assemblies of the confreres of Arriaga or of the freemen of Biscay had aimed at serving as channels for the qualms and ambitions of those they represented, just as the Brotherhoods now sought to do. To the Parientes, both kinds of assembly had been the paramount stages upon which their claims to supremacy were displayed and acknowledged. Elected as deputies by their clients and communities, they had used these gatherings as platforms to further their goals. Here, they could see themselves—and be seen by others—as the biggest fish in their ponds. After all, a man's true worth could only be gauged in the company of his peers.

Despite these echoes from the past, Brotherhoods differed from previous parliaments in three key respects. First, their authority emanated from above. Be it the king or the lord of Biscay, it was only the ruler that could ratify the ordinances and decisions the *Hermandad* sought to uphold. This did not mean, of course, that monarchs could impose their will heedless of discordant voices, but it granted them a freer hand in governance than the ancient laws ever did. Second, these assemblies were not the exclusive domain of an aristocracy of householders. Chartered bourgs, too, had a seat at the table and a vote in the decision—an acknowledgment of their jurisdiction that the Parientes had no other choice but to stomach. And, finally, the mandate of Brotherhood was conceived as a territorial one, stretching uniformly over all the lands and peoples under their charge.

Insofar as it mirrored the *fuero* of a city in this last point, a *Hermandad*—if permitted to follow their logic to its fullest extent—also threatened the means of social control set in place by the Parientes. Vassals of the king though they were, they saw it as their duty to stand as the voice of their communities before the monarch, and any institution that could challenge this role was, by default, met with suspicion. While they might attend a Brotherhood's meetings and even try to monopolize its offices and appointments as coveted markers of status, no magnate ever felt truly bound to its fate. The king might decree the establishment of a *Hermandad*, yet in the last reckoning it fell to the Parientes themselves to make sure that its effectiveness remained as limited as possible.

Other deputies, and particularly those elected by chartered towns, were nonetheless unwilling to cede ground so easily to the ambitions of the greatest families, and before long a fateful battle for control of these Brotherhoods and their prerogatives was set in motion. In those places in which the Parientes held the reins of power, these quickly became rather ineffectual, spiritless institutions. On the contrary, where urban centers had a larger territorial projection and the magnates were either disorganized or of more modest standing, like in Guipuzcoa, the *Hermandad* swiftly fell into the hands of urban patricians.

In fact, town oligarchies—especially in Guipuzcoa's coastal municipalities—were not gutless operators daunted by the intimidating displays of the Parientes. Far from it. Most members of the urban elite, rather than seeing in a career of arms the culmination of their ambitions, had always been preoccupied with broadening their investments, securing socially and economically advantageous marriages, and embedding themselves within the mechanisms of local administration. Insofar as they pushed forward the rights and privileges of their communities, they did so as a means of extending their own. Over time, these circuits of interest had put many of them in contact and had fostered an increasing sense of sympathy and shared ambitions. A camaraderie which had ended up making them aware of how different their lifestyles were from those of the lineages that ruled the unchartered countryside.

This growing sense of solidarity among their leading families was precisely what had pushed city councils in Guipuzcoa to collaborate with each other. Careful businessmen as they were, they could all recognize that to surrender their autonomy to strengthen the *Hermandad* might end up being, if they played their cards well, a very good deal. By the late fourteenth century, the Brotherhood of Guipuzcoa had already become, under their management, an instrument to extend their reach at the expense of both the peasantry and the Parientes. These assemblies had sanctioned, for example, the marginalization of the magnates, stripping them of offices and failing to show them the respect they so eagerly craved. The Parientes, threatened with irrelevance, responded by mobilizing their supporters and working behind the Brotherhood's back. Guipuzcoan society split in two: on the one side, the self-styled virtuous, peaceful dwellers of the bourgs; on the other, "the knights, squires, and the chieftains of the land."[9]

The favorable conditions encountered by urban authorities in Guipuzcoa were not necessarily applicable to the rest of the Western Pyrenees. Elsewhere, circumstances happened to conspire to prevent towns from asserting a similar degree of control. In Alava or Navarre, for example, the upheavals of the age had placed many bourgs under the control of noblemen. Others had never possessed the economic strength nor the political privileges necessary to challenge the preeminence of local barons to begin with. The relentless factionalism of the urban *bandos*, supported by neighboring chieftains, was a constant presence in these towns, and one which threatened to tear the social fabric apart and weakened any sense of civic pride. Be it as it may, the end result was the same. Those who, contemplating the successes of Guipuzcoa's urban oligarchies, had sought to emulate them were in for a bitter disappointment.

Those systematically excluded from municipal offices by the entrenched lineages needed not the sight of flame-engulfed Mondragón to be convinced of the benefits of getting rid of the prevailing order. As early as 1435, amid a brutal confrontation between local parties, the king's appointed representative had been sent to Bilbao to erase the root of the problem. He did not act alone. Merchants and prosperous townsmen, eager to unshackle themselves from the grip of the principal families, put their case in stark terms. Under the prevailing system, they argued, citizens were forced to court the favor of the lineages to access the city's upper echelons. To bring such a pitiful situation to an end, they proposed a radical solution: to abolish these alliances altogether. Everyone in the city, from the mayor to the pettiest commoner, was to be explicitly forbidden from maintaining bonds of loyalty to the most prominent houses. Paying homage to a Pariente would be deemed a major crime. Every post in the government of Bilbao should be filled through a system explicitly devised to render alliances with the magnates politically inoperative. In all, the goal of these measures could not have been clearer: to sever the city, as much as possible, from the destructive logic of lineage warfare. Insofar as this was its objective, it was hard not to consider the entire experiment an utter failure. Amid the increasingly polarized climate of the region, they must have appeared a sort of utopia, an outlandish method that did not take into account the limitations imposed by reality. And yet, at the same time, it constituted a reminder of the deep resentment that some urban factions harbored against the Parientes.

If there was any land where the forces of the bourgs and the magnates were evenly matched, this was Biscay. Here, cities were not only numerous but, in telling examples such as Bilbao, Bermeo, or Durango, of key economic and social importance. Unlike Guipuzcoa, the Lordship was also home to a large number of villages and communities not ruled by city councils but rather by a fractious class of middle-ranking, quarrelsome freemen. The name given to these lands—*Tierra Llana*, "flatland"—was less a recognition of its geography, rocky and mountainous, than of their lack of special privileges. For in them it was not law nor royal decrees that were obeyed, but the kind of customary norms that had once governed all of northern Iberia. Slowly eroded and rooted out by dozens of royal clerks, judges, and legislators, these traditions had elsewhere been lost. Only in the *Tierra Llana* of Biscay could such a system still be said to function in earnest. An immemorial tradition, for the most part orally transmitted, and for this reason rather malleable to circumstance. In other words, a fertile soil for a Pariente's aspirations.

Which is not to say that the *Tierra Llana* was a social paradise of sorts, ever encroached against any royal meddling. In fact, just as in Guipuzcoa, it was initially Biscaynes themselves who in 1394 had appealed to their Trastámara master to request the creation of a Brotherhood "because the wrongdoers were many . . . and the old law of the land did not suffice to chastise them."[10] A sizable portion of its inhabitants must have welcomed the news that the forces of the *Hermandad*, under the command of an energetic royal appointee, had trampled down the towers of some particularly unruly Parientes. The age of unchecked impunity—or so it must have seemed to those involved—was in Biscay, just as in Guipuzcoa, drawing to a close.

These hopes, though, were not bound to come to fruition. While the Biscayne *Hermandad* had shown some success in curbing the abuses of the most predatory Parientes, it was not destined to become the source of political transformation it was in Guipuzcoa. Royal bureaucrats, supportive in the eastern territory of the ambitions of city oligarchies to extend their authority, dared not to challenge so directly the leaders of the Biscayne *Tierra Llana*. As they recognized, the balance between the two sides was, for all that the newly formed Brotherhood appeared to have tilted it in favor of the bourgs, too delicate to undermine without reason. The Parientes, at any rate, seem to have reached a similar conclusion. The leading Biscayne urban oligarchies, on the other hand, perhaps did not.

In 1415, with starvation and scarcity once again preying upon the land, the Brotherhood accused the king's representative in Biscay of having smuggled grain out of the Lordship, and taking matters into its own hands, it set out to punish the offender. The royal appointee, gazing directly at the abyss, was left with no alternative but to summon the Parientes of the *Tierra Llana* to his aid. The defeat of the *Hermandad*, when it came later that year, was momentous. Two of its highest-ranking officials, along with many of its men, were left to rot on the field.[11] The power of the Brotherhood was shattered. The attempt at wrestling the control of the countryside away from the lineages was stamped out. The lord's administration, left with no other choice, was compelled—if not openly, then in practice—to accommodate itself to the interests of the Parientes.

So it was that Brotherhoods had attempted with varied fortune to stop the *bandos*. In most places, with the exception of Guipuzcoa, they proved mostly powerless to do so. Attacks, challenges, raids, and sieges continued on all fronts. The king, in need of both soldiers and loot, did not hesitate to pander to the Parientes and to reward them for their military assistance with land, payments, and privileges that only nourished their ambitions. The more city oligarchies sought, through their representatives in the

Hermandad, to regulate as many aspects of the social and economic life of its inhabitants as they could, the more the Parientes responded with resistance and outright aggression. Any attempt to diminish their social esteem was rebuked on the grounds that they were faithful vassals of their king and lord. Any attack upon their properties or rights was opposed either by force or lawsuit. And, while this was going on, the Parientes continued to press their advantage. Tribute was extracted, rivals were extorted, challengers were confronted. Let the Brotherhood protest as it might—some of them must have thought. In the end, its delegates would be left with no alternative but to recognize them for what they already were: a breed of men above the rest.

Mondragón, however, had broken something. The events had been too polemic, the behavior of the Parientes too rushed and reckless, the consequences too stark and horrendous to simply gloss over them as if nothing had happened. The head of a major lineage had died in battle; a chartered city had ended up a pile of charred rubble. These were the kinds of calamities that even a distant and distracted king could not overlook. A royal commission was immediately dispatched to inquire about the episode, and its verdict was categorical. The Guevaras were condemned "to death by drowning, each with weights tied around their necks. Their other noble accomplices were to suffer the same fate, and those who were not nobles were to be hanged."[12]

The culprits were doomed—or so it seemed. For in Castile, a realm that had proven so prone to backstabbing and factionalism, there was no charge so shameful and no treason so overt that it could not be tempered by the soothing hand of self-interest. Enemies, if treated with affection and forgiveness, could even be transformed into allies—and loyal allies were always in short supply. Less than a year later, most of the accused had already been exonerated from their charges. Justice, as ever, had bowed to the demands of power.

Such a brazen display of impunity did not, at any rate, fall well with city oligarchies and representatives of the *Hermandad* of Guipuzcoa, who quickly took action to exact as much retribution as possible from the Parientes. In 1450, they obtained from the king a document that legally forbade any person in the *Hermandad*-administered territory from taking part in the truces of the lineages. Then, in the following year, the forces of the Brotherhood razed two fortified towers near Mondragón.[13] More strongholds would be toppled in 1455 and again in 1456. The mightiest Parientes, brought to accept that this time, perhaps, their aura of prestige alone would not be enough to shield them from the vindictive actions of the Brotherhood, tried to poise staunchly as loyal vassals of the sovereign and dutiful servants of the *Hermandad*. But the Brotherhood's wrath, ignited as it was by the memory of Mondragón's burning, could not be fooled. A dam had been broken. The people now craved justice. And for the urban lineages of Guipuzcoa, the hour finally seemed ripe to break the authority of the Parientes for good.

Maybe it was in recognition of this fact that an almost-miraculous event took place in July 1456. For generations, the greatest families had conducted an implacable struggle to determine who among them was "worth more." Wealth, power, esteem—all rested for the Parientes upon this ideal of shared honor. No expense nor thought had been withheld in the pursuit of superiority. But now, it was not a particular family, nor a single house, nor an individual Pariente that was threatened with annihilation, but an entire worldview. For those who took for granted that not all men were born equals, the attacks of the *Hermandad* could not but threaten doom upon all that was sacred and good. With the erasure of their laws and the king rejecting their supremacy, the Parientes would have become pariahs in a world governed by councilors and petty merchants. From the standpoint of a magnate that felt himself entitled to respect, this was the ultimate in humiliations. Reaction, therefore, was inescapable.

> For having formed brotherhoods or alliances and conspiracies against [us], and for having made them destroy [our] strongholds, killing [our] relatives and taking [our] goods, and for turning [us] against the King, and ultimately for having tried to ruin [us] and erase [our] names from the land, and for attempting to take [our] churches and monasteries and for many other reasons . . . , and by the nature, superiority, and loyalty that we owe to the said lord King, it is our right . . . to turn friendship into enmity against you, and to challenge you, and to wage war and cruel destruction upon your persons and goods, as enemies of our said lord King.[14]

The text of the challenge, nailed at the doors of the chartered city of Azpeitia, reverberated across the land. The glove had been thrown. The old ways would not die without a fight.

A challenge such as this, which threatened those who had most earnestly opposed the ambitions of the Parientes with war and ruin, was naturally one that no self-respecting authority could leave unanswered. The king of Castile, a man named Enrique IV, resolved to march northward to put an end to the turmoil in Guipuzcoa. But what would he do? On the one hand, the challenge was an overt declaration of private war and an intolerable threat to communities and institutions the sovereign himself had long endorsed. On the other hand, as the example of the perfidious burning of Mondragón and its aborted consequences had shown, the Parientes were adept at swaying the royal will while pushing forward their cause. As Enrique made his way north to Vitoria, all rested in the balance. Parientes and urban oligarchs all caught their breath.

In the event, the king would decisively take the side of the wronged town authorities.

> In the year of our Lord 1457, the Brotherhoods of the province of Guipuzcoa rose up against all the major families . . . because they committed and allowed many robberies and wrongdoings in the land, on the roads, and everywhere. And they made them pay for all the misdeeds and demolished all their strong houses, not leaving a single one in the entire province. . . . And they took away all the members of their retinues, leaving not a single one. . . . And they exiled the said major families from the entire province for a certain period of time, and they have lived in justice ever since.[15]

Exiled, their revenues frozen and their towers a pile of timber and rock, the Parientes of Guipuzcoa had gambled their survival upon a decisive, coordinated action—and they had lost.

Once again, as had happened so many decades before in the field of Arriaga, the ancient ways of the land had been thwarted by a king's endorsement of the chartered bourgs. The following year, adding insult to injury, a royal appointee personally selected the officials of those cities and villages whose elites most favored the pretenses of the lineages.[16] The dismantling of their towers would not be, however, the last act in the humiliation of the Parientes. In 1460, the heads of the principal families of the land, returning from their exile in far-off Andalusia, were forced to undergo a final chastisement: swearing that they would not, ever again, oppose the rules and decisions of the Brotherhood.[17]

The law dictated by the bourgs had become, with the backing of the monarchy, the only law in the Province of Guipuzcoa.

Notes

1 García de Salazar, *Libro de las Buenas Andanças*, 814.

2 Aguirre, *Lope García de Salazar. El primer historiador de Bizkaia (1399–1476)*, 92.

3 Laborda, *El Señorío de Vizcaya. Nobles y fueros (c.1452–1727)*, 79.

4 García de Salazar, *Libro de las Buenas Andanças*, 788.

5 Etxeberria, "Guerras privadas y linajes urbanos: violencia banderiza en el Bilbao bajomedieval," 86–7.

6 Ayerbe, "El señorío guipuzcoano de la casa de Lazcano. De Parientes mayores a grandes de España de segunda clase (s.XIII-XXI)," 34–6.

7 Garibay, *Los XL libros del Compendio Historial*, XVI, I, 1069.

8 García de Cortázar, "Álava, Guipúzcoa y Vizcaya en los siglos XIII a XV," 221–2.

9 Marin, *"Semejante Pariente Mayor,"* 128.

10 Monreal, *Fuentes del Derecho Histórico de Bizkaia*, 105–6.

11 Aguirre, *Las dos primeras crónicas de Vizcaya*, 249.

12 Garibay, *Los siete libros de la progenie y parentela*, II, 4, 237.

13 Garibay, *Los XL libros del Compendio Historial*, XVI, XLII, 1144. Also, "Anales Breves de Vizcaya." In Aguirre, *Las dos primeras crónicas de Vizcaya*, 179.

14 Martínez de Zaldibia, *Suma de las cosas cantábricas y guipuzcoanas*, 91–6, XXIII.

15 García de Salazar, *Libro de las Buenas Andanças*, 790.

16 Irijoa, "Gobierno urbano en San Sebastián a fines de la Edad Media: Crisis de linaje, conflictos y reestructuración política," 122.

17 Díaz de Durana, *La otra nobleza*, 95.

CHAPTER 14
THE WHITE LORD

While the situation in Guipuzcoa eroded in the years before and after 1448, Biscay, too, was facing a decisive moment. The defeat of the *Hermandad* in 1415 had left it powerless and little more than a shadow of its former self. For decades, as a result, the monarchy had been left with no other alternative but to seek accommodation with the great lineages of the land. But here, just like in Guipuzcoa, the ruin of Mondragón had done much to publicly discredit the *bandos*. Many, even in the *Tierra Llana*, feared what an uncontrolled escalation of competition might precipitate next. Sensing the shift and buoyed by a groundswell of renewed backing, the weakened Brotherhood was re-launched. Towers were cast down, and the retinues of the most warmongering Parientes were chased. In response to these events, and pretty much like their Guipuzcoan counterparts, the leaders of the countryside opted for a policy of contention and compromise. Accepting the conditions imposed by the assembly, they signed a truce whose goal it was to preserve peace in the Lordship.[1]

The lessons of the crisis, on the other hand, were simply too evident for anyone to dismiss. Even if the *Hermandad* still lacked the strength to crush the power of the Parientes for good, no one could doubt that feelings toward the latter were at an all-time low. Those who, like the reformers of Bilbao in 1435, had once been sidelined by the competition of the lineages, now found themselves joined by a growing number of discontented and exasperated compatriots. Even within the ranks of the *bandos* themselves, anxiety was on the rise. Voices emerged, uneasy with the possibility that the escalating arms race that swept the Lordship, for all that it was justified by the uppermost Parientes as a means to protect the ancient liberties of Biscay, would only accelerate their demise. Who doubted, should the flames of factionalism consume the Lordship as they had ill-fated Mondragón, that retribution would be swift and definitive? Unruliness was hardly a great greeting card for a system of self-government toying with survival.

Which is why, in the frail state of peace enforced by the Brotherhood, those most disillusioned householders in Biscay began to contemplate a different course of action.[2] The defense of their customs, they argued, rather than depending on the capricious influence provided by magnates and their webs of clients and patrons, might be better served by a unified and unchanging administrative organ. An unwritten version of the old norms might have been workable in the past, when the lord had lived in their midst. But ever since the advent of Juan Trastámara, distance threatened to make the monarch disinterested and impatient with his northern subjects. This reason alone made it necessary to write down all the treasured heirlooms of Biscayne legal tradition. Only thus could the venerable laws of the Lordship, just like the Ordinances of the *Hermandad*, be presented before the king as part of a deal—one that promised the total pacification of the *Tierra Llana* in exchange for a single, inescapable condition: the perpetuation of the traditional system.

The logic was sound. A century prior, the confreres of Arriaga had already understood that the surest path to preserve their position was to yield to royal authority. Now, it was the turn for these reformers to accept that no better way existed of preventing Castilian legal innovations from eroding the liberties of Biscay than to make the monarch their steadfast protector. With the silent acquiescence of royal appointees, unsure about opposing the de facto powers of the land, they set about the task of codifying what they considered their rights. And so, in 1452, the first comprehensive compilation of the *fuero* of Biscay was finally completed.

Castilian monarchs, naturally, had long been aware of the existence of these norms. As lords, they knew that custom dictated that, in order to receive the obedience and payments their vassals owed them, they ought to enter the country and there, in front of an assembly gathered beneath the mighty oak of Guernica, swear a solemn oath to uphold Biscayne liberties and privileges.[3] The same ritual was then to be re-enacted at various other spots across the Lordship. Much less clear was what exactly each sovereign was swearing to preserve. Did these liberties include only the written statutes, like those compiled in the times of Juan Núñez de Lara? Or were they instead those ancient, orally transmitted agreements that, by their very nature, were likely to be altered or to be forgotten over time? In absence of records, it was difficult to say. What was certain, however, was that court advisers and royal officials alike had long grasped an inescapable reality: that the freemen of Biscay "always wanted their *fueros* sworn and safeguarded and to possess their own judges . . . and [that] the Biscaynes are men of their own will who wish to be very free and very well treated."[4]

To determine the reach and validity of the *fuero* of Biscay was no mere exercise in legal abstraction. Quite the contrary: It was a matter of profound consequence. Not only did custom sanction certain precepts that were contrary to Castilian legal practice, like the possibility of passing down one's inheritance to a unique member of the family rather than dividing it among all heirs, but it did something else: It presented these rights as impeachable and untouchable. Rather than seeing these as the result of a slow evolution and the ups and downs of circumstance, across the Western Pyrenees, from Navarre to Biscay, the wardens of local self-government had long been in the business of viewing their respective traditions as exceptions born out of pristine moments of foundation.[5] The primordial "contract," they said, had been voluntarily entered by both the community and the ruler and its reenactment was necessary upon the coming of each new lord. In other words, it constituted a claim, made in the name of an entire people, to self-government and independence.

Yet, in a land as bereft of scholarly tradition as Biscay, there existed as many interpretations of what this contract really entailed as there were interests vested in its meaning. It was for this reason that, in 1452, those entrusted with setting down the *fuero* saw their task as urgent. For they sought to define, to their advantage and once and for all, the true nature of such an agreement, and what it might mean for the future.

The version they propounded, in its essentials, went as follows. Long ago, shortly after the arrival of the Muslims to Spain, there lived in Biscay a man of singular renown—one whose lineage stretched back to the kings of Scotland and better known in the land as Jaun Zuria, "the White Lord." On one occasion, "a son of the king of Leon, accompanied by a large number of people, entered Biscay burning, plundering and murdering . . . because the territory had shaken their ties of dependence." The dwellers of the *Tierra Llana*, appalled by the pillaging army, resolved to fight, but the Leonese prince refused to meet them in battle unless they were led by a captain of royal blood. The men of Biscay, after the initial confusion and forced to elect a suitable candidate, had immediately thought of Jaun Zuria. The struggle that ensued, as expected, was a decisive triumph for the locals—so great, indeed, that the very spot where it took place would from then on be known, in reference to the blood spilled by the Leonese, as *Arrigorriaga*, the "red stone."

But the true turning point came after the victory. The Biscaynes, as they gathered in solemn assembly at Guernica, had understood a harsh reality. They would never be able to defend their lands from their enemies if they were not themselves led by a powerful chieftain. And so they turned once more to Jaun Zuria, "and they took him as Lord and divided with him the mountains and the meadows . . . and they gave to him all the best plots of land in every shire . . . and granted to him the civilian and criminal justice." In exchange, he swore an oath, binding for all time, to uphold and protect the liberties of the freemen of Biscay.[6] And so it was that the Lordship had been born.

Of course, few halted to ponder the historical veracity of such an account. That no chronicle—Leonese nor otherwise—so much as alluded to the battle of Arrigorriaga, to Jaun Zuria, or to the supposed contract signed between the prince and the community of householders of Guernica must have scarcely weighed in the consciousness of those writing down the *fuero*. What mattered most, for Biscaynes at any rate, was that the narrative offered a satisfactory answer, tailored to the interests of the dwellers of the *Tierra Llana*, to the most pressing questions they sought to resolve. What were the juridical roots of their rights and privileges? How much could the monarchy ask in return? Could a king, without their explicit consent, alter the terms of this relationship? Herein lay questions that, for long, had been the matter of heated dispute.

And these disputes, at a time at which the resolute onslaught of the *Hermandad* threatened to extend royal jurisdiction all over Biscay, were ever more pressing than ever. Yet in the tale of Jaun Zuria, the Parientes could find a perfect answer to their predicament. Just as they were the heirs of a free people that had never submitted to foreign rule, so too was the monarch the successor of that first lord who had sworn never to strip them of their liberties. The contract stood in place and—so it followed—no amendment could be made to the terms of their allegiance without first securing their consent. The historical foundations of such a claim, for all its shakiness, could always be argued to be scarce precisely because Biscay's past had been preserved orally, rather than in parchment. In turn, what little scraps of testimony did survive—passing mentions to the occasional oath sworn by lords beneath the oak of Guernica—could easily be cast, thanks to their ambiguity, as re-enactments of that original pact between Jaun Zuria and the Biscaynes. It was all a perfectly defensible approach. And not in the least because the

Parientes had proven time and again to be specialists in the art of turning unprecedented demands into rights immemorial.

Insofar as the text put limits on its authority, it was hardly surprising that the king himself would meet the writing of the *fuero* with little excitement. When Enrique IV arrived in the region in 1457 to curb the challenge of the Parientes of Guipuzcoa, the tremors of his campaign were also felt in nearby Biscay. Here, too, towers and strongholds were torn apart, and the heads of famous lineages were exiled to the southern frontier on charges of having disrupted the public peace.[7] Taking his oath as lord of Biscay that very year, Enrique shied away from any mention of the *fuero* written in 1452, with all its stipulations and precisions, and reverted instead to the customary reference to abstract liberties and privileges. The omission spoke volumes. It was, without doubt, a deliberate maneuver to keep his hands free of the shackles that the document imposed upon his power. A power that, in the wake of recent events in Guipuzcoa and Biscay, appeared to be more secure than ever.

But then, these certainties dissolved. In 1462, Enrique IV, a faint-hearted, childless man who a contemporary would describe as "always being ruled by his own will, fleeing from any sane advice,"[8] announced the birth of a daughter, Juana. This was troublesome news for two reasons. First, because it displaced his half-siblings Alfonso and Isabella from the royal succession and, second, because rumors began to spread about the dubious paternity of the newborn princess. As the monarch stepped up to make Juana the royal heiress, factions within the upper echelons of the Castilian court began to do what they always did and maneuvered to elevate the teenager Alfonso to the throne. What followed was a descent into chaos—conspiracies, betrayals, murders. For Biscay's great lineages, crumbling at the time under Enrique's heavy foot, this unraveling of royal authority was a lifeline that could not have come at a better time. With Castile in flames, the *bandos* were free once more to press their claims to dominance. Meanwhile Enrique, overwhelmed by events, tried to keep his position afloat. Royal appointees, desperate to secure the allegiance of the Biscayne nobility, ratified the *fuero* of 1452 in 1463. Unfortunately for Enrique's cause, it proved too little too late. The following year, Castile had already become a battlefield. The authority of the monarchy fell apart.

With the king's gaze turned elsewhere, it did not take long for the Parientes to cast aside their endorsement for an administrative solution and to resuscitate their ambitions over cities and ports. Competition spread, and with it, the resort to private war. In 1468, the great houses gathered their allies and pitted their forces against one another for control of the bourgs of Durango and Elorrio. So savage was the carnage that Guipuzcoan authorities even submitted a document to the king manifesting their anxiety about the calamitous situation of Biscay.[9] The specter of Mondragón loomed large in the minds of all. But unlike in 1448, little help could be expected now from a monarchy more concerned with its own survival than with maintaining any semblance of order in the realm. The maneuvering required to secure the throne made a bargaining chip out of every royal resource, and kingmakers, just as in the previous civil war, were quick to realize their opportunity. The same year the Parientes had staged their bloody spectacle in Elorrio, a mighty nobleman, Count Pedro de Velasco, had made its bet in support of Enrique IV. He was rewarded, first, with a lordship over Bilbao. A few months later, the king added to this prize the rest of Biscay and Guipuzcoa.[10]

Such promises, lavished by the king to his favorite, did not fail to excite an irate response from the locals. Their representatives, immediately upon hearing news of the concession, raised irritated complaints to the sovereign.[11] These, however, proved useless. Enrique could not hope to hold his ground without the support of the nobility, and Velasco's price, for all that it may spell disaster for many across Biscay, had been set. To mercantile oligarchs in Bilbao, the arrival of the count presented an intolerable dilemma: either to endure the violence of lineage confrontation, which constantly threatened their commercial interests, or to submit instead to a new master and relinquish their own town's destiny. To those who had championed the *fuero* of 1452 and defended a contractual connection between the Lordship and the monarchy, Velasco's grant was nothing short of a deathblow to their plans. And yet, not even they found the arrival of the new master so personal a threat as did the Parientes. "For I, Don Pedro de Velasco, by order and with the authority of our lord, the king, have had and still have the responsibility . . . to pacify and quell any uprisings and disturbances . . . in the Province of Guipuzcoa and the county of Biscay."[12] Few could have missed the true meaning of these words, as well as what they entailed. Shortly after the arrival of the count, the heads of the two main Biscayne *bandos* were exiled from the country. The Parientes, it seemed, had been defeated yet again.

Had Velasco succeeded in pacifying the Lordship as was his intention, then the course of Biscayne—and Western Pyrenean—history would have undoubtedly been very different. Ruled by a lord with jurisdictional powers over their lives, the inhabitants of the Lordship would probably have seen their ancient liberties vanish at a stroke. Cities which had once sought to extend their privileges in the name of the king would immediately have been put in the hands of agents with no stake in confronting noble prerogatives. The freedoms enshrined in the *fuero* of 1452, which the document had cast as immemorial and unassailable, would have been reduced to little more than bribes that the lord could revoke at will. The Basque exception would have been no exception at all.

As it happens, though, time would thwart these plans. If there was a timeless constant in medieval politics, it was that disproportionate influence always summoned its own enemies. Therefore, the exiled Parientes had soon found themselves in the presence of a magnate whose resentment against the new ruler of Biscay was as vivid as theirs. Thanks to his endorsement, they had achieved what might, in another age, have been deemed a miracle. In a scene reminiscent of the alliance signed by the Guipuzcoan *bandos* before staging their challenge against the *Hermandad*, the heads of Biscay's most formidable families had cast their blood-feuds aside and had pledged their children to each other in marriage. The erstwhile enemies had then joined their forces against Velasco.

The war that followed was short and brutal. The Parientes were besieged in their towers; Velasco's men were expelled by force from Bilbao. The count might have hoped that time would fracture the fragile confederation of his enemies. But such a possibility failed to materialize. When the two sides met in battle in Munguía later that year, the outcome was a decisive one. Velasco, crushed without hope of a comeback, "escaped with great luck . . . and embarked in Bermeo and from there went to France."[13] The cause of Enrique IV in the Western Pyrenees crumbled at the flight of his favorite.

The aftermath of the battle of Munguía, coupled with the death of King Enrique himself in 1474, ushered in an entirely new situation for Biscay. Only a year prior to the monarch's passing, the soon-to-be Queen Isabella of Castile had already sworn to uphold the text of the *fuero* of 1452. Far more significant was the gesture made by the two great leaders of the *bandos*, former enemies now turned into allies in the wake of Velasco's defeat. When they paid homage to the princess as was their obligation, they did so not as chieftains in command of large private clienteles. Rather, they did so as spokesmen for a singular Biscayne community.[14] The strategy of the reformers had been vindicated. The guarantees agreed by the new monarch, coupled with a general exhaustion from internecine warfare, had convinced the foremost Parientes to accept that their pursuit of absolute dominance might be futile. Vassals of the monarchy, they would continue to rule themselves according to their own laws. The difference lay in that, from now on, they would do so under a system backed by the power of the crown, and not set in direct opposition to it. Power and privilege would remain intact, but now, public peace would be their price.

At any rate, the pacification of Guipuzcoa and Biscay, those most troublesome pits of instability in the Western Pyrenees, could hardly be secured without tackling the problems that lay at their root. For all the outward unity recently professed by their elites, urban *bandos* still controlled the means of accessing city councils. These were even more coveted prizes now that the northern trade routes, long stagnant after the crisis of the previous century, were once again starting to revive. In 1474, for instance, the neighbors of Mondragón still complained about a local official who, far from concealing his family's ties with the destroyers of the town, overtly displayed them by riding "armed on horseback like a men-at-arms with the lord of Guevara and his soldiers."[15] Demonstrations of misplaced devotion such as these, because they recalled the behaviors that had put the entire region on the brink of collapse, could no longer be tolerated. More important than relatives, allies, friends, or patrons, there stood something else: the good of the entire community. To risk fragmentation was to threaten society itself.

So it was that to root out of the urban *bandos* once and for all, a sweeping regulation was enacted in 1476. First applied to Vitoria and later extended to other cities, the essentials of the new order, sponsored by the new kings of Castile, bore a striking resemblance to those attempted in Bilbao three decades earlier. Municipal government was tightly restricted, the long-standing practice of duplicating offices to accommodate rival factions was abolished, and elections were to be decided through a lottery of suitable candidates. Crucially, a prohibition was set to prevent all inhabitants from taking part in a lineage's retinue. Anyone found guilty of such an infraction would be branded "an offender of his homeland and a destroyer and violator of its peace and common good."[16] Under the new system, access to the magistracies would rest solely on reputation and financial standing. Resorting to personal connections or to the favor of the scions of the most important families, both of which had once been key to office, was now deemed not only illegal behaviors but also deeply immoral ones.

By 1480, the pacification of the Western Pyrenees was, for all intents and purposes, a *fait accompli*. There remained, of course, bouts of local disagreement between commoners, city councils, and the heirs of the Parientes, and these would continue for decades. Regardless, rarely would these debates escalate, as they had often done before, into armed struggle. Increasingly, the soldiers and skirmishers that had once accompanied the heads of the lineages were cast aside in favor of an altogether no less threatening, albeit more civilized, retinue: lawyers. In a twist laced with irony, the very triumph of those who saw in the exertion of violence the main disruptor of public life would hand the Parientes a more secure way of preserving their privileges. "[B]ecause it is no longer the time to go around in factions like in the old days," they would now fight their struggles in the courts rather than on muddy battlefields.[17]

The transition was swift. By 1514, for instance, when the townspeople of Azcoitia sought to challenge a local Pariente's claim over their church, they did so in a lawsuit. Unfortunately for them, royal justice, despite its veneer of impartiality, remained a bureaucratic affair in which personal connections and carefully cultivated networks mattered no less than they did in battle. Commoners, who might have expected the defeat of the Parientes to usher in a betterment of their conditions, were soon to be disappointed. The people of Marquina, in 1490, claimed that through "tricks and deceits," and despite their clear legal entitlement to the full revenue from the local church, justice had allotted them only half of it.[18] Their frustration was extensible to many other places across the Western Pyrenees.

The transformations brought by peace were profound, but few fully grasped all their implications at the time. One of the most striking consequences was that territorial identity gained in compactness and solidity. Once upon a time, Alava, Biscay, and Guipuzcoa had been mere geographical designations whose borders were blurred by feudal claims and shifting alliances. Thanks to the regulations enshrined in the *Hermandad* or the *fuero*, they now emerged as provinces—or in Biscay's case, a lordship—with definite administrative boundaries and codified commandments.[19] Even in this latter territory, where pacification had come as much from a defeat of the Parientes as from an accommodation with them, the assemblies that were to rule the Lordship gathered not as representatives of lineage interests, but rather as delegates of territorially defined circumscriptions.[20] The case was similar in Alava.

To live within the limits of these jurisdictions now meant to accept the legitimacy of the institutions and laws created to rule over them. The days when alternative power structures competed for control were over. From the mightiest magnate to the lowliest shepherd, everyone would be swayed by the same regulations. The kind of social fractures that the *bandos* had so long exploited—and from which they had acquired their power—were to be erased forever.

But though internal peace had settled over the Western Pyrenees, and for all that the forces that had shaped the resolution of the conflict—the monarchy, the merchants, the disillusioned members of the lineages—had played out in parallel across the region, this did not translate into a sense of common political identification. The violent clashes and the remedies applied to contain them had favored the transformation of what were once fuzzy jurisdictions into more internally consistent provincial orders. However, this newfound solidity had come at the expense of separation. The Provinces of Alava and Guipuzcoa and the Lordship of Biscay neither shared institutions nor followed a uniform set of laws. The cross-pollinating networks of patronage that had once transcended these spaces, the kind that had once allowed a lord of Biscay to stand as representative of the Alavese nobility in Arriaga, had disappeared. Culturally, of course, a sort of friendliness lingered on, nurtured by a common language, similar lifestyles, and the frequent intercourse expected from vicinity. Yet politically, because provincial authorities saw their interests as confined to their own administration, these were of little consequence. The only true link between them was the monarch, to whom all of them, in unison, paid homage and obedience. A monarchy that, in ratifying its legal codes and overseeing reconciliation, had secured for itself a position as the sole and undisputed arbiter of justice.

One had not to go far to glimpse what might have been. In Labourd, just beyond the Bidassoa River, people spoke in a tongue not dissimilar to that of Guipuzcoa or Biscay. Their ways of life, too, were rather comparable: peasants, fishermen, artisans. Like their neighbors to the south, their freemen upheld an analogous custom of meeting to settle communal matters, had once founded a Brotherhood to chase criminals, and even claimed to follow a customary law inherited from their elders.[21] None of these shared traits, however, could outweigh the single most decisive factor that separated them: their political allegiances.

When Bayonne fell to forces of the king of France in 1451—the last territory in Gascony under the English monarchy to do so and the conclusive act of the Hundred Years War—witnesses, among them Guipuzcoan and Biscayne soldiers allied to the French,[22] were said to have spotted a vision in the sky: a crowned cross that, only a few moments later, changed into a fleur-de-lis.[23] The miracle was not unearned. For three long centuries, Bayonne had been staunchly loyal to their distant sovereigns. Its conquest, at any rate, must have seemed to their enemies not unworthy of divine intervention.

But the fall of Bayonne, just as it was the final act in the longest and most brutal war of the Middle Ages, marked also the beginning of a new chapter for the Western Pyrenees. 1476, the year the ordinances that ended the *bandos* in Vitoria had been promulgated, also witnessed a French army laying siege to the frontier bourg of Fuenterrabia. Former allies, Castile and France, in the fluctuating game of diplomacy and in the absence of their previous common enemy, had lost no time in turning on one another. Eager to show their loyalty to their respective sovereigns and attracted by promises of booty and further concessions, the inhabitants of the Western Pyrenees rushed to the fray. The newly formed provinces, anxious to strip the Parientes of their last remnants of social power, saw the conflict as an opportunity to demonstrate that it was they, and not the old noble lineages, that best could protect the monarch's interests.[24]

Internal pacification, in tidying up the sources of law and binding them incontestably to a single authority, had thus the paradoxical result of exporting these conflicts to the outside. The Western Pyrenees, after having long suffered calamities born out of the weakness of central power, now found itself the scenario of a confrontation between two of the richest and best-coordinated states in all of Europe. The frontier thus hardened. And so too, in their wake, did outlooks.

Notes

1 "Anales Breves de Vizcaya." In Aguirre, *Las dos primeras crónicas de Vizcaya*, 177–8.

2 Laborda, *El Señorío de Vizcaya. Nobles y fueros (c.1452–1727)*, 125.

3 See, for example, López de Ayala, *Crónicas de los reyes de Castilla*, II, Año Tercero, Enrique III, XIX, 488–92.

4 López de Ayala, II, Año doceno, Juan I, II, 298.

5 "Fuero General de Navarra" (*c.* 1238). In Jimeno, *Los fueros de Navarra*, 29. The same tradition can be found in the *fueros* of Sobrarbe of Aragon. See Villanueva, "Francisco Calça y el mito de la libertad originaria de Cataluña," 79–80.

6 García de Salazar, *Libro de las Buenas Andanças*, 691–2.

7 García de Salazar, 884.

8 "Memorial de diversas hazañas" (1487). In Rosell, *Crónicas de los reyes de Castilla*, 3, C, 95.

9 Martínez de Isasti, *Compendio Historial de Guipúzcoa*, 54.

10 Laborda, *El Señorío de Vizcaya. Nobles y fueros (c.1452–1727)*, 139–41.

11 "Memorial de diversas hazañas" (1487). In Rosell, *Crónicas de los reyes de Castilla*, 3, LIV, 55.

12 Quoted in Aguirre, *Lope García de Salazar. El primer historiador de Bizkaia (1399–1476)*, 356.

13 "Crónica Ibargüen-Cahopín" (1558–1620). In Arriolabengoa, "Ibarguen-Cachopín Kronika. Edizioa eta Azterketa," XLIII, 556.

14 Laborda, *El Señorío de Vizcaya. Nobles y fueros (c.1452–1727)*, 145–6.

15 Díaz de Durana and Fernández de Larrea, "Las relaciones contractuales de la nobleza y las élites urbanas en el País Vasco al final de la Edad Media (*c.*1300–1500)," 307.

16 "Ordenanzas de Vitoria" (1476). In Díaz de Durana, "La reforma municipal de los Reyes Católicos y la consolidación de las oligarquías urbanas: el capitulado vitoriano de 1476 y su extensión por el nordeste de la Corona de Castilla," 224.

17 Quoted in Fernández de Larrea and Díaz de Durana, "La construcción de la memoria," 161–2.

18 "Relación anónima de los sucesos ocurridos en torno al patronato de la villa de Marquina desde la fundación de la misma hasta la sentencia arbitraria de 1490" (*c.* 1490–1). In Enríquez, *Colección Documental del Archivo Municipal de Marquina (1355 1516)*, 21.

19 García de Cortázar, "Álava, Guipúzcoa y Vizcaya en los siglos XIII a XV," 233–4.

20 García de Cortázar, 232.

21 Although the first mention to the Assembly (in Euskera, *Biltzar*) of Labord dates from 1567, the institution must be of older origin. See Goyheneche, *Le Pays Basque*, 130. The *fueros* of Labord were compiled in 1513. See Mounole and Lacarra, "El Euskera arcaico," 374.

22 Pontet, *Histoire de Bayonne*, 72.

23 Wade, *Gascony, England's first colony, 1204–1453*, 221.

24 Soria, "La Hidalguía Universal," 309–10. Also, Díaz de Durana, *La otra nobleza*, 187–8.

PART III
PRIVILEGE

Figure 1. Courtyard in The Assembly House in Guernica. The tree of Guernica stands as the eternal symbol of Basque liberties. Across generations, saplings, beneath whose branches deputies from Biscay have governed the affairs of the Lordship, have succeeded one another. And yet, the adoption of the tree as a symbol for all Basques is much more recent, dating back—at most—a century and a half: an attempt to forge a collective identity out of previously differentiated territories. Photo: Cristina Arias/Cover/Getty Images.

Figure 2. Bronze sculpture of the God Helios from the Roman site of Oiasso, around second–third century AD. Although later authors would come to claim that Western Pyreneans had resisted Roman domination, the truth was that, in their customs and their beliefs, locals were not, by any means, impermeable to their influence. Photo: Fundación Arkeolan.

Figure 3. View of the shrine of Saint Michael in Excelsis (twelfth century) with the mountain range of Andia in the background. Over the course of the convulse decades that preceded the end of the Western Roman Empire, the Western Pyrenees became a conflictive frontier. The struggle between local strongmen—derisively referred to as *Bacaudae*—and the aristocratic classes for control of the territory led not only to the destruction of much of the region's Roman infrastructure. It also rendered it a periphery whose trajectory would diverge markedly from that of their neighbors. Photo: Xabier Cañas Arenaza, Wikimedia Commons.

Figure 4. *Chronicles of St. Denis*, miniature by Jean Fouquet, Charlemagne discovering Knight Roland's remains at Ronceveaux, fifteenth century, France. The *Chanson of Roland* bestowed literary immortality upon Charlemagne's defeat at Roncesvalles. The poem presented it as a battle against the Muslim. Contemporaries, on the contrary, offered a very different account: "On the heights of the Pyrenees, the Wascones prepared an ambush, attacked the rearguard, and threw the whole army into confusion." Photo: Photo12/Universal Images Group via Getty Images.

Figure 5. Porta Speciosa from the Monastery of Leyre, eleventh century. Enneco Arista, the first king of Pamplona, styled himself a protector of Christians—especially the monks of the monastery of Leyre. In reality, he was a competent political operator who benefited largely from the support of the Emirate of Cordoba and the Muslim Banu Qasi dynasty. Photo: Kent Wang. Wikimedia Commons.

Figure 6. Sculpture of Sancho III the Great on the exterior of the Palacio de Oriente, Madrid. In the early eleventh century, the kings of Pamplona were the most powerful dynasty in the Iberian Peninsula. More important for nineteenth- and twentieth-century Basque nationalists, though, was that Sancho the Great had ruled over every territory once associated with the Vascones. Was this a proto-Basque state? Not really, for his authority owed little to the will of a single people, and more to Sancho's ability to navigate the political dynamics of his time. Photo: Javier Pérez Montes. Wikimedia Commons.

Figure 7. Sancho IV Garcés, king of Pamplona (1054–76), being pushed into the void from the top of a ravine by his brother Ramón during a hunt in Peñalén. The "King's Cliff," near the Navarrese town of Funes, marks the location where Sancho of Peñalén, grandson of Sancho the Great, met his doom at the hands of his own brother. In the aftermath of the fratricide, the kings of Castile and Aragon advanced to dismember the kingdom of Pamplona, thereby ensuring a future in which powers beyond its borders would rule the Western Pyrenees. Photo: Juan Alaminos/LTL/Heritage Images via Getty Images.

Figure 8. The tower of Mendoza in Alava, thirteenth century. The ultimate aim of the violence and extortion perpetrated by the Parientes Mayores was to secure recognition as titled lords and achieve, in regions like Guipuzcoa and Biscay, a level of social hegemony comparable to that enjoyed by more prominent families, such as the Mendozas or the Guevaras. Photo: Basotxerri, Wikimedia Commons.

Figure 9. View of the city of Mondragón (Guipuzcoa). The burning of the chartered bourg of Mondragón in 1448 signaled the end of social tolerance toward the activities of the Parientes Mayores. This would prove a momentous event in the eventual consolidation of the provinces of Guipuzcoa, Alava, and Biscay. Photo: Marisol Murua, Wikimedia Commons.

Figure 10. Iron ore mining by Darío de Regoyos y Valdés, c. 1900. Ever since Roman times, metallurgy had been vital occupation for many inhabitants of the Western Pyrenees. Crafted tools and weapons oiled trade routes that extended into northern Europe. By the end of the fifteenth century, in fact, the production from Biscay alone accounted for more than ten per cent of that of all Christendom. Photo: Fine Art Images/Heritage Images via Getty Images.

Figure 11. Glasswork inside the Assembly House in Guernica. In 1526, all inhabitants of Biscay and Guipuzcoa were formally recognized as noblemen. While this distinction, unparalleled across Europe, did not eliminate internal social hierarchies, it allowed the population to play an outsized role within the Spanish monarchy and laid the groundwork for the development of Western Pyrenean exceptionalism. Photo: Dosfotos/Design Pics Editorial/Universal Images Group via Getty Images.

Figure 12. View of Potosi, engraving from an atlas, Bolivia, seventeenth century. Potosí, the richest city in the world, boasted in the sixteenth century "a large population, though without order, harmony, or planned streets." And, at the helm of this vast economic powerhouse, were the *vascongados* from the Western Pyrenees. Photo: DeAgostini/Getty Images.

Figure 13. Portrait of Jeanne d'Albret, queen of Navarre (1528–72), by François Clouet, *c.* 1570. Although widely recognized throughout the Western Pyrenees and beyond, the concept of *Euskal Herria*—that is, a community united by knowledge of *Euskera*—held special resonance in the northern territories ruled by Jeanne d'Albret. To the south, on the contrary, the provincial elites proved either indifferent or openly hostile to an idea that threatened their privileges and status. Photo: Fine Art Images/Heritage Images via Getty Images.

Figure 14. A gathering of witches. The Basque term *Akelarre*—interpreted by inquisitors as "pastures of the billy goat"—was regarded by prosecutors as evidence of nocturnal gathering of witches plotting the ruin of their neighbors. In reality, the term seems to have simply referred to a field of herbs, highlighting the considerable cultural and linguistic distance that often separated the judge from the prosecuted. Photo: Culture Club/Bridgeman via Getty Images.

Figure 15. Monument to the Count of Peñaflorida in Vitoria (Alava). Xavier María de Munibe e Idiáquez, Count of Peñaflorida, was not only described by his contemporaries as an "exceedingly obese" man but also as a major patron of the sciences. Kickstarting a transformative movement in the Spanish Enlightenment, he had sought to build "upon the remnants of the unhappiness of our beloved Homeland, . . . a throne of Public Happiness." His influence would echo across the continents. Photo: Asier H. Aguirresarobe.

Figure 16. Monument to the *fueros* built in 1903 in Pamplona (Navarre). After 1876, the trauma caused by the abolition of the *fueros* of Biscay, Guipuzcoa, and Alava would manifest in overt displays of devotion such as the magnificent monument to the *fueros* in Pamplona (1903). Discontent with the abolition drove many radical *fuerists* to adopt an ever more hostile stance toward the Spanish government and, in some cases, even to join the ranks of Basque separatism. Photo: José Luis Filpo Cabana, Wikimedia Commons.

Figure 17. Picture of Sabino Arana Goiri in the prison of Larrinaga (Biscay), *c.* 1902. Sabino Arana Goiri, the father of Basque nationalism, combined an aversion to industrialization with a rejection of all things Spanish. His thought—encapsulated in the slogan *Jaungoikoa ta Lagi Zarra* ("God and the Ancient Law")—evidenced a profound indebtedness to the belief in Western Pyrenean exceptionalism. To his adversaries, he was a traitor; to his followers, however, he became a martyr comparable to Jesus. Photo: Wikimedia Commons.

CHAPTER 15
DE GLORIA ET NOBILITATE

When the representatives of Seville's city authorities first found themselves brought before the royal tribunal in 1520, they could not have imagined that the case against them would amount to anything more than a minor inconvenience. After all, their accusers—Nicolás Sánchez and Juan Sánchez de Aramburu, father and son, natives from the Guipuzcoan town of Azcoitia—had staged what to them appeared a claim so far-fetched as to verge on the absurd. The charge was simple: The two men insisted that, being of noble ancestry, they should not pay any other tribute in the city save those other noblemen paid as well. This was, of course, a substantial privilege for merchants in a foreign land to demand—and made all the more striking by the fact that neither of them possessed a single valid document to support their allegation. Summoned before the judges, Juan and Nicolás were frank in their admissions: They had no titles, no certificates, no seals of authentication. Wholly absent was any indisputable evidence that might constitute proof of their nobility. Under these circumstances, the authorities of Seville had every reason to feel confident. The case, they must have thought, was as good as won.

Fast forward three years to the day of the sentence, and these certainties appeared all but trampled on their heads. Against all expectation, the judges and notaries that made up the Royal Chancellery in Granada ruled in favor of the two merchants. The arbiters of the case, in explaining their verdict, did not delve into the reasoning behind it, but it seemed clear that the witnesses brought forward by Nicolás and Juan Sánchez de Aramburu had had a massive role in their decision. Not for nothing, an exceeding number of elderly and respected citizens of Azcoitia had been called upon by the accusers to back their claims. One after another, they had come forward, and their testimony had been as unanimous as repetitive: The two men were noblemen. In fact, these witnesses had gone further, asserting an even bolder claim—that "in the aforementioned town of Azcoitia and in the Province of Guipuzcoa, there was not one that was not a nobleman, for there were no serfs in those places, nor the kind of tributes that serfs pay."[1]

The defeated party, as was only to be expected, was dumbfounded and perplexed. That two mere merchants—men without title, without distinction—should have won for themselves privileges reserved for only the highest echelons of Sevillian society was an outcome so implausible as to defy belief. The appellation was not long in coming. The case, they insisted, reeked of manipulation. The witnesses had been drawn from the accused's circle of relatives and friends, and their accounts, conspicuously similar to one another, bore the resemblance of a well-rehearsed script. And there was, of course, the staggering claim that a man, just for the sole reason of being a natural of Azcoitia or

Guipuzcoa, should be counted as a noble. The royal attorney scoffed at this idea. That the townsfolk of such a nondescript settlement had ceased to pay taxes, he claimed, obeyed only to a royal exemption: a privilege to the town itself that in no way could suggest any universal nobility to its inhabitants. To hint at the contrary was to twist reality almost to the breaking point, and, regardless, demonstrating the truth of such reasoning would require firmer evidence than the fading memories of a handful of white-haired men. If such logic were allowed to stand, after all, what would prevent other Guipuzcoans from launching similar claims all across the kingdom?

After a long exchange of accusations, the two sides agreed upon a course to find a solution. This would apply not only Nicolás' and Juan Sánchez's case but also to the mounting number of similar lawsuits involving natives from the province that had started to alarm authorities in the south. According to its terms, an agent would be dispatched to Valladolid to seek clarity on a single issue. Were the exemptions these Guipuzcoans enjoyed the result of royal privilege, or did they stem from something altogether more fundamental—perhaps nature itself?

The outcome of the inquiry, when it was made known in Granada, reverberated like a thunderclap. The scribes and officials in Valladolid, far from backing the arguments presented by the royal attorney, had instead lent the full weight of their authority to his opponents. Illustrious civil servants had confirmed, under oath and without flinching an eye, "that all the natives of that province, young and old alike, were noblemen and were taken as such, but that the humblest paid courtesy and obedience to the greatest, wealthiest, and most respected." More striking, perhaps, was their sanctioning that this status applied "both within the province and beyond it, wherever they might be." The accounts matched those provided by the witnesses back in Granada almost to the letter. But now there was more. Among the documents uncovered in Valladolid was a missive, issued in 1476 to Guipuzcoan authorities by King Ferdinand himself, in which he referred to the inhabitants of the province, collectively, as "my good and loyal noble vassals." It was the final blow. The judgment, when it finally came in 1526, was no longer a surprise. All Guipuzcoans—no matter their profession nor their appearance—were, indeed, of noble stock.

Looking back on this extraordinary conclusion, many would later wonder how such a decision could have ever been reached. The nobility recognized to all inhabitants of Guipuzcoa—and acknowledged, in an update to the *fuero* made in 1526, to those of Biscay as well—was, after all, a legal concession unparalleled not only within the Spanish monarchy, but across Western Europe. It was a badge of honor, a mark of distinction that conferred meaning and pride to those who possessed it, and which would profoundly shape the ways in which Western Pyrenean peoples would come to see themselves and others. Before long, all kinds of narratives, arguments, and legends would emerge to justify this status and to present it as natural and self-explanatory. And yet—perhaps paradoxically—the person who had most clearly grasped the true nature and implications of this astonishing transformation was neither a chronicler nor a historian, not even a Western Pyrenean himself, but rather that baffled attorney of Granada. He, in denouncing the means by which provincials had tried to pursue their claims before the tribunal, had put his finger on the radioactive core of what had taken place. He had understood, better than anyone, that at the heart of what would later be known as *Hidalguía Universal*—"universal nobility"—stood an attempt, overt but subtle, audacious yet confident, to transform what had erstwhile been conditional privileges into unchallengeable rights.

Contrary to the complaints raised by the royal attorney, though, the presumption that there existed a kind of widespread liberty common to the inhabitants of Biscay and Guipuzcoa enjoyed a certain pedigree. In both regions, freemen made up indeed the largest proportion of the population. This owed as much to their peripheral situation relative to the great Christian kingdoms as to their weak internal hierarchization prior to the founding of the first chartered towns. For, where could freedom come from in the first place, in a world which conceived liberty merely as the absence of subjecthood, but from the failure of the lords to suffocate it? Freedom could only thrive where enforcement declined. The defeat of the Parientes, fresh in the collective memory, had been only the last nail in the coffin of seigneurial ambitions. Now, their inability to put their neighbors in their shadow had given rise to the largest concentration of exempt peoples anywhere in the peninsula.[2]

Local authorities had likewise come to accept that absence of effective vassalage could indeed be taken as a mark of nobility. As early as 1397, for example, the Ordinances of the Brotherhood of Guipuzcoa had justified the prohibition of torture as a punishment on the grounds that "in the said land, they are commonly all noblemen," a status also recognized for Biscay in 1394.[3] Years later, in 1417, the main authorities of Guipuzcoa had once again rejected the imposition of a royal tax because "they are noblemen and have been and remain in possession of the privilege of said nobility."[4] Even kings, as the document presented to the Chancellery of Granada demonstrated, had found it suitable, on occasion, to pay lip service to this idea.

But why? How was it possible that anyone—not to say the royal court—had come simply to admit that the tremendous gap which elsewhere separated the free from the dependent had been effortlessly bridged in Biscay and Guipuzcoa? How could, in fact, those serfs of, say, the lord of Biscay leave behind the taint of subjection and be taken for impeccable noblemen?

The example of the Guipuzcoan town of Tolosa, founded in 1256, offered an illustration of the ways in which such an apparent miracle might have taken place. Initially, and in accordance with the customs of the land, Tolosa had been populated by men and women of both free and unfree origin. Confronted with the requirements of the city council to contribute to the costs of running the town, the former had soon demanded—and obtained—a royal validation of their right not to pay their share of these obligations. The exemption, as the order explicitly clarified, did not apply to the tax-paying residents of the town—in other words, to serfs.

A crystal-clear utterance, and one which might have solidified the distinction between noblemen and dependents for good, had it not been for the unstable circumstances of Guipuzcoa in the late Middle Ages. With both struggles between local Parientes and the lurking presence of the kingdom of Navarre constantly casting their shadow over Tolosa, many found their willingness to settle inside the walls diminishing into nothingness. To fight back this tendency, which threatened to depopulate a valuable position in a disputed border zone, the monarchy had issued, in 1326, a powerful incentive: the granting of the immunities that were proper of a nobleman to all new migrants to the city. Crucially, the document said nothing about those citizens who had been serfs when their ancestors had first populated the town and who remained a second-class of neighbors. Yet this difference, which no doubt must have been both difficult to enforce and potentially volatile in a small community such as that of Tolosa, was finally discarded. By 1374, in response to certain requirements by the royal treasury, the town council was already arguing that the franchise of 1290—which originally had only affected freemen—applied instead to every single inhabitant. The court, in accepting this interpretation and confirming it in various instances over the following century, merely solidified the dogma posited by urban authorities. That in Tolosa there were not, and had never been, serfs of any kind.[5]

Over time, what had once been a perk of border and marginal regions became, thanks to tax exemptions and other benefits that the crown had lavished upon them, something more for many of its inhabitants: an article of faith. Serfs, in abandoning their lands to settle in communities populated only by freemen, had sought exactly the same as had those who migrated into chartered cities like Tolosa. All of them took for granted that being exempt from personal taxation was the primary marker that separated a serf from a noble. Another conclusion, then, was short in coming. If being reduced to servile behaviors could lead to a fall from grace, would not the continued exercise of one of the main privileges of nobility eventually become indistinguishable from nobility itself? Just as much as a Pariente, in extorting payments and gifts from his compatriots, wanted to demonstrate that he was an equal to a titled lord, so too the dependent who opted for not disbursing these tributes and challenged their lawfulness was gripping firmly onto the ladder of social advancement. Faking it, for both the mighty and the meek, was indeed a prerequisite for making it.

The long years of the struggle of city and peasant communities against the violence of the *bandos* had seen the ideological divide between the Parientes and their opponents increasingly widened. The more the former would claim that they were worthy of ruling jurisdictional lordships, the more city oligarchies made a public display of their privileges and exemptions. Every time the Parientes wished to present themselves as the only authorities in the land, their rivals made sure to undermine these presumptions. By the mid-century, with the flames of private violence and unruliness reaching their peak, a new frame of mind had slowly coalesced among the leading citizens and householders.

And it was a dumbfounding one. According to the new ideology, no member of society, let alone those despicable fosterers of endless confrontation, was "worth more" than anyone else. Instead, every head of family was lord of itself and his household. Insofar as everyone—citizen, peasant, serf, or nobleman—was equally committed to contributing to the costs of the *Hermandad* or to paying off the plethora of lawsuits levied against the most troublesome Parientes, everyone was—juridically speaking, at any rate—an equal.[6] Combine this conclusion with the parallel extension of city privileges and the leveling of runaway serfs to the legal status of their neighboring freemen, and it is not hard to see how the trend might undermine the pretensions of the mighty. The Parientes denounced that, due to these developments, "it is not known which are freemen and which are serfs and children and grandchildren of serfs."[7]

The clauses contained in the *fuero* of 1452, which distinguished between the liberties and exemptions of freemen in Biscay and those of the rest of the inhabitants, would mark the death rattles of the mental world that the Parientes had so earnestly fought to preserve. Occasionally, administrative inertia might see such distinctions refloat, as happened in some provincial ordinances of Guipuzcoa from 1463. But, in all, even the Parientes themselves had begun to accept the new *status quo* and to incorporate peasants and citizens into their entourages—regardless of the fact that military service was the preeminent marker of the nobility.[8] Increasingly overpowered by the monarchy and the Brotherhoods and urged to vie for terms, the painting was finally on the wall. In a society long exposed to individuals who threatened to cast the rest in their shade, the notion that everyone was "worth the same" was an intoxicatingly revolutionary one.

However, defeating the nobles was easier than rejecting nobility itself. As the Parientes had long taken for granted that only a handful of distinguished houses—their own—could boast the innate superiority to stand head and shoulders above their fellow compatriots. Castilian law, too, made it clear that knights, just like clerics and peasants, were "one of the three estates by which God willed the world to be sustained."[9] Their genealogies, passed down the generations, were filled with symbols that backed these interpretations: stories about their descent from glorious Gothic warriors, memories of services paid back by grateful kings with handsome favor, lands won by lance and sword. How could anyone—so their descendants argued—doubt that they deserved to tower above their neighbors, whose deeds history had forgotten, if they had ever achieved any at all? The failure of their plans to rule over these communities had not altered this logic in the slightest. Though their ambitions had been crushed, they still wielded in the new society a more powerful discourse than even the sharpest steel. A land without nobles was as unthinkable as a land without peasants. Which in turn meant that if the new provincial institutions wished to prevent the resurgence of old lineages and ensure social stability, they would need a narrative of their own. One that would solidify provincial power against the rise of ambitious warlords.

The challenge, naturally, lay in how to do it. Could it truly be argued that the provincial institutions, far from being a recent innovation, were in fact older—and therefore more legitimate—than even the most ancient of lineages? How was it possible to convince anyone of the fact that a shoemaker or a farmer was entitled to the same rights as a knight? To many, at any rate, these were positively otherworldly scenarios. And not only that. For the provincial justification, while ultimately aimed at dismantling the narrative put forth by the noble lineages, had also to double down as a defense mechanism against another potential rival: the crown's centralizing ambitions. For the time being, a fragile social peace had taken hold in the provinces. Yet, if this was to endure, it would need to be safeguarded by protecting the very conditions that had allowed it to emerge in the first place. The favor of kings, as those who had seen Mondragón burn and its culprits go unpunished knew all too well, was a resource too unreliable to count on. Instead, the provinces would have to find a way to avoid appearing as the mere outcome of a royal whim, for that would imply, in turn, that they could just as easily be undone at the monarch's will. Only thus, in short, could their permanence be assured.

A final factor had to be added to this calculation. The Castile upon which the southern territories of the Western Pyrenees had been incorporated, back in the early thirteenth century, had been an embattled kingdom. Now, in the early sixteenth, it was instead the pulsing heart of a global empire which included almost the entire peninsula and a vast range of colonial possessions. Conquest, inheritance, and lucky discoveries had all made its monarchs the most formidable in all of Christendom. A majesty, though, that bespoke peril to those willing to secure their privileges. For, against the might of such dazzling figures, what were the ambitions of provinces such as Guipuzcoa or Biscay, if not the petty labors of meek insects? The realization pushed local oligarchies to try and render the administration of these provinces untouchable to the royal hand. And this endeavor, in turn, meant casting their allegiance as being conditional to the swearing of their laws. Unfortunately, this was a privilege that established legal and scholarly doctrines recognized only to independent kingdoms and duchies like Aragon, Flanders, or Brabant—all of which were leagues above any Western Pyrenean territory in both riches and political clout. And yet, if their efforts were to be fruitful, these qualms would have to be surmounted. Out of their traditional regional obscurity, Western Pyreneans would have to bring their arguments to the stage of the grandees.

In this regard, Biscay enjoyed a considerable advantage. Being as it was a lordship separate from the rest of Castile, the *fuero* of 1452 had already cast the pact with the lord as a contract, binding to both parties, and dating back to the very moment of its foundation. As the story had it, Jaun Zuria had agreed with the Biscaynes on the distribution of power, and successive kings had implicitly accepted it. Neither Guipuzcoa nor Alava, despite having emerged institutionally strengthened from recent confrontations, could boast a similar tradition. Even the position of the inhabitants of the Lordship, however, was far from unassailable. After all, who had given those original residents the right to establish their own laws and to enforce them? Under what authority had they opposed the control of the kings of Asturias and Leon, from whose lineage the current sovereigns of Spain descended? The original freedom of Biscay, if not properly grounded in both law and history, threatened to end up providing, rather than proof of the entitlement of its dwellers to preferential status, the ultimate demonstration of their disloyalty.

It was therefore a legitimacy contested both internally and externally that ultimately would push the *foral* institutions in Biscay and Guipuzcoa to take an untrodden path: to extend nobility to all their inhabitants. Untrodden, but potentially revolutionary. *Hidalguía*, the name by which the lowest class of nobility was known in Castile, had always promised substantial benefits to those who could prove it: exemptions from certain taxes and services—including mandatory military service—access to higher offices and positions, and immunity from torture and other servile punishments.[10] But *Hidalguía* was also the legal expression of something else: liberty. Were it to be accepted, then the Parientes would have no other alternative but to recognize the freedoms of their neighbors and, in consequence, their supposed superiority and unquestionable right to represent the community would finally be undermined. Not only that, for only a land of nobles could present its compliance to the crown's command as a voluntary act and not an imposition. *Hidalguía* might mean individual freedom, yes, but it also meant communal self-governance. In the extension of nobility lay the cement that promised to definitively consolidate the authority of the provincial institutions. As had happened in Tolosa and in numerous other towns in the Western Pyrenees the privileges of some, if cards were played right, could become the privileges of all.

The attempt at seeing the nobility of Guipuzcoans and Biscaynes confirmed that it was staged during the 1520s could be seen, therefore, as the logical culmination of the ideological transformations of the preceding period. But in the early sixteenth century, there were other advantages to be gained from it as well. The pacification of private wars had not merely brought the triumph of an educated provincial oligarchy of city-dwellers; it had also provided new opportunities for the social ambitions of this class. It was not a coincidence that Seville, the place where men like Nicolás and Juan Sánchez de Aramburu had tried to make their fortunes, was the burgeoning center through which passed all the trade from the recently discovered Indies. For the kind of merchants and shipowners that made up the ruling class of Biscayne and Guipuzcoan coastal towns, the benefits to be reaped from recognition of nobility in such a trade post were indeed stupendous. Moreover, the expansion of royal power had also furthered the need for scribes, lawyers, soldiers, sailors, and clerks that could run the endlessly growing apparatus of the monarchy and enforce its claims across Europe. Faced with the choice between a land which had always offered little sustenance to its children and the opportunity of a prosperous career elsewhere, it was not hard to understand the hundreds upon hundreds of Western Pyreneans that opted to take the road leading away from home. Here, too, nobility could prove an advantageous perk to possess. In their competition for status and wealth, against the Parientes within and against other Castilians without, the attainment of *Hidalguía* was not only a prize worth pursuing, but a means toward ever greater horizons.

The problem lay in turning what was in essence a mutually recognized juridical equality, born out of the particular circumstances of a territory, into a claim to full-fledged nobility to be accepted both by foreigners and the court. Never before had anyone in the Western Pyrenees—not even the most ambitious Parientes—attempted such an astonishing exercise in public relations and outright deception. But staggering though the scale of the purported objective might have appeared, the methods to attain it were—just like the idea of a shared, universal freedom—deeply rooted in the customs and traditions of the past. After all, the Parientes, in trying to pose as the natural chieftains of the land, had invented for themselves a whole array of stories and half-truths. They had treasured mentions and concessions gained at the service of the monarchy, had produced emblems and symbols that distinguished their families, and had sponsored writers and artists to pen narratives and images that placed their houses at the summit of social achievement. Now, with their aspirations drenched in blood and opprobrium, their vanquishers were ready to make their own bout for glory. And, for all that their goals stood in direct opposition to the ideals endorsed by the Parientes, they would prove in their methods to have been their most advanced apprentices.

No one doubted, of course, that there were dark and difficult alleys that had to be navigated before such a radical idea could take root. In the bourgs, the final step before proclaiming nobility had been to completely erase the memory of servitude. Never, their representatives repeated again and again, had anyone walked their streets who was not of noble status. But under the current predicament faced by the General Assemblies of Guipuzcoa and Biscay, the problem was not precisely a handful of serfs, but rather other groups who, because they were marked by difference, could ruin the illusion of that homogeneous community of noblemen which deputies sought to impose. The whole affair reeked of more than a little dose of self-reflection. Who better than a recently enfranchised social climber, after all, to identify the potential pitfalls that lurked in the confusion between peoples of different conditions? Ambiguities had to be erased. Which is why the first collective endeavor undertaken by the new elites of Guipuzcoa and Biscay after the pacification of the land was none other than the persecution of all religious minorities.

As early as 1476, the Lordship's authorities had already requested "that no infidels, whether Moors or Jews, be allowed to reside in or remain within the county," and six years later a Guipuzcoan ordinance similarly prohibited Castilians—especially Jews or converts—from settling within the province.[11] In 1510, amid the general climate of anti-Semitic persecution that had followed the establishment of the Inquisition and the expulsion of all Jews from the kingdom, Guipuzcoa once again erupted in xenophobic fury against the newly converted. "No person, whether a new Christian of Moorish or Jewish origin or of such lineage, shall be permitted to settle in any of the said cities, towns, or places of the Province of Guipuzcoa, nor within its jurisdiction, and if any are found to be residing there, they shall be ordered to leave."[12] Biscay followed suit. In the same update to the *fuero* that so proudly proclaimed that "all natives, residents, and inhabitants of this Lordship . . . were known noblemen," the monarchy recognized the imaginary boundaries provincial authorities had so long sought to patrol. Any immigrants wishing to settle in Biscay would have to prove the religious purity of their lineage.[13] The following year, 1527, and perhaps in response to the recent sentence gained in Granada, an analogous exclusion of non-noblemen was put in place for Guipuzcoa.[14]

Considered against the background of the expulsion of all Jews from Castile in 1492, Biscayne and Guipuzcoan authorities were, in their persecution of religious minorities, pretty much children of their times. But, both in the precocity of their religious intransigence and the vehemence put on display to defend it, they also showed the extent to which the physical presence of these groups threatened the imagined community of equals they had wished to craft. Once upon a time, the Parientes had kept their claims to supremacy grounded upon the superiority of their bloodline. Fast forward to the present and the hegemony of the General Assemblies was similarly made to have resulted from an impeccable and immaculate succession of Christians.[15] "All in that land are clean of lineage thanks to God Our Lord," declared the sixty-year-old Pedro de Olano, one of the witnesses of the trial of Granada.[16] An assumption upon which every last Guipuzcoan and Biscayne could take pride, and an illusion on behalf of which all those who did not fit the bill, local or foreign, had to be singled out, identified, and ousted without remorse. Equality was not, at any rate, a privilege to be shared by all.

While expelling minorities from the land was one means of furthering provincial objectives, it was far from the only one. Another crucial strategy to prepare the way for the recognition of universal nobility was to propagate a view by which the services paid by both cities and General Assemblies to the monarchy could be regarded as military contributions. This, which might appear to be a minor point, was, on the contrary, an essential part of the whole endeavor. Both the Parientes and all previous noble families like those of Haro, Mendoza, or Guevara had taken for granted that their claims to lordship derived from their role as defenders of the community. As captains and leaders, they had early on identified in military service the paramount avenue for attaining their desired dominance.

But if they had come to learn this lesson, so too had their rivals. Cities and Brotherhoods had taken part in funding and provisioning the royal armies from the onset. The same boats that had honed the iron trade with Flanders were those that, back in 1415, had encircled English-ruled Bayonne and had put Biarritz and Saint-Jean-de-Luz to the torch.[17] However, such financial and material contributions, even though undeniably essential to the success of campaigns carried out against neighboring kingdoms, were short of exhibiting the same distinguished patina that only direct military service could bestow.

However, this could perhaps change as well. Provincial authorities began to take steps to reframe their contributions in terms worthy of almost-nobility recognition and this, as anyone could have expected, infuriated their opponents. In a heated dispute in the early sixteenth century between the foremost Parientes and the provincial deputies of Guipuzcoa, the assembled heads of lineage reiterated their standing as the leading protectors of royal interests in the territory. As they explained, they had

> not only serve[d] against the enemies of the Faith, but in all times of necessity, . . . ha[d] defended this entire homeland in all the wars that have arisen on these frontiers with France, Navarre, and England, as knights, noblemen, and defenders of the homeland. . . . For to such knights . . . it is proper and natural to defend, fight, and wage war against enemies with their arms, horses, squires, and relatives; for it is not their lot to guard livestock in the fields, nor to plow or break the land.[18]

The final condemnation summarized the way in which these powerful chieftains still treasured, almost a century on from their public surrender to the Brotherhood, the image of their ideal society. One in which the recourse to arms was part and parcel of a warrior class—and not of anyone else.

Against such views, the province deployed a very different argument. Dusting off services on men, coin, gear, and ships made on behalf of the monarchy in the recent past, the deputies of the Guipuzcoan Assembly set off to demonstrate that it was they who managed the chains of supply and recruitment in the territory of the Brotherhood. In return for these services, these delegates explained, Guipuzcoans had received rewards, such as the easing of grievous taxes, whose advantages for the local trade were nothing to sniff at. What, on the other hand, had the preponderance of the Parientes ever added to the common good? Only turmoil, destruction, and calamities. The implication was clear. The province could defend itself, and therefore the pretense of the Parientes was entirely unfounded, "for the number of the said Parientes Mayores would not be, nor is, sufficient to defend the said province or to render the services that have been performed for Your Majesties on behalf of the said province. And to claim that [they] alone could defend the said province or wage war . . . would be, and is, untenable."[19]

By the mid-1520s, when the provincial authorities finally decided to try their luck at the recognition of widespread *Hidalguía*, both the transformation of social realities and the legal arguments needed to support it had been decades in preparation. Pair this with some favorable circumstances and the presence of influential supporters—some of whom, in fact, would join the list of witnesses in the trial of Nicolás and Juan Sánchez de Aramburu—and it is not therefore surprising that the chances of receiving this unparalleled recognition were at an all-time high. Even the monarch, for all that he seemed to be fooled by the attempt, conceded that the whole endeavor had, in keeping the inhabitants of a distant and sensitive frontier content, some valuable advantages too.

In time, both Biscay and Guipuzcoa would see their *Hidalguía* recognized. However, the particulars of how this status had been gained and codified were unique in each of the territories, as were also the specific arguments deployed in its defense. Even the magistrate from Valladolid who had so effusively backed the pretensions of the Guipuzcoans noted that, in terms of nobility, "there were differences from Guipuzcoa to Biscay."[20] For one, the authority of the Province in Guipuzcoa had been premised on the total triumph of city oligarchies and the complete sidelining of the Parientes. In Biscay, on the contrary, matters were more complex. The General Assembly was, owing to the way in which the Lordship had been pacified, a clumsy juxtaposition of two different assemblies—that of the cities and that of the *Tierra Llana*—all under the unstable aegis of a royal official. In fact, so discontent were Biscayne cities with the settlement that in 1514 they had even attempted to detach themselves altogether from the rest of the Lordship.[21] Therefore, it should come as no surprise that the arguments deployed by Guipuzcoans were, on the whole, much more radical and deprecative toward the Parientes, whereas a cautious collaboration marked the way in which Biscayne *foral* authorities would usually proceed.

And then, of course, there was the pesky question of why Alava, which shared so much—in its history and its culture—with these two Western Pyrenean provinces, would never attain a similar legal status. Here, due probably to a longer story of subjection to feudal customs, the proportion of freemen in the sixteenth century was about a quarter of the population. Under such conditions, the extension of *Hidalguía* was neither a desirable nor a likely outcome. First, because it made it almost impossible for serfs to find a place populated entirely by exempt peoples to settle in. And second, because the hidalgos themselves, reminded daily of the differences between these subjected individuals and themselves, would treasure these valuable privileges much more staunchly than any of their northern counterparts ever did.

Notes

1 The following extracts come from the "Ejecutoria de Hidalguía de Juan Sánchez de Aramburu." *Archivo General de Guipuzcoa*, Juntas y Diputaciones, July 1, 2025.

2 However, the proportion of freemen was extraordinarily high (in Western European terms) all across the northern crust of Castile. See Díaz de Durana, "La hidalguía universal en el País Vasco," 56.

3 "Cuaderno de Ordenanzas de la Hermandad de Guipúzcoa" (1397). *Archivo Provincial de Guipúzcoa*, S.1, N.11, L.7. S.1, N.11, L.13: XXXIV. Also, Monreal, *Fuentes del Derecho Histórico de Bizkaia*, 116.

4 Orella, "El control de los judíos, conversos y extranjeros en Guipúzcoa durante el siglo XIV y la afirmación de la hidalguía vasca," 107–8.

5 Soria, "La Hidalguía Universal," 287–8.

6 Díaz de Durana, "La hidalguía universal en el País Vasco," 58.

7 Monreal, *The Old Law of Bizkaia (1452)*, 280.

8 Lema, "'Por los procuradores de los escuderos hijosdalgo': de la Hermandad general a la formación de las juntas de la provincia de Guipúzcoa (siglos XIV-XVI)," 88.

9 *Las Siete Partidas*, II, Título XXI.

10 Martínez de Isasti, *Compendio historial de Guipúzcoa*, 44–7.

11 We only have notice of this document thanks to a complaint made by Fernando del Pulgar to Pedro González of Mendoza. See Orella, "El control de los judíos," 109–10.

12 Quoted in Orella, "El control de los judíos," 110.

13 "Fuero Nuevo de Bizkaia" (1526). In Monreal, *Fuentes del Derecho Histórico de Bizkaia*, 299, XVI; 297–8, XIII.

14 Lema, "Por los procuradores de los escuderos hijosdalgo," 112.

15 Lema, 100.

16 "Ejecutoria de Hidalguía de Juan Sánchez de Aramburu." *Archivo General de Guipuzcoa*, Juntas y Diputaciones, July 1, 2025.

17 García de Salazar, *Libro de las Buenas Andanças*, 662.

18 Lema, et al., *El triunfo de las élites urbanas guipuzcoanas. Nuevos textos para el estudio del gobierno de las villas y de la Provincia (1412–1539)*, 325.

19 Lema et al., 329.

20 "Ejecutoria de Hidalguía de Juan Sánchez de Aramburu." *Archivo General de Guipuzcoa*, Juntas y Diputaciones, July 1, 2025.

21 Zabala, "Las Juntas Generales de Bizkaia a principios de la Edad Moderna: desequilibrios y enfrentamientos anteriores a la concordia," 86.

CHAPTER 16
CHILDREN OF THE PROPHETS

By the early 1530s, the idea that all the inhabitants of Biscay and Guipuzcoa were of noble standing was a legally accepted and sanctioned one, yet nowhere were the implications of the new ideology more overtly displayed than in naming conventions. For centuries, surnames in the Western Pyrenees had developed under pretty structured lines. The name of a person was usually coupled, first, with a reference to his or her father: for example, Sánchez—"son or daughter of Sancho"—or González—"son or daughter of Gonzalo." This was then followed by a mention of the extended lineage, such as Butrón, Oñaz, or Mújica. The Parientes had once attempted to structure all society by means of such familiar identifications, which of course placed them at the top of the social pyramid.

Insofar as these onomastic rules had grown and developed, sheltered by the practical benefits they bestowed in a turbulent society shaken by civil struggle, challenges to the towering position of the Parientes could not help but problematize these as well. If, according to the new orthodoxy spreading from the most important cities, everyone was indeed worth the same, why would places like Loyola or Balda be the only ones distinguished enough to grant their name to their residents? For the longest time the Parientes had defended that it was their position at the head of these famed lands which granted them dominion and command over their neighbors. But now their compatriots were hardly willing to accept any such assumption. Any house, they argued, even the humblest hamlet of an impoverished peasant, was as worthy of recognition as the most formidable of manors.

The unseating of the Parientes from political life thus had its reflection in the social realm, which is why the use of the lineage surname had begun to grow increasingly rare. What emerged, in its place, was a new convention: one that tied each individual, regardless of his or her resources, descent, or provenance, to the house they currently inhabited. As Andrés de Poza, an apologist of the provincial order, would put it, "there is no nickname or true surname of an original Biscayne that does not correspond to some house, place, district, quarter, mountain, river, or grove within this same Lordship."[1] By his time the transformation was mostly complete. Names had come to single out these peoples, not as members of a given Pariente's retinue, but instead as inhabitants of a legally delimited territory.[2]

Not that as momentous a concept as that of universal nobility, which promised to put an end, simultaneously, to internal instability, pacify the factions, and guarantee all sorts of exemptions and benefits across the empire, could ever rest on political measures alone. After all, nothing was more anathema to the mindset of the age than the nakedness of novelty. Any innovation had to be duly justified by tradition, scholarship, and custom, and in such an environment, the rejection of history could never be the same as a contempt for memory. The councilors of Tolosa, in making their claims derive from a privilege issued nearly a century before, had already grasped what this meant. Inventing the future meant reinterpreting the past, not eliminating it. The universal nobility that the new institutions so eagerly aspired to establish did not thus require any political manifesto nor justification listing its social or economic benefits. On the contrary, it only needed a good story.

It is almost impossible to determine when the narrative began to take shape, nor who were the first to conceive it. It remains unknown how it was passed on, altered, and expanded, from mouth to mouth through streets and castles, docks and hamlets, in a society where rarely anything was written down unless absolutely necessary, nor how the march of the years slowly made it evolve in the tongues of these peoples. Many of the notions that later became its pillars—such as that all dwellers of Guipuzcoa and Biscay were indeed noblemen—had been crafted during the long years of the struggle against the Parientes. Others, on the contrary, came most likely from distant lands, new thoughts heard in the classrooms of famous universities or in the relentless bustle of the ports, only later appropriated because they seemed to confirm the biases and needs of the locals. In any case, approximately half a century after the end of the civil wars, the story already existed in its fundamentals, from which it was later only superficially altered.

At the outset, however, its later success was hardly a given. The provincial authorities of the Western Pyrenees might have been forced to rewrite their past to justify their new situation, but the rest of the monarchy was likewise immersed in a true literary effervescence. Politically obsolete legends, all across the empire, were being replaced with others more in line with contemporary concerns. The myth of the Gothic inheritance, for example, which had so firmly underpinned the Reconquista against the Muslims during the times of the kingdoms of Leon and Pamplona, outlived its usefulness once the kingdom of Granada, the last bastion of Islam in the peninsula, was conquered in 1492. The defeat of the old boogeyman, however, had not diminished the regularity of attacks against the interests and claims of the monarchy. Others were now pouring their venom against the subjects of the kings of Castile and Aragon. And among them, thanks to the extent of their influence, none could compare to the Italians.

"The entire kingdom was full of Jews and heretics, and the majority of the people were tainted with this depravity; they held all the main offices and leases of the kingdom, and with such power and numbers that it was evident that, without intervention, in a few years all of Spain would abandon the Catholic faith."[3] The verdict, issued by a Florentine ambassador in 1513, furnished an image that many shared in Italy. The populations of this peninsula, battered by the recent expansion of Spanish interests in the region, had quickly developed a poisonous rivalry with the newcomers. In the writings of their intellectuals, the Spaniards often played the role of barbarians, and the ancient Gothic myth was turned on its head to rationalize the savagery and brutality of their supposed heirs.[4] Many feared, in fact, the stain that centuries of acquaintance with Jews and Moors might have left on these peoples—a charge that even extended to the Aragonese Pope Alexander VI himself.[5] The Italian humanists, steeped in the reverence for classical tradition, thus condoned their resistance with descriptions that presented them as the sole heirs of ancient Rome and of true religion.[6] In their outrage, the response of Spaniards, as in the case of the provinces, had been to seek an even older antiquity to appropriate.[7] In both cases, it was a matter of proving not only that their claims were older and more legitimate than those of their opponents but, even more generally, that God was on their side.

Luckily, there were alternative traditions that could boast a more brilliant pedigree than even Greco-Roman sources, and, among these, none shone more brightly than Holy Scripture. For centuries, across Christendom, intellectuals and clerics had painstakingly traced the origins of peoples and kingdoms to their biblical ancestors. In the case of the inhabitants of the Iberian Peninsula, this process had resulted in the identification of a single progenitor: Tubal, the grandson of Noah. Isidore of Seville, back in the age of the Visigoths, had already recorded this parentage in his *Etymologies*.[8] But it would not be him, but rather a Castilian chronicler from the late twelfth century, Rodrigo Jiménez de Rada, who would ultimately set the narrative in stone: "The fifth son of Japheth was Tubal, from whom the Iberians descend, who are also called Spaniards."[9] The message left no doubt and, for this reason, proved the perfect ammunition for the ideological battles of the present. The Spaniards, far from a heretical mixed race or the heirs of savage barbarians, were instead the descendants of the noblest and purest lineage of the patriarchs of Israel.[10] Tubalism became the foundation of Spanish claims to proclaim, as foreigners disapprovingly noted, "that no nation can compare with theirs."[11]

Interestingly, this newly discovered ascendancy of the story of Tubal, which contributed so much to the international propaganda of the monarchy, would end up being a lifeline for Western Pyrenean provincial institutions. As the story went, the patriarch and his companions, leaving the east after the construction of the Tower of Babel, had made "the peaks of the Pyrenees" their new home.[12] Tradition dictated that this referred to the central areas of the mountain range, and this was also how generations of Biscaynes, Guipuzcoans, and others had interpreted it. Nothing better to demonstrate this point than noting that the Parientes, little susceptible to missing an opportunity to highlight the nobility of their houses, had never echoed the story. And why would they? If their genealogies were to be believed, their dynasties had been founded by kings and knights, or at the very least by courageous Goths proficient in feats of arms. Weighed against this, a generic reference to a supposed biblical descent could not add that much.

For those at the helm of the provinces, in contrast, the situation was quite different. The new collective institutions could not rest satisfied, like lineages did, with singular ancestors, progenitors of a single family branch. What they needed was a common origin that could equalize—at least in imaginary terms—all those living under their jurisdiction, and this rendered the Tubalian myth one of vital importance. Convince even the humblest Biscayne that, regardless of his wealth or position, he was as much a descendant of the patriarchs of the Old Testament as the most aristocratic of Parientes, and the right of the latter to primacy would soon collapse under its own weight.

Naturally, the story had to be appropriately tweaked. The circulation of the story of Tubal, as the crown's propagandists understood it at any rate, was based on the certainty that all inhabitants of the peninsula could trace an equal line of descent from this distinguished ancestor. But this equality, while valuable on the European stage, jeopardized the provincial's goal of putting the Tubalian discourse at the service of their selfish interests. How to prove otherwise that only they, among all the king's subjects, were entitled to see their elevated status legally recognized? After all, it was at this point—in its acceptance by foreigners—where most talk of superiority tended to fail.

Fortune, however, had placed in the hands of the authorities of Guipuzcoa and Biscay a perfect and indisputable instrument to uphold their ambitions; an unapproachable enigma of unknown origin and completely unique in its kind; a remnant that could very well, as some dared to speculate, be a relic of humanity's golden ages. A language whose very antiquity—and its widespread ignorance outside the Western Pyrenees—made it the perfect weapon with which to defend anything, even the most radical of revolutions. In a world that was but beginning to pay heed to the import of the popular speech of the masses, the mantle of mystery that surrounded *Euskera* could easily be stretched so as to conceal—or so it seemed—the true origins of those who spoke it.

And, certainly, *Euskera* was the language of the masses in the Western Pyrenees. Outside the city walls, it was the only language spoken in Biscay, Guipuzcoa, and Labourd, while in Alava and Navarre the spread of Castilian only became more noticeable the more one traveled south.[13] It was also the mother tongue of most of the local aristocracy. The fleets bound for Flanders and England, and which transported the country's valuable iron cargo, were managed and operated in *Euskera*, and it was also in *Euskera* that the blacksmiths who extracted the dark metal from the depths of the earth communicated. Children running in front of churches played games in this language, the same in which sellers approached their customers in the loud market squares.

And yet, despite its prevalence, it remained a despised dialect. Sidelined by the Romance languages from all spheres of power—political administration, the church, long-distance commerce—it nevertheless survived precisely because it was truly distinct from them. While the Romance speech of Navarre or Gascony was endangered by contact with Castilian or French, with which they shared much of their grammar and vocabulary, nothing of the sort happened with *Euskera*. And yet, for all that its survival seemed assured, a functional diglossia, founded upon a separation of tasks, lowly and superior, popular and snobbish, was at any rate starting to set in. As a traveler to Alava would record in 1572, "here, you can see that the common people speak Biscayne, or *vascongado*, as they call it, which is a hard language to learn, while the nobles speak excellent Castilian very clearly."[14]

However, even though the widespread use of *Euskera* was an undeniable reality, never before had the natives of the Western Pyrenees made use of it as part of any political discourse. The language, at least since the times of Strabo, had been considered a barbaric and savage tongue, and the medieval testimony that compared its sound to the "barking of dogs" was regrettably famous.[15] But now, surprisingly, the provincial institutions had discovered for the first time in *Euskera* an irrefutable argument to back their claims to exclusivity. "It can be truthfully said that the language [these provinces] still maintain, a manifest testimony of their antiquity, is one of the seventy from the Babylonian confusion of tongues, inspired by God, and this, as it was granted to their first man, [is] so eloquent that in each of its words it connotes the secrets of all things."[16] In other words, *Euskera* was nothing short of the language of Tubal: a divine relic preserved since the darkest antiquity among the mountains and forests of the Western Pyrenees.

Of course, it remained to be explained how it was possible, given that all Spaniards were descendants of Tubal, that *Euskera* was only spoken in a remote part of the peninsula and nowhere else. Was it not to be expected, if the language was indeed that of Tubal, that there would be some communities still speaking *Euskera* elsewhere or, failing that, employing a large number of loans from this language? The thought must have crossed the minds of Western Pyrenean ideologues for, soon enough, they began to "uncover" extravagant etymologies in *Euskera* for cities and regions all across Iberia. Asturias, for example, became in their writings "ahaztu herria"—"the forgotten land"—while the Ebro River became "Ibero," singularly translated into Castilian as "you hot."[17] This fervor for etymology, however, extended not only to landmarks outside the Western Pyrenees. The name of Guipuzcoa, for example, was made to derive from "Guk puska"—a boast meaning "we will tear you apart." Baseless translations and inventions, most of them, but of a kind which, in the intellectual climate of European humanism, where philology and vernacular languages had become the latest fashion, were often accepted as valid. Under the weight of such abundant and earnestly repeated erudition, after all, who could be surprised that many came to be convinced of the fact that *Euskera* had been, indeed, "the first language of Spain"?[18]

Few Asturians, to cite but a single case, would have recognized their own country in that "forgotten land" writers from the provinces so carelessly described. And that was because nowhere in this territory—nor anywhere else in the Iberian Peninsula—was it possible to hear as much as a hint of *Euskera*. According to the propaganda poured from Biscay and Guipuzcoa, this constituted no refutation of their claims. If anything, it only strengthened them even further. Everyone knew that the rest of Spain had been repeatedly conquered by Roman, Gothic, and Arab hordes, and these invasions had doubtless erased the pristine customs and the language brought by Tubal. The Western Pyrenees, on the contrary, had never bent the knee to the foreigners. This was the sole reason, and not any other, why *Euskera* had been preserved in this mountainous bulwark. In an all-too-fortunate coincidence, it was also why no other territory nor community in the entire kingdom could claim as distinguished a descent as could Biscaynes and Guipuzcoans.

A definitive and politically useful verdict, of course, but also a historically dubious one. The intellectual acrobatics required to maintain this fiction were of such magnitude that they demanded nothing less than the reinterpretation of each and every available historical source. But once again, luck favored the designs of the provincial elites. The territories of Biscay and Guipuzcoa, which for much of their history had lingered on the margins of a periphery, were almost barren when it came to documents and testimonies. The Parientes, in pursuing what they had considered their time-honored rights, had once taken advantage of this very fact to push forward their supremacy. As they had masterfully recognized, in a world dominated by orality and by the recourse to folk memory, any narrative, if repeated with enough regularity, could eventually come to resemble a self-evident truth. What was the overwhelming absence of documents issued by the Leonese or the Castilian monarchs, for example, if not proof of the ghostly control their kingdoms had exercised in Guipuzcoa and Biscay? Even the few surviving charters issued by long-dead kings could, if read appropriately, come to buttress this outlandish conclusion. The ancients had once regarded a sort of civilizational obscurity as the distinctive mark of Western Pyrenean barbarism. Now, in the sixteenth century, this same obscurity was being repurposed as the main confirmation of the high-class status of their inhabitants.

To so shamelessly proclaim the invincibility of these lands naturally required arguments to match, and local authors immediately set off to the task. The memory of the numerous encounters between the Vascones and the Visigoths was dusted off, as was also the record of the battle of Arrigorriaga that had—allegedly—pitted the Biscaynes against the Leonese. Each of these episodes was then transmuted into a valiant struggle in which nothing short of the primordial freedoms of the children of Tubal had been at stake. The only issue arose when one tried to apply this literary framework back to the Roman period. Was it not indisputable and well-known that the legions had subjugated the Western Pyrenees, as they had done the rest of the Peninsula? Did not their most populous city, Pamplona, even bear the name of one of their generals? The argument of eternal resistance appeared to have met a dead end. But again, scholars tasked with defending the Spanish monarchy's European ambitions had inadvertently given wings, in their defense of the peninsula's antiquity, to their provincial counterparts. The latter might reluctantly admit that the Vascones, as reputable historians confirmed, had been subjects of Rome. But there was another mountain population, further west, who had been not.

The Cantabrians, back in the first century AD, had fought a series of bloody campaigns against Augustus' legions and had been the last of all the peoples of the peninsula to accept the Roman yoke. Most crucially, there was some ambiguity regarding the geographical location of ancient Cantabria. Some scholars argued that it was located to the west of the Western Pyrenees—near Asturias or even in Galicia. Others, by contrast, identified it with Rioja or northern Castile. And, as it could not have been otherwise, there existed a third group of authors, including prestigious ones, who took for granted that ancient Cantabria had included in its bosom the Provinces of Guipuzcoa and Alava and the Lordship of Biscay.[19]

Those willing to emphasize the Tubalian heritage of these lands needed little more than that. In a display of inventiveness and historical forgery worthy of the best masters of the time, apocryphal stories began to circulate about the Western Pyrenean Cantabrians. One of them, accounted for by Juan Martínez de Zaldibia, spoke of a ritual combat staged in Rome between 100 Cantabrian soldiers and 100 Romans. The Cantabrians, thanks to their victory, had gained recognition from Caesar "as friends and confederates, retaining their ancient freedom and nobility."[20] Another text exhibiting the modest name of

Crónica General Española y Sumaria de la Casa de Vizcaya offered, even more startlingly, the very hymn these Cantabrians had chanted on occasion of their triumph, in which it was made clear that "Otabiano /[m]unduco jaun/ leco bydi/ Vizcaicoa": Octavian—Augustus—may have been lord of the world, but not of Biscay.[21]

These and other retellings imprinted on the minds of many cultured individuals that the Lordship and the provinces had indeed been part of the ancient and unconquerable Cantabria, and that it was *Euskera* that most vindicated such conclusion. The pieces, it seemed, were finally falling into place. And even the Romans, who had once prided themselves on being masters of the known world, were now widely recognized to have fallen utterly short of putting an end to the freedoms of Tubal's descendants.

A moral that could also apply to Castilians. Biscayne freemen had been the first, thanks to their political and legal particularities, to present their allegiance to the peninsular monarchs as a binding contract between equals—and thus revocable in case of transgression by either party. Observance of the *fuero* was, in such a reading, the counterpart for Biscayne loyalty. But the interpretation, which appeared so self-evident in the Lordship, was a farce that was difficult to maintain in the rest of the territories. In Guipuzcoa, unlike in Biscay, the vast majority of inhabitants had fallen under the privileged jurisdiction of chartered cities. The very documents of these franchises showed that they had been favors granted by the monarchy and not the result of any mythical agreement. In Alava, too, the privileges granted by Enrique Trastámara to reward those who had helped him secure the throne also made a pact-based interpretation hard to abide by. Chroniclers and historians at the service of both provinces would spend long decades trying to solve these obstacles to their advantage. Their success, in the long term at any rate, would be ambiguous.

And yet, for now at least and amid the intellectual environment of the Renaissance and the Reformation, the biblical and philological arguments deployed by the intellectuals of the Western Pyrenees appeared sufficient to establish a curious comparison. Almost uncritically, and overlooking occasional scholarly debates, those places where *Euskera* was predominantly spoken came to be considered the last refuges of the people of Tubal, for "only this nation among all the provinces and kingdoms of the world preserves its laws as given in the law of nature . . . and only this one has preserved its original language."[22] The people of the patriarch, the ancient Cantabrians, and the modern provincials of Biscay and Guipuzcoa were one and the same people, pure in their roots, which they had preserved thanks to a stubborn and everlasting overwatch. Not only that, but they could even boast that all the great triumphs that the Spanish monarchy had achieved, both in the peninsula and beyond, were ultimately a consequence of their reluctance to forfeit their God-ordained customs. Through literary confusions and half-truths, a lineage of incomparable nobility had been born in the Western Pyrenees.

As for the Parientes, the whole affair of universal nobility, the Tubalian myth, and the strengthening of the provincial framework bespoke bad news indeed. For the heirs of chieftains whose predecessors had set cities on fire in revenge for affronts to honor and reputation, the new conditions were hardly a match made in heaven. Unlike members of the city oligarchies, most of them were, in fact, ill-prepared for the kind of legalistic and Castilian-speaking environment that emerged in the wake of the pacification. The result was that it took them precious time to benefit from the economic and social opportunities that had opened by the end of the fifteenth century. In addition, the entire project of collective ennoblement had not only been a direct rejection of their attempts at social domination but also had been framed through arguments that demonized their activities. The new ideology had made sure to depict the Parientes, not as the great men of the land as they pretended to be, but instead as fosterers of public turmoil and provokers of discord and misery. This held true even in Biscay, where the heads of the greatest families took part in the new institutions. But even here their preponderance had come to be filtered through the procedures of a territorial assembly which denied them any inherent superiority over the rest of the inhabitants of the Lordship.[23]

Once they became convinced that the new settlement was bound to stay, the Parientes closed ranks and tried to find ways to thrive even under such unfavorable circumstances. In Biscay, for example, they sought to transform their traditional dominion of the *Tierra Llana* into a way to obstruct, in the General Assembly, the aspirations of emboldened city authorities such as those of Bilbao. In Guipuzcoa, because delegates were elected by city councils and the Parientes themselves were barred from attending the meetings of the General Assembly, they opted instead to create a separate assembly of "vassals of the king." Strikingly, in the ensuing contest between the latter and the Province of Guipuzcoa—which began in 1516—and apart from vindicating yet again their position as protectors of the land, the Parientes made sure to also deploy a never-before-seen argument. Rather than enemies of the province, they proclaimed, they were in fact "its founders, as well as the bedrock, trunk, and root from which all the other noblemen of this homeland" had originally emerged.[24] In their outrage, and to a portrayal broadcast by urban elites, of the lineages as unruly warmongers, they opposed a view that took them as the epitome of the noble community of Guipuzcoa.

The move was not only audacious but hard to refute. For if lawyers at the service of the province took pains to explain that the community of Guipuzcoa was indeed far older than the individual lineages, there was also the fact that the defense of the *Hidalguía* had been premised upon a staunch belief that the liberties of the provincials predated even the foundation of chartered cities. In other words, the exemptions and liberties granted by a succession of monarchs were, to the mainstream provincial discourse, nothing but the "trappings" of nobility, whose essence lay elsewhere. But where exactly? The only option was, naturally, to assume that these were still observable in the non-chartered countryside. Thus, and for all that the pursuit of universal nobility had been spearheaded mostly by urban oligarchies and upwardly mobile freemen, its results were paradoxical. Key to the elevation of the standing of all naturals was proclaiming the existence of an idealized countryside—the same countryside that the Parientes had geographically, politically, and symbolically made their abode.[25] Tubal, the Cantabrians, the men who resisted the Moors: All of them were much easier to link to those with deep ties in the rural world than to the merchant and administrative class of city-dwellers. So it was that, albeit with some delay, the door opened for the great families to join the victors of the wars of *bandos*. A century later, the Guipuzcoan author Lope Martínez de Isasti would pen the perfect summary of what this imbrication had truly entailed.

> It cannot be denied that the Parientes Mayores in Guipuzcoa have been powerful and esteemed in their time. Although all natives and original inhabitants of this land are of noble lineage, some are more distinguished than others, and in saying this, no offense is given. Two silver vessels are both valued for being made of such fine metal, but if one is gilded, it is clear that it is held in even higher esteem.[26]

Some might find in such a conclusion a rebuttal of all the aspirations behind universal nobility. But, in fact, it did not have to be so. After all, the new systems were no paradise of social justice. *Hidalguía*, for all that it might constitute for many a source of pride and identity, had not spawned the idyllic brotherhood of man that perhaps testimonies poured in its defense so fervently proclaimed. For starters, getting written proof of nobility—that is, a document stating that a person was indeed a true native of Guipuzcoa or Biscay and which made recognition of status possible outside these territories—was a long, arduous, and costly process. As such, it lay only within reach of the high achievers; in other words, members of the city oligarchies and the heirs to powerful families. Likewise, appointment to local and provincial offices was barred behind an income-wall better known as *millares*, "thousands." This system marked a minimum patrimony, measured only in goods and lands passed down through *mayorazgo* and which kept, in practice, the reins of the government in the hands of the wealthiest. It was thanks to the *millares* that the new provincial aristocracy—who had increasingly married into the most distinguished lineages—would monopolize the administration of the territory and would prevent anyone else from meeting the requirements needed to access any politically significant offices.[27]

Ordinances and rulings, in addition, prohibited artisans from being elected as delegates, and peasants, too, were barred from attending the meetings of the General Assemblies. The whole voting system, rigged as it was to suit the needs of the grandees, effectively took any measure of power off the hands of commoners. [28] In Guipuzcoa, many rural communities which in the previous decades had sought security under the wing of chartered cities now saw these towns' delegates usurp the right to speak on their behalf.[29] It was not an isolated trend. In fact, throughout the sixteenth century, the competences of the General Assembly, barely an egalitarian institution to begin with, were systematically diminished, as more compact councils such as the Regiment and the Deputation emerged to carry the lion's share of the administration of the land.[30] It goes without saying that these new institutions, too, were rapidly monopolized by those with *millares*.

A final but telling demonstration of the extent to which the ideology of universal nobility could be a tool for internal domination had to do with language. *Euskera* might have been a crucial pillar in the ideological defense of the Provincial order, a language valued not only for its antiquity but also endowed with the distinguished pedigree of having been created by none other than God Himself. However, the new ruling class was not in the business of letting these lofty ideas threaten their dominion. While *Euskera* might be a badge of honor to be dusted off, if necessary, every time a foreigner challenged provincial privileges, it was precisely its second-class status that most secured the right of the wealthy and the powerful to exercise their authority. Which is why, rather than doing away with its subordinate position, members of these groups sought to reinforce it. The General Assembly of Guipuzcoa, in 1529, had already made it a requisite for delegates to know how to talk and write in Castilian: a measure that effectively excluded all but the upper crust of urban society from its meetings.[31] Similar approaches were taken elsewhere.

All in all, the results of the revolution carried out by the victors of the war of *bandos* in Biscay and Guipuzcoa were indeed stupendous. On the outside, a community entirely comprised of noblemen had been created. Not only that, for it had been successfully defended with proofs that linked legal arguments, historical narratives, and even Holy Scripture itself in a tangle which proved almost impossible to unravel. The endeavor had singled out a political space that now rested, thanks to its contractual nature, beyond the reach of the most powerful of monarchs and, moreover, an entire class of Western Pyrenean clerks, merchants, and military officials—like Philip II's personal secretary, Juan de Idiáquez, or Esteban de Garibay, royal chronicler for the same king—now flooded the posts of an ever-expanding administration in Europe and the Americas. Within the provincial territories, too, the basis of the power of the Parientes had been decisively broken and brought to submit. Here, provincial institutions had secured their calling as the main—the only—spokesmen of the community.

But these achievements had come at a cost. The equality so enthusiastically paraded in books and letters had led to the physical exclusion of minorities and the political sidelining of the popular classes. Everywhere, wealth—and, more precisely, wealth that could be passed down the generations in *mayorazgo*—had substituted honor and military service as the main axis to measure the value of a given person. In such a society, the enemies of the new ruling class were no longer the Parientes—who were rapidly absorbed into it—but instead the mass of the excluded. With just as much vehemence as they had once deployed to prove that none in their land was inherently superior to another, members of the elite now thundered about the existence of a supposedly contingent—yet suspiciously unchanging—hierarchy of worth. Soon, this too would become an almost unchallenged dogma. As the orthodox view declared, "as for esteem, there have never been a lack of hierarchies in Biscay, even though nobility is common, as can be inferred from the houses of great distinction."[32] A similar verdict applied to the rest of the Western Pyrenees.

Even after the trampling of the hopes of the Parientes, and for all that the learned might state otherwise, some were still worth much more than others.

Notes

1 Poza, *Fuero de hidalguía Ad pragmaticas de Toro & Tordesillas*, 275–7.

2 Azurmendi, *Nombrar, embrujar. Para una historia del sometimiento de la cultura oral en el País Vasco*, 17–18; 20; 31. Also, Aranzadi, *Milenarismo Vasco. Edad de Oro, etnia y nativismo*, 334. Martínez, *Casa, Provincia, Rey*, 14–15.

3 Guicciardini, "Relazione di Spagna." In Giucciardini, *Scritti Autobiografici e rari*, 135.

4 See, for instance, the case of Antonio de Ferraris, quoted in López, "'Non placet Hispania'. Los orígenes de la leyenda negra," 76.

5 Arnoldsson, *La Leyenda Negra. Estudios sobre sus orígenes*, 21–2.

6 A similar process, concerning depictions of the French made by Italians, has been studied by Hirschi, *The Origins of Nationalism: An Alternative History from Ancient Rome to Early Modern Germany*, 142–52.

7 Álvarez and De la Fuente, *El relato nacional. Historia de la historia de España*, 60.

8 Isidore of Seville, *Etymologies*, IX, II, 22, 193.

9 "Historia Rebus Hispaniae," I, 3. In Jiménez de Rada, *Historia de los hechos de España*, 64.

10 Remarkable among these are Giovanni Nanni (better known as Annio de Viterbo) and Antonio de Nebrija, official chronicler of King Ferdinand and Queen Isabella. See Álvarez and De la Fuente, *El relato nacional*, 61–2.

11 Guicciardini, "Relazione di Spagna," 129.

12 "Historia Rebus Hispaniae," I, 3. In Jiménez de Rada, *Historia de los hechos de España*, 64.

13 The limits of Euskera in this period appear to have included the cities of Estella and Tafalla in Navarre. See Mounole and Lacarra, "El Euskera Arcaico," 388–9.

14 Giovanni Battista Venturino (1572). Quoted in Madariaga, *Anthology of Apologists and Detractors of the Basque Language*, 109.

15 Klaus and Santos, *Liber Sancti Jacobi Codex Calixtinus*, V, 7, 240.

16 Poza, *Fuero de hidalguía Ad pragmaticas de Toro & Tordesillas*, XIII, 247.

17 Poza, I, 3. Also "Crónica Ibargüen-Cahopín" (1558–1620). In Arriolabengoa, "Ibarguen-Cachopín Kronika," I, XXXV, 482–4.

18 Garibay, *Los XL libros del Compendio Historial*, IV, IV, 91.

19 Morales, *Coronica General de España*, VII, XIII, 85.

20 Martínez de Zaldibia, *Suma de las cosas cantábricas y guipuzcoanas*, 58.

21 "Crónica Ibargüen-Cahopín" (1558–1620). In Arriolabengoa, "Ibarguen-Cachopín Kronika," LXXI, 90.

22 Martínez de Zaldibia, *Suma de las cosas cantábricas y guipuzcoanas*, IV, 10.

23 One of these approaches, particular to Biscay, was to institutionalize the bandos of Gamboa and Oñaz for the election of delegates to the Assembly of the *Tierra Llana*. See Zabala, "Las Juntas Generales de Bizkaia a principios de la Edad Moderna: desequilibrios y enfrentamientos anteriores a la concordia," 90.

24 Lema et al., *El triunfo de las élites urbanas guipuzcoanas*, 325.

25 Soria, "La Hidalguía Universal," 299–300.

26 Martínez de Isasti, *Compendio Historial de Guipúzcoa*, 78.

27 Martínez, *Casa, Provincia, Rey*, 263.

28 Celaya, *Los Fueros de Bizkaia. I. Como nacieron. II. El licenciado Poza y la defensa de la hidalguía*, 215. Also, Azurmendi, *Nombrar, embrujar*, 198.

29 Azurmendi, *Y se limpie aquella tierra. Limpieza étnica y de sangre en el País Vasco (siglos XVI-XVIII)*, 37–8.

30 Intxaustegi, "Las instituciones territoriales y locales en el Señorío de Vizcaya durante la Edad Moderna: Convergencias y divergencias," 173–4.

31 Díaz de Durana, "La hidalguía universal en el País Vasco," 52.

32 "El Tordo Vizcaíno" (*c.*1638). In Mañaricua, *Polémica sobre Vizcaya en el siglo XVII: El búho gallego y El tordo vizcaíno*, 137.

CHAPTER 17
EUSKAL HERRIA

A colossal triangular mass, black against the canvas of the night like the jaws of a primordial beast, was the main attraction of the richest city in the world. A mountain that—as had been tested by countless teams of miners—was literally made of silver. Nowhere else in the world, except in Potosí, in the Viceroyalty of Peru, could such a treasure be found. Only six years after the city's foundation it was already contributing more than three million ducats to the Spanish monarchy, "an amount greater than what the Spaniards obtained from Atahualpa or what was found in the city of Cuzco when it was discovered."[1] And indeed, drawn by the allure of quick wealth, entrepreneurial adventure, and the scent of opportunity, both new conquerors and nearby indigenous populations had flocked to the shadow of the mountain. "In this way, they formed a large population alike, though without order, harmony, or planned streets,"[2] inhabited by people of all backgrounds: Castilians, Indians, Andalusians, Italians, Potosí remained, a hundred years after the exploits of Cortés and Pizarro in the New World, a mosaic of individuals aspiring to make their fortunes in the Indies and enrich themselves with their gifts. And at the helm of this city, which fueled the Spanish monarchy's aspirations for dominance with its silver harvest, were men and women from the Western Pyrenees.

Upon deeper scrutiny, there was nothing unusual about this. The heirs of families from the region, accustomed as they had grown to solving matters through force, had found fertile ground for their talents in America, and many had held positions of power and honor in the newly discovered lands. From Oñate came Lope de Aguirre, nicknamed "the Madman," who tirelessly sought the mythical city of El Dorado. Juan Ortiz de Zárate, a native of Orduña, took part in the conquest of Peru and governed the Río de la Plata. Diego and Francisco de Ibarra, whose lineage of Parientes originally hailed from Eibar, founded the kingdom of New Biscay in northern Mexico in the mid-sixteenth century—and the latter even gave its capital the name of Durango. The founder of Santa Fe and Buenos Aires, Juan de Garay, was also from Biscay, and the conqueror of the Philippines, Miguel López de Legazpi, came from Guipuzcoa. Even Juan Sebastián Elcano, the captain of the expedition that completed the first circumnavigation of the world in 1522, had been born in Guetaria.

Many of these early colonizers, as invariably happens with most migrants, had looked for the support of their fellow countrymen upon arriving in Potosí. While this was indeed a trend common to all newcomers, Western Pyrenean individuals had proven especially prone to setting up their own closed communities and to becoming a sort of minority within a minority. Naturally, there were practical reasons for such apparent isolation. Speaking as many of them did a broken and halting Spanish, they instinctively sought the company of those with whom they could communicate in their native language. Their neighbors had not failed to notice this, and thus had, from early on, referred to them as *vascongados*—that is, as "*Euskera*-speakers." However, as the years went by, and the riches of Potosí came to be renowned across the world, linguistic affinities had given way to more prosaic considerations. The community of *vascongados* had grown in number, and so too, in parallel, had grown the opportunities available to its members. The networks of clients and useful contacts that the most influential among them could tap from extended not only throughout Peru but across all of America and at both sides of the Atlantic. Anticipation of what an individual might attain through them was only comparable to the deals they allowed to broker in Potosí itself.

Already in 1589, well-doing families native to Biscay, Alava, Guipuzcoa, or Navarre had chosen to solidify their bonds by sponsoring the cult of the Guipuzcoan Virgin of Aranzazu. By 1602, these *vascongados* already controlled more than two-thirds of the city's shops and estates.[3] Not all of them, of course, could still speak the language of their ancestors, which they must have found rather unserviceable in their routine dealings with Indians and other Spaniards. Nevertheless, they cultivated a strong sense of shared ancestry and a distinct identity all the same. And so, while back in their homeland, politicians and judges sought to harden the jurisdictional, legal, and mental barriers that separated their respective provinces and lordships from one another, here in America, "[. . .] without distinction, united in these vast kingdoms of the Indies with love and benevolence, we call ourselves *vascongados.*"[4]

Innocent though this feeling of camaraderie might appear at first sight, many of their neighbors, especially those less favored in the distribution of the New World's riches, could not help but perceive a sinister reminder in the tendency of Western Pyreneans to form exclusive communities. "The fact that you are not Jews by profession does not mean that you are not so by blood, ancestry, and nation," thundered a treatise published in Potosí in 1624.[5] Coexistence among settlers, far from being harmonious in a city so blessed with unparalleled wealth, had always been marked by envy and hostility. So, too, by the periodical eruption of uprisings that threatened to drown the streets in blood. As early as 1552, for example, the "words of great presumption, vanity, and arrogance" of a *vascongado* had resulted in the open insurrection of other Castilians.[6] Thirty years later, a similar clash between factions had left a royal magistrate wounded, whereas in 1609, the support given by his successor to the *vascongados* had been regarded by his enemies as reason enough to plot his assassination.

And yet it was now, in 1622, that the situation had taken an especially terrifying turn. Financial difficulties had struck the poorer Spanish settlers, who—unsurprisingly—were those most resentful of the *vascongado*'s relatively well-off position. The latter's economic and political dominance in the city was a stain in the eyes of many, a constant reminder of how their ancestors had been cheated out of their rights over their conquests. The *vascongados*, who were the object of such disdain, rather than throw a heavy veil over the entire issue, paid their accusers back with haughtiness. When in the summer of 1622 a *vascongado* magnate was found dead in an alley with evident signs of violence on his body, their kin cried out for revenge. Roaming the town, they searched for the culprits.

Soon, anarchy and vendettas spread through the streets, "and it should be noted that it was a scourge of God's wrath for the sins of Potosí . . . , for of the twelve nations that inhabited it, they tore each other apart, and the same happened among the natives."[7]

The eruption of factional violence in Potosí would lead to three years of intense confrontations, followed by a long series of prison sentences and summary executions. Yet even after all of this, once the town had finally recovered some measure of peace, the issue of the *vascongados* would remain a sensitive topic in the social life of its citizens. And not just there. Across the domains of the monarchy, the previous decades had seen the rise of many Western Pyreneans and their descendants to high positions in the administration and economic life of the colonies. These high achievers had then made use of the perks of their position to propel a whole array of relatives and fellow Western Pyreneans on their trail. In Lima, as in Potosí, there had existed since 1612 a brotherhood dedicated to the Virgin of Aranzazu and which brought together natives from Biscay, Guipuzcoa, Alava, and Navarre. In Seville, too, the newly arrived had possessed their own congregation since 1540: The century would see the rise of parallel organizations in Mexico and other parts of the Americas. Across all Hispanic territories, these *Biscaynes*—as they were also commonly referred to—appeared to display a similar awareness of their common origin and a solemn commitment to remaining distinct.

But why? The fact that this trend toward collaboration outside of the Western Pyrenees would coincide with attempts by provincial institutions to harden their internal boundaries cannot be regarded as a coincidence. While deputies and councilors in Guipuzcoa or Biscay took pains to frame their contribution to the wars with Navarre or neighboring France as campaigns conducted against foreign foes, their compatriots, forced to fend for themselves abroad, were all too happy to seek the company of these same enemies whenever the opportunity presented itself. Not for nothing, in the boundaries between these territories, permeation had always been the norm. Impervious to the drawing out of clear-cut frontiers by university-trained clerks and courtly policymakers, family ties, friendships, business, trade operations, and cultural exchanges continued there with normality. Defiant to the unremitting expansion of bodies of law, justice, and governance that sought to monopolize the allegiance of those subjected to them, there continued to exist, on the margins, an unquenched sense of commonality. It was here, in lands obscured by the shadow cast by competing jurisdictions, that the seeds of resistance to the order proclaimed from the provinces had been sown, watered, and tended with care. A harvest that bespoke of cultural fraternity and which, in contact with foreign worlds, was bound to give abundant fruit.

Of course, these ties were hardly new. The Parientes Mayores, who held little respect for the attempts of councils and assemblies to constrain their power, had often regarded neighboring territories, vague administrative divisions notwithstanding, as fair game for their aspirations. Guipuzcoan lineages had been key players in the endemic internal confrontations of Navarre. Navarrese factions, in turn, had always kept a keen eye upon the lands beyond the Pyrenees. The heads of the most prominent Biscayne households had been active both in Alava as well as on the territories that extended on their western flank. The situation, for as long as political instability and social turmoil had continued to prey upon the dwellers of the Western Pyrenees, had largely stood in place.

Yet as the fifteenth century had slowly given way to the sixteenth, so too had the spaces upon which the heads of the *bandos* could exert their influence been gradually made to match the new hardened frontiers. The Parientes of Guipuzcoa, either in challenging their provincial opponents in 1457 or in feeding their internal tensions afterward, had tacitly accepted this shortening of horizons. So too had their Biscayne counterparts done in their battle against the Count of Haro. The trend was analogous across the Western Pyrenees. After all, the more provincial assemblies and institutions managed to tighten their grip on power, the more those interested in wielding such authority were encouraged to play by the rules. Against the fuzziness of the past, the predicament of the regional establishment was to institute a clean new order.

Obstacles to this goal, though, were manifold. Long centuries of dubious management, intermittent warfare, and royal indifference had resulted in a patchwork of institutions and networks that only occasionally matched the definitive territorial limits of the provinces. In distant Bruges, for instance, the supervision of the profitable trade between Flanders and the Western Pyrenees had fallen, ever since 1455, upon the hands of an organization aptly referred to as the "Nation of the Coast of Biscay." This association had not, despite its name, included merely natives from the Lordship but also merchants and mariners from neighboring regions. In 1527, the same year Biscaynes had proclaimed their universal nobility, the foremost posts of this "Nation of Biscay" had been monopolized by Alavese and Riojan managers.[8] In Antwerp, too, Guipuzcoan and Alavese businesspeople were similarly habituated to self-identify as *Biscaynes*.[9]

Perhaps this, rather than a repudiation of their own territorial origins, might indeed be nothing more than a cunning marketing strategy. After all, the iron extracted in Biscay was famous across Europe and, by the end of the fifteenth century, as the violence of the *bandos* was finally being put out for good, the production of the forges of the Lordship amounted to more than 10 percent of that of all Christendom.[10] Peace had only increased these rates. William Shakespeare, in describing the internal suffering of one of his characters, could still compare it, more than a century later, to iron restraints—*bilboes*—which bore in their name the unmistakable trace of their Biscayne origin.[11] Guipuzcoans too prided themselves on the quality of their steel weapons and tools, which as they boasted were dispatched to "many kingdoms and provinces, being so necessary that without them even the lands would not bear fruit, . . . nor the people be able to produce things, nor live with any comfort."[12] All of them great things to claim. And yet, as everyone knew, it was in the Lordship that ore of the utmost quality was extracted and worked by the locals. So much so that the *fuero* severely punished anyone trying to smuggle as little as a single ounce. The result was a monopoly on exclusivity. An ingot, if it happened to parade the name of Biscay, was as straight a shorthand as any for exquisite quality. Which means that traders from the Western Pyrenees, who, as their Biscayne counterparts, spoke *Euskera* and faced fierce competition in the crowded hubs of Flanders and beyond, had every incitement for taking a shot at ambiguity. Obscure though the names of their provinces might sound to the foreign ear, they could still default to a designation with remarkable brand recognition.

For all that having to turn to the name of Biscay to secure foreign trade could from time to time annoy other Western Pyreneans, few regarded these petty transgressions as a threat to the discipline promoted by the General Assemblies. What happened in Bruges or Antwerp, after all, was unlikely to have an impact on how people thought of themselves back home. However, other challenges could not be met with comparable leniency. The new age, just as it had witnessed the humbling of the Parientes, the hardening of provincial jurisdictions, and the discovery of a wholly unknown continent, had also brought with it an expanding preoccupation with boundaries and limits. Nominal allegiance to a distant king had been replaced, over the course of the sixteenth century, with carefully established regulations, courts, and political institutions. The landscape, too, had been altered. In Fuenterrabia, which back in 1476 had been besieged by French troops, the battered medieval fortifications had been surrounded by a vast ring of walls and bastions, an impressive upgrade that unmistakably displayed its new role as sentinel over a delicate frontier. San Sebastian's battlements, equally outdated, were refurbished and modernized, and watchtowers and lookouts were set in place to stand guard over any movement from the north. There, on the French side, plans for the strengthening of Bayonne advanced with ebbs and flows. What had once been a nondescript periphery now stood revealed as a delicate pressure point between the two most powerful monarchies of Europe.

Two kingdoms now vied for supremacy in the region. Two, but not three. For long centuries, ever since the times of the incorporation of Guipuzcoa and Alava to Castile, the Western Pyrenees had been a chessboard disputed on three sides. Now, a seat at the table had been left vacant. After the demise of the plans of Sancho the Wise to recover his western domains from his Castilian neighbor, successive kings of Navarre had been reduced to playing the part of regional potentates. The extinction of the local dynasty early in the thirteenth century, which brought in rulers from beyond the Pyrenees largely uninterested in developing the small kingdom, had only compounded the feeling of abandonment. For fifty years, the title of King of Navarre had fallen to the king of France, and although the union of the two crowns had ended in the early fourteenth century, later monarchs had been unable—and unwilling—to shake their indebtedness to the French connection.

In all, Navarre had increasingly grown to be—as plague, economic crisis, and social conflict preyed upon it—an appendage at the mercy of more powerful interests, a minor in the hall of the sovereigns, a territory in-between. The cards at its leaders' disposal were few and hard to play, and yet, they were not without opportunities. For as long as the kings of Castile, Aragon, France, or England had been unable to secure their dominance in the region, their Navarrese counterparts had been more or less free to leverage their position, playing one against the other for survival. But now, faced with the French conquest of the north and the consolidation of a Castilian-Aragonese monarchy in the south, the deck seemed to be running perilously thin.

The monarchs of Navarre, of course, had not failed to read the omens. Catherine I and Juan III, the reigning couple, had tried ever since 1494 to modernize the administration and reestablish their supremacy in the kingdom. More than anything, this had meant recovering control over their finances. Not for nothing, and to a degree even more acute than in Castile or in France, sovereigns in Navarre had, over the decades, only secured the support of their nobility at the expense of exorbitant grants and concessions. Cities had been alienated from the royal patrimony, large payments had been disbursed to ensure peace between the factions, and the ever-rising debt had been covered only at the cost of all kinds of promises and bribes. In all, this policy had made, as it was bound to happen, even more difficult to face future expenses. Throughout the fifteenth century, the vicious circle had starkly impoverished the Navarrese monarchy.[13]

More worryingly, perhaps, it had rendered many noblemen dissatisfied with the benefits to be reaped from their faithful service, and thus willing to complement their income with foreign subsidies even. The monarchs themselves, their efforts to strengthen the crown hindered by the risk of alienating their own support base, had been reluctantly obliged to turn to Paris and Castile for coin and guarantees. Their hesitancy was well merited. After all, as Catherine and Juan knew well, interest for these advances was often paid, not in cash, but in political commitments. Contemplating the growing climate of hostility that reigned across the frontier, and with many of their subjects increasingly invested in the triumph of one side or the other, the kings of Navarre must have been deeply aware of the frailty of their position.

In the event, the chance to elucidate these dilemmas for good had arrived in the summer of 1512. As part of a coordinated attack by England and Castile against France, King Ferdinand had asked Juan III for safe passage through his kingdom. The Navarrese monarch, who readily understood that bending to the demand would put the rest of his domains north of the Pyrenees at risk of confiscation by the wronged king of France, opted to drag out negotiations with the Castilians. Naturally, this was not a neutral move by any means, for it had given the French garrison valuable time to reinforce their line. After several days of inaction, the Castilian general, frustrated that the king of Navarre "swayed more by Gallic promises than by the honor of God," had twiddled his thumbs no longer.[14] Crossing the border, the invading army set up camp before the walls of Pamplona only a few days later.

Juan III, who at first had appeared steeled in his determination to resist the invaders, opted on occasion for crossing the Pyrenees and seeking refuge in his family's Bearnese domains. News of his excommunication, sanctioned by a Pope with more than two feet on the Spanish camp, reached a capital already demoralized by the flight of the royal couple and deprived of any natural fulcrum of resistance. Before long, the nobility and public authorities of Navarre began to look after their own particular survival. Pamplona, in exchange for confirmation of its privileges, surrendered without a fight. So too did most of the realm. Navarre accepted Ferdinand as king.

The result was as surprising to the victors as it was to the defeated. Forays into the lands of Navarre by military contingents, in a previous century marked by factionalism and widespread violence, had not been an uncommon way of pressing compliance with

Castilian interests. As in 1512, all participants had on those occasions recognized these raids as merely one of the tools of pressure—alongside financial and political ones—that their neighbors could use against the little kingdom. This time, however, rather than forcing the submission of an untrustworthy ally, Juan's flight had revealed the ruler's failure in aligning his interests to those of his subjects. While all kinds of ties—linguistic, economic, cultural—connected most of the Navarrese to their Castilian neighbors, almost none of these existed between them and the Bearnese. If by sheltering himself in the north, the fleeing monarch had expected his subjects to opt for the path of resistance, then he was primed for disappointment. Confronted with a monarch that seemed to have forgotten his responsibilities and the likely loss of their livelihoods, few in Pamplona had hesitated before suing for terms. Between the dynasty and the kingdom, it was clear which the Navarrese population had chosen.

The decision would be made painfully clear in the following years. After the initial success of Castilian arms, it did not take long before the frontier turned into a stalemate, with frequent attacks and counterattacks on both sides. In 1516, after Ferdinand's death, the dispossessed king had once again entered Navarre with a small army, banking on the love and longing of his former subjects. The summons, however, were left mostly unanswered, and Juan was forced into a dishonorable retreat. Five years later, though, conditions had proven more auspicious. Taking advantage of the internal problems that the succession of Charles V was provoking in Castile, and at the head of a large French army, Henry, Juan's successor, had once again marched south to gain back his kingdom. This time—perhaps attentive to shifts in the direction the political winds were blowing—many Navarrese noblemen accompanied his retinue. Pamplona, as a decade earlier, capitulated without much resistance. The kingdom—it seemed—had been restored. And yet, the French high command, in what would prove a huge miscalculation, decided to push even deeper into Castile. Charles' armies, coming to the relief of the besieged city of Logroño, chased the enemy as it began a disorganized retreat toward the Pyrenees. Then, a handful of leagues from Pamplona, the two armies clashed and victory, decisive victory, fell to the Castilians. Henry's family lost their kingdom for the second time in less than ten years.

The aftermath of this aborted reconquista had done much more than merely get things back to where they were. Charles V, recognizing the cost in manpower and coin of keeping constant watch over the French, had gradually ordered his officials to fall back to more defensible positions. The ensuing works had seen castles toppled and Pyrenean garrisons reinforced. What lay beyond these, though, an area of their kingdom that the Navarrese had known as *Ultrapuertos*—"beyond the peaks"—was abandoned for good. Surrounded as it was by Henry's and the French king's domains, the position had proven a compromised one to maintain. Better off, then, to give it away altogether. Members of the twice-expelled royal family, in returning to claim sovereignty over this north-Pyrenean redoubt of their inheritance, had done so as rulers of an independent Navarre. A realm whose authorities, despite its reduced dimensions, are still identified as the successors of the great kingdom of Sancho the Great.

Unsurprisingly, the confusing events that had led to the emergence, by the 1530s, of not one, but two separate kingdoms of Navarre were seen by many contemporaries as in need of explanation. The need to deflate any reclamations made by the enemy only made this urge ever more pressing and, before long, wildly different accounts of what had transpired were spreading in manuscripts or being put to press at both sides of the curtain. Some testimonies, delivered by witnesses who had taken part in the initial incorporation of the kingdom in 1512, regarded it as a full-on annexation, a glorious conquest that, by merit of its indisputable success and the excommunication of the foe, had rendered Castilians free-handed to tailor Navarre to their own interest. Such one-sided, optimistic narrations, though, had soon been tempered by prudence. Castilian intellectuals, striving for arguments that would sustain their masters' legal claim over the territory, increasingly glossed over the right of conquest and offered subtler reasons: the dynastic right of King Ferdinand to the throne, the geographical unity of Spain, the strategic weaknesses it addressed. Take into account "the uniformity it brings with the other kingdoms of this country" and the fact that its incorporation "had closed off the route of entry into Spain from that area," and the capture of Navarre, rather than a waste of resources, could appear to Castilians a "magnificent" occurrence indeed.[15]

In Navarre, naturally, that kind of triumphalist discourse found a small audience among the population. Just as their kings had been famed for their ability to walk a tightrope without falling, so too their erstwhile subjects, in this time of uncertainty, knew better than to put all their eggs in one basket. That was why most citizens and noblemen had chosen not to resist the Castilian advance in 1512. That, also, was why they had not hindered King Henry's expedition either. However, as the military situation had stabilized from the late 1520s onward, and once it had been clear that the restoration of the old kingdom was not likely to ever happen, members of what were still the public institutions of the realm had sought to get the best out of their circumstances. Their main goal, as ever, had been to keep for themselves as many areas of independent decision-making as they could possibly secure. And the issue, naturally, was how to render these demands palatable to those who had to approve them back in Castile.

Luckily for the attempt, their new Castilian overlords were more than willing to make the administration of the realm more straightforward. While Navarre already possessed a legal compilation sanctioned by its sovereigns, not only had the document become unmanageable in its extent, but it was also plagued with a plethora of exceptions, nuances, and dubious footnotes. As the Navarrese legislators themselves admitted, "there were many *fueros*, some of which were observed in certain places and parts of the Kingdom of Navarre, and others in different ones. And among them, there were some that were contradictory, many that were superfluous, and others that, due to their antiquity, were written in such a style that they were barely understandable."[16] The times, then, seemed ripe for an update. One of the last measures of Catherine I and Juan III, in the months prior to being expelled by the Castilians, had, in fact, been to publicly pledge a rationalization of law.[17] Now, with the conquest completed, the task had befallen their vanquishers.

Neither those in the highest echelons of Navarre's bureaucracy nor the viceroys appointed by Charles V were exactly lacking in examples from which to draw inspiration. The institutional problems preying on the kingdom, despite the exceptionality of recent events, were hardly unique even within its immediate surroundings. Just like their Navarrese counterparts, for instance, the authorities of Biscay were also trying to defend their laws from the intromission of Castilian norms. Just as the Navarrese, they too looked upon their land as a territory "united" to Castile, yet "distinct" and "detached" from it.[18] This claim, which could be initially interpreted as an exhortation for independence, was however moderated in practice by the recognition that being a Castilian, too, was worthy of appreciation. By 1528, the realization would lead Navarrese authorities, endowed with the unpleasant task of compiling a refurbished document that included the most important laws of the kingdom, not to clarify their ambiguous position in the slightest. Heirs to a proud kingdom though they professed themselves to be, these powerbrokers openly declared as well their right to share in any privilege reserved to any Castilian. The game of shadows that had once allowed Navarre to endure in the face of adversity could—within, rather than without the global monarchy of Charles V—be played still.

Whereas the reality of the division of Navarre was tacitly accepted by those propounding the new compilation, this was a pill not everyone was willing to swallow. If to the south, tax collectors and accountants still included the lands of *Ultrapuertos* in their figures and tables in expectation perhaps of a possible change in the state of the frontier, to the north, the expelled dynasty never ceased to treasure the increasingly unachievable dream of recuperating their realm. The decades that followed Juan III and his son's failed attempts to attain this objective had only served to exacerbate differences on both sides of the mountain range. And yet, and for all implausibility, it remained possible to believe that the distant tremors of the age could perhaps help in rendering this goal a feasible one.

Ever since the excommunication of the king of Navarre in 1512, there were those in the region—as there were in many other parts of Christendom—who had come to regard the Pope less as the indisputable deputy of God than as a key participant in all-too-earthly geopolitical struggles. Among these, of course, were the members of the royal family itself. Henry II of Navarre had married Margaret, the widowed sister of King Francis I of France, in 1527. A learned woman and a polyglot who mastered five languages, the new queen had soon cut a dash among the retinue of her husband.[19] She was a splendid writer and an acutely perceptive observer of society, and as such, even before coming to Navarre, Margaret had already come to grasp much of what other disillusioned contemporaries criticized in the spiritual corruption of the Papacy. True, she never abandoned the faith of her ancestors. Yet it was equally true that many could appreciate the trace of her teachings in the upbringing of her daughter.

Jeanne, heiress not only to the throne of Navarre but also to the duchy of Albret, the counties of Foix and Bigorre, and the viscounties of Béarn, Tartas, and Marsan, was an independent and strong-willed woman, pretty much in the line of her mother. Some, failing to square this character with the expectations imposed on her gender, referred to her as "a princess who possessed nothing of a woman but her sex, her soul filled with manly concerns, a powerful mind inclined toward great matters, and a heart impervious to adversity."[20] A praise that bespoke the fact that the daughter, pretty much like the mother, was an innate mold-breaker. No sooner had she come to the throne of Navarre in 1555 than she had embraced Calvinism. The fateful step, at a moment when severe tensions threatened to tear up the very fabric of Christendom, had, beyond the Pyrenees, gained her the epithet of "sectarian princess."[21] Yet such manifestations of disdain were not bound to stop her. In 1564, Jeanne had already declared the liberty of cults, Catholic and Protestant, in her Pyrenean dominion in Bearne. Two years later, she had furthered her support for the reformed religion, pushing Catholics to the side and all but banning their congregations. These measures would also later be extended to the rest of her personal dominions.

Many in Bearne, willfully or compelled by circumstance, had chosen to follow the example of their ruler and converted as well. But to the west, in Soule and Navarre, the old creed had managed to hold fast. The strong rejection of what many saw as a "Bearnese captivity" was exacerbated in these parts by a whole array of local rivalries and vendettas, often dating back to the days of the conquest and even beyond. Influential members of the higher nobility and close confidants of the queen might endorse the program of reformation, sponsor Protestant priests, and lend their backing to the whole endeavor. But the mass of the people, for the most part, remained unconvinced. While it was possible to find a few reformed priests in Saint Palais and other scattered towns, the reality was that the isolation—both geographical and cultural—of Navarrese and Soulentine peasants was proving to be, in all, a hard nut to crack for the new doctrines. "It is their fear"—a plea to the queen adduced in explanation for their slow rate of conversion—"that there are some who want to take away the Mass and the practice of their religion, as was done in Bearne."[22] Needless to say, this was precisely Jeanne's ultimate goal.

Naturally, once her subjects had realized that there was no compromise to be reached, they had opted for resisting the enforcement of the new laws. By mid-January 1568, "the inhabitants of the said viscounty [of Soule] rose up in arms . . . and went into the land of Navarre" to partake in rebellion. Jeanne, in response, dispatched an army of 2,500 men accompanied by her son, the fourteen-year-old Henry, to reinstate order in the region. Entering Saint Palais, the teenager had once again issued the anti-Catholic laws of his mother. Then—at least as the tendentious testimony of his rivals had it—he had entered the local church, cast down an image of Christ on the cross and had "stabbed it repeatedly with a dagger, tied it with a rope, and had it dragged through the streets. . . . The church was then turned into a stable, where horses and other animals were kept."[23]

True or not, stories such as this one showcased the heightened hostility that existed between both camps. Jeanne, in trying to enforce compliance with her religious legislation, had not merely displayed the kind of missionary fervor so proper of recent converts. While she felt herself, both by the circumstances of her family and her own upbringing, destined to illuminate those enthralled by Papist ignorance, there was more to her conversion than mere theological preoccupations. The population of her dispersed and fragmentary domains, united neither by culture nor language, was hardly exemplary as a brotherhood of man. Solidarity between them, fifty years on from the defection of the southern Navarrese to the Castilian side, had hardly improved. A fierce localism and a half-veiled antipathy still lurked under the surface of their common allegiance to Jeanne. The queen's religious policy could thus be interpreted as a risky attempt to overcome such differences and set all her subjects on a shared venture. The violent reaction of the Soulentines and the Navarrese, however, had only demonstrated how difficult overcoming these disagreements truly was.

The queen, despite these setbacks, would not give up so easily. She, as a convert herself, had come to recognize that the surest route to the heart of a man passed through the Word of God. Mistaken and entrenched in their own old ways though her western subjects might be, there was none among them so villainous, none so wicked that, if taught correctly, might remain beyond salvation. Which is why, even before the first bouts of insurrection had sparked in Navarre and Soule in 1566, Jeanne had already set out on a path as noble as it was reminiscent of antique endeavors. Tasking an ecclesiastic with the commission, she had ordered him to provide the ultimate tool for the conversion of her subjects: a translation of the Gospels, for the first time, to the tongue of the *vascongados*.

Joanes Leizarraga, the man chosen by Jeanne to undertake this great feat, was in no illusion as to the many problems implied in the assignment. Originally a Catholic priest from Briscous, in Labourd, he had become, after his conversion, a preacher in the Navarrese town of Labastide Clarence. By then, he was sixty: a man among the increasingly few who could remember, albeit fuzzily, a time when peoples at the two watersheds of the Pyrenees had obeyed a single ruler. Maybe for that very reason Joanes could better grasp the crux of what was truly expected from him. "[E] veryone knows," Leizarraga wrote in reference to the various geographical dialects of *Euskera*, "[. . .] how different the ways of speaking are from almost one house to the next." Men from Labourd such as himself, if they happened to travel to the east for a few dozen miles, found it difficult to make themselves understood in a place like Soule. To find a solution to this problem, important though it certainly was in these northern territories, was ever the more urgent if the Word of God was ever to reach those beyond the mountain peaks as well. What hope was there of ever gaining back the ancient realm—Leizarraga must have wondered—if not even the holy text could overcome these petty linguistic hindrances?

Which is why he would opt, in the event, for creating a language that, rather than pandering to a single audience, could meet all of them halfway. Challenging and technical, erudite and rich in grammatical flourishes though it was, his version of the Gospel aspired to serve as the bedrock from which a common understanding could ultimately arise. In this, he was doing more than simply pushing forward Jeanne's dynastical aspirations. While in his French dedication of the Gospel, published in 1571, Joanes had defended his zealous endeavor as an attempt to extend God's unaltered message across the "country of the Basques"—meaning the territories that lay north of the Pyrenees—the rendering of that same preface into *Euskera* carried out a sensibly different meaning.[24] In that version, Joanes emphasized that his efforts, rather than merely being a means to convert Jeanne's unruly subjects and bring them to submission, were instead targeted at a much wider constituency: those able to understand his words. A community bonded, not by rulers nor kingdoms, but by a shared knowledge of *Euskera*. What, in their own language, many Western Pyreneans would call an *Euskal Herria*.

Hearsay about the existence of such a group certainly predated the publishing of Leizarraga's Gospel, nor was he the first to put them to print. More than a quarter of a century earlier, another priest, this time a native from *Ultrapuertos*, had already made sure to voice them. Bernat de Echepare, unlike Leizarraga, was not a loyalist of the expelled royal house of Navarre. Instead, he was one of those who, ever since the first arrival of the Castilians in 1512, had opted to cast their lot with the newcomers. This support had brought the man little happiness. When Henry II had tried to seize back his kingdom and had entered Navarre in 1521, the ill-fated Bernat had been summoned to court to Bearne and put in chains. While in prison, he had given himself to despair:

> Lest I should die in captivity, an innocent man, give me,
> I pray, the wherewithal to come out a healthy man
> so that my enemy will not later chuckle:
> "He was guilty and there he lost his life".[25]

In the event, Echepare's prayers were answered, and by 1545, he seemed to have already made peace with his former jailers. A parish priest in a small locality of *Ultrapuertos*, he would become, also, the author of the first ever printed book in *Euskera*.

Linguae Vasconum Primitiae, or "The Novelties of the Language of the Vascones," was, in all, a pretty unremarkable book. An anthology of poems ranging from Christian doctrine to love verses, its colloquial eastern-Navarrese vocabulary was as distant from Leizarraga's commitment to precision and universality as anything that could be imagined. Echepare, however, shared with the Protestant priest from Briscous the awareness of being a pioneer of untrodden roads. The preface of the *Primitiae*, the first words ever printed in the language of the *vascongados*, already betrayed the sense their author had of himself as an innovator. He had written them so

> that all of us might have, in this way, . . . a precious jewel, the Basque language in print, something which has not existed hitherto; so that it might grow, endure, and spread throughout in the future from your auspicious beginning; and that Basques might have, in their language, in the same manner as the rest, some doctrine and written matter whereby they might amuse themselves, converse, sing and spend their time.[26]

It had been Echepare's dream that *Euskera*, which ranked already as the indisputable language of the people, could perhaps, should it be treated with respect, become much more than that.

> Among tongues were thou held in low esteem;
> but now thou art due honor among them all.
> *Euskera*, come forth into the whole world![27]

A daring proclamation, but not an unprecedented one. Echepare's work, just as Leizarraga's more than two decades later, was part of a larger movement in favor of vernaculars sweeping Renaissance Europe. From Castile to Germany, and from Italy to England, scholars and writers had set out to elevate the standing of their mother tongues against the preeminence of Latin. To this end, linguistic comparatives had been issued, works of literature sponsored, and comprehensive grammars distributed. Protestant reformers, who participated in a shared reverence for the letter of the Gospel, had likewise contributed, with their translations, to the valorization of these languages. So too had kings. Francis I of France, for example, had decreed in 1535 that all administrative documents in his kingdom ought to be written in French. In 1561, Jeane III of Navarre had issued a similar order, only that this time it favored the Bearnese language.[28] These rulings, increasingly accepted across what had up until then been a Christendom linked by their common use of Latin, had done much to constrain the ability of those on the margins to blend in. New powers, after all, needed not only new voices. They needed, as well, the silence of the old.

Euskera, for all that it was no less the vernacular of increasingly institutionalized regions, had never fared well in this regard. Not once throughout its long history had anything but the most derisive and poisonous of venoms been poured over this Western Pyrenean tongue. While long gone were the days in which its sound had been compared in the disgust it produced to the barking of the dogs no one had, up until the times of Echepare and Leizarraga, done as much as to think of it as anything beyond the patrimony of the deprived and the uneducated. It had never occurred to the Parientes of Guipuzcoa, Navarre, or Labourd, for example, that something as solemn and serious as a nobiliary title, or a law, or even the ruling of a court, might be written in *Euskera*. Nor had their rivals. Cities in the Western Pyrenees, be it in Navarre, or in Alava, or in Soule, were wholly accustomed to the stark separation of linguistic functions that the new provincial authorities had recently sought to impose. While no one doubted that French and Castilian were king in this regard, other Romance languages such as Bearnese, or Gascon, or even Occitan had all enjoyed at least some amount of time in the spotlight. All—but not *Euskera*. And so, when in 1529 the General Assembly of Guipuzcoa had established that fluency and literacy in Castilian would from then on be a requirement for holding a public position in the province, no one had raised as much as an eyebrow. It was obvious, after all, that for certain tongues to be destined to greatness, others had to be condemned to ignominious obscurity.

But why? What explanation could there be for the fact that local elites in the Western Pyrenees, at a time when their counterparts across Europe were pushing forward their rights as vernacular speakers, would decide instead to set the exclusion of their mother tongue on even firmer grounds? Knowledge of *Euskera* among the learned of *Ultrapuertos*, as Echepare's and Leizarraga's examples demonstrated, was not unheard of. Nor was this a northern exceptionality. A manuscript, written in Alava and probably contemporary to Leizarraga's Gospel, proved that, among the Parientes-turned-courtesan, poems in this language were hardly an oddity.[29] And not only that, for the text, just like the Protestant Gospel, also made play with the idea that, on a dimension detached from the schemes of princes and the jurisdiction of their officials, there might exist a common heritage to all *Euskera*-speakers.

Why hath thou God upon *Euskal Herria*
so many advantages bestowed
that if the seas would be ink
and the sky a wide book
not even then could
the gifts of Alava be counted?.[30]

Ambiguous though the term certainly was, ambiguity was of course precisely the point. No one could, after all, hope to find *Euskal Herria* on a map. No one could, therefore, be condemned nor chastised for using the term. While delegates in Biscay, or in Guipuzcoa, or even in the two Navarres might find it reassuring to imagine that some kind of common solidarity and shared history had given birth to their provinces, no such connection linked all *vascongados* together. True, linguistic and cultural ties might lead them closer, but it was no less correct to say that there were many other factors, from political allegiance to business and family networks, that pulled them ever apart. Appeals coming from Labourd and Soule, for example, were expected to be resolved, not there, but rather in the distant Parlement of Bordeaux. Northern Navarrese individuals like Echepare, too, had learned after the conquest that much of their future rested in the hands of authorities in Pau. Better then to make sure that one's voice was heard in these two cities—and to have friends in high places there—than to bank on the camaraderie of neighbors who could hardly lend a hand. The more Guipuzcoans, Biscaynes, Alavese, and Navarrese looked toward Castile in search of status, profit, and confirmation, the more too their northern counterparts did as much in the opposite direction. *Euskal Herria*, like a Janus-faced god, was not a single community, but rather two—each one gazing in exactly opposite directions.

Which is not to say that everyone resigned themselves to this conclusion. After all, as recent events in *Ultrapuertos* and Soule had laid bare, there were many individuals among the popular classes who were rather discontented with being categorized as second-class subjects of distant sovereigns. Especially in northern Navarre, where the memory of independence was still a vivid one, the supremacy of Bearne was looked upon with suspicion. No wonder, then, these northerners would be more prone to imagine *Euskal Herria* as a community spanning both sides of the Pyrenees. Deprived by conquest and indifference from rights and institutions they saw recognized to southerners, these Western Pyreneans had first-hand experience of what it meant to be at the mercy of others' whims. Now, in the midst of a convulsive struggle for the minds and the souls of their compatriots, these notions had only taken on an ever more urgent semblance. Any *Euskal Herria*—whatever its definite contours—appeared to them a path to self-government and to prestige. In other words: to significance. It offered, to a culturally distinct and marginal land, gradually left without means to control its own destiny, the promise of a better future.

A lofty goal perhaps, but one that, naturally, could scarcely entice their counterparts in the south. Advocates for the rights of the freemen of Biscay or Guipuzcoa took for granted that, for all its many local variations, a single language was spoken from Bilbao to Soule.[31] And yet, they never made use of it in their documents, nor pandered to those who did. It seems to have never occurred to members of these elites to propose that any particular solidarity, nor affinity—not to say any political relationship—should derive from the fortuitous coincidence of employing a similar speech. Provincials, entangled as they were in networks of business and patronage that extended over the entire span of the Spanish empire, were scornful of identifications that could end up estranging their source of both wealth and honor. A Guipuzcoan, an Alavese, even a dweller of the recently incorporated Navarre: All could feel reassured in their position as vassals to a mighty king, wardens of a sensitive frontier, and descendants from the unbroken lineage of a patriarch. Not only because these were honorable badges by themselves, but also because they had much to gain from them. A *vascongado*, in contrast, was nothing. Worse than that, it was a pariah, a menace to these coveted perks. For what would happen were the monarch to realize that the border was manned by peoples who felt more sympathy for the enemy than for their realm? What then would become of the *Hidalguía*? What then of the privileges? What, in summary, would be the fate of the entire provincial order? It was not enough for cultural and linguistic ties such as those carefully cultivated by Echepare and Leizarraga to be ostensibly ignored. For the future of the provinces to remain secure, any bridge these authors had sought to strengthen should be put to the torch.

Paradoxically, it was these two books, premised on the assumption that *Euskera* could be a tool in the hands of the learned, that did much to cast the language as a symbol of backwardness. Even before the publishing of Leizarraga's Gospel, some inquisitors had already denounced a certain religious relaxation in the region's most cosmopolitan trade hubs. Through the streets of Bilbao and San Sebastian, they cried, pamphlets and books containing heretical teachings found an easy way into Castile. According to their records, an entire sect of apostates was lurking in clandestinity. The prospects of the true faith in the Guipuzcoan city appeared so dire, in fact, that one of these priests suggested nothing short of punishing those who displayed the most familiarity with foreigners and who, as always, were thought to be the source of the corruption.[32] A Spanish ambassador to Bearne had confirmed the veracity of these accusations. "There are in the country of the Basques many [Protestant] books, catechisms, and psalms in the Biscayne language . . . , and also they are read to many of those who come from Navarre."[33]

The notion that many Western Pyreneans, at both sides of the border, might be on the verge of turning their backs to both God and their rightful lords must have loomed large on the mind of many onlookers, especially as tensions in France between Protestant and Catholic factions intensified. To deal with the danger, more punctilious and extensive censorship was set in motion in the south. A muscular approach—and perhaps an excessive one. For—the pervasive climate of anxiety notwithstanding—the prospect of the Basque-speaking population converting to Calvinism en masse after having the Gospel translated into their own language, as Leizarraga might have desired, had ultimately failed to materialize. War and conflict, in radicalizing and hardening opinions, had left little room for any unemotional comparison of creeds. At any rate, the text, pretty much like the rest of Jeanne's and Henry's policies to curb the particularities of the region, had only exacerbated these differences even further. The more Protestants clung to vernacular preaching, the more Catholics, in response, made overt ostentation of their disdain for it.[34] By 1585, Henry of Navarre was finally forced to call an end to the whole experiment. Revoking the anti-Catholic measures first set in motion by his mother, he accepted the right of his subjects to believe as they may. Fifteen years later, the full extent of his defeat in this regard was evident: In the entirety of northern Navarre, only a single, lone priest still dared to sing the praises of the reformed religion.[35]

The fading of the Calvinist cult, however, had not completely dispelled the preoccupations of its opponents. The wars of religion in France might be drawing to a close, but the blurry lines of allegiance in the frontier remained a very real concern. Even the recent confrontation had proven it. Just as some residents of San Sebastian had contributed a fair amount to the proselytization of Protestantism, so too had those defending the Catholic cause, in *Ultrapuertos* and Soule, counted on the endorsement of influential southern patrons. Under the shade cast by the mountain peaks, and with ready access to foreigners with whom they had more in common than with compatriots, the loyalty and service owed to the sovereign was perceived by locals as only a type of bond among many.

How could such people be trusted—and not only that, be granted free hand to watch over the enemy? Isolated from the rest of the realm due to the scarcity of adequate roads and infrastructure, these villages remained, more than a century on from the defeat of the Parientes, a world apart. One governed by its own rules and traditions and largely unaffected by what happened beyond. Naturally, such a state of affairs had been reluctantly tolerated when the entire region had risked becoming an every man for himself. But now, with the resources and personnel available to monarchies growing year after year, the time had come to finally address the problem. Discipline—strict and unerring discipline—had to be imposed over the border.

That mountains were the abode of rustic, ignorant peoples had long been taken for granted by city-dwellers. Seen from behind the security of a stone wall, the world in the countryside appeared unruly, mysterious, and even occasionally corrupting. Curses, spells and magical creatures, expelled long ago from the urban landscape, became ever more real the more one stepped out into the wild. Which meant that, when back in 1527 two little girls from an obscure mountain village had arrived before the highest court of Pamplona and had denounced the attacks of witches, few had doubted their testimony. A commission had been duly appointed, and a report had been dispatched to the see of the Inquisition in Logroño. In all, the episode had resulted in more than fifty sorcerers being put to death.[36]

The seriousness of the topic merited no less. As every learned person knew, it was on the margins, on the remote expanses that eluded the stern gaze of authorities put in place by God Himself, that the devil found it easier to make his abode. Constantly intriguing and plotting, his lies struck truer among the unknowing peasants. And as was also notorious, it was there that he recruited his workforce, for it was witches and sorcerers that spread, in his name, ruin among the people.

As was to be expected, rustic communities were mildly cautioned about the peril. These men and women knew, as did most Christians, of the power of soothsayers and dispensers of auguries, of the abilities of blabbermouths to stir jealousies among their fellows, of the ominous powers contained in curses and damnations. They had some familiarity, too, with how pure hatred could be distilled into poison; not in the least because, in times of internecine rivalries and low-scale violence, these treatments had been employed with uncaring assiduity.[37] For as long as anyone could remember, individuals trading in such secrets had been frowned upon and regarded as vessels to forces that could be bargained with, yet not entirely bent to one's will. Occasionally, it is true, at desperate times when a family member fell ill, or entrenched rancor threatened the dissolution of the solidarity upon which the community depended, a villager may turn to the supernatural for assistance. And yet, help could not always be counted on. When these prescribed ointments and magic words, purchased at grievous cost, proved incapable of averting death, or heartbreak, or miscarriage, then it was a most human reflex to see in the beneficiary of the payment the very cause of the problem. For who gained anything at all from the malady if not these weirdos? A vile gaze cast from the corner of the eye, or an invocation of torment muttered while crossing paths with a neighbor: These were the signs that betrayed the involvement of a witch. In a world of personal face-to-face relations, in which the word of a neighbor remained the most important marker of a virtuous life, these outcasts played a despised—yet necessary—role. For they served, first and foremost, as perfect scapegoats to blame for disgrace.

Peasants understood these things, but they were still pretty much in the dark when it came to the true nature of witchcraft. Not for nothing, only recently had even those most learned scholars come to grasp it themselves. In 1484, the Pope had issued a bull describing how

> very many persons of both sexes, unmindful of their own salvation and deviating from the Catholic faith, abuse demons, . . . and by their incantations, spells, conjurations, and other nefarious superstitions and acts of sorcery, . . . they destroy the births of women, the offspring of animals, the fruits of the earth, the grapes of the vineyards and the fruits of trees.[38]

The implication was clear. As the most influential theorists of witchcraft explained, for a person to become a witch "it is necessary that there should be made a contract with the devil, by which contract the witch truly and actually binds herself to be the servant of the devil and devotes herself" to him.[39] Rather than outcasts tapping at their own risk from unknown sources, witches had been revealed to be nothing more than agents of Satan who took part in nauseating ceremonies where they mocked the rites of the servants of God. That such a vile sect could not be suffered to exist, of course, went without saying. Secular and religious authorities, when confronted with accusations of witchcraft, had thus good reason not to falter. For in those spots where witches thrived, God's order was ultimately bound to collapse.

And not only God's. In 1608, only a few years after the apparent quenching of Protestantism in the Western Pyrenees, King Henry of Navarre—by now also King Henry IV of France—received news of a bout of sorcery in Labourd. The accusers this time were not peasant girls, but instead two of the greatest noblemen in the entire land. The prince, alerted by their disturbing reports, immediately instructed a commission to be appointed by the Parlement of Bordeaux to deal with the issue.

That there might exist an underground covenant of heretics in Labourd appears to have struck one of the men chosen to carry out the job, the 56-year-old lawyer Pierre de Lancre, as not exceedingly surprising. For, as he put it,

> one must understand that this is a mountainous country, at the edge of three kingdoms . . . , a mixture of three languages . . . enclosed by two bishoprics. . . . Now, all these diversities give Satan marvelous opportunities to hold his gatherings and Sabbaths in this place, especially considering that it is also a coastal region, which makes the people rustic, rough, and poorly civilized.[40]

Trailing the villages of Labourd for over six months, De Lancre and his fellow judges confronted the reality of such claims. Reports only confirmed their worst fears: The land was full of witches. Seemingly normal in their looks, these agents of the devil were masters in disguising their true semblance. Fortunate, then, that witch-hunters had come to develop means to expose their wickedness. In some cases, it took only some torturing for these offenders to accept the charges. Many, appropriately softened by threats and thrashings, even provided fresh lists of accomplices who had attended their unspeakable reunions, parodies of the Christian mass in which the devil, enthroned with a book of dark scriptures to his side, presided over scenes of fornication, sacrilegious baptisms, and even the blessing of a dark holy host.

Other witches, however, were more difficult to discover. Only those most gifted or innocent—oftentimes little children—could search for the mark of the demon with any guarantee of finding it. A talent that men like De Lancre, who over the months had come to learn of the various aspects that Satan's deceit might take, had managed to master.

> They summoned me to see whether I would recognize the mark in the eye of a young girl of seventeen years. I recognized her as soon as I entered the room and said that she had it in her left eye, which was somewhat cross-eyed, misaligned, and more wild-looking than the other. They looked inside and found something like a small cloud that resembled a toad's paw. The girl confessed.[41]

Witches, who had never before been exposed to such inquisitive examinations, suddenly found themselves at the mercy of justice. As expected, many tried to escape retribution by crossing into Spain. De Lancre saw this as proof of the effectiveness of his approach. For, as he put it, these sorcerers were "an evil piece of furniture you should not bother to take inventory of."[42]

On the other side of the frontier, however, the arrival of these suspected heretics was met with lesser enthusiasm. News of De Lancre's success in stamping the king's authority over the witches of Labourd, and the staggering reports of dark covenants and dream-like abductions, all contributed to creating a climate of heightened alert in Spain. In places like Zugarramurdi, a village only a few miles from the frontier, the arrival of peoples from the north rapidly sparked new accusations. The Inquisition, yet again, took to its job, interrogating anyone assumed to be a witch, gathering information from anonymous informers, and schooling the rural flock on how to best spot the devil's hand in their surroundings. The results were appalling. Out of all the inhabitants living at the shadow of the snowy peaks, more than a quarter were cast as suspects, and the proportion, in some villages along the border, rose to three-quarters of the population.[43]

Naturally, such a vast transgression of the divine mandates required an equally extensive response. Collecting as many testimonies as could be gathered, and after bringing the most entrenched witches from Zugarramurdi's whereabouts to Logroño in 1610, an astounding spectacle was made out of their punishment. As many as 30,000 people from Biscay, Guipuzcoa, Alava, Navarre, and beyond congregated to witness the burning of the sorcerers and the uncovering of the perfidious assemblies. A speaker, raising his voice over the assembled crowds, detailed one by one, to the audience's bewilderment, all and every sign that singled out a witch: the mark of the toad's paw in their left eye, their gusto for eating human flesh. More than anything, the man spoke of the "pastures of the billy goat"—*akelarre*, in *Euskera*—where these sorcerers were summoned to plot the ruin of their neighbors and of all mankind.[44] The message was transparent: A dangerous peril had been exposed, and yet, thanks to the unwavering overwatch of the inquisitors, justice had ultimately prevailed.

For all that the events of Logroño had thus trumpeted the legitimacy of the authorities' actions, there were some individuals, even among the latter, that could not shake the feeling of having committed a terrible mistake. Their reports, as they were made known to their superiors in the months that followed the pyres of Logroño, told a very different story from the one the speaker had so self-assuredly proclaimed on stage. That among elderly people who had been interrogated and even confessed to partaking in the rites, "not one knew what it was to be a witch nor anything which savored of this evil art, nor what an *akelarre* signified."[45] How, in fact, prior to the executions carried out by De Lancre in Labourd, no one in these parts had heard of these things. That young, attractive "witches" put into the custody of local priests to prevent them from attending the Sabbaths, had declared themselves, a few months later, mysteriously pregnant.[46]

Irregularities went on and on. Documents stated that alleged sorcerers, faced by the stern gaze of examiners bent on extracting an admission of guilt out of them, had simply given up their resistance and had confessed whatever their accusers had wanted them to say. Others pointed out how both in France as well as in Spain, the lists extracted from these confessions aligned all too well with local quarrels and disputes.[47] Most insidiously, there was the fact that the majority of witnesses, whose mother tongue was *Euskera*, had been forced to rely on the goodwill of hostile translators and intermediaries to defend their cause. Metaphorical expressions—like that most cherished toad paw in the left eye—had been given literal meanings. Words such as *akelarre*—probably a field of herbs—had metamorphosed into pastures dedicated to a goat-headed deity.[48]

In all, and for skeptical Spanish inquisitors at least, the entire affair stank of corruption and embarrassment. Which is why they, rather than continuing the persecution of the thousands of purported sorcerers that still roamed the mountainsides, opted instead for issuing a general pardon. As the new doctrine had it, "the testimony of accomplices alone—even if they had not been submitted to violence and compulsion—without further support from external facts . . . is insufficient to warrant even an arrest."[49]

The years of persecution, loud as they had been in accusations, rebuttals, and in the suffering of those chased by witch-hunters, had been nonetheless quite silent in other regards. Provincial authorities in the Western Pyrenees, so prone to denounce any interference of extraneous bodies into their internal functioning, had been staggeringly quiet as inquisitors had roamed the countryside interviewing incriminated individuals, imparting justice, and carrying out incarcerations. Guipuzcoan and Navarrese deputies, so touchy when it came to being subjected to external jurisdiction, had nonetheless put up with the situation with formidable restraint. And not only that, for they, rather than complain about the plethora of irregularities that had characterized the process, had chosen instead to throw more wood into the fire. They had policed the borders to prevent witches from crossing the Pyrenees, had supported inquisitors with all means at their disposal, and had even allowed their fellow compatriots to be taken to Logroño to receive punishment and damnation.

Of course, some saw in this merely a consequence of the rising climate of thrill and anxiety that had ensued during the witch craze. But, for all that it was true that most provincial delegates shared in their neighbors' belief in covenants of sorcerers, there were also more mundane motives at play in their actions. One had only to think about how the entire persecution had started. The two Labourdine noblemen who had presented their worries to Henry IV, members of the local aristocracy as they were, might in other times have refrained from bringing the issue to the monarch's attention. In a bygone age, disagreements of this kind, involving as they did humiliating and hard-to-shake accusations, had been commonly sorted out in local assemblies or at the intercession of particularly respected inhabitants. Such popular courts, founded on prestige and personal influence, had been the natural abode of the Parientes.

But now, those days were over. In summoning royal assistance, the two noblemen had made a choice. Above their role as representatives of their fellow communities, they had underscored their position as loyal vassals of the French sovereign. De Lancre, roaming the marginal areas of Labourd dispensing merciless rulings, had done so as the unmistakable agent of his monarch's prerogatives. Witchcraft, after all, was not dissimilar to a kind of treason. For,

> if the agreements made by certain subjects with someone who is the sworn enemy of their Prince are punished by death without remission, how then can one excuse or pardon these abominable pacts, which have been and continue to be so closely

> and perniciously tied with the mortal enemy of God, of the Church His spouse, of Religion, and of all good Christians?[50]

The Basques of Labourd, in being found guilty of one charge, might as well have been admitting the other.

Similar patterns had played out to the south. Tidings of new bouts of witchcraft had not come from within the small community of Zugarramurdi, but rather from a priest of a nearby town—coincidentally a translator of De Lancre's manual to recognize sorcerers—who was a close associate of one of those noblemen that had sparked the persecution in Labourd.[51] Here, too, inquisitors had arrived, not only as representatives of God's justice but also as that of their sovereign. They had brought to the region's inhabitants an understanding of definite borders, of the virtues of crystal-clear morality, and of the perils of corrupting influences: the same goals that the provincial authorities were trying to uphold. Breaking prisoners in a rack, or rendering necessary the presence of a judge to heal a torn community, or even demonstrating that the oral culture of these marginal societies was unsuitable both for tending to the soul and to the business of state: All contributed to the same purpose. Those on the margins, disciplined into the machinery of modern institutions, were to be made to comply. The benign law of the state, which meant of course the law of the provinces, had to leave no area in the shadow, small or peripheral though this may appear at first glance. Suppressing any alternatives to provincial society demanded no less.

And yet, the end of the witch craze had brought something else. The years of confessional and military conflict that had shaken the Western Pyrenees ever since the early sixteenth century had once given wings to the idea of a community that, worshipping one way or another and under one sovereign or another, hoped to span both sides of the mountain range. Now, however, this dream was almost dead. Under the pressure of secular and religious apparatuses of power, the frontier had been solidified, both in space as well as in the minds of those who lived in it. Naturally, the notion of a possible union of the Basque speakers, just as it had emerged in the lands surrounding *Ultrapuertos*, was also treasured for longer in those parts. Scholars and writers, following in the inaugural footsteps of Echepare and Leizarraga, would continue throughout the seventeenth century to occasionally abandon French and Gascon to pen works in *Euskera*. Likewise, they would emphasize how few differences existed between the "Basques and the Iberian Basques, [who] had almost the same qualities and the same defects."[52]

Not that they could harbor high hopes about their readership in the south. Observing that their counterparts at the service of the Spanish crown praised *Euskera* as the tongue of the patriarchs and the proof of the nobility of their provincials, these authors regularly raised irate complaints at the fact that their texts were written invariably in Castilian.[53] Some, taking a more despondent tone, lamented that "if only there were made in *Euskera* as many books as they are written in Latin, French, and other languages, then Basque would be as rich and praiseworthy as these tongues, and that if this is not the case, then it is the fault of its speakers and not of *Euskera* itself."[54]

But such a prospect—of *Euskera* becoming a tongue of culture—was now more unfeasible than ever. In the wake of the defeat of Protestantism and after having to quench a widespread bout of sorcery, few among the ruling classes had any eagerness to take chances. Better to reestablish a full diglossia, to teach Christian doctrine in the language of the church and to keep the affairs of men under the aegis of officials fluent in French and Castilian, than to risk pernicious—and dangerous—associations. Naturally, those at the short end of this policy, members of the popular classes, might from time to time seek to alter the terms of the deal. In Bilbao, during a virulent uprising in 1630, the "people were shouting for *Euskera* to be spoken so that everyone could understand what was being said, [and] that those who wore black hose—that is, those who lived like gentlemen—should not be the deputies, but rather the simple folk."[55]

And yet, in all, Echepare's vision of a time in which Basque speakers would see their speech appraised and esteemed missed the mark. Provincial authorities, and all who benefited from their existence—be it the heirs of the Parientes, the merchants and traders scattered across the empire, or members of the urban patriciate who longed for a post in the court—rather than stimulating the growth of *Euskera*, had become its most ferocious opponents. For its failure in developing into a vehicle of culture, Basque would thus pay a grievous price: to remain, in its own land, a language on the fringes.

A lingering whisper of this doomed utopia, however, persisted. Silenced and dim though it was at home by voices that defined belonging according to rules, statutes, and privileges, it was still possible to pick up its melody if only one traveled far enough from the Western Pyrenees. Never anything but a minor echo among the strenuous trumpeting coming from the court and the General Assemblies, the notion that speakers of *Euskera* shared in a brotherhood of its own never wholly vanished either. From Potosí to Antwerp, and from Seville to Newfoundland, it continued to shape the lives of Western Pyrenean communities around the globe. The hegemony of the provincial order, secure though it might appear on the surface, was not as complete as to manage to erase the notion for good.

Euskal Herria might be nowhere to be found on a map. And yet, unbeknownst to all but those most attentive of observers, it still clung to life. *Euskera*, indeed, had come forth into the world.

Notes

1 Cieza de Leon, *Parte primera de la chronica del Peru*, CXXIII, v.

2 Arzáns, *Historia de la villa imperial de Potosí*, II, IV, 42.

3 Méndez, "El fraude en la Casa de Moneda de Potosí. Otro episodio de la lucha entre vicuñas y vascongados por la preeminencia local," 92.

4 Quoted in Hausberger, "La guerra de los vicuñas contra los vascongados en Potosí y la etnicizaci6n de los vascos a principios de la edad moderna," 40.

5 Zaragoza, *Castellanos y vascongados. Tratado breve de una disputa y diferencia que hubo entre dos amigos el uno castellano de Burgos y el otro vascongado en la villa de Potosí, reino del Perú*, 48.

6 Arzáns, *Historia de la villa imperial de Potosí*, III, VII, 78, 1552.

7 Arzáns, VII, I, 322, 1621.

8 Fagel, "Los hombres de la lana y del hierro: mercaderes vascos en los Países Bajos Siglos XVI," 60.

9 Aernouts, "Presencia vasca en Brabante en el siglo XVI: ¿Licenciado Poza Antwerpensis?," 70.

10 Laborda, *El Señorío de Vizcaya. Nobles y fueros (c.1452–1727)*, 99–100.

11 Shakespeare, *Hamlet*, Scene II. Also, Garate, *Viajeros extranjeros en Vasconia*, 1989, 7.

12 Garibay, *Los XL libros del Compendio Historial*, XV, XV, 971.

13 Floristán, "Conquista e incorporación del Reino de Navarra a la Monarquía de España," 320.

14 Yanguas y Miranda, *Historia de la Conquista del Reino de Navarra por el Duque de Alba*, 63–4.

15 Francesco Guicciardini (1512). In Floristán, "Conquista e incorporación," 335–6.

16 "Fuero Reducido de Navarra" (1528). In Arregui, "El trasfondo político de las recopilaciones del Reino de Navarra," 194.

17 Arregui, "El trasfondo político," 195.

18 Floristán, "Conquista e incorporación," 340–1.

19 Pérez, "El ejemplar regio de un libro real," 15–16.

20 Théodore Agrippa d'Aubigné, "Histoire universelle depuis 1550 jusqu'en 1601" (1616–1626). Quoted in Pérez, "El ejemplar region," 23.

21 Garibay, *Los XL libros del Compendio Historial*, XXX, XIV, 639.

22 Quoted in Ritter, "Jeanne d'Albret et la Réforme chez les Basques," 173.

23 Ritter, 176.

24 Leizarraga, *Iesus Christ Gure Iaunaren Testamentu Berria*, IV.

25 "The song of Monseigneur Bernat Etxepare," vv. 93–7. In Dechepare, *Linguae Vasconum Primitiae*, 229.

26 Dechepare, *Linguae Vasconum Primitiae*, 193.

27 "Contrapas," vv.14–19. In Dechepare, *Linguae Vasconum Primitiae*, 230.

28 Mounole and Lacarra, "El Euskera arcaico," 395.

29 Aldekoa, "El Renacimiento en la literatura vasca: Juan Pérez de Lazarraga," 148.

30 "Loa de las damas y galanes vascongados." In Bilbao et al., *Lazarraga eskuizkribua: edizioa eta azterketa*, 18 or. v-r, 32–3.

31 Garibay, *Los XL libros del Compendio Historial*, IV, IV, 91.

32 Quoted in Martínez, *Casa, Provincia, Rey*, 168–9.

33 Francisco de Álava (1564). Quoted in Ritter, "Jeanne d'Albret et la Réforme chez les Basques," 172.

34 Jimeno, "La Contrarreforma en la Navarra incorporada a la Corona castellana: las instituciones educativas (1515–1630)," 357.

35 Goyeneche, *Le Pays Basque*, 227.

36 Azurmendi, *Y se limpie aquella tierra*, 127–8.

37 Bazán, "El crimen de lesa majestad divina: brujería y superstición vasco-navarra (s. XIII-c.1530)," 88–9.

38 Innocent VIII. *Summis desiderantes affectibus* (1484).

39 Kramer and Sprenger, *Malleus Maleficarum*, I, I, 2.

40 De Lancre, *Tableau de l'inconstance des mauvais anges et demons*, I, 30.

41 De Lancre, *Tableau de l'inconstance*, III, 192–3.

42 Azurmendi, *Nombrar, embrujar*, 217.

43 Quoted in Henningsen, *The Witches' Advocate: Basque witchcraft and the Spanish Inquisition (1609–1614)*, 129–30. Also, Gari, "La brujería en los Pirineos (siglos XIII al XVII): Aproximación a su historia," 340.

44 Fonseca, *Relación summaria del auto de la fe que los señores Doctor Alonso Bezerra Holguin, del Abito de Alcantara, Licenciado Ioan de Valle Albarado, Licenciado Alonso de Salaçar Frias, Inquisidores Apostolicos en el Reyno de Navarra y su destricto, celebraron en la Ciudad de Logroño, en siete y ocho dias del mes de Noviembre, de mil y seyscientos y diez años*, 12.a.

45 "The Bishop's Report." In Henningsen, *The Witches" Advocate*, 128.

46 Henningsen, *The Witches' Advocate*, 140.

47 Henningsen, 130–1. Also, Azurmendi, *Nombrar, embrujar*, 218–19.

48 Azurmendi, *Nombrar, embrujar*, 226–7.

49 Alonso de Salazar Frías. In Henningsen, *The Witches' Advocate*, 304–5.

50 De Lancre, *Tableau de l'inconstance*, VI, 554.

51 Azurmendi, *Nombrar, embrujar*, 218–19.

52 Oihenart, *Notitia utriusque Vasconiae tum Ibericae, tum Aquitanicae*, 408.

53 Joannes Etcheberri de Ziburu. Quoted in Martínez, *Casa, Provincia, Rey*, 172–3.

54 Axular, *Gero*, 10; 12.

55 Laborda, *El Señorío de Vizcaya. Nobles y fueros (c.1452–1727)*, 173–4.

CHAPTER 18
IRURAC BAT

That the Idiáquez were the most important family in Guipuzcoa was as indisputable a statement as saying that the touch of water got things wet. Its members, natives from Azcoitia, had for generations—and under the protection of the provincial institutions—thrived in earnest. Early on, they had been one of the first to dip their toes in the profitable business of the iron trade. Then, as this commerce dwindled and became less and less lucrative through the seventeenth century owing to both foreign competition and the unpalatable consequences of European-scale warfare, scions of the family had changed course and had started to opt for military careers instead. Many had served as officials and soldiers in the battlefields of Flanders, Italy—and even at sea.[1] These experiences had allowed the family to mingle with and befriend many Castilian aristocrats as well as other great men of the empire. Women of the lineage, too, had played their role in the elevation of their house, securing alliances and giving birth to children that would, in turn, follow the upward trend initiated by their ancestors. In all, the results were impressive. Holders of a myriad of *mayorazgos*, well-connected to the empire's transmission belts, and with a legion of employees, dependents, and relatives both in the province and across the dominions of the Spanish king, the Idiáquez were as successful as any Western Pyrenean had ever dreamed to be.

But if their accomplishments were positively impressive, then recent events only promised to render them ever more dazzling. Charles II, the last of the Spanish Habsburgs, had been a sickly, mentally challenged individual. A barren one, too. And so, when at his death in 1700 a new monarch—a French Bourbon nothing less—had come to the throne, all hell had been let loose. Across Europe, the shockwave of the possible alliance between Spain and France had engulfed every court and, before long, both within and outside the domains of the Spanish monarchy, war had raged in earnest.

The young and inexperienced Philip V, grandson of Louis XIV and the French candidate for the Spanish throne, might not have seemed, initially, the most suitable individual to face such a volatile situation. Luckily for him, he was not alone. The aspiring king could count on his side many trustworthy members of his grandfather's retinue, as well as valuable contacts south of the Pyrenees. In December 1700, as he made his way to his new kingdom, the teenage sovereign met in Bayonne a delegation of Spanish noblemen. There, procuring to the teenage king's enjoyment, they staged the first ever bull-fighting spectacle ever carried out anywhere in France.[2] Philip had been overjoyed.

But pleased with the show though the king certainly was, and curious though the strict etiquette of the Spanish Habsburg court must have appeared to a man accustomed to the pleasures of Versailles, the initial reaction would soon give way to mounting tensions. As it happens, the empire he aspired to rule was a kneeling giant, burdened by more than a century of expensive foreign wars and an endemic shortage of funds. Its political institutions, too, appeared to French observers little more than outdated relics. The system of government, largely set in place by the successors of Isabella and Ferdinand in the early sixteenth century, resembled, more than 200 years on from their passing, a machine kept alive only by the barest of threads. The army was largely ineffective; so too was the collection of taxes. In the peripheries and throughout the vast colonial possessions, where smugglers drained the lifeblood of the empire and offered it to its rivals, the rule of the monarch had become an ever more contested one to wield. Reform of some kind was long overdue. And it was this project—the modernization of the Spanish state according to the latest French innovations—that Philip V and his aides had, amid a continental war, come to set in motion.

A project of such magnitude, it goes without saying, required money and able men. In other times, perhaps, when the economic buoyancy of the Spanish monarchy had been less questioned by pirates and corsairs, and the high nobility of the kingdom had seen in the funding of distant campaigns an investment worthy of their resources, these might have been easier for the sovereign to come by. Now, however, supply was severely cut off. High-ranking aristocrats, many of whom felt threatened by the centralizing measures Philip wished to sponsor, had flocked to the Habsburg candidate's camp. Others, indecisive and unsure of what the future had in stock, offered only the most ambivalent of endorsements. And yet, the march of hostilities, and the expenses that came naturally from ruling a worldwide empire, had not decreased at all—quite the opposite. Despite the shipments that his grandfather would continuously send to alleviate his predicament, Philip's situation remained precarious. As his ministers explained, the elderly king of France had his own troubles to attend to. And so, if the Spanish alliance was to endure—and if the Bourbons were to elevate themselves as the most prominent dynasty in Europe—then Philip would have to muster coin for his reforms all by himself. The problem, as ever, was where to find it.

The Idiáquez family had favored the French candidate ever since the start of the conflict. They were hardly the only northerners to do so. While blue-blooded aristocrats had chosen, for the most part, to oppose Philip's plans, there were many in these lands that had seen in the rise of the young king their own path to the summit. For many generations, ever since the defeat of the Parientes, the provincial oligarchies had increased their patrimonies through trade, industry, marriage, and inheritance. Their position then secure at home, they had enrolled their children in prestigious universities, there to engross the ranks of the Habsburg administration, the army, the navy, and the clergy.[3] Never had any of these gray figures, lacking high-flown titles and vast estates, ever come close to threatening the position of the mighty dukes and counts of the empire, but they had thrived under their wing nonetheless. Some had been clerics or admirals, while an Idiáquez—as the family never let anyone forget—had even become a member of Philip II's personal council. And yet, by 1700, these were already old news. The later Habsburgs, in promoting their favorites to the government, had dampened the hopes of these middle-ranking servants of ever reaching the top.[4] Which is why, when members of these families heard about the pecuniary troubles that plagued the new ruler of Spain, they had immediately opened their coffers to support him.

Philip's regime, naturally, had accepted the lifeline that was being thrown its way and had made sure to pay it back with largesse. Before long, a whole retinue of peoples from northern Spain, and mostly from the Western Pyrenees, found their way to official appointments, state-sponsored contracts, and careers in the army. Juan de Idiáquez, as only befitted one of the foremost members of his family and a veteran of the wars of Flanders at that, saw his endorsement outstandingly rewarded. In 1704, and under a personal recommendation by the all-powerful Duke of Berwick, he was tasked with the creation and command of the king's personal bodyguard troop. The position demanded that he follow the monarch wherever he may go, to check the lodgings in which he would stay, and to personally close the gates of the royal palace every night.[5] Most importantly, perhaps, it made its responsibility the recommendation—and ultimate selection—of any recruit willing to join the king's escort. Both physically and figuratively, it was Juan de Idiáquez that held the keys to the king.

Back in the provinces, the meteoric success of Juan de Idiáquez and other compatriots, suddenly elevated to the post of ministers, secretaries, and stewards of Philip V and his family, was contemplated with excitement. After all, as had always been the case in the region, the rise of a man could likely become the rise of many. The warlike Parientes, in signing truces with cities and freemen, had once promised a better deal to those cast under their protection. Now, under a very different political and social system, realities treaded on similar patterns. Many in Guipuzcoa, be it because they worked their forges, rented their houses, or transported their goods, owed their livelihoods, in some way or another, to Juan de Idiáquez and his family. Others, while perhaps less directly dependent, knew nonetheless better than to dismiss the family's friendship. For as long as anyone could remember, after all, their endorsement had opened many doors across the province—and even beyond.

But unlike the Parientes, who had always tried to put others in their shades, outstanding members of the Idiáquez lineage, for all that they stood at the top of the social pyramid, had made sure to give something back. Individuals from minor branches of the family tree had, for example, been employed as overseers in important trade hubs like Seville or Brussels. Others had, on the contrary, remained back at home to take responsibility for the correct exploitation of the family's resources. And yet, the distribution of profit went much further than the household's boundaries. The heads of the family, always attentive to the subtle fluxes in the balance of local power, had made sure to oil their networks carefully. Sponsorships, favors, information, marriages: All had been dispensed to the advantage of both patron and client. Even the community, which was so often forgotten in the higher spheres of the province, had received its fair share. In addition to providing them with seasonal employment, these grandees had also funded the building of monasteries, primary schools, and hospitals. That this might, in turn, revert to the greater glory of those paying the bill was, of course, only natural. The head of the Idiáquez clan, either in presiding over a military parade in Azcoitia, in being allotted first place in a local procession, or in being courted by ambitious social climbers in the General Assembly, could experience what it meant to be the greatest man in the land. For he was the head—as a French minister would say—of "one of the most important families [and the one] that makes the rest of the province move."[6]

Now, with Juan's dramatic rise, the floodgates for further promotions lay wide open. Not only was the captain of the king's bodyguard a relevant figure in the palace, but he was also a close confidant of the king himself. And not only Philip's: for the prince—the future Ferdinand VI—being fifteen at the time, was said "to secretly drink chocolate in mister Idiáquez's room because, by order of the king's doctor, it [was] forbidden to him."[7] Details such as these betrayed a closeness that, grounded in devout service and personal affection though it was, could just as easily result in all kinds of appetizing opportunities. The young prince, in seeking the elder soldier's protection to contravene his physician's orders, was just as much acting on his own volition as playing the role Juan had set up for him. And this because patronage was all but a reliable affair. While Philip's support might, for the time being at any rate, be assured, who could guess, politics in the court being what they were, how long this favor might last? The long-term prospects of Juan's family—and of those Western Pyreneans elevated on their trail—might one day depend on such banalities as a chocolate bowl. No wonder then that Idiáquez was "overjoyed" with how things were turning out: "because he believes [the prince] will be the salvation of the world due to his great talent and affection for the Spanish, and especially for the *Biscaynes*."[8]

Those *Biscaynes*, indeed, were doing exceedingly well under the new regime. While successful northerners in general had managed to attain posts of responsibility in the administration, the army, and the church in recent years, the proportion of individuals from Guipuzcoa, Biscay, Alava, and Navarre dwarfed their numbers. Dozens of Western Pyrenean youngsters, forcibly expelled from a society in which only the firstborn could inherit the familial patrimony, flooded to Madrid in search of juicy appointments and the prospect of a better life. Here, granted that their families had cultivated the required contacts, they could count on the help and instruction of the high achievers of the previous generation to guide them through the twisted paths of the court. Such a pattern of masters and apprentices was one that enjoyed a decades-long pedigree in Madrid, and yet, the arrival of those provincials raised by Philip had only exacerbated its importance.[9] Now, more than ever, it was crucial to tap on the necessary contacts to succeed. And so, these *vascongados* had soon, as their forefathers had previously done in Seville or Potosí, chosen to park their differences to better pursue preeminence. In the early 1710s, they began to push for an association of natives "from the three most Noble and most Loyal provinces of Cantabria."[10] In 1713, these rather informal gatherings were granted royal approval as a Royal Congregation of Saint Ignace of Loyola—a Guipuzcoan and the favorite patron saint of all *vascongados*. Thanks to this foundation, there now existed in Madrid, in the center of the empire, a lobby of Western Pyreneans which closely resembled the ones that for more than a century had been functioning on its margins.

A lobby which could boast an empire-wide network and permanent access to the monarch's ear was, in the turbulent years that followed Philip's advent to the Spanish throne, a formidable asset to possess. If the stated policy of the sovereign was the reform of the structure of the imperial administration, such an effort depended, ultimately, on the recruitment of a suitable class of shock troops to dispel the qualms of the most entrenched elements of the outmoded regime. The regiments of bodyguards raised by Juan de Idiáquez were perhaps the readiest example of this. And yet there were others who, although they did not physically protect the royals, were no less the defenders of their prerogatives for that. Sidelining the great judges and magistrates, scions of mighty Castilian lineages, that populated the higher echelons of the administration, Philip V recruited a new class of servants of the crown. These were men without titles, without great patrimonies, who owed their position in the court both to their talents and to the king's own favor.[11] Louis XIV was said to have given his grandson, before the latter's travel to Spain, a succinct piece of advice: "do not let yourself be governed by anyone; be the master."[12] And if the anecdote was indeed true, then Philip had for sure taken note of it. Affairs of all kinds, which had previously been dispatched by opaque councils controlled by haughty clerks, were increasingly being redirected to purposefully created organs of decision-making in which the monarch had the last word.[13] Many of Philip's enemies saw in these measures a trampling of the old traditions. His supporters, on the other hand, regarded them as a necessary antidote to ensure the correct functioning of the realm. The king might be bound by law and custom just like anyone else, but as warden of society, it was his ultimate duty to apply extraordinary remedies to any problems for which the ancient rulings could not find a viable solution.[14]

The willingness of the royal administration to go further than any of its predecessors was blatantly obvious in Aragon. Here, as a punishment for the kingdom's support of the Habsburg candidate, Philip and his advisers had conducted what could only be described as an unprecedented labor of uprooting. From 1707 onward, a series of decrees had stripped the limitations of royal power encoded in the kingdom's legislation. These included, among others, the erasure of its particular assemblies and its political and fiscal institutions.[15] Then, with these obstacles out of the way, the monarch had sought to extend to Aragon the ample prerogatives he possessed in Castile.[16] In all, the results were traumatic. So much so that peace in the country could only be maintained in their aftermath thanks to a permanent stationing of tens of thousands of soldiers.[17] But if the debacle of the Aragonese particularities paraded the hubris of a regime that had inherited from its French exemplars the impatience with the obstructions of petty regionalists, it could also bear witness to the powers such a government might wield. If not even the venerable institutions of a powerful realm like Aragon, which had successfully contained so many a great king, were enough to stop Philip's plans of reform, who—in Castile and beyond—could rest entirely confident in what the future held in store?

A warning that struck especially close to home in the Western Pyrenees. Not for nothing, after the cataclysmic alterations that had recently shaken Aragon, there remained in the entire peninsular possessions of Philip only four territories in which Castilian laws did not apply: Biscay, Guipuzcoa, Alava, and Navarre. Of course, these territories had supported the Bourbon candidate and thus were safe from the kind of vendetta the new monarch had visited upon the former kingdom. But the same could not be said about Philip's reforming appetites. Never a man to tolerate limits upon his powers, he could hardly regard the protections granted by the legal paradigms of these territories as anything but challenges to overcome. And these, when it came to the supply of coin and soldiers—the two aspects that most interested his government to obtain—were especially uncooperative. Troops from the provinces, according to their laws, could not be freely conscripted and dispatched to the raging battlefields of the empire, but had to be paid off for the trouble. Likewise, when the time came to garner funds, the provinces boasted unique tax systems. Biscay, shielded in its status as a separate lordship, had managed for centuries to protect its inhabitants from the most grievous taxes levied on the Castilians, as had the Navarrese. Guipuzcoans and Alavese, on the other hand, although not entirely dispensed from all payments, had seen many of them either fossilized or abolished for good.[18] In all cases, the particulars of these exemptions, concessions, and partial agreements had varied from province to province and nothing resembling a common fiscal organization was anywhere to be found. A succession of kings had tried to find creative solutions and favorable interpretations to alter this situation. And yet, the reality was that, for the most part, the inhabitants of these territories had contributed far less than they should have done were they subjects of the Castilian king.[19]

If there was an aspect of these provincial systems that particularly irritated reformers it was the arrangement of tariffs. The agricultural poverty of the land—made notorious in a stanza which described a certain Lope the Biscayne as "rich in apples, poor in bread and wine"—had always rendered the task of feeding the population of the coastal provinces a difficult proposition.[20] To deal with these shortcomings, Western Pyrenean cities in the Middle Ages had often been granted sizable advantages to buy foreign grain at competitive prices and prevent these trade hubs from slowly depopulating.[21] These measures had, in turn, been inherited by the provincial order. The only problem lay in that, to make sure that the discounted goods were strictly confined to these disfavored territories as intended, custom houses, rather than on the coast, had to be established in the limits between them and the rest of Castile.

As time went on, this settlement had bred its own set of problems. The smuggling of colonial goods, whose commercialization in Castile had been up to this point fiercely monopolized and taxed by the monarchy, found in these northern districts a perfect vehicle for its goals. Shipments of tobacco and cocoa from the Caribbean, illegally extracted and after a stopover in Lisbon or Bayonne, were then unloaded without duties in Bilbao or San Sebastian, there to be shipped undercover to the captive Castilian markets and sold at skyrocketing profit. The whole enterprise, dangerous though it was, provided many impoverished youngsters and peasants—not to say the merchants and shipowners that oversaw the operations—with an abundant harvest of coin. Before long, smuggling was already a key economic activity in the Western Pyrenees, and one for which bravery was the sole requirement. "Since their wealth has no other foundation than the rashness of their recklessness, they rush into danger with little foresight, believing it is less of an evil to endure it than to live in continual misery."[22]

Both as a warden of God-ordained harmony and as a monarch starved of resources, the issue of smuggling, because it meant the trespassing and bending of royal and provincial jurisdictions, was one that Philip V could not look upon fondly. Already in the late years of his Habsburg predecessor, royal advisers had toyed with the idea of transferring Biscayne custom houses to the coast and thus integrate the Lordship into the Spanish inner market.[23] The new regime, as part of its purported reforms, soon sought to revive the idea. First off, between 1713 and 1714, a series of unpopular measures—like the stationing in the provinces of royal officers to watch over potential smuggling—had already showcased the firm hand with which the government pursued the matter.[24] Then, in late 1717 and early 1718, a decree commanded the immediate establishment of coastal tariffs in Bilbao, San Sebastian, and other ports.

It proved a major miscalculation. Scared and stirred by local agitators with the prospect of having to pay "stamped paper, a salt tax, and all the taxes of Castile; and that when they married they would have to pay a fee, as also when they were buried and when they baptized their children," the population of the villages around Bilbao took arms and harassed the delegates of the Lordship to force them to revert the measure.[25] A primal fury spread over the city, as foreign merchants were beaten and magistrates were tortured for their alleged collaboration in the trampling of Biscay's liberties. Most horridly for the powerful, Enrique de Arana, General Deputy for the Lordship, was murdered in cold blood by an uncontrollable mob.

> He came, and the republic of Erandio surrounded him; and after he had signed in the middle of the Arenal, he was struck a blow that split half his head open. So many followed with swords, pikes, and lances that it is dreadful to recount; in the end he died soon after, at eleven in the morning, and every villager who passed by to see him thrust their swords into him.[26]

Similar scenes repeated in other towns. In Bermeo, the discontented assassinated a local potentate and threw his corpse to the city square.[27] In Azpeitia, members of the local oligarchy had managed to prevent a bloodbath only by giving particularly violent protesters money and wine—a policy that, in their own words, cost them dearly.[28] The inhabitants of Biscay and the western side of Guipuzcoa, it seemed, had expressed their opposition to the royal policy. Viewing in this only a plot to deprive them of the benefits of their *Hidalguía*, they had rejected the attempts to transfer the custom houses to the hinterland in the strongest of terms: with fire and with blood.

The uprising, especially in Biscay, had shown the extent to which the locals could be touchy when it came to their most sizable privileges—relatively low taxation and exemption from military service. And yet, many both within and without the Lordship feared that this staunch aversion to change, so fervently lauded in provincial rhetoric, might prove, paradoxically, the source of the whole system's undoing. Everyone had the pitiful example of Aragon fresh in their minds. What if the king, contemplating the vicious resistance his plans had produced in the north, were to take a similar approach toward its solution? This thought was especially worrisome for Western Pyrenean oligarchs, many of whom had proven elsewhere to be apt tools of royal reformism. Now they were torn between the king's favor—upon which their success in the court depended—and the defense of their provinces' prerogatives—which sustained their dominion of the native homeland. But, why, some of these influential men wondered, might the two not prove compatible? The reform of the custom houses, so recklessly chased by Philip's ministers, was indeed a succulent prize to pursue, but it was also one that could not be obtained in the absence of suitable compensation. As early as 1705, after all, the commercial elites of Guipuzcoa had already shown their willingness to alter the current tariff system in exchange for the establishment in San Sebastian of a hub with royal authorization to trade with America.[29] The king's mistake in 1717, it followed from this, had been simply trying to deprive the provinces of their privileges without giving anything in return.

For all that Philip V might feel hardly at ease with such bargains, he and his ministers had to admit that the whole affair of the custom houses had been a major fiasco. The quenching of the revolt in Biscay, after the dispatch of royal forces to the Lordship, had been swift. And yet the cost of such an operation had taxed scant resources the monarchy, embroiled in complex military entanglements all over Europe and America, could hardly do without. The revenues obtained in the years that followed the decree, likewise, had fallen utterly short of the dazzling expectations painted by the champions of the measure. And to this it ought to be added that an impending war with France and England had rendered the thought of a bunch of discontented territories on a sensitive frontier an especially unsettling one to entertain.

Envoys from Guipuzcoa, Biscay, and Alava, sensing the turning of the tides—and under the attentive guidance of their respective associates in Madrid—had taken advantage of the shift. First off, they had managed to get the restoration of the custom houses to their usual locations in 1723. Negotiating with the court for a definite solution to the problem of smuggling in 1727, they had done so separately, as befitted their status as standalone provinces. Behind the curtain, though, their agents had made sure to oversee in common what was agreed by each one of them, so that it might not hurt the standing of the rest. A massive effort of trust and coordination, for sure, and one that, in turn, was aided by the precedent of the Royal Congregation of Saint Ignace of Loyola, of which many of these negotiators were fellow members.[30] The end result was, thanks both to the ability of the *foral* negotiators and to the sticky circumstances the monarchy was going through, a major triumph for the provinces. The customary tariffs were kept in place. The causes of the revolt were, by attributing it solely to the unfathomable fury of the peasantry, separated from any debate about the usefulness of the provincial system. The issue of smuggling in these territories was glossed over with a resigned confirmation on Philip's part of his "trust in their Governments" to undertake "the necessary measures for this purpose."[31]

The episode, in putting the exemptions of these northern districts at risk, had done much to showcase their mutual imbrication. However, it was no less true that not all of them had profited equally from its conclusion. After all, neither the governments of Biscay nor Alava could count on the invaluable assistance and persuasion that an individual like Juan de Idiáquez could summon in Madrid. Idiáquez, who had been raised to the title of Duke of Granada de Ega back in 1708, had not hesitated in working with other *vascongados* to find a suitable resolution to the thorny affair of the custom houses. And yet, he was, first and foremost, a Guipuzcoan, and this meant that the interests of his motherland had priority over the ties that linked him to the other Cantabrian provinces. Now, these interests—given that the petty trade and fishing ventures the locals relied on to survive had been ruined, among other things, by the pernicious transformations of the tariff system—pointed, more than ever, toward America. Only colonial trade, with its exotic goods and its rising demand, could fill the void in Guipuzcoan coffers. Which meant that, when one of Philip V's ministers, Juan Bautista de Orendain—another Guipuzcoan—expressed his interest in the creation of a commercial corporation that could take charge for some American territories and relieve the crown from these expenses, Juan de Idiáquez had made sure to mobilize his networks to secure the appointment for Guipuzcoa.[32] The culmination of his labors would come in 1728 with the creation of the Guipuzcoan Company of Caracas.

Venezuela had been, of all the American possessions of the Spanish monarchy, the one that, up until this point, had received the least attention from the metropolitan government. Over the course of the decades, this oversight had made it the most prone to get embroiled in the kind of smuggling that so many headaches had given to royal administrators. The foundation of the *Company*, then, was envisioned as a deal that could kill two birds with one stone. First, it pandered to the government's needs by fully externalizing the cost of the state apparatus in the region to a commercial corporation while effectively ensuring the enforcement of Spanish interests and the dutiful paying of taxes. But, in addition to this, it gave those investing in the venture the chance of importing colonial goods like cocoa which promised abundant profits. And not only them, for the needs of the *Company*—which soon became the biggest industry not only in Guipuzcoa but in all the Western Pyrenees—[33]spilled all over the province. Haulers, carpenters, forest rangers, sailors, dockworkers, ship captains, weaponsmiths, the list of personnel required to make sure that the ships bound to Venezuela were adequately supplied reinvigorated the decaying economy of the province. A few years later, this American connection was already shaping the destinies of hundreds of locals:

> Boys and slightly older youths, bachelors and married men, enlist on ships—especially those bound for the Indies—and begin with the lowest tasks, then as common sailors, petty officers, constables, guards, boatswains, first and second pilots, clerks, captains, and many other ranks. All go off cheerful and full of hope. Caracas has been the grave of countless Guipuzcoans: this is public and notorious; and nevertheless, Caracas is where they aspire to go, as if each one were destined to become one of those officers who, in six or eight years, have grown fabulously rich by some Merlin's art, unknown here but learned there.[34]

And at the head of such a momentous enterprise, which promised to serve both Guipuzcoa and the empire at once, stood embodiments of what a well-nurtured web of connections might achieve in a changing world, men like Juan de Idiáquez.

The quick succession of political triumphs these Western Pyrenean provinces had attained in the 1720s did not fail to have an impact on how others perceived them. In a monarchy that had recently ruled out the distinctions in law, taxation, royal prerogatives, and military assistance which had made up the matter of life in Aragon, the example of Biscay, Guipuzcoa, Alava, and Navarre, which seemed to have not only weathered the reformist storm but even to have turned it to their advantage, must have shone bright in comparison. Once, the dominions of the Habsburgs had contained a scattered patchwork of territories and jurisdictions: counties, kingdoms, dukedoms, and city-states of all kinds. Now, after the first quarter of the eighteenth century, there remained of that world only the provincial institutions of the Western Pyrenees. Many, upon realizing this fact, weighed heavily on what it truly meant. Did the survival of these autonomous districts owe to any exceptional character, or was it rather a product of mere chance?

Truth be told, little up until this point had singled out these Western Pyrenean lands from other small political and territorial constituencies, beyond perhaps their meager resources and the curious egalitarian ideology they had fostered among their population. From this standpoint, the maintenance of the *foral* order appeared to be indebted more to a succession of lucky decisions and favorable events than to any ingrained uniqueness. However, and as had been so many times demonstrated in the Americas, in Seville, or in Madrid, the *vascongados* seemed to have been especially well-suited to building networks and endeavors that vastly exceeded their relative importance within the composite monarchy. Now, the restoration of the custom houses and the creation of the Guipuzcoan Company of Caracas only lent more credence to those who had come to consider Biscaynes, Guipuzcoans, Alavese, and Navarrese as members of a protected caste of sorts. Malicious rumors began to spread in Madrid that highlighted the favor men like Juan de Idiáquez and his northern clique enjoyed in the Bourbon court:

> With evasions and outrages
> it dominates and devours Spain
> from the uncultivated mountain
> a troop of savages:
> those who were once pages
> and today are nothing but vanity.
> It is true.[35]

Even American creoles, irritated for having to sell their production at prices set by the *Company*, complained "that the metropolitan bureaucracy was generally subject to the will of the Basques."[36] And indeed, if imitation is the sincerest form of flattery, then the fact that between 1723 and 1753 no less than fifteen regional congregations had been founded in Madrid on the example of the Royal Congregation of Saint Ignatius, bespoke an inescapable reality.[37] That natives from these "exempt provinces" constituted, for all intents and purposes, the new imperial elite.[38]

But if disfavored strangers had every reason to view the principal *vascongados* as the objects of unmerited favoritism, the latter, too, had come to regard their position as a manifestation of their own exceptionality. Provincials-turned-noblemen imagined themselves wholly free from the vices that they thought preyed on the minds of the aristocracy, who sought "only the preservation of their lineage through successive generations, but not that they should have the character required to be useful men in the state."[39] In the Western Pyrenees, the question of what precisely had prevented the native institutions from following other similar ones to the grave was increasingly answered with references to a self-evident uniqueness. The ancient virtues of the Cantabrians, the proverbial loyalty deployed by the provincials in the defense of the monarchy's interests, and the theory of the contract between the provinces and the monarchy were all, of course, dusted off to support such conclusions. And yet, in the wake of the perilous scenario so closely avoided in 1727, such arguments were no longer enough. The court, in trying to single-handedly trim the privileges of Biscay, Alava, and Guipuzcoa, had committed an unjustifiable transgression. And one, what is more, that had counted, if not with the complicit silence, at least with the tacit consent of the elites. Deputies to the General Assemblies, councilors in towns, delegates in Madrid, all had seemed less interested in standing up in support of the ancient liberties than in complying with any order that could guarantee them a profitable rise. That the end result of the entire affair had kept the old tariffs in place was no excuse for this misbehavior. These privileges, the sacred legacy of Tubal, should absolutely be non-negotiable.

Such, at any rate, was Manuel de Larramendi's indictment. Larramendi—a man "tall in stature, with a beautiful countenance, of iron constitution"[40]—had been appropriately schooled to understand the way of thinking of the *foral* aristocracy. A Jesuit trained in Salamanca, he had accompanied the widow of the deceased King Charles II to Bayonne, acted as her confessor until 1733, and then settled down for good in the Guipuzcoan shrine of Loyola. It was from this shelter that he, in the following decades, had set out to admonish members of the elite about their duties, preaching at times in front of the General Assembly itself.[41] If his oratory resembled his writing style in the slightest, then Larramendi's discourses must have been nothing short of incendiary. A fellow Jesuit, tasked with reviewing his works for publication, had once praised his style as "fluid, eloquent, nervous, [and] lively" but had pointed out against it that it was inundated by "a harsh vehemence, an offensive shaking, with expressions foreign, not only to urbanity, but also to religious circumspection, calling foolishness, simplicity, ridicule, nonsense" anyone who opposed his views and opinions.[42] Local potentates, foreigners, the ministers of the king themselves, anyone, if they had the misfortune of finding themselves on the wrong end of Larramendi's pen, could be assured of one thing: that he would speak his mind without holding his tongue.

And as it happens, Larramendi's tongue had an uncontainable inclination to looseness. A passionate Guipuzcoan, he took special offense from anyone who dared to criticize or even cast a shadow of doubt over the entitlement of this province to its newly found prosperity. In his opinion, the current buoyancy of the territory owed nothing to any ridiculous partiality, and everything, instead, to its exceptional character.

> In Guipuzcoa, you don't see men with ugly, monstrous, deformed bodies and brutish faces like in other kingdoms. They are agile, lively, quick, strong, and robust, all with faces of men that do not degenerate into feminine features due to poor

> diet, weak constitution, or effeminate upbringing. . . . The women in Guipuzcoa are the most beautiful in all of Spain, with vivid color, well-built, plump, strong, agile, and healthy; with few affectations and histrionics, very active, going up and down to their farms and mountains with the same air and vigor as if there were no slope.[43]

Honest strength and a stern sense of morality: these were the qualities that, according to Larramendi, had made the peoples of Guipuzcoa great.

Not that these features were themselves the product of fortuitous happenstance. Instead, they all derived from a revelation. Every kingdom and province around the world, past and present, had been the result of human action: the outcome either of bloody wars, public agreements, or a succession of marriage alliances. But this description, which held true for every single government on earth, was inappropriate when it came to Guipuzcoa. Only this little, rugged province, among all that dotted the surface of the globe, could boast the honor of having at its origin the Divine itself. "I establish God—Larramendi proclaimed—as the particular founder of Guipuzcoa . . . in bond and inheritance; and I am not surprised that you find it strange, since you do not find it in all those who have spoken of jurisprudence in all its extent."[44] A tantalizing thought, no doubt, and one that drank directly from biblical examples. If God, in granting a law to the Israelites, had once fashioned them a distinct people, the same could be said about the primitive inhabitants of Guipuzcoa, followers of Tubal who had been entrusted with commandments and privileges no less inspired and beneficial than those of the Old Testament. It went without saying that this legacy, just like any other *mayorazgo*, was one that could not be renounced at will.

> Consequently, although God may permit, as He has permitted with others, that our small inheritance of Guipuzcoa be violently and tyrannically destroyed, Guipuzcoa can never voluntarily yield its inheritance to others without contravening the original institution of the inheritance and the will of its founder, who is God—and this it cannot do in justice or in conscience.[45]

In other words, Guipuzcoan authorities had no right to either modify or renounce these laws: for theirs was a power only to preserve, to defend, to safeguard. And this, because unlike other territories, Guipuzcoa was "free because it was born free, was raised free, grew old free, and remains free in every stage since its founding, which was that of Spain."[46]

Larramendi lamented that knowledge of these self-evident truths had gone almost extinct by his time. He mournfully noted that foreign, Castilian customs—of which the attempted alterations to the tariff system were but the latest—had slowly eroded the unblemished purity of his homeland. It was possible to recognize in this the usual reservations that most Jesuits in Spain harbored about the reformist program deployed by Philip V. But it was no less true that Larramendi had felt a special sense of moral mission all throughout his life. Back in 1729, when he had noticed that the teachings of the church were passed down to locals in Spanish—and acknowledging that "Romance languages were of little use with the common man"—he had attempted to ensure the salvation of his fellow countrymen by authoring a concise grammar of *Euskera*.[47] On another occasion, he had met the accusations of a bishop who had described the public dances staged in Guipuzcoan towns as "spectacles of Satan" by offering a lengthy dissertation that presented them as innocent and edifying festivals.[48] A distinct object of his anger had been "the foolishness of the Castilian commoners and other Spaniards . . . when, in speech and writing, they refer to all *vascongados* by the name of Biscaynes."[49] A particularly damaging charge; for although "Biscay and Guipuzcoa are sister provinces," Larramendi could not suffer the former monopolizing the glory and esteem garnered by the latter.[50] After all, he wondered,

> where does the Frenchman enter with blood and fire in times of war? Is it not Guipuzcoa where he unleashes his fury, his fires, his logging, and his looting? . . . Yes, it is Guipuzcoa. Not Biscay, not Alava . . . nor any other province, where they live without fear nor worry, while Guipuzcoa suffers the pitiful devastations of war.[51]

Adding these episodes together might have amounted, perhaps, to little more than a fastidious series of equivocations and misunderstandings, had they not been but symptoms of a deeper malady. Larramendi believed that it was somewhat to be expected that those less favored among the king's subjects would look up in envy to Guipuzcoan and other Western Pyrenean privileges and would seek to snuff them out. What he could never tolerate was the complicity of native well-to-do families. Many, blinded by the sheer brightness of the opportunities made available to them across the empire, gave the impression of having forgotten that they were, first and foremost, children of Guipuzcoa. These men "dress up, from top to bottom, according to French or Spanish fashion"; their women, in turn, "go about . . . uncovered, bare, half-exposed, immodest, indecent."[52] Shameful displays of immorality all of them, of course, that stood in marked contrast with the traditional sobriety and religiosity Larramendi ascribed to the provincials. The mighty, so contaminated by foreign etiquette in Madrid or Seville, parading their disdain for the speech of the land, were at risk of becoming turncoats. And, if that were to happen, calamity would befall the land. A little taste of what lay in store had been offered by the events of 1718, and although Larramendi readily admitted that "popular tumults are not a means for a fair and rational defense, but to multiply folly, horrors, and scandals," he would not deny, either, that it was a horror that members of the elite had called upon themselves.[53] The only viable solution to prevent more revolts lay in abandoning the sources of the pollution, and in bringing back in earnest the pristine ideal set by God upon Guipuzcoans. Only thus would the community be united again, and only thus would the privileges of the motherland stand secure.

Larramendi's moralizing against the degeneracy of the provincial system constituted a confrontational and anti-Castilian strain of the old *foral* propaganda, but it was not, by any means, a revolutionary manifesto. The old Jesuit still prided himself on the loyalty that, on condition of respect for their exceptionality, Guipuzcoans and other *vascongados* would pay to the king of Castile. Similarly, he never challenged the right of the great families to monopolize the offices in the General Assembly or in the Deputation, dedicated one of his books to the Duke of Granada de Ega, took the functional diglossia between Castilian and *Euskera* for granted, and went as far as to defend the requirement of *millares* as a way to "serve as security for the republic [and] to protect itself from the harm that a bad officeholder might cause it."[54] Instead, his denunciation focused squarely on the transformation that Juan de Idiáquez's generation and that of his successors had undergone in order to become an imperial elite. Larramendi agreed with the critics in accepting that the position enjoyed by these *vascongado* ministers vastly exceeded the size of their native province. But this was not a problem in need of correction: It was merely the natural recognition by the king and his confidants of the natural superiority of these Western Pyreneans. Herein lay the source of their success, and it was exactly this fountainhead of virtue that, in contact with the profligate fashions currently in vogue in the court, Larramendi found so urgent a task to preserve.

One could argue that the old Jesuit had put his finger on a particularly sore spot, not only in his beloved Guipuzcoa, but across Western Pyrenean society. The reservations held by Larramendi mirrored those of many of his fellow neighbors in the provinces, and this was because, all throughout the eighteenth century, the cultural and behavioral distance which separated the elite from the common folk had been widening at a precipitous pace.[55] Previously, and despite the very real variation in economic and social standing, the preponderant lineages had kept a sort of symbiotic relationship with their compatriots. Their scions had been friends in school, had attended the same public balls, and had shared a cultural universe that had rooted them both firmly in the traditions of the land.

Now, however, this connection was being dissolved. Families like the Idiáquez and their many imitators, their eyes fixed on the careers of their members and clients, had over time developed an innovative dynamic to achieve their goals. While the firstborn, as befitted his status as householder, took responsibility for the family *mayorazgos* and thus stayed in the province, any remaining siblings were quickly dispatched to serve as apprentices to well-positioned relatives. There, they had learned the ins and outs of a career in the highest spheres. Over the course of a couple of generations, this procedure had hoisted up dozens of *vascongado* military officials, pages, ministers, secretaries, and church administrators and had joined them in an intricate web of marriage alliances.[56] Accomplishment in attaining imperial-scale success, in other words, depended as much on the personal talents of the candidate as on the quality of the patrons a family could tap for his advancement. Which meant that while youngsters, in their early years, might be "raised entirely in the local style and almost without knowing any language other than Basque," once they arrived in Madrid, they were hard-pushed by the stern tutors endowed with their education to learn to read, to count, and to speak in Castilian—and to completely forget their mother language.[57]

In this sort of meteoric ascent, as men like Larramendi no doubt noticed, the provinces' inhabitants and institutions were relegated to playing a very modest role.

The theoretically virtuous and egalitarian General Assemblies were packed either by the most accomplished householders, who thanks to their intimate contacts across the monarchy had—unlike their less connected compatriots—access to riches to dispense or to exclusive information to take advantage of, or by individuals aspiring to obtain the latter's favor.[58] Larramendi was hardly the only one to have denounced the kind of abuses and irregularities this situation tended to provoke.[59] And given that this dominion ultimately depended on a top-down relationship, its beneficiaries had little incentive to avoid a slow assimilation to the manners and demeanors of the greater partner. In fact, those clothing fashions so reviled by the Jesuit were only one among the manifold ways in which members of the elite now sought to manifest their superiority. Preeminent lineages, ennobled by Philip V and his successors, began to bask in their Castilian titles. On other occasions, the division was translated into physical space. In 1756, oligarchs in Bilbao, going against all precedent, had held a ball in a large boat garnished with all kinds of fantastic decorations and luxuries and had forbidden commoners from joining in.[60] Similar public entertainments, previously celebrated in the town square, were over the course of the century gradually staged behind barred doors for the sole enjoyment of a sophisticated—and minuscule—audience of selected attendees. Increasingly, as these grandees' sense of indebtedness and dependence toward their fellow provincials dwindled, so too swelled the sense of moral and cultural disgust they felt about the latter's traditions. Just like Philip V and his associates when they had first confronted the Spanish administrative system, the Western Pyrenean families that now operated the gears of the empire had come to identify themselves as archetypes of a new social order. One that, to flourish, felt entitled to correct the sins of an older regime they thought well on its way to extinction.

A man armed with such convictions arrived in Azcoitia in 1746. Xabier María de Munibe and Idiáquez, Count of Peñaflorida, was both in his origins and his upbringing an exemplar of the new winds blowing in the Western Pyrenees. His ancestors, enriched by American trade, had later come back to Guipuzcoa to buy lands and found *mayorazgos*, and thanks to a succession of advantageous marriages and the patronage of powerful relatives, they had soon joined the ranks of the local oligarchy.[61] Xabier, as corresponded a scion of such a family, had been sent to study to a suitably exclusive institution. In recent years, it had become somewhat of a commonplace for the children of well-to-do lineages to receive their education in places where they could rub shoulders with the *crème de la crème*. While some preferred the Seminar of Nobles in Madrid, others settled instead for royal Military Academies. And yet there were other parents, preoccupied with the need to provide a first-rate foundation for the ambitions of their offspring, that opted for a more exotic alternative and sent them abroad.

This had been the case with the young Xabier. Taken away from his native town, where he had received his first lessons in the local school "confused even with the lowest class of the attendees," the future count had been enrolled in the Jesuit school in Toulouse.[62] The experience must have been transformative for the teenager. Intellectual circles in the French city in the early 1740s were, owing to a poignant campaign to gain royal patronage for the local *Académie des Sciences*, at an all-time high. The ideal of practical knowledge, inspired by the groundbreaking example set by Isaac Newton, was presented in their meetings simultaneously as the most valid way to explain the natural world and as a panacea that promised a solution to all of mankind's troubles. Such a notion the young Xabier must have found exhilarating. Thanks to the intercession of his lecturers, he got to know many of the members of the exclusive and pioneering academy. More telling of his enthusiasm was, perhaps, his decision to inscribe himself in other related endeavors, such as the *Académie* of Bordeaux. And so, when his father passed away in 1746 and he was forced to go back to Azcoitia to take hold of his inheritance, Xabier did so with a declared purpose: to carry these wonderful innovations to his motherland.

An enormous task, at first glance—but one for which the modest town offered at least some promising traits. The newly appointed Count of Peñaflorida might have drunk from one of the main spring-wells of the French Enlightenment, but the reverberations caused by the latter's transformative impact had not failed in sending waves through the provinces even before his arrival. Rural aristocrats, many of them well acquainted with the most exclusive spheres of Bourbon administration, had been in the custom of indulging in evening meetings of—as they called them—"games and munchies."[63] In these informal gatherings they had discussed news and scientific discoveries. "Already in this corner of Azcoitia Nollet and Franklin had his own followers in their respective systems for explaining electrical phenomena; while for many leagues around, in more spacious halls, time was being wasted on useless questions of a barbarous metaphysics, and on ancient, interminable controversies."[64] Peñaflorida's effort, then, had merely consisted of transforming these reunions into "a more elegant academic society," with more structured statutes and in which knowledge of useful topics, ranging from mathematics to geography and from physics to music, could be discussed and spread among attendees in an orderly fashion.[65]

Those in Guipuzcoa most suspicious of what they perceived as foreign innovations did not, as could be anticipated, welcome these meetings. And yet, although they dared to anonymously criticize Peñaflorida and his closest associates in terms reminiscent of Larramendi's incendiary language, their animadversion did little to stop their efforts.[66] After all, the so-called "Triumvirate of Azcoitia"—made up of Peñaflorida and his relatives and friends the Marquis of Narros and Manuel Ignacio de Altuna—were not only the main representatives of a new generation of enlightened reformers: They were also major political players in their own right. Between the late 1740s and the 1760s and even beyond, the three of them would be elected mayors of Azcoitia on five occasions and General Deputies of Guipuzcoa on nineteen. It was an evident demonstration of their central standing in the provincial system, but also of the way in which they understood their own roles.[67]

> They were well persuaded that there existed but the single path to acquiring truths, and that this passed through experience and observation; that abstract knowledge and purely imaginary discussions contributed little to the well-being of nations; that those who observed the most, who asked nature the most questions, were the wisest; and, in a word, that all the science under the heavens was reduced to a store of well-answered questions drawn from nature itself.[68]

Just as much as science, politics depended on experimentation. Changing the world necessitated firsthand familiarity with its functioning.

Xabier's small hometown, however, was hardly enough to satiate the thirst for change blazing inside a man like Peñaflorida. But it was not until 1758, when he was appointed Guipuzcoa's delegate to the court, that he began to entertain a more ambitious and pioneering proposition: a plan for the creation of a society that, going beyond the interest in scientific matters, would export its practically minded approach to the management of the monarchy. An impressive project, of course, and one for which, as ever, Peñaflorida counted on the collaboration and intercession of well-placed *vascongados* among the king's advisers.[69] By 1763, when he finally presented his scheme to the General Assembly of Guipuzcoa, Peñaflorida could be certain of its success. He and the fifteen other members who signed the proposal made up the upper crust of Guipuzcoan society, possessed unbeatable ties with the court, and, when all was said and done, promised to take only an advisory role that did not constrain the General Assembly's powers in the slightest. In all, it was at the same time a state-of-the-art undertaking and one specifically designed to minimize internal frictions. One that would not last long, too. Before a year had gone by, influential figures from the Province of Alava and the Lordship of Biscay, members of lineages related to or well acquainted with Narros or Peñaflorida, began to campaign for the institution's immediate dissolution. In its stead, they suggested the creation of a society that, rather than being limited to Guipuzcoa, would extend its activities to the other two territories as well. Peñaflorida and the rest of the directive board immediately accepted. On December 24, 1764, in the crowded hall of the Intxausti palace of Azcoitia, it was born the *Sociedad Bascongada de Amigos del País*.

It is not hard to realize that the emergence of this "Royal"—after its endorsement by King Charles III of Spain in 1770—"*Vascongado* Society of Friends of the Country" owed much to the transformations of the previous half century. The rise of the provincials in Madrid, the unavoidable need for friendly contacts in the capital, and the decades old experience of the Royal Congregation of Saint Ignace all had done much to give rise to a core of amenable provincials willing to collaborate in the attainment of common goals. Now, for the first time, the birth of the *Sociedad* had imported this understanding of reciprocal relations back to the Western Pyrenees. The motto of the institution, in fact, left little doubt about this fact. *Irurac bat*—a Basque expression translatable either as "the three are one" or "the three at once"—was a definitive expression of the kind of shared *vascongado* collaboration that so good results had yielded in 1727. And yet, in making what had erstwhile been a fact-of-life, tacit relationship an officially sanctioned one, it also lent its weight to the idea of these territories as exceptional constituents within the fabric of the monarchy.

Not that this meant an attempt at unification of any kind. Happy though its founders were with boasting about the "union" and "equality" that existed between the "three provinces," the *Sociedad* was also quick to allocate resources, offices, and duties according to cautions inspired by the strictest *foral* orthodoxy.[70] The whole institution was divided into three different branches—one for each of its comprising territories—and each section only met with the rest once a year in an assembly held, alternatively, in the

Guipuzcoan town of Vergara, in Bilbao, or in Vitoria.[71] All of these were measures that evidenced a rigorous protectionism that appeared to stand in stark contradiction to the collaborative spirit implied by the organization's slogan. They, nonetheless, betrayed the debts Peñaflorida and the rest of the reformers had incurred with the provincial system. It might have been a common goal of all Friends to see "ignorance . . . succeeded by knowledge, indolence by diligence, inaction by industry, discomfort by ease, misery and poverty by opulence and wealth" and to raise "upon the remnants of the unhappiness of our beloved Homeland, . . . a throne of Public Happiness."[72] But, in the final reckoning, the reality of what could and could not be achieved, as ever, was still marked by rules and sensibilities that rarely went beyond the limits of the province. While it was possible, from time to time, to bask in the advantages of a special *vascongado* connection, the success of the *Sociedad* ultimately depended on the willingness of local administrations to apply its proposed policies. So, when in 1771 the *Sociedad* suggested alleviating the agricultural deficit of the region by favoring the relocation of Guipuzcoan peasants to Alava, the General Assembly of the latter territory rejected the plan on grounds that such a migration of freemen would undermine the local preeminence of Alavese noblemen.[73] Likewise, any talk of tariff reform was understandably out of discussion. The "three" might be content for the time being to act as one, but they were no less the wardens of their own distinctiveness for that.

These occasional clashes with provincial particularities did not rarify for long the relationship between the provinces and the *Sociedad*, nor did they detract from its activities. As Charles III himself referred in congratulatory terms, its members

> undertook agricultural experiments on lands they leased for this purpose; they encouraged certain manufactures, supporting them with their resources and knowledge; they acquired machines, instruments, and books; they established annual prizes to serve as incentives for diligence; they devoted themselves to teaching their Students Mathematics, History, Languages, Military Art, and the principles of Drawing, and they wrote various Dissertations, Memoirs, and Reports.[74]

It was, at any rate, a vast exertion in the name of progress. And one that—as demonstrated by the passage above—was widely admired outside the Western Pyrenees. A leading member of government would pen a text in 1774 encouraging local oligarchs all around the empire to follow Peñaflorida's virtuous example. His call would be answered with enthusiasm. Between 1775 and 1808, in places like Madrid, Seville, Asturias, or Murcia, almost a hundred institutions were created which treaded, with little in the way of innovation, the path marked by the *Bascongada*.[75]

And yet, none of these sister organizations could compare, in the dazzling quality of its charisma, to the *Sociedad*. Membership in it, ever since its conception, had been limited to *vascongado* groups and their descendants, but Peñaflorida—with the infallible eye of a born entrepreneur—had soon extended this clause to include anyone who inherited, even by means of marriage, a *mayorazgo* in any of the three provinces.[76] A decision that, considering that much of the higher nobility of Castile descended from or were relatives with Western Pyrenean families, rapidly made the most blue-blooded figures in the realm flock to this modern and fashionable institution. Even the Duke of Alba, whose wealth and illustrious ancestry dwarfed the pedigree of all the founders of the *Sociedad* combined, applied for membership all the same on behalf of his descent from the line of Mendoza.[77] Everyone, both in the peninsula and in America, wanted the right to boast about their implication and support of this most important institution of Enlightened, state-sponsored reformism. In consequence, membership figures shot up. Offshoots of the *Sociedad* were established in Mexico and Habana in 1773, in Manila in 1780, and in Lima in 1783. The success of these implantations—which, in the case of the Mexican one alone, included more than 500 members—was no doubt helped by the traditional associationism of *vascongado* communities in the territories beyond the sea.[78] Such precedents, in combination with the glamour granted by royal support, meant that by the early 1780s there existed, dispersed throughout the vast territories of the Spanish empire, almost 2,000 Friends of the Country—and of these only about one in five lived in the Western Pyrenees.[79]

Great news, of course, because new members meant new subscriptions, and the plethora of projects carried out by the *Sociedad* could not function without a steady influx of coin. Neither the *foral* institutions nor the monarchy itself had contributed much to these, and thus, the improvements planned by its director tended all too often to meet with the harsh realities of insufficient funds. "The Patriotic Societies"—a member of the Society of Madrid explained bluntly in an indictment that could have very well applied to the *Bascongada*—"have various defects that will prevent or delay the advantages that the state expects from them. They need money."[80]

Luckily for the *Bascongada*, though, its enviable entrenchment in America and the collaboration of creole elites, eager to imitate metropolitan fashions, had allowed it to weather such a crippling circumstance better than most. Thanks to these overseas contributions, the most magnificent of all the projects of the *Sociedad* would see the light of day in 1769: the creation in the Guipuzcoan town of Vergara of a Seminar for the instruction of noblemen. The institution, whose declared goal was "to shape, refine, and strengthen the youth, and to strip them of rusticity and roughness," would be responsible for the education of hundreds of students over the course of its thirty-year-long existence.[81] Here, pupils were presented with a teaching program that embodied the scientific and courtesan ideals of its founders: mathematics were balanced with the study of humanities; that of religion with experiments in physical sciences; knowledge of history was paired with dancing and fencing lessons.[82] A well-rounded education that promised, in its elitism and refinement, to become the ultimate stepping stone for anyone—*vascongado* or otherwise—aspiring to be somebody.

An allure further compounded by its achievements. It was in the Seminar that Wolframium was first discovered, that new methods were developed to make the exploitation of iron and coal more efficient, and that pioneering techniques of navigation were taught to future navy officers.[83] These all in addition to the already impressive advancements the *Bascongada* had sponsored and which included, among other things, extensive vaccination campaigns, the printing of more than sixty books on scientific topics between 1768 and 1794, and the diffusion of new seeds and fertilizers brought from Britain, France, or Holland to improve the yields obtained by neighboring peasants.[84] Even the polemic—and otherwise banned—*Encyclopédie* of Diderot and D'Alembert was made accessible to its members by special inquisitorial license, on condition, of course, that they would not read "any chapter relating to Religion."[85]

The clause was strictly adhered to. And this, better than anything, demonstrated the extent to which the *Sociedad*, for all its efforts to modernize the monarchy, remained in its moral and social standing a fairly conservative organization. The conclusion should not come as a surprise. A project led by the most important lineages of the land, wealthy and admired by their peers, could hardly have laid the foundation for revolutionary thinking. The exceptional legal and political conditions of the provinces, from which many of the problems the *Sociedad* aimed to tackle ultimately stemmed, were beyond critical questioning. The diglossia which deprived commoners of even the humblest education; the *millares* that prevented their voices from being ever heard in the institutions; the *mayorazgos* that put much of the territory's harvest in the hands of a class of magnates always ready to speculate in times of need: None of these were the objects of the reformist spirit of the *Bascongada*. In fact, its leaders, who never pulled punches when it came to mauling the stubbornness of their superstitious opponents, felt no scruple in quenching these sensitive debates in their cradle. So happened, for instance, when a radical Friend was immediately censored for daring to criticize the speculative custom of assigning "an exorbitant value to grain and refus[ing] to sell it, waiting for the price of a *fanega* to rise by two or three *reales*."[86] Similarly, an attempt by merchants from San Sebastian to create their own society to push for the liberalization of trade with America was thwarted due to the obstruction of the *Bascongada*'s benefactors in Madrid.[87] Over time, and owing precisely to the heterogeneous composition of the *Sociedad*, the ideological distance between these conservative and radical positions was bound to grow larger and larger. And yet, by 1785, when the Count of Peñaflorida—"the most zealous citizen, the most indulgent man, . . . the best Friend"—passed away, the prestige and power of the institution was still capable of containing these frictions.[88]

Not everyone, looking back upon the count's impressive career and upon the Seminar he had founded in Vergara, could resist the temptation of remembering Larramendi's indictment. What was this Seminar, with its sophisticated laboratories and celebrated teachers, if not the most perfected way of isolating the provincial elites from the rest of the people? It constituted a parallel reality; a world where—despite the *Bascongada's* motto—no *Euskera* was spoken and access to which, thanks to its steep fees, was barred to everyone but the wealthiest.[89] Some individuals, pondering these arguments, might retort that members of the *Sociedad* were at least respectful of the provincial order. But it was equally true that this respect amounted less to the sacred commandments Larramendi had described than to a set of rules and privileges that allowed them to direct the provinces' destinies and to thrive outside of them. The Seminar was the perfect embodiment of such a conception. Rooted in the heart of Guipuzcoa though it was, and sponsored by its most prominent children, the knowledge taught in its classrooms was not Western Pyrenean by any stretch of the imagination. Instead, it owed everything to the etiquette of a distant court and to a horizon of success whose ultimate measure was, as ever, a worldwide empire.

Just as much like their fathers and grandparents in the turbulent times of Philip V, the leading members of the *Bascongada* still staked their future in the favor of the king. The success of the Royal Congregation of Saint Ignace and the Guipuzcoan Company of Caracas, first, and that of the Seminar and the *Sociedad*, later, all were interpreted as vindications of the judiciousness of their wager. They, too, came to regard themselves as members of an exclusive caste. But they knew better than to impute this preeminence merely to the benignity of some ancient *fuero*. Theirs was instead an interprovincial superiority, grounded on analogous career paths, blood ties, and patterns of socialization, and which had, for the most part, emerged outside of the Western Pyrenees. However, it was hard not to divine the presence, behind these notions, of older assumptions inherited from provincial discourses. *Vascongado* reformers would take for granted that they were entitled to lead the rest of Spain out to the Lights. And yet, when it came to their modest territories, they demonstrated a firm determination to prevent anyone else from ever meddling in their affairs.

The Marquis of Narros, Peñaflorida's chief collaborator, offered in 1786 an emotional public obituary of the late count. In it, apart from praising his curiosity and fondness and highlighting his "extreme obesity," he described what he saw as the most important guiding light of Peñaflorida's career.[90] "He was born to gather, combine, and direct knowledge for the greatest happiness of his fellows."[91] The *Sociedad*, its Friends dispersed all over the globe, bore testimony to his success. But such a task, in simultaneously bringing to the surface the massive scale of the *vascongados*' reach and preeminence, had likewise sown the seeds of a perilous future. Within the ranks of the *Sociedad* clerics could be found alongside royal reformers, Western Pyreneans alongside Castilians, merchants alongside *mayorazgos*. For a time—and under favorable conditions—all of these elements had relished in the sheer allure of the institution. But topics such as the unresolved issue of the American trade, the commercial tariffs decreed by the provincial system, or the increasing conceptual equalization between the three provinces all threatened to tilt this precious balance for good. And there was, of course, the fact that the influence of such a kind, regardless of the Enlightened intentions behind it, was always bound to produce a sense of envy and unfairness among the rest of the sovereign's subjects.

These were not, as of yet, hopeless strains. But they showed that, below the surface, the calm waters that had once allowed a class of petty northern freemen to reach the highest spheres of power in the monarchy might be less secure than they might have wished for.

Notes

1 Guerrero, *Las elites vascas y navarras en el gobierno de la monarquía borbónica. Redes sociales, carreras y hegemonía en el siglo XVIII (1700–1746)*, 296.

2 Laborda, *El Señorío de Vizcaya. Nobles y fueros (c.1452–1727)*, 329–30.

3 Guerrero, *Las elites vascas y navarras*, 85–6.

4 Bermejo, "La caída de una clase política—Los reformistas vascos en la crisis del Antiguo Régimen," 54. Also, Guerrero, *Las elites vascas y navarras*, 295.

5 Guerrero, *Las elites vascas y navarras*, 73. Also, Dedieu, "La Nueva Planta en su contexto. Las reformas del aparato del Estado en el reinado de Felipe V," 128.

6 Guerrero, "Familias en la encrucijada. Redes sociales, lealtades y resistencias durante la Guerra de Sucesión (País Vasco y Navarra, 1680–1715)," 124–5.

7 "Letter from José de Aguirre y Acharán to his brother Pedro" (1728). Quoted in Guerrero, *Las elites vascas y navarras*, 328.

8 Guerrero, 328.

9 Angulo, "Una década peligrosa (1717–1727). Los provincianos en Madrid y la negociación del traslado aduanero," 129–30.

10 Guerrero, *Las elites vascas y navarras*, 287–8.

11 Imízcoz, "La clase política del reformismo borbónico: las redes sociales del cambio," 19–20.

12 Quoted in Dedieu "La Nueva Planta en su contexto," 137.

13 Dedieu "La Nueva Planta en su contexto," 118.

14 Garriga, "Orden jurídico y poder político en el Antiguo Régimen," 17–18.

15 Delgado, "Construir el Estado, destruir la nación. Las reformas fiscales de los primeros borbones. El colapso del sistema de equilibrios en el imperio español (1714–1796)," 68–9.

16 Dedieu, "La Nueva Planta en su contexto," 130–1.

17 Delgado, "Construir el Estado, destruir la nación," 71.

18 Porres, "Las contribuciones vascas a la hacienda real en la Edad Moderna: algunos contrastes provinciales," 90–1.

19 Porres, 98–9.

20 Quoted in Mañaricua, *Vizcaya, siglos VIII al XI: los orígenes del Señorío*, 203.

21 Goyeneche, *Bayonne et la région Bayonnaise du XIIe au XVe siècle*, 149. Also, García, *Gobernar la ciudad en la Edad Media*, 122. Also, Tena, *La sociedad urbana en la Guipúzcoa costera medieval*, 154. Also, Laborda, *El Señorío de Vizcaya. Nobles y fueros (c.1452–1727)*, 191–2.

22 Quoted in Lamikiz, "La matxinada de 1718 y su trasfondo socioeconómico," 116–17.

23 Laborda, *El Señorío de Vizcaya. Nobles y fueros (c.1452–1727)*, 316–17.

24 Laborda, 431.

25 Quoted in Laborda, *El Señorío de Vizcaya. Nobles y fueros (c.1452–1727)*, 476.

26 Laborda, 492.

27 Laborda, 531.

28 Alcibar, Francisco. "Prudente conducta y proceder con que se manejo D. Francisco Ignacio de Alcibar Jaúregui en las revoluciones que hubo en la villa de Azpeitia en el mes de noviembre de 1718" (1718), fol. 14.

29 Alberdi, "Reforma de la administración de los recursos navales de Guipuzcoa a principios del siglo XVIII. La búsqueda de un nuevo equilibrio entre la política naval y económica de

la Monarquía y las actividades de los principales hombres de negocios de la provincia," 192. Also, Garate, *La Real Compañía Guipuzcoana de Caracas*, 12–14.

30 Angulo, "Una década peligrosa," 142.

31 Angulo, 150. Also, Laborda, *El Señorío de Vizcaya. Nobles y fueros (c.1452–1727)*, 523.

32 Bermejo, "La caída de una clase política," 73–4. Also, Guerrero, *Las elites vascas y navarras*, 386.

33 Martínez, *Casa, Provincia, Rey*, 287–8.

34 Larramendi, *Corografía o descripción general de la muy noble y muy leal Provincia de Guipúzcoa*, 172.

35 *El Duende Crítico de Madrid. Obra histórico política del siglo pasado*, 18.

36 Quoted in Bermejo, "La caída de una clase política," 76.

37 Angulo, "Una década peligrosa," 137.

38 Zabaltza, *Mater Vasconia. Lenguas, fueros y discursos nacionales en los países vascos*, 27.

39 Imízcoz, "Las élites vasco-navarras y la monarquía hispánica: construcciones sociales, políticas y culturales en la edad moderna," 111.

40 Larramendi, *Corografía*, 5.

41 Martínez, *Casa, Provincia, Rey*, 256–7.

42 Larramendi, *Sobre los fueros de Guipuzcoa. Conferencias curiosas, políticas, legales y morales sobre los fueros de la M.N. y M.L. Provincia de Guipuzcoa*, 342.

43 Larramendi, *Corografía*, 154–5.

44 Larramendi, *Sobre los fueros de Guipuzcoa*, 131–2.

45 Larramendi, 136.

46 Larramendi, 19.

47 Larramendi, II.

48 Reguera, "El mundo del ocio," 235–6.

49 Larramendi, *Corografía*, 15.

50 Larramendi, *Sobre los fueros de Guipuzcoa*, 296.

51 Larramendi, 30.

52 Larramendi, *Corografía*, 183–6.

53 Larramendi, *Sobre los fueros de Guipuzcoa*, 282.

54 Larramendi, *Corografía*, 142. Also, Azurmendi, *Y se limpie aquella tierra*, 258. Also, Guerrero, *Las elites vascas y navarras*, 331.

55 Imízcoz, "La clase política del reformismo borbónico," 270–1.

56 Bermejo, "La caída de una clase política," 20–1.

57 Pedro Agustín Girón. Quoted in Bermejo, "La caída de una clase política," 134. Also, Urgell, "Primer Vasco Moderno," 600, 613–14.

58 Bermejo, "La caída de una clase política," 93–4.

59 Ayerbe, "'Defensa de las regalías y beneficio de la causa pública,' de Don Joseph de Zabala y Miranda (Vizcaya, 1746)," 233–7.

60 Imízcoz, "La clase política del reformismo borbónico," 299.

61 Bermejo, "La caída de una clase política," 55.

62 Silvan, *La vida y obra del Conde de Peñaflorida, fundador de la Real Sociedad Bascongada de Amigos del País*, 11.

63 Eguía, "Elogio de Don Xavier Maria de Munive Idiáquez, Conde de Peñaflorida," 39. Also, Imízcoz, "La clase política del reformismo borbónico," 288.

64 Eguía, "Elogio," 40.

65 Astigarraga, *Los ilustrados vascos. Ideas, instituciones y reformas económicas en España*, 30–1. Also, Eguía, "Elogio," 39.

66 Iñarra, "La razón de la sinrazón. Actitudes hacia las ideas ilustradas en las provincias vascas (1748–1839)," 42.

67 Bermejo, "La caída de una clase política," 103.

68 Eguía, "Elogio," 54.

69 Bermejo, "La caída de una clase política," 106.

70 *Estatutos aprobados S.M. para gobierno de la Real Sociedad Bascongada de los Amigos del País (1774–1765)*, 7–8, 165.

71 Arias de Saavedra, "Educación y economía. Las Sociedades Económicas de Amigos del País en el reformismo de la Ilustración," 26.

72 Munibe, "Discurso preliminar. Leído en la primera Junta General Preparatoria de la Sociedad, celebrada en Vergara el día 7 de febrero de 1765," 18.

73 Astigarraga, *Los ilustrados vascos*, 92–3.

74 *Estatutos aprobados S.M. para gobierno de la Real Sociedad Bascongada de los Amigos del País (1774–1765)*, 2–3.

75 Arias de Saavedra, "Educación y economía," 19.

76 "Letter from Xavier María de Munibe to Pedro Jacinto de Álava," October 23, 1771. In Tellechea, *La ilustración vasca. Cartas de Xavier María de Munibe, conde de Peñaflorida, a Pedro Jacinto de Álava*, 141–2.

77 Bermejo, "La caída de una clase política," 148.

78 Astigarraga, *Los ilustrados vascos*, 67.

79 Arias de Saavedra, "Educación y economía," 17. Also, Imízcoz, "Las élites vasco-navarras y la monarquía hispánica," 112.

80 Francisco Cabarrús (1786). Quoted in Arias de Saavedra, "Educación y economía," 37.

81 Arias de Saavedra, "Educación y economía," 18. Also, Imízcoz, "La clase política del reformismo borbónico," 278.

82 Martínez, *Casa, Provincia, Rey*, 224–5. Also, Angulo and Reguera, "Los valores de la sociedad vasca en la Edad Moderna," 130–1.

83 Angulo and Reguera, "Los valores de la sociedad vasca en la Edad Moderna," 130–1.

84 Astigarraga, *Los ilustrados vascos*, 62. Also, Iñarra, "Las luces en penumbra: Proyectos ilustrados y conflicto comunitario en las provincias vascas (1748–1833)," 284. Also, Arias de Saavedra, "Educación y economía," 32.

85 "Letter from Xabier García de Munibe to Pedro Jacinto de Álava," February 5, 1772. In Tellechea, *La ilustración vasca*, 160.

86 Valentín de Foronda (1778). Quoted in Otazu, *La burguesía revolucionaria vasca a fines del siglo XVIII*, 83–4.

87 Martínez, *Casa, Provincia, Rey*, 218–19.

88 Eguía, "Elogio," 66.

89 Martínez, *Casa, Provincia, Rey*, 223–4.

90 Eguía, "Elogio," 60.

91 Eguía, 37.

CHAPTER 19
THE TEARS OF THE *VASCONGADOS*

The Western Pyrenean territories under French dominion were never, in political terms at any rate, an amazing sight to behold. Unlike their southern counterparts, who had cultivated for themselves an exclusive identity reluctantly accepted by foreigners, nothing marked the peoples from Labourd, *Ultrapuertos*, or Soule as exceptional in any way within the fabric of France's monarchy. Their institutions, in stark contrast to those of the provinces, had never managed to gain a comparable monopoly over their own affairs. For this reason, they had usually cast jealous looks at the preferential treatment their neighbors received from the Spanish administration. On more than one occasion these northerners had attempted to weaponize the idea of *Euskal Herria* to pursue privileges that could match those of Guipuzcoa, Biscay, or Alava. For example, an *Essai sur la noblesse des Basques*, penned in 1761 and published in 1785, described, echoing notions that were familiar south of the Pyrenees, the men and women from these three districts as "nobles by origin, and prior to all feudal laws; [and] consequently, . . . exempt from all the rights of feudalism to which one might wish to subject them."[1]

For the most part these arguments fell on deaf ears. Royal absolutism, which was making inroads in France as it had in Bourbon Spain, shared with the latter a disdainful opinion of the meager legal and juridical particularities of these peripheral communities and increasingly sought to sideline the obstacles these raised to the king's executive authority. The approach would prove particularly effective in Soule and *Ultrapuertos*. The Labourdines, though, managed—despite the mounting fiscal and political pressure—to arm a legal resistance to make sure that "new regulations would be published in vain if they ran counter to the manners of the Basques and the traditions of their forefathers."[2]

But now, as the summer of 1789 approached, the political climate was shifting. The French treasury was in shambles and Louis XVI, in a last-ditch attempt to prevent the system's collapse, had agreed to summon the Estates General. Even in far-off Labourd the feeling of momentousness was hard to shake off:

> News has arrived of the death of the state
> But after singling out the source of the malady
> It should suffice, to heal it
> to cut off some limbs to preserve the rest.[3]

The surgical approach would, eventually, lead European society to enormous transformations and many French citizens to the chopping block. More immediately, though, it would result in an amazing reconfiguration of France's political landscape. On

August 4, 1789, the delegates gathered in the Estates General, as part of an overarching renunciation of all feudal laws, declared "that all the particular privileges of the provinces, principalities, *pays*, cantons, cities and communities of inhabitants, whether financial or of any other kind, [would be] abolished without return and shall be merged into the common right of all French people."[4] Back home, as it could not be otherwise, local institutions were dumbfounded. Labourdine authorities complained that their current constitution was "the only one under which they could exist."[5] Delegates from *Ultrapuertos*, on the other hand, sheltering themselves behind the territory's status as a kingdom—and therefore not as one of France's provinces—rejected the jurisdiction of the Estates General altogether.[6] It was all in vain. By late September, royal officials had already dissolved these supposedly "feudal" gatherings.

These were only appetizers of what was to come. Accepting begrudgingly that they could no longer operate as particular bodies within the monarchy, and confronting rumors coming from Paris that spoke of the impending creation of new territorial demarcations, members of the local elite began to campaign for the creation of an all-Basque *département*. "Navarre, being incorporated into France, can only be joined with the province of Soule and the land of Labourd, whether for provincial organization or for the administration of justice"—wrote the authorities of *Ultrapuertos* in the winter of 1789.[7] Their Labourdine and Soulentine neighbors, too, endorsed the compromise. Theirs was a sensible project, after all, grounded on the many ties—linguistic, cultural, social, economic—shared by the three neighboring regions. And yet, it was also possible to find in their grievances an effort to emulate what the southern *vascongados*, barricaded behind their particular institutions, had learned to take for granted. That the allegation held some truth was betrayed by the complaints aired by the French and Gascon-speaking oligarchs of Bayonne.

> Isolated by their character, by their customs, and essentially by their language from Frenchmen, who are like strangers in their midst, the Basques would only double this wall of separation if they were left to themselves. Now that the National Assembly has the essential goal of destroying the solidarity of provinces, how can it tolerate and even foment the particularism of the Basques?[8]

A damning accusation that echoed the anxieties of many Spaniards alarmed by the *vascongados*' meteoric rise.

However, the particularism discussed by revolutionaries in Paris that winter was very different from the one that Larramendi had so vehemently defended. Its supporters might refer in passing to the "excellent character and the patriarchal customs" of the Basques, but the crux of their argument was, just as much as in the times of Echepare and Leizarraga, related to language. "The union that is being proposed to you"—explained a Labourdine delegate balking at a plan to join the three territories with Bearne—"is physically almost impossible. Bring together men, some of whom speak one language and others another: what do you expect them to say to each other?"[9] The recourse to *Euskera* as a marker of difference was, at any rate, predictable. To peoples toying perilously with the loss of even the paltriest of political autonomies, recourse to a united *Euskal Herria* still offered a comforting reassurance. But on this occasion, as in centuries past, their plans did not bear fruit. On March 4, 1790, the *Département des Basses-Pyrénées*—which merged the three districts of Labourd, *Ultrapuertos*, and Soule with Bearne—was created. Any remnant of Basque exceptionalism in France was entombed in its womb.

That a destiny so pitiful as that of their northern kin could befall the Spanish *vascongados* seemed, in the eve of the revolution, almost an impossible concept to entertain. But the events unfolding from 1789 onward, in addition to stark political transformations in France, also bred war in the Western Pyrenees. After Louis XVI's execution in 1793, conflict had rapidly erupted between the Spanish Bourbons and the new Republic, and as more and more levies were desperately mobilized by French generals, the weight of manpower had begun to take its toll. The frontier bastion of Fuenterrabia fell in July 1794. Shortly after, and under threat of a hopeless siege, San Sebastian too surrendered to the invader. The sudden disintegration of the northern front paved the way for total anarchy. Levied soldiers, radicalized by counterrevolutionary priests fleeing from France, threatened mutiny against their commanders for not facing the foe head-on. The General Assembly of Guipuzcoa was taken hostage by the enemy and drafted a humiliating agreement. By its terms, the province, making explicit use of its original independence, would abandon the Spanish and join the French Republic. Immediately, a second Deputation, formed in a rush by many members of the *Bascongada*, rejected the treaty and pledged to continue a doomed resistance against the invader.[10] The French advance, however, could not be stopped. By 1795, when the Spanish government managed to snatch an ignominious peace agreement from the jaws of defeat, any semblance of order in the frontier had entirely collapsed.

Unsurprisingly, the search for culprits started as soon as the buzz of muskets died out. Reports accounting for the less-than-exemplary behavior of the *vascongados* over the course of the conflict flooded the desk of Manuel Godoy, the sovereign's new favorite. Commanders of the royal army complained about the pettiness with which provincial authorities had conducted themselves during the campaign, preventing their soldiers from advancing beyond their territories' boundaries and thus hindering the operations.[11] *Foral* authorities retorted with a time-honored argument: that they had carried out the service they owed the monarchy "in accordance with [their] natural exemptions and the invariable custom in which [they have] always remained."[12]

But their position, this time at least, seemed a difficult one to cling to. It was clear to most onlookers that provincials, so full of themselves when it came to their role as the shield that guarded Spain, had failed miserably in their duty. In the advisory boards that surrounded the king's favorite, voices began to suggest nothing short of the overhaul of the provincial system in its entirety.

> If to this peace were to follow the union of the provinces and the rest of Navarre, without the *foral* hinderances that distinguish them and make them almost a dead limb of the Kingdom, Your Excellency would have accomplished one of those

> works we have not seen since Cardinal Cisneros or the great Philip V. These are the times that must be seized to increase the resources and strength of the Monarchy.[13]

As in 1722, a promised increase in revenue made such ruminations even more enticing. Godoy, the sharpest and the least compromising of all the tools ever to be employed by Bourbon reformism, needed little more to act.

The favorite's plan was as simple in theory as it was challenging to put into practice. For more than two centuries, delegates from the provinces had checked the king's authority thanks to two intertwined mechanisms. The first one was the rulings and laws that framed the monarch's power in the Western Pyrenees as resulting from a pact between sovereign and community. These rules, in turn, were imagined to be the primordial liberties passed down the generations from the times of Tubal. The second element was the firm grip with which local oligarchies held the reins of the political institutions of the land. Thanks to their ascendancy in the General Assemblies and in towns and villages, aristocrats like Peñaflorida had managed to create a whole net of contacts and clients that could, simultaneously, limit royal meddling and tame the most violent outbursts of peasant discontent. The resulting system had proven itself, ever since the defeat of the Parientes, a particularly stable one. But what—Godoy must have thought—if that was no longer the case?

For decades, scholars had been casting doubts upon the historical accuracy of the stories Biscaynes, Guipuzcoans, Alavese, and Navarrese had grown used to telling about themselves. Reputable men of letters across the empire, for instance, had questioned the notion that these Western Pyreneans could be the heirs of the Cantabrians.[14] Occasionally, some of these voices had come from within the region itself. In 1638 Arnauld Oihenart, the Soulentine author of a history of all the communities of *Euskal Herria*, had already picked up these scholarly threads to rebuke what he characterized as little more than "pure dreams from those wide awake."[15] For the most part, the exacting standards and refined arguments presented by these historians had tended to weigh far less than the brute facts of official endorsement. Neither the provinces nor the monarchy, after all, were to gain much from alienating one another over a bookish dispute. And so, when in 1768 Enrique Flórez, a rigorous Augustine monk and compiler, had published a direct attack against the Cantabrian origin of the *vascongados*, the response of the General Assembly of Biscay had been simply to push for stern censorship against these "indecorous expressions contrary to the prerogatives, exemptions, and antiquity of this illustrious land."[16] The *Bascongada* too, casting aside its so-publicized devotion to intellectual inquiry, rejected the work and offered a response that amounted to little more than a regurgitation of the old tales.[17] The affair, it seemed, had been put to rest.

Godoy, however, had not lost track of the touchiness with which Western Pyrenean aristocrats and intellectuals had met Flórez's work. The minister had realized that the monk, in claiming that the existence of *Euskera* "does not exclude the subjection of the land to the Romans," had also implied much more: that the Tubalian liberty—if it existed to begin with—had been lost; that the provinces were not the remnants of an idyllic past; that the idea of a pact between them and the king was nothing but a farse.[18] Like an arrowhead flying directly to the heart of the provincial ideology, the debunking of these myths posed a threat to all that generations of Biscayne, Guipuzcoan, and Alavese oligarchs had taken for granted—their entitlement to privilege.

The realization was precisely why Manuel Godoy now made sure to take over the helm of the attack. Soon enough, books appeared that echoed Flórez's verdicts—among them a historical dictionary of Spain which, coincidentally, only focused on the Western Pyrenees.[19] In the pages of these state-sponsored publications, every brick of the account of the Western Pyreneans as heirs to Tubal was targeted, dismantled, and torn down with unrelenting efficiency. The pact between the king and the provinces was cast as a "political dream"; the ancient religiosity and excellence inherited by every *vascongado* and manifest in the survival of *Euskera* met with incredulity. "In *Euskera* there is no trace of religious tradition"—critics noted—"neither true nor false . . . whatever of religion it contains is posterior to Christianity and was taken from the Latin language during the barbarian centuries."[20] One by one, the onslaught cut down the ropes that sustained the whole edifice of the exceptionality of the *vascongados.*

An attack spearheaded with ink but followed up with actions. Godoy, who controlled the strings of courtly favor in Madrid, had made sure to deprive the provinces of one of their most valuable assets: their ready access to the monarch. Cut off from this source of patronage, the kind of virtuous apprenticeship that had marked the lives of so many Western Pyrenean youngsters ever since the coming of Philip V disappeared overnight. Now, all that remained for this class of trained courtesans was to go back to the comfort of the homeland and resign themselves to managing their properties. But here, too, the wave of disrepute provoked by the defeat in the war against France had rendered their future far less secure than before.[21] Debt and despoilation had forced many commoners to take up arms and become bandits; daughters of impoverished families had been reduced to becoming women of ill-repute; the homeless roamed the streets.[22] New taxes, levied to assist the war effort, burdened the peasantry. In the Guipuzcoan valley of Oyarzun, close to the border, people would lament that, "at that time, everything was lacking . . . : bread, wine, oil, soap, and other necessary items for sustenance were nowhere to be found, nor was there hope of obtaining them, except by bringing them in from Navarre at great risk and at very high prices."[23]

In hindsight, the situation recalled the worst moments of the custom house affair. And now, as in 1718, the hostility against the mightiest *mayorazgos* did not take long to surface. There was, however, a crucial difference. If on that occasion violence had proven a somewhat anarchic eruption, in the first years of the nineteenth century, on the contrary, there were men ready to weaponize the people's discontent to serve their own ends. Not everyone, after all, had profited equally from the triumphant star of their compatriots. Many were the delegates from small towns and villages who, although locally prominent, had been excluded time and again from the prestigious circuits set in place by Peñaflorida and his peers. This had nurtured an aversion toward the lifestyles of these titled noblemen, and now, sensing their rivals' strengths falter, some were not willing to let pass the opportunity to avenge their grudges. Pandering to the dissatisfied multitudes, they denounced the foundations of the oligarchs' power: the unattended properties and estates they possessed in *mayorazgo*; their arrogance and haughtiness, as demonstrated by their desire "to distinguish their households and families from the rest"; their propensity to go off to Madrid, there to "squander their incomes amid luxury, vice, and the corruption of morals."[24]

All of which made for quite a Larramendian denunciation, but one whose goal, rather than educating the families that ruled the provinces, was instead to supplant them. Coincidentally, Godoy shared that same objective. And thus, when on top of a wave of populism, the faction of those dissatisfied with the *mayorazgos* rose to power in Biscay, the king's favorite made sure to stand by their side. Officials loyal to the minister were appointed to oversee customs revenues. A project was approved for the construction of a massive port—nicknamed the "Harbor of Peace"—that would overshadow that of Bilbao. Plans that, had they been carried out, would have certainly compromised the smuggling and trading operations upon which the notables of the Lordship depended for their prosperity.

And yet, if Godoy's efforts to stamp out the privileges of the provinces were indeed stupendous, so too could they—on occasion—miss their target and provoke outrage. When rumors of an agreement to extend the terms of military service spread in the summer of 1804, the vengeful roar of the masses, which had until then rallied behind the new government of Biscay, suddenly turned against it. Once again, the streets of Bilbao flooded with violent peasants and artisans calling for the derogation of the measure and the heads of its promoters. A new Deputation was summoned on the spot to placate the riots, but to no avail, and by mid-September, a royal army of 80,000 arrived in Biscay. Plans for the Harbor of Peace were put off indefinitely. Normality, though, was not restored. The political life of the Lordship would be shadowed, in the following years, by military occupation.[25]

The episode of 1804, in hindsight, would prove premonitory. For one, it uncovered the depth of a cleavage that prosperity and the political hegemony of the *mayorazgos* had previously concealed. Commoners, impoverished by recent calamity and exacerbated in their hatred of revolutionary ideas by preachers and monks, no longer looked up to the values the *Bascongada* represented with benignity. Nor did, in fact, others in more relevant offices. The inquisitorial permit that had once allowed Peñaflorida's colleagues to access the *Encyclopédie* was withdrawn in 1793 and only recovered with difficulty. In 1804, the Seminar of Vergara itself was expropriated—although by that time it had already become a shadow of its former self.[26] In such testing times, locals found comfort in their own sense of superiority. "This hostility from outsiders is not strange, for they always look at us out of the corner of their eye, since they cannot bear our privileges and exemptions, which they themselves lack."[27] And yet, as current events in Biscay had shown, this was no longer a rivalry confined to the courtesan circles of Madrid. The disruption of communal life brought by the war had upturned the internal balance that had once hoisted the rise of the *mayorazgo* class—and there was no shortage of those willing to take advantage. Bereft of royal favor and giving up any dreams of becoming an imperial elite, the grandchildren of Peñaflorida's generation were forced to resign themselves to a more pressing—albeit less glamorous—endeavor. Making sure that their control of the Western Pyrenees, that last redoubt of their inheritance, would not, too, slip from their hands.

Luckily for them, the early nineteenth century would witness the collapse both of Bourbon administration and of their attempts at meddling in *foral* affairs. As the pyres lit by revolution in France came, in time, to consume Spain, and as the survival of the monarchy stood at stake between 1808 and 1814, few had time to continue the onslaught let loose by Godoy upon the provinces. Not that the advent of an age of unprecedented convulsion had erased the underlying anxieties. Despite their many differences, both royal reformers and liberals inspired by the language of liberty agreed on their instinctive revulsion toward privilege. Be it in the name of the king's sovereignty, or in the more fashionable language of the nation, the concept of exemption ran anathema to their plans to transform public life.

No surprise, then, that when a liberal Constitution was proclaimed in Cadiz in 1812, it would declare a paramount duty of all the king's subjects "to contribute, without any distinction, according to [their] ability, to the charges of the state."[28] A deathblow to the immunities enjoyed by nobles and churchmen, of course, but one which also put in jeopardy the very concessions that stood at the core of the *vascongado*'s sense of self-importance. For the time being, King Ferdinand VII would swear the various ordinances and laws that made up the *fueros* of Biscay, Guipuzcoa, and Alava in 1814, and he would prove a staunch opponent to the constitutional text.[29] But these could hardly pass for anything more than momentary respites amid an unresolved struggle. A sense of dread settled in among the Western Pyrenean oligarchy, as "never, as in the present time, has our unity been more necessary in order not to make it easier for our enemies to achieve the triumph they seek by attacking us individually."[30]

Regardless of whether they came from absolutist ministers or their liberal opponents, many in the Western Pyrenees thought it advisable to put the idea of the abolition of the provincial institutions definitely to rest. Some, following the most revered orthodoxy, opted for parading the old stories of Cantabrians, patriarchs, and medieval battles despite the blows dealt by Flórez and his many adherents. Others, updating these accounts to the vocabulary of the Enlightenment, saw in them the result of a social contract which, in their eyes, promoted public happiness.[31] And yet there were a few who, rather than accept the terms in which their opponents framed the debate, rejected these altogether. The entitlement of Western Pyrenean peoples to their laws, they wrote, did not depend on some doubtful documents or parchments; rather, it was plain for everyone to see. Not only was it possible to demonstrate empirically that *Euskera* had been the first—and therefore the most perfect—language of the peninsula, but it followed from such a conclusion that its speakers were as free from taint or corruption as the speech they used.[32] What did it matter, then, what Tubal or the Cantabrians might have done? What if, the mists of time being as dense as they were, some details had been forgotten or been altered? The essence of the story persisted. The exceptional status of the *vascongados*, once backed up by tweaks and amendments made to classical luminaries, could now very well do without them. It was clear to these apologists, as it had been clear to Larramendi, that all Western Pyreneans had a divine origin, and that their contamination by strangers could only result in their damnation.[33] And while human reason might say otherwise, and although "enlightened" notables occasionally mocked their claims and asked for the "terms by which scribes, tailors, and shoemakers were called in the Earthly Paradise," few could find it easy—when confronted with the evidence—to refute their point.[34]

The assumption that Basque-speaking, virtuous peasants might rank as the moral superiors of their corrupted and greedy urban neighbors was one that had long enjoyed a following in the Western Pyrenees. Echoes of this belief could be picked up in the writings of Larramendi, in the chants of the rebels who had stormed the streets of Bilbao in 1804, or—even before that—in the rivalry between the Parientes and the provincial institutions. And yet it was now, in an age of unparalleled convulsion and ideological transformation, that they became the cornerstone of a new way of imagining the region.

While Peñaflorida and his associates had once dreamed of freeing their compatriots from the chains of superstition and to usher the Lights upon them, their ideals, increasingly associated with the revolutionary cause, came to lose much of their previous mainstream appeal. Not for everyone, though. Ever since the previous century, merchants and businessmen in hubs like San Sebastian, Vitoria, or Bilbao had seen in some elements of the provincial system a hindrance to their ability to conduct business. Now, in the early nineteenth century, as war, first, and independence from Spain, later, had cut off the American territories from the metropolis, the transferring of the custom houses to the coast seemed no longer an attempt at enrichment, but rather a requirement for survival. After all, if trade with America dried away, and if the *foral* institutions barred them from getting into the Spanish market as well, what alternative awaited these middlemen, if not bankruptcy? The liberal promise of a single, unified nation, without barriers of any kind, was one that must have immediately appealed to such individuals. As it did, coincidentally, the prospect of wealth being the only stipulation for social prestige. Therefore, and while in the countryside both the *mayorazgos* and the commoners—albeit in support of their own selfish ends—agreed in a staunch defense of the traditional superiority, in the largest and most prosperous cities many started to dream of the day in which that very uniqueness would be erased for good.

In reality, the controversy over the legitimacy of the provincial order was but a manifestation of a wider tremor shaking the foundations of the *ancien régime* all throughout Europe.[35] In Spain, Ferdinand VII's reign was to be marked by the vicious opposition between traditionalists and liberal adherents of the 1812 Constitution. Over time, the two cliques had crowded around two competing successors—Don Carlos, the king's brother, and Isabella, her newborn daughter—and had prepared for the inevitable clash. While the liberals chose to frame the traditionalists as tyrannical and old-fashioned, the latter, often radicalized by churchmen zealous of their privileges, were described as an execrable bunch of *philosophes*, Jews, freemasons, or even heretics.[36] Thus, when the king passed away in late September 1833, the long anticipated breakout did not take long in coming, and the pawns started to move to prevent this malignant sect of "wicked men" from reaching power.[37] The "Carlists," taking to the streets, hailed the news of King Ferdinand's death with hurrahs to his brother and songs promising "Death to the liberals, Cristinos, and heretics!"[38]

Considering the inner tensions that had been fermenting underground ever since the war with France, it was barely a surprise that Western Pyreneans would, for the most part, side with the Pretender's cause. Carlism, although ostensibly a party born from dynastic power struggles, masterfully exploited the animosity that existed between the commercial cities and the well-connected *mayorazgos*, on the one hand, and the God-fearing peasantry, the rural oligarchies, and the anti-liberal clergy, on the other.[39] A contemporary observer, reflecting on the enthusiastic support the provinces had granted Don Carlos, concluded that finding an explanation for it was rather "easy": "All secluded people, and mountaineers especially, have a great reverence for old customs, and a sort of instinctive horror of change. The apostolic party, having the clergy on their side, soon enlisted all the superstitions of the country on their behalf."[40] In all, a few weeks on from the uprising, circumstances were appalling for Isabella's cause. In the entirety of Biscay, Guipuzcoa, Alava, and Navarre, only the garrisons of San Sebastian, Bilbao, Vitoria, and Pamplona upheld her right to inherit her father's crown. Elsewhere, it was Don Carlos' forces that held sway. The *Bascongada* might have once tried to demonstrate that modern reforms were compatible with revered traditions. Now, however, the split loyalties of the war transparently displayed how deep the chasms threatening to tear apart Western Pyrenean society truly ran.

The Carlist war would rage on for six long years, from 1833 to 1839, and, given the failure of Don Carlos' supporters in taking up major positions in the peninsula, it would for the most part be constrained to the Western Pyrenees and Catalonia. It would linger in memory as a ruinous period in which raids, banditry, and forced exertions upon the locals became commonplace:

> The sons [are] soldiers
> and prisoners their parents
> for they cannot pay
> the contributions.
> The remaining neighbors
> are forced to work in the trenches.
> Painful are
> today our steps.[41]

The climate of calamity only grew bleaker as the end of the war appeared more and more remote. As conflict intensified, and as the Carlists besieged the main cities and were repelled with difficulty, so too did the propaganda war radicalize at a similar rate. The Pretender's supporters, with an eye cast at ensuring the endorsement of the local population and at concealing their incapability to gain adherents in the rest of Spain, began to adapt their messaging for a Western Pyrenean audience. They did so by pandering to the anti-modernist tropes deployed by the previous generation in defense of their exceptionality. Was it shocking, after all, that it was the *vascongados*, heirs to the primordial and most gifted of all the peoples that made up the king's subjects, who had risen in arms to defend the monarchy and the true religion? After all, what might happen to their rightful liberties were liberals to gain the upper hand? Only if Don Carlos' claim prevailed—or at least so Carlist propagandists proclaimed—could such a thing as the preservation of the *foral* order be accomplished.

Or could it? Some contemporaries may well recall that, in the days that had immediately followed the Carlist uprising, few among their number had even mentioned the defense of the *foral* system as one of their goals. Not only that, for "it was only afterwards, when their own territory was invaded, and their hopes of a simultaneous rising all over Spain disappointed, that they began to assume the character of a virtuous race struggling for their ancient laws and liberties."[42] Don Carlos' cause was then not, by necessity, that of the provinces. In fact, only a few months after the beginning of the conflict, provincial delegates in Madrid had already strived to decouple the outcome of the confrontation from the survival of their exclusive system of government. These politicians had realized that, among members of the Spanish liberal government, there were many who "considered [these Western Pyrenean territories] as a conquered country who must suffer all kinds of vexations."[43] Therefore, the risk of connecting the future of the *fueros* to the fate of Carlism appeared, especially to moderate liberals, a catastrophic one to take. Against such views, they began to propound a vastly different thesis. According to it, the privative administration of these provinces, rather than anathema to the unifying purpose of the liberal cause, was instead fully compatible with it. Not only that, but "the Government and the Cortes of Isabella II, far from annihilating them, should examine them, study them carefully, and, in view of their excellence, preserve them as a model of provincial administration, in order to extend and establish them in the other provinces of the monarchy."[44] The message was clear. The exceptional *vascongados* were not the enemies, but rather the most valuable component, of the Spanish nation.

A far-fetched take, perhaps. And yet, as the conflict carried on without a victor in sight, the benefits of embracing such an illusion for Isabella's government began to outpace the disadvantages. If in 1837 the Spanish Cortes had voted for the abolition of the provincial institutions on grounds of their rebellion, only a year later—and given the impossibility of breaking Carlist resistance—the liberal party was already pushing for reconciliation under the motto "Peace and *fueros*."[45] Following a major victory in the Guipuzcoan town of Hernani in May 1838, the leader of the Isabeline forces, Baldomero Espartero, reinforced this commitment by issuing a statement in which he promised that the *fueros* would be preserved.[46] The strategy worked wonders. The Carlist high command, realizing that continuing the fight would only alienate their supporters without getting them any closer to victory, began to make moves toward pacification. The following year, the war ended. And "the *fueros* of the *vascongado* provinces and Navarre," as per a law signed by the queen of Spain herself, "[were] confirmed, without harm to the constitutional unity of the Monarchy."[47]

The agreement was, in all, a triumph for Western Pyrenean moderate liberals. Not only did they get the so-desired transfer of the custom houses to the coast—which allowed them to access the Spanish market on equal terms as other Spaniards—but they retained, for the time being at least, the political, fiscal, and military autonomy that constituted the cornerstone of the previous system. Likewise, and thanks to their ideological harmony with the Spanish administration, their position at the head of the new administration was hardly to be disputed from the outside. The deal seemed to offer them the best of both worlds while, in addition, unmistakably underpinning the government's recognition of *vascongado* distinctiveness.

The agreement, however, did much more than that. The confirmation of the reformed *fueros*, by soothing the sorest points of friction that had nourished the antagonism between urban liberals and rural elites, seemed to carry the olive branch of reconciliation attached to it. Even the heads of the Carlist party, who might have otherwise been accused of bowing to the terms imposed by the liberals, moved away from the Pretender's camp and reframed their actions during the war as a conscious fight for the *fueros*—and "only for them."[48] And so it was born, as a transfigured conception of the *vascongado* exceptionality, a new one: *fuerism*. A shorthand for the virtuous lifestyle of a people which—if ever deprived of it—would not hesitate in taking up arms in its defense.[49]

That the shadow of blackmail loomed behind these words was precisely the point. It was also indicative of the different ways in which politicians in Madrid and in the provinces interpreted the *foral* confirmation of 1839.[50] For *fuerists*, the new law was an acknowledgment of the entitlement that the inhabitants of Biscay, Guipuzcoa, Alava, and Navarre had to their own particular administration; a pact between the nation and these communities which mirrored those allegedly signed between the *vascongados* and Augustus, Alfonso VIII, or Jaun Zuria. The new *status quo* put an end to almost half a century of ideological attacks and political meddling of the central state in the Western Pyrenees. Likewise, it rendered wholly unnecessary to defend these particularities with problematic references to Strabo or Tacitus. The *fueros* had been confirmed, and this was all that mattered.[51]

Spanish liberals, on the other hand, extracted from the law a very different conclusion. In their eyes, the confirmation of the *fueros* meant the acceptance, by everyone in the provinces, of the superiority of the Spanish Constitution, as well as the right to alter these rules every time "the constitutional unity of the Monarchy" required so.[52] An example of what this could mean in practice was ready at hand. On August 16, 1841, Espartero—the liberal general who by now ranked as regent to the minor Isabella—agreed with representatives of the kingdom of Navarre on a new way of government for the territory that transformed the former realm into a province of Spain.[53] While the change was defended by the Navarrese deputies and other *fuerists* as a compromise between two distinct communities, there were many who, in the following years, would retort that it was but a law like any other, and thus amendable as such.[54] After all, circumstances in the wake of the civil war had rendered the issue of the *fueros* a sensitive one to undertake directly, for the time being at any rate. But, for all that some in Madrid proved willing to wait and play to the *vascongados*' wounded sense of invulnerability, there was simply no accepting that the confirmation of 1839 was anything but an internal Spanish affair.[55]

Not everyone saw matters that way, and not only in the Western Pyrenees. Many intellectuals in France and Germany, for example, had looked upon the Carlist war as a struggle between a centralizing state and a community of "fervent patriots who are proud of the privileges of their homeland and of the age and the glory of their nation."[56] The mid-nineteenth century was the heyday of Romantic effusions, after all, and the thought of a virtuous race rejecting the damning advance of modernity was an appealing one indeed. Some foreigners, for example, did not shy away from comparing the traditional government of these provinces to "the small republics of Greece and Italy in their best days."[57] Others, more radical or eccentric in their sources, read in the Carlist struggle more than a mere rejection of the liberal state. Rather, they caught in it a glimpse of something far more momentous: a war between two very different, irreconcilable peoples.

Joseph Augustin Chaho, born in Soule, had from the beginning of the war manifested overt support for the Carlist cause. A writer as daring in his intellectual endeavors as bold in his public life—he would be wounded in a duel and was buried without any religious ceremony—Chaho had come to assume, after a prolonged exposure to esoteric works, that Western Pyreneans held the key to the future of mankind.[58] These men and women were, in his eyes, a race of "seers," endowed with an intrinsic knowledge of the divine grounded on teachings passed down the generations "without symbols, without sacrifices, without priests, and without cult."[59] A startling statement, perhaps, but one inspired nonetheless in the claims of local propagandists who for a long time had styled themselves the heirs to the first inhabitants of Iberia. Chaho's mysterious insights, however, went much further than any of his forerunners. If the latter had made use of the Tubalian myth to demonstrate that they were the first and most exceptional of all Spaniards, Chaho now challenged the fundamentals of that story. Tubal—he admitted—was indeed the forefather of the Spanish peoples. But he was not, crucially, the forefather of these "Basques."

> You know . . . that the Basques trace their origin to the Iberian patriarch Aitor, and that every peasant of Cantabrian blood, every distinguished soldier, every free man is considered noble among us, and a child of Aitor—*Aitoren seme*? . . . I will now tell you that this name Aitor is allegorical: it means "universal father," "sublime," and was imagined by our ancestors to recall the original nobility and ancient lineage of the Basque race.[60]

Chaho, by adopting and reinterpreting notions of *Euskal Herria* that had for centuries been current on the northern side of the Pyrenees, now sought to provide a mythical alternative to the Tubalian tale. Every Western Pyrenean—to whom he applied the name given to *Euskera*-speakers in France, "Basques"—was part of the last remnants of an ancient race, but one entirely distinct from that to which belonged the Spaniards that surrounded them. An argument vindicated by history. While the former exhibited an "essential preeminence resulting from their lineage and an inherited independence," the latter had never managed to rise beyond being "serfs under the Visigoths, slaves under the Moors, . . . a herd of men, penned on barren lands."[61] For millennia, the two communities had struggled with one another, and it was as part of this eternal conflict that the stories told about the Cantabrians, Jaun Zuria, or Roncesvalles had come into shape. Now, in the age of revolution, the time had come yet again for the immemorial confrontation to be staged, with the Basque liberties—"their noble independence and the individuality of our primitive and solar race"—as ever, the prize at stake.[62]

Staggering and verging on the heretical though Chaho's writings might be, it was their reception south of the Pyrenees that proved more surprising. His *Voyage en Navarre pendant l'insurrection des Basques (1830–1833)*, published in 1836, might be full of invented episodes, interviews that did not take place, and a saturating esotericism that rendered all its Western Pyrenean characters less flesh-and-blood humans than omniscient prophets. But beyond these qualms, the text's principles, to an extent unparalleled for any other work penned in *Iparralde*—as the northern Pyrenean territories were known in *Euskera*—in the preceding 300 years, were eagerly appropriated by southern *fuerists* in the wake of the conflict. Initially, such an enthusiastic response might appear paradoxical, especially considering that, if anything, it was precisely the Carlists Chaho had supported that had come out defeated. However, upon further scrutiny, it was not difficult to see why, in the aftermath of the *foral* confirmation of 1839, there were many, both in the liberal and in the Carlist camps, open to listening to what an eccentric Soulentine would say about the true essence of Basqueness.

After all, the mid-nineteenth century was an age of reinvention. Across Europe—in Ireland, in Germany, in Italy—a wave of Romantic sensibility swept away the unifying and faceless principles of the Enlightenment and highlighted various alternative modernities.[63] At the same time, the rediscovery of ancient poems and the publishing of best-selling historical novels—such as Walter Scott's *Waverley* in 1814—contributed to granting these decades an "antiquary" flavor. Talk of races, of spirits, of essences took over the main stage. And, unsurprisingly, these developments also affected post-1839 Western Pyrenean society. At first, the fuzziness of the *foral* agreement and the general exhaustion after the Carlist war muted overenthusiastic expressions about the exceptional character of the locals. But when the Spanish government sought to undertake in Biscay, Alava, and Guipuzcoa a similar project of uniformity as the one recently carried out in Navarre, the dormant discourses were yet again reawakened. It was unfair—*fuerist* politicians ardently proclaimed—to deprive the provinces of what were, in essence, the most venerable and democratic institutions of the peninsula. Others, lamenting the fixation of their rivals with their downfall, staged dramatic acts of mourning and retorted "that the tears of the *vascongados* will not make the Castiles bloom, nor would raise them to opulence."[64] And so—and even though the Spanish cabinet's attempt would ultimately be unfruitful—these episodes demonstrated that the *foral* issue, despite the pacification of 1839, was still far from a thing of the past.

In 1851, the Guipuzcoan writer José María Goizueta published a book titled *Leyendas Vascongadas* and thus kickstarted the interest in Romantic novels with a Western Pyrenean twist.[65] The rediscovery of local folklore, initiated by none other than the eccentric Chaho in his search for the primordial teachings of the Basque seers, was but an outgrowth of similar *renaissances* elsewhere in Europe. In fact, to an extent even more acute than in those other experiments, this "Basque" rebirth owed much more to fantasy than to immemorial traditions passed down orally. This was clear, for example, in the fact that these works were, for the most part, written in Spanish rather than in the vernacular, in that they did not hesitate from blatantly copying characters and tropes from Scott and other Romantic authors, or in that many of them mentioned characters—like the patriarch Aitor—only recently invented by Chaho.

Details, all of them, that did not prevent these stories from enjoying a sizable audience. The *Leyendas*, for one, would have five editions between 1851 and 1890.[66] There was good reason for this success. After all, tales set in foggy forests and windswept hills offered a transcendent and mysterious view of the past to a people who, in more recent times, had come to regard itself an unjustly persecuted one. They showed—in the words of one of these authors—how Western Pyreneans,

> obeying that traditional spirit which is the hallmark of our race, and entrusting to it the preservation of their institutions and their history, have never taken care to transmit in writing to their descendants either the accounts of their great deeds, or the key to their strong organization, or, finally, the secret of the immense power they attained—a power that can hardly be understood given the limited conditions of their territory and their wealth.[67]

Now, finally, that silence was being amended. And what stood revealed was the uniqueness, timeless and eternal, of a race endowed by fate with all kinds of virtues.

Mystery—linguistic, regarding the origins of *Euskera*, and historical, owing to the few ancient mentions of the region—provided a perfect setting for these tales. However, the constant recourse to that very mystery was, in a sense, an admission of defeat. Unable to maintain, in the face of an increasingly rigorous historical scholarship, the veracity of the old stories, Goizueta and his many imitators would opt instead for promoting an alternative yardstick of reliability. Shielded against criticism by the literary garments of their novels, they nonetheless updated and breathed new life into the old myths.[68] The children of Tubal were repurposed, in a stage now almost completely removed from serious history, as the children of Aitor: a race that "held what was pure and authentic in great esteem, regarded what was impure with horror, and looked down on what was degenerate."[69] Chaho's ideas about the primitive religiosity of the Western Pyreneans were uncritically adopted. The Cantabrians and their forged songs were rehabilitated. The most damning attacks of the Soulentine against other Spaniards were appropriately muted.[70] As demonstrated by newspapers, books, and pamphlets, a narcissistic view of their own extraordinariness came to imbue the minds and hearts of the provincials.

This essentialization of the Western Pyrenean exception, in doing away with documents and legal rulings, and transferring this notion instead to the fields of culture, language, and emotion, triggered unforeseen consequences. Ever since the imperial heyday of the *vascongado* elites in the eighteenth century—and as manifested outwardly in the foundation of the *Bascongada*—a mood of collaboration had prevailed in the dealings between the provinces of Biscay, Guipuzcoa, Alava, and Navarre. Connected by ties of friendship, interest, and lifestyle, the elites of these territories had often considered each other close allies in their dealings with the royal court. However, and slogans such as the famous *Irurac bat* notwithstanding, each province, with its own idiosyncrasies and particularities, had largely retained the allegiance of those under its sway. Proof of the veracity of this claim had come in 1821 when, upon hearing of plans for the creation of a united *vascongado* province, the General Assembly of Biscay had rejected it as "unattainable" given "the moral division" that existed between the inhabitants of these territories.[71]

Now, however, matters had changed. That so revered law of 1839, which *fuerist* politicians regarded as the landline for their institutions, made reference, not to Biscay, Alava, or Guipuzcoa, but rather to the "*Vascongado* provinces."[72] Chaho's view of the Basques—and for all that it could also apply to the French territories—was similarly premised on the existence of a fundamental sameness connecting all Western Pyreneans. Popular books and anthems, like Goizueta's *Leyendas* or José María Iparraguirre's hit from the 1850s, *Gernikako arbola*—which described the oak of Biscay as "blessed among the Basques"—spread an identical message.[73] Thus, as the *foral* issue, on the one hand, and the Western Pyrenean exception, on the other, both came to coalesce in a discourse that made them surface elements stemming from the racial spirit of the Basques, so too did notions of a *vascongado* identity begin to trample the previous barriers that existed between Biscay, Alava, and Guipuzcoa.[74] For, "in fact, the same are the principles and fundamental bases upon which the three rest; the same their character, their nature, their tendency, and their results; one their origin, just as one were the needs whose satisfaction they sought."[75]

Considering the speed with which *fuerist* writers and politicians embraced these notions of racial distinctiveness, it remains noteworthy that his teachings would garner much less success on the northern side of the mountain chain. To the inhabitants of *Iparralde*, talk of primordial races, of unconquerable Cantabrians, and of antediluvian monotheism had never appeared as enticing as to their southern counterparts. The abolition of their frail autonomy in 1789 had only exacerbated their indifference. While Romantic epics about the creation of Spain and the lineage of Aitor spread in the peninsula, a few miles north, the debate about the place of the locals in the modern world was very different indeed. Here, French nationalists, heirs to the unitary ideals of the Revolution, had proven less receptive than their Spanish equivalents to the thought of the nation as a composite amalgam of various communities. This had left the Basques with only a single perk to distinction: their language.

Long before the times of Chaho, philologic studies about *Euskera* had been a regular endeavor for the leisured classes of France.[76] Now, in 1851—the same year of the publication of Goizueta's *Leyendas*—the Irish-born Antoine d'Abbadie staged the first *Koplarien Guduak*—"Wars of Singers." These were literary and musical contests in *Euskera*, aimed at raising awareness about the customs of the commoners.[77] Against the *Irurac bat* of the *fuerists*, the message these meetings paraded was that of *Zazpiac bat*—"the seven at once" or "the seven are one": an evident updating of notions of *Euskal Herria* that had been circulating ever since the times of Echepare. Sadly, just as the writings of the latter, word of these competitions never seeped into Biscay, Guipuzcoa, Alava, or Navarre. Focused as the elites of these territories were on the defense of their autonomy on grounds of their status as the primordial inhabitants of Spain, they had little time to dynamite such efforts by displaying a confraternity with their northern brethren. Despite Chaho's claims to the contrary, the mountains had proven, yet again, too-mighty a barrier for the alleged brotherhood of the Basques to coalesce.

As it happens, by the 1860s a precarious equilibrium had been reached in the Western Pyrenees. The *fueros*, stemming from the wellspring of the Western Pyrenean spirit, had survived under a watchful defense, political and otherwise, carried out by liberals and Carlist alike. External factors had also contributed to this outcome. The leaders of the Spanish state, moderate liberals, no longer looked back fondly at the radical example of 1812, and contented themselves instead with tempering the supposed panaceas of the modern world with the hierarchical instincts proper to the *ancien régime*. In this endeavor, the maintenance of the *fueros*—volatile though their assimilation promised to be—reinforced their own party goals.[78]

There existed, of course, controversy about what the *fueros* themselves, particularly about the kind of spirit that had breathed life into them. Were they, as left-wing radicals proclaimed, "a democratic republican system"?[79] Or was the destiny of Western Pyreneans, rather, to stand as the last bearers of the standard of the true faith "that once led the hosts of Pelayo in Covadonga"?[80] Finding an answer to these questions was obviously a hard ask. And yet, in their sheer variety, they remained expressive of the extent to which resorting to the *fuero* had already become a strategy that promised votes and support. For this was "much more than a good law; it [was], if we may be allowed to say so, almost a second religion—cherished and revered."[81] And this reverence, a double patriotism that had as its object both the Spanish nation and the Western Pyrenean homeland, was founded on the assumption that it, rather than diminishing the status of the former, could indeed be taken as its most perfected manifestation.[82]

This delicate balance was starting to show signs of exhaustion, nonetheless. The entire edifice of *fuerism* rested, in hindsight, upon a single, crucial factor: the tolerance displayed toward it by politicians in Madrid. This apparent lenience had been caused by an all-too-sensible hesitation to stir a hornet's nest that could result in the resurrection of Carlism. And yet, as discontent for moderate rule began to spread in the Spanish capital, so too did, accordingly, the thought of attaining a final settlement to make Biscay, Alava, and Guipuzcoa common provinces within the Spanish state. As early as 1850, parliamentary debates had occasionally been dotted with attacks from the most radical liberals. In the words of these critics, anyone who defended the privileges and exemptions of the *vascongados* were the "declared enemies of the rights of other Spaniards."[83] Not for nothing, these "progressive" individuals—whose star was on the rise in the 1860s—had grown weary of the kind of conciliatory attitude toward Western Pyreneans exhibited by the moderates. Liberty—by which they meant a restoration of the ideals of the single, unitary nation proclaimed in Cadiz in 1812—could not be bargained with. On the other hand, liberal leaders in San Sebastian, Vitoria, or Bilbao knew better than to stake their local dominance on an unpopular plan for the abolition of the *fueros*. Rather, they responded with the phlegm proper to a race of unjustly accused heroes. "They never start from here"—a *fuerist* delegate concluded—"the aggressions always come from Madrid. It's important to keep this fact very much in mind."[84] A soothing message that could barely conceal the volatility of the situation. Trapped between the renewed star of Spanish nationalism, on one side, and the self-interested conviction of *fuerist* politicians, on the other, the dilemma of the age—whether the privileges enshrined in the *fueros* could be compatible with a modern constitution—was once again brought into the light of day.

The problem was, of course, that the interests of the "progressive" party went far beyond the *vascongado* question. Religious freedom, reform of the monarchy, payment of the national debt, these constituted their main goals. And so, when in 1868 the Spanish moderate government collapsed, and a new radical cabinet rose to power, provincial Deputations, rather than directly opposing the change, simply caught breath and waited.[85] So too, did the Carlists. The change of regime had brought the expulsion of Isabella II from the throne and had rekindled, in conservative hearts, the fear of what modern and impious ideas might portend: two developments that played directly into the movement's hands. In Bilbao, for example, foreigners were surprised by the exceeding Carlist devotion of most women, who were "influenced" in their political opinions "entirely by the priests."[86] Other fearmongers, upon hearing news of projects aimed at the liberalization of religious worship, warned that these would result in Christian prayers being silenced by "the cries of the rabbi, the santon, the brahmin, or perhaps the shameless Mormons."[87]

Fuerist propaganda, which had for decades depicted the locals as the first and most staunch defenders of the Christian faith, seamlessly fueled such conservative readings. While some intellectuals continued, even in these fraught circumstances, to assimilate the *fueros* to the democracy propounded by the progressive party, they remained a negligible minority.[88] The first elections with universal male suffrage in the provinces resulted in a landslide victory for the Carlists. And so, when the promises of the progressives in Madrid failed to materialize and a grandson of Don Carlos proclaimed in 1872 his determination to stand as king of Spain, the old liberal nightmare of the Carlist uprising was raised from its slumber.

Once again, war
with the clamor of death
strikes the ears
of free Spain.
Once again, ungrateful Vasconia ignites it,
insolently breaking
venerable pacts.
All too generous,
the lion now understands
that within its breast
it carries hostile serpents.
If your shadow, [Tree of Guernica]
protects such traitors
oh, accursed be you,
accursed a thousand times!.[89]

For more than thirty years, ever since the agreement that had brought the first Carlist war to an end, the tendency to associate the cause of the Pretender with the defense of the administration of the provinces had been a mainstay of conservative propaganda. "God and *Fueros*"—a Carlist author wrote—"this is the banner from which this privileged land shall never part: a glorious and beloved standard in every Basque heart, a sacred and inviolable emblem for all the Euskeric race."[90] These messages, inflamed by the waves of criticism that the Western Pyrenean exception had recently endured, exploded in earnest with the war. The masses of the dependents, who had suffered the most from the increase in prices that had followed the transfer of the custom houses, rallied to the conservative camp.[91] In Bilbao, "many of the foreigners left the town; [and] every steamer out had more than its full complement of passengers."[92] The situation was not unlike that of 1836, when Carlist forces had controlled the countryside and the representatives of the liberal state had maintained but a feeble holdout in the main cities. However, and for all that in the provinces Carlist propaganda battered incessantly about the need to preserve the *foral* order, its advocates did not lose sight of the true prize. "Charles VII will respect the *fueros* and liberties of the provinces, and he will leave nothing undone to ensure that, within the great Spanish family, all may live in peace and happiness under the protective aegis of the throne of Saint Ferdinand."[93] In other words: The destiny of the provinces, for good or ill, was to be that of the rest of Spain.

As in the previous conflict, liberal delegates tried in earnest to dissociate the fate of the provincial administration from that of the Carlist uprising.[94] This time, however, their efforts would prove unsuccessful. Carlist forces, which thirty years earlier had proven insurmountable, were this time defeated on the battlefield. It took some time, for the war lasted until early 1876, but, when all was said and done, it was a calamitous defeat for the conservative cause all the same. The press in Madrid, emboldened by the military victory, passionately advocated for an immediate application of the provisions included in the law of 1839. It was, in their view, within the government's prerogatives to reform or abolish these institutions if "the constitutional unity of the Monarchy" was at stake, and this was precisely what the uprising had threatened. Provincial delegates, on the other hand, answered such utterances by claiming that the government could not single-handedly erase what they interpreted as laws resulting from a pact between equals.[95] The inevitable debate that followed only served to exacerbate anti-Castilian sentiments among all sectors of Western Pyrenean society.[96] Biscayne, Guipuzcoan, Alavese, and Navarrese liberals, incapable of finding a middle ground amid the radicalization, tried in vain to prevent the Spanish parliament from drafting a new project they judged "the death of the *fueros*."[97] Even the sitting Spanish president, Antonio Cánovas del Castillo, conceded that, although he would have it otherwise, he felt impotent to attend to the delegates' pleas, for "the spirit of the nation is angered against the majority of the Basque inhabitants."[98]

In the event, the law to abolish and modify the *fueros* of the provinces of Biscay, Guipuzcoa, and Alava would come on July 21, 1876. According to its contents, the military and fiscal advantages that the dwellers of these provinces had enjoyed for the best part of three centuries were rescinded. The law did not say anything about the political institutions of the land, which initially remained in place. But, even these, following a bout of resistance against the implantation of the new norms, were duly dissolved.[99] New Deputations, this time made up of moderates more willing to cooperate with the Spanish government, then rushed to salvage what they could from the previous order.

It would prove—despite its lack of popularity—a sensible policy. Neither the public trauma that the erasure of the *fuero* had produced nor the extremism it fostered did play well into the objectives of either the local elite or national parties. If the provinces were not to fall yet again into anarchy, wounds needed healing—and fast. Thus, behind closed curtains at first and more overtly with every passing week, the gears of the Western Pyrenean exception began to move once again. In private talks, in confidential meetings, in the corridors of parliament, a new privilege was conceived. As per the ruling of 1876, the provinces had been compelled to pay, as their contribution to the budget for 1877–8, an amount of money determined beforehand by the Spanish government. But what—these pragmatic politicians thought—if this extraordinary system of quotas was to be rendered the usual one? In late 1877, they managed to secure such a right. The provinces would pay what they owed to the coin-starved cabinet—but they would do so after a negotiation better known as the "economic concerts."

In hindsight, that these "concerts" would mark the end to almost a century of controversies around the *foral* issue was indeed paradoxical. On the one hand, the *fueros* themselves—that is, the codes and institutions that had emerged from the defeat of the Parientes Mayores around the late fifteenth century—had been either completely abolished or transformed beyond recognition. In this sense, the law of 1876, for all that it might state that it "modified" the *foral* system, was nothing short of the deadly blow that *fuerist* authors had suspected. On the other hand, the new "concerts," a fiscal procedure unparalleled in any other Spanish territory, not only kept the memory alive of a previous age in which rule had been framed as a pact but also granted, de facto, a very real advantage to Western Pyreneans.

Not that this, of course, left everyone content with the outcome. The accommodating *fuerists* who had pushed for the establishment of the quotas were, in the following years, routinely pressured by hard-core factions and the Carlist, both of whom—for one reason or another—saw in the full restoration of the *foral* system a goal all in and of itself.[100] However, and despite the apocalyptic outbursts of these individuals about the loss of the *fueros*, the very existence of the new privilege, no longer tied to dubious documents nor to far-fetched primordial qualities but to scrupulous legality, was a vindication of all that Western Pyrenean oligarchies, for almost a century, had fought for. Conceived as a compensation by the Spanish government, the new "concerts" tacitly implied that there was something that had been unfairly—even if legitimately—taken away from the dwellers of the region. This newfound exemption, no less than the previous one, was grounded on the idea that the Basques had contributed something more to the Spanish nation than anyone else. The unique spirit of the race who, in the words of US President John Adams, had "preserved their ancient language, genius, laws, government, and manners, without innovations, longer than any other nation of Europe" could not be erased overnight by a simple act of legislation.[101] For it was, as both Chaho and many others had proclaimed for more than thirty years of Romantic exaltation, an exemption born out of blood and landscape, a natural fact of life, "an essential preeminence."[102]

Notes

1 Sanadon, *Essai sur la noblesse des Basques, pour servir d'Introduction à l'Histoire générale de ces Peuples*, 9–10.

2 Dupré de Saint Maur (1780). Quoted in Lafourcade, "L'autonomie administrative du Pays Basque de France sous l'Ancien Regime," 137–8.

3 Salvat Monho (1789). Quoted in Goyhenetche, *Histoire Générale du Pays Basque. Tome IV: La Révolution de 1789*, 95.

4 Goyhenetche, *Histoire Générale du Pays Basque*, 195.

5 Goyhenetche, 184.

6 Polverel, *Tableau de la Constitution du Royaume de Navarre et des ses rapports avec la France*, LXIII.

7 Quoted in Goyhenetche, *Histoire Générale du Pays Basque*, 174–5.

8 Quoted in Ilacqua, "Territory and the Politics of Identity in the Basque Country during the French Revolution," 329.

9 Joseph Garat (1790). Quoted in Goyhenetche, *Histoire Générale du Pays Basque*, 200–1.

10 Porres, "Los medios y los miedos humanos," 103–5.

11 Sarasti, *Memoria de la Revolución Francesa y de la Guerra de España por la parte de Navarra y Guipuzcoa en los años de 1793, 1794 y 1795*, 77. Also, Bermejo, "La caída de una clase política," 177.

12 Ibáñez, *Manifiesto histórico de los servicios que ha hecho el muy noble y muy leal señorío de Vizcaya en la última guerra con la Francia*, 26.

13 Francisco Antonio de Zamora. Quoted in Bermejo, "La caída de una clase política," 192–3.

14 See Iglesias, "Estudio preliminar," 33.

15 Oihenart, *Notitia utriusque Vasconiae tum Ibericae, tum Aquitanicae*, 15–16.

16 General Assembly of Gernika, July 22, 1768. Quoted in Mañaricua, *Historiografía de Vizcaya. Desde Lope García de Salazar a Labayru*, 233–4.

17 Astigarraga, *Los ilustrados vascos*, 178–9. Also, Azurmendi, *Y se limpie aquella tierra*, 365. Also, "Letter from Xavier Munibe to Pedro Jacinto de Álava," November 25, 1769. In Tellechea, *La ilustración vasca*, 101–2.

18 Flórez, *La Cantabria. Disertación sobre el sitio, y extensión que en tiempo de los romanos tuvo la región de los cántabros*, 133.

19 Real Academia de la Historia, *Diccionario Geográfico-Histórico de España. Sección I, II*. Also, Llorente, *Noticias históricas de las tres provincias vascongadas*.

20 Conde, *Censura crítica de la pretendida excelencia y antigüedad del vascuence*, 5.

21 Bermejo, "La caída de una clase política," 326.

22 Martínez, *Casa, Provincia, Rey*, 367–73.

23 Sarasti, *Memoria de la Revolución Francesa*, 95.

24 Juan Antonio Zamácola, "Historia de las Naciones Bascas." Quoted in Bermejo, "La caída de una clase política," 228.

25 Bermejo, "La caída de una clase política," 251–2.

26 Bermejo, 210, 221.

27 Sarasti, *Memoria de la Revolución Francesa*, 104.

28 Constitution of Cadiz 1812, II, art. 8.

29 "Conversation between the Biscayne deputy Echezarreta y Arribi and the Guipuzcoan delegate Alzaga." Quoted in Rubio, *La identidad vasca en el siglo XIX. Discursos y agentes sociales*, 70.

30 José Joaquín Echezarreta Arribi (1817). Quoted in Rubio, *La identidad vasca en el siglo XIX*, 70.

31 Martínez, *Casa, Provincia, Rey*, 354–5.

32 These were the themes of the two most important works penned by this group: Pablo Pedro de Astarloa's *Apología de la Lengua Bascongada* (1803) and Juan Antonio Moguel's *Peru Abarca* (1802).

33 Artola, "La antimodernidad en el País Vasco: Practicas sociales y discursos (1765–1833)," 142–3.

34 "Letter from Félix María Samaniego to Benito María Ansótegui." Quoted in Artola, "La antimodernidad en el País Vasco," 134–5. Also, Sánchez-Prieto, "Constitución, fueros y democracia. Motivaciones, discursos y actitudes políticas con relación a la permanencia o abolición de los fueros vasco-navarros," 107–8.

35 Storm, *Nationalism: A World History*, 67–8.

36 Bacon, *Six years in Biscay. A personal narrative of the sieges of Bilbao in June 1835 and October 1836 and of the principal events which occurred in that city and the Basque provinces during the years 1830 to 1837*, 18.

37 Quoted in Vázquez, "La cultura política aranista: genesis y definición del nacionalismo vasco," 216–17.

38 The mention of the Cristinos is a reference to Ferdinand's wife, María Cristina of the Two Sicilies, who was blamed by Carlists for the sidelining of Don Carlos in favor of Isabella. Quote from Bacon, *Six years in Biscay*, 88.

39 Imízcoz, "Las élites vasco-navarras y la monarquía hispánica," 117.

40 Bacon, *Six years in Biscay*, 76–7.

41 "Muñagorriren kantak" (1838). Quoted in Antxustegi, *El debate nacionalista. Sabino Arana y sus herederos*, 67.

42 Bacon, *Six years in Biscay*, 126.

43 "Letter from Fausto de Otazu to Iñigo Ortés," February 6, 1834. Quoted in Bermejo, "La caída de una clase política," 366.

44 *Observaciones sobre la necesidad de examinar el régimen administrativo de las Provincias Vascongadas para fallar con acierto en esta materia*, 12.

45 Rubio, *La identidad vasca en el siglo XIX*, 103. Also, Sánchez-Prieto, "Constitución, fueros y democracia," 114.

46 Monreal, *Fuentes del Derecho Histórico de Bizkaia*, 615.

47 "Law confirming the *fueros* of the *Vascongado* provinces and Navarre," October 25, 1839. In Monreal, *Fuentes del Derecho Histórico de Bizkaia*, 618.

48 "Speech by José Churruca in the Spanish Congress in December 6, 1844." Quoted in Rubio, *La identidad vasca en el siglo XIX*, 108.

49 Rubio, *La identidad vasca en el siglo XIX*, 105–6.

50 Aller, "El Fuero como retórica. De reliquia positiva a canon identitario," 61.

51 Monreal, "La ley abolitoria de fueros de 21 de julio de 1876 (antecedentes y paso por el congreso)," 50–1.

52 "Law confirming the *fueros* of the *Vascongado* provinces and Navarre," October 25, 1839. In Monreal, *Fuentes del Derecho Histórico de Bizkaia*, 618.

53 Monreal, "La ley abolitoria de fueros," 144–5.

54 Monreal, 146.

55 Monreal, 52.

56 Rahn, "Deutsches Staats-Wörterbuch" (1857). Quoted in Mees, *The Basque Contention: Ethnicity, Politics, Violence*, 34. Also, Zabaltza, *Mater Vasconia*, 227–8. Also Juaristi, *El linaje de Aitor: La invención de la tradición vasca*, 77.

57 Bacon, *Six years in Biscay*, 61–2.

58 Juaristi, *El linaje de Aitor*, 78–9.

59 Chaho, *Voyage en Navarre pendant l'insurrection des Basques (1830–1833)*, 233.

60 Chaho, *Voyage en Navarre*, 87–8.

61 Chaho, 271, 420–1.

62 Chaho, 91.

63 Storm, *Nationalism*, 61–2.

64 Gaminde, *Impugnación al arreglo de los fueros de las Provincias Bascongadas por la Comisión de Gobierno de las mismas Provincias*, 63.

65 Goizueta, *Leyendas Vascongadas*.

66 Juaristi, *El linaje de Aitor*, 108–9.

67 Araquistain, *Tradiciones vasco*-cántabras, 5.

68 Juaristi, *El linaje de Aitor*, 59.

69 Navarro, *Amaya o los vascos en el siglo VIII*, I, 7.

70 Juaristi, *El linaje de Aitor*, 124.

71 General Deputation of Biscay, March 19, 1821. Quoted in Rubio, *La identidad vasca en el siglo XIX*, 91.

72 "Law confirming the *fueros* of the *Vascongado* provinces and Navarre," October 25, 1839. In Monreal, *Fuentes del Derecho Histórico de Bizkaia*, 618.

73 Luengo and Delgado, "El árbol de Gernika. Vicisitudes del símbolo foral de los vascos," 28.

74 Rubio, *La identidad vasca en el siglo XIX*, 39.

75 Julián Egaña, "Ensayo sobre la naturaleza y trascendencia de la legislación foral de las provincias vascongadas" (1850). Quoted in Rubio, *La identidad vasca en el siglo XIX*, 32.

76 Rubio, *La identidad vasca en el siglo XIX*, 256–7.

77 Urgell, "Primer Vasco Moderno," 598.

78 Sánchez-Prieto, "Constitución, fueros y democracia," 119–20.

79 Quoted in Rubio, *La identidad vasca en el siglo XIX*, 78–9.

80 Sánchez-Prieto, "Constitución, fueros y democracia," 130–1.

81 Casimiro Jausoro. Quoted in Rubio, *La identidad vasca en el siglo XIX*, 111–12.

82 Sánchez-Prieto, "Constitución, fueros y democracia," 127.

83 Manuel Sánchez Silva, "Semblanzas de los 340 diputados a Cortes que han figurado en la legislatura de 1849-1850" (1850). Quoted in Sánchez-Prieto, "Constitución, fueros y democracia," 122.

84 Ramón Ortíz de Zarate (1856). Quoted in Sánchez-Prieto, "Constitución, fueros y democracia," 126–7.

85 Monreal, "La ley abolitoria de fueros," 53.

86 Borges, *Vizcaya or, life in the land of the Carlists at the Outbreak of the insurrection 1872–73*, 108–9.

87 Arístides de Artiñano, "Jaungoicoa eta foruac" (1869). In Garmendia, *Jaungoicoa eta foruac. El carlismo vasconavarro frente a la democracia española (1868–1872)*, 145–6.

88 Rubio, *La identidad vasca en el siglo XIX*, 78–9.

89 Ruiz, "El Árbol de Guernica. Eco nacional," 13.

90 Rezusta, *Apuntes sobre la historia de la revolución en Guipúzcoa*, 11.

91 Vázquez, "La cultura política aranista," 203.

92 Borges, *Vizcaya*, 151–2.

93 Juan Rico Amat, "La unidad católica" (1868). Quoted in Garmendia, *Jaungoicoa eta foruac*, 15–16.

94 Rubio, *La identidad vasca en el siglo XIX*, 113.

95 Monreal, "La ley abolitoria de fueros," 169–70.

96 Rubio, *La identidad vasca en el siglo XIX*, 169. Also Molina, "Delenda est Carthago? La nación española y los fueros vascos (1868–1898)," 82.

97 Quoted in Rubio, *La identidad vasca en el siglo XIX*, 114–15.

98 Antonio Cánovas del Castillo. Quoted in Rubio, *La identidad vasca en el siglo XIX*, 170–1.

99 Molina, "Delenda est Carthago?" 79.

100 Aller, "El Fuero como retórica," 74–5.

101 Adams, "The Works of John Adams" (1856). Quoted in Monreal, *The Old Law of Bizkaia (1452)*, 17.

102 Chaho, *Voyage en Navarre*, 271.

CHAPTER 20
THE BASQUE JESUS

Once upon a time, back when the Muslims first arrived in Iberia, there had lived in the Western Pyrenees a girl called Amaya. In a world devastated and strained after centuries of conflicts between the locals and the pull from the Visigothic kings of Toledo, the girl's own existence was nothing short of an anomaly. Her mother had been a Vascon princess; her father, in turn, a Gothic count. Theirs had been a forbidden love, of course, yet one whose main result—the very birth of the girl—had been largely stepped over by contemporaries. Amaya's mother had died in mysterious circumstances shortly after childbirth. The child, taken under his father's custody, had been raised as a Gothic maiden. The shadow of her bloodline, however, had proven an impossible one to outrun. For one day, when she was only a teenager, Amaya had discovered the truth of her deceased parent's lineage. That she had been the eldest heir from the house of Aitor, the patriarch of the Basques, and that she, in giving birth to a daughter, had made her the depositary of a life-altering secret. A secret that led straight to the treasure of Aitor, and to the emergence of a Christian king among the Basques.

Not that the revelation had made matters easier for her. She might fancy calling herself a Basque, but to their alleged brethren, especially in the deepest valleys of the north, she could not appear anything but a Gothic maiden. How could such a girl—the scion of the inveterate enemy—uphold her rights to the inheritance of Aitor? No such thought could be entertained, even by the most moderate of Basques. And if that was the case among Christianized Western Pyreneans, naturally less isolationist thanks to their religion, what could be said about their pagan counterparts? The latter had twice as many reasons to deplore Amaya's claims: For she was a Goth as well as a Christian. And so, her own aunt—a stubborn and fierce lady called Amagoya, who still clung to the ancient rituals—regarded Amaya as nothing but a barbarian and a fraud. The treasure of Aitor should never be allowed to fall into such an enemy's hands.

Had this been the end of Amaya's story, though, it would be hardly noteworthy. An illegitimate child of a distinguished family often suffered, after all, the scorn of those who should have loved her most. Amaya's destiny, on the other hand, was to soar much higher than that. For the year was 711, and the time of reckoning was approaching for the kingdom of the Visigoths. First, a deep-seated plot against King Rodrigo was uncovered; shortly after, news reached his camp of the arrival of Muslim forces to the south. Confronted with these tidings, which should have been merely read as a threat to Toledo's own dominion, some Basques suddenly underwent a startling transformation. Foremost among these was García Jimeno who, rallying behind the banner of the Cross, had marched alongside his former enemies to battle the heathen invader. And so, a new dawn was promised to Spain, one in which the division between Basques and Goths would be overcome by their own shared defense of the Christian truth. And one in which Amaya's own descent, rather than an obstacle to be sidelined and commended to oblivion, would instead hold the key to a better future for a united Spain.

This, in essence, was the plot of Francisco Navarro Villoslada's *magnum opus* "Amaya or the Basques in the eighth century": a family struggle pitting the Basques and the Goths, Christianity and paganism, all against the backdrop of a pivotal moment at the imagined origins of the Reconquista. Of course, most of the characters in the play were fruits reaped from their author's outsized imagination. These had either never existed—like Amaya and Amagoya—or were—like Pelayo or the last Visigothic king, Rodrigo—unrecognizable from their historical counterparts. Not that these caveats had ever stopped novelists enamored of the *fueros*. In 1851, the same year in which Navarro Villoslada had begun work on his epic, another Western Pyrenean author, Pedro Novia de Salcedo, had defended the kind of historical escapism these literates cultivated. "The Basques know the respect that the traditions of peoples deserve, but they also want the observance of this same reciprocal principle of justice regarding their own: there may be, indeed, in them something or much that is fabulous and supposed, but this does not destroy the essence of the fact."[1]

An approach, in other words, that allowed novelists to play fast and loose with the kind of fastidious inconvenience that so much tormented historical defenders of the provincial privileges. Scarce though the worth of "Amaya" as a piece of historical scholarship might appear at first, this did not necessarily entail that the book would not hold a massive impact in shaping the ways in which contemporaries imagined their own past. The novel, ever since its initial printing in 1877, never stopped being applauded and avidly read.[2] It was a success to which its many talents certainly contributed. In its pages, the readers could find a thrilling adventure of larger-than-life figures, of kings and seers, of Providence and Doom, and a text with tinges of Walter Scott in which the wickedness of the antagonists only served as a contrast to the humility and Christian zeal of its main characters.

Navarro Villoslada's success did not, however, merely stand on top of the epic's own worth. While "Amaya" might have been packed with memorable episodes and remarkable personalities, there was much of the period's *Zeitgeist* flowing freely through its many lines, and many readers who, in the wake of the *foral* abolition of 1876, desperately sought out the reassurance its pages provided. The main crux of the argument, after all, was precisely that old grudges ought to be parked, and that "Basques and Goths"—placeholders for contemporary Spaniards—"must unite to create the Christian kingdom, and with it, peace."[3] Everything, from the setting at the outset of the Reconquista to its fervent Catholicism, without glossing over its overt and furious anti-Semitism, seemed calculated to pander to the tastes of a generation of *fuero*-fetishizing Western Pyreneans suddenly estranged from the object of their desire. Even Vasco-Iberianism, an eleventh-hour attempt at salvaging the notion of the Western Pyreneans as the first Spaniards, featured prominently in it.[4] Spain and the Basque provinces, or so "Amaya" took pains to assure, were distinct, yet entirely compatible realities. And so, just like the pagan Amagoya was presented as the last exemplar of a species approaching the edges of extinction, with her cause a long-lost one and her resistance, pathetic and doomed, so too were Gothic kings, in their attempts at stamping out Basque liberties, cast as equally misguided. In the eyes of the *fuerists*, heirs to a venerable tradition, the Basques could never—had never—been curbed by the sword. "Those whom you see as so rebellious, untamed, and wild—when left in peace, in freedom, and to their own ways—become a people of children who amuse themselves singing and dancing in the meadows."[5] The message was clear: Restore the *fueros*, and everything would be right.

There were some who, in reading "Amaya" and similar historical novels which dealt with a mystified Basque antiquity, would extract from their pages a very different conclusion.

In September 1902, Bilbao trembled in anticipation of the visit of the king of Spain. Public buildings, balconies, streetlights, fences, all were garlanded with flags and flowers. Newspapers filled their pages with every detail of the preparations, and the climate of elation was compounded by an entire program of public spectacles and entertainment for the citizens organized by the city council. In the Arenal, it was a show of weirdly shaped, multicolored balloons. In the Old Square, a pyrotechnic display starring a bull-headed cart whose horns spewed a gleaming cascade over the crowds. Biscayne authorities, albeit in a more institutionalized and respectable fashion, also took part in the celebrations. At their orders, a massive timber frame, flanked by two actual-size lion sculptures and two dragons and garnished with dozens of white and red-light bulbs, had been installed on the riverside. In it, it was possible to discern the coat of arms of Spain, and on top of it the motto *Viva el Rey Alfonso XIII*. A sign of deference for a monarch, who—as the president of the Deputation of Biscay declared—had ever since his youth been "notorious" for his "interest in the growth of this province's industry and prosperity." A prosperity, naturally, that not only benefited the locals. The royal boat, as it made its way up the waters of the Nervion toward Bilbao, would also be greeted by a red and yellow placard set in place by the British *Orconera Iron Ore Company*. In it, written in English, the sovereign could read "Welcome to King Alfonso XIII."[6]

While representatives of public institutions and private corporations alike salivated at the scent of opportunity the royal visit promised, there were those who awaited it for very different reasons. "On Thursday the King is coming to Bilbao. The entire city is in turmoil, gathering signatures to request my release. . . . People are very stirred up. . . . If they do not grant me freedom now, I think the King's farewell won't be very warm."[7] No one could blame the convict for harboring such hopes. For more than two months he had been kept in custody in expectation of either a trial or his liberation. However, none of them had yet come. The king's visit, for all the certainties of the prisoner, would likewise lapse without a trace of the so-anticipated discharge. It was, his friends and family agreed, a harsh punishment for the grievous crime of sending a telegram. But it was a punishment whose roots, as Sabino Arana Goiri knew well, went much, much deeper than that.

Sabino—or Sabin, as he would have no doubt preferred—was, at the time of writing this letter, not yet forty40. He was the eighth child of a well-to-do, fervently Catholic family from Abando which had had some fortune in the world of shipbuilding and which had reinvested the benefits in land properties. Santiago, the father, had also reached the post of mayor of the town prior to its absorption by Bilbao in 1890 and had even been nominated as deputy in the General Assembly of Biscay. However, in addition to these entrepreneurial adventures, Santiago had also proven to be a devoted Carlist. In 1872, as war was brewing in the provinces, he had sheltered members of the Pretender's high command in his house and had even bought weapons and supplies in London for the Carlist battalions. Laudable exertions, all of them, which had not failed in putting the entire family in a compromised position. The young Sabino had spent his first years exiled in Bayonne, and only in September of 1876, with the conflict concluded and the *foral* system abolished, had he managed to come back to Biscay. By then, however, the economic circumstances of the family had suffered a stark downgrade. While they remained affluent enough to sustain themselves with ease, they now encountered many erstwhile open doors and avenues of enrichment closed to them. In the ardent heart of the teen Sabino, the experience must have planted the seeds of a profound hatred for the governing liberal regime.[8]

The young man had then grown up to become a committed Catholic and, as was common in late century bourgeois circles, a protective family man. In his letters, especially the ones addressed to his sisters or to Nicolasa, the peasant girl that he would one day marry, Sabino always appeared a tender and attentive person. "I love you, Nikole"—he once confessed to his fiancée—"just as you are now, without adding nor taking anything away."[9] At other times, such emotional attachments, rather than bringing him pleasure, appeared to have almost taken him to an early grave. In 1883, after his father's death, Sabino had fallen ill from sadness. In 1888, when it came the turn for his mother to pass away, he once again was forced to stay in bed.

And yet, for all that his correspondence lent credence to those who saw the young man from Abando as a loving and caring son, brother, and husband, it sporadically also uncovered a very different facet of his character. On those occasions, the younger of the Aranas could be a determined, confrontational, and almost authoritarian individual. "Don't call me Sabino, but Sabin"—he would instruct Nicolasa—"my name in *Euskera* has in your lips a special kind of sweetness. Yours write always with *k*."[10] But even the high standards he applied to others came, in the end, from a place of love. Fearful of the Almighty as he was, Sabino had come to learn that only through sacrifice could anything like true victory ever be attained—and he was more than willing to become a martyr himself.

> Between living with that material comfort in our little corner of Iturburu, and living a life of toil and hardship far from our land and separated from our relatives, never again able to see these mountains and shores, I prefer the latter—if that is the only way I can fulfill the duty God has imposed on me: to show my brothers of the same race the only path that can lead them to save their homeland.[11]

The Bilbao into which Sabino Arana had been born and in which he would spend most of his life was, in a sense, as Janus-faced as the young man. No longer could it boast, as a British traveler in 1823 had described—and despite the insidious presence of "numberless insects of all kinds, with rats and mice"—to be "the cleanest town in Spain."[12] For centuries, its streets had been packed with shops and traders. Hundreds of wool sacks, after arriving in the city from across Spain, had awaited in the Arenal the moment of being brought aboard the lazy vessels on the Nervion to their destination in Flanders or England. The river itself had been brimming with tiny boats like nutshells and the buildings of the old town, four or five stories high, had doubled down as residences, warehouses, stores, offices, and workshops for its inhabitants. And yet, the crisis of the century had not spared this Biscayne trade hub. The rapid succession of wars—against England, against France, against other Biscaynes—had seen the commercial standing of Bilbao plunge into the abyss. The wool no longer paid the bills; the ironworks, most of them hardly altered since the times of the Parientes, were insufficient to make up for the difference. Incapable of paying the skyrocketing rents imposed by its narrow municipal boundaries and the greed of the *mayorazgo* class, the demand for new housing and industry—which could have revitalized the town—rotted unattended. Even shipwrights like Santiago Arana had been, by the mid-nineteenth century, reduced to the construction and repair of old-fashioned sailing ships, which in the rest of Europe were being substituted for steamboats. Bilbao, wherever one might fix the gaze, toyed with obsolescence.[13]

Fast forward to the last decade of the century, and the gloomy picture had been massively altered—for better or worse. After the absorption of large territories in the villages of Begoña and Abando, the city had escaped its suffocating limits, and not only there. Across the river, a massive new neighborhood had been built from scratch, exhibiting luxurious apartments and villas and all kinds of modern comforts unheard of in the craggy old town, while a network of train rails fastened the city to nearby factories and holiday spots. Not for nothing, Bilbao had revived to be regarded as the "El Dorado of Spain."[14] "The river here is thronged now by ships of all nations"—the English traveler Ellen Borges would write in 1872—"the largest seem to be steamers, but they are all here on the same errand. The cargoes they bring are various; coals from England, cod, or 'baccalau' from Newfoundland, timber from Norway; but they all carry back the same burden—iron, iron, iron."[15]

The sturdy metal had been the defining export of the region ever since the Middle Ages. But never during the long centuries in which Biscay had been governed by its *fuero* had anything like the massive boom in its trade attained the scale it had now that the latter had been abolished. The elimination of the obstacles the provincial system had set up upon the export of iron ore—paired with the exquisite quality of the raw material in Biscay—had created a feverish climate of free-for-all.[16] Huge furnaces like dark fingers cast their shadows over the hills. On the shores of the Nervion, mines, industries, docks, warehouses, shipyards, and train stations all vied with the rapidly dwindling rural exploitations for space.[17] So, too, did workers. If Bilbao had 17,969 inhabitants according to a census carried out in 1860, by 1910 the number had grown to an unbelievable 93,536.[18] Nearby towns underwent similarly staggering transformations. Baracaldo saw its population multiply by eight, as did Santurce; Portugalete's shot up from 1,527 to 5,663—and there was, of course, the mind-boggling case of Sestao: in 1860 a small hamlet of 341 which, fifty years later, housed almost 12,000 individuals.[19] But, where did these extraordinary increases come from? A figure might shed some light over what had happened. For by the time Sabino Arana had reached adulthood, of all individuals living in Bilbao, one in three had been born outside Biscay.[20]

Foreigners had recently discovered in the Western Pyrenees an appealing destination. The Euskarophile Antoine d'Abbadie, in building for himself a picturesque holiday cottage on a promontory overseeing the beach of Hendaye in 1864, might have been a trailblazer, but he was hardly the only one. Even before the first Carlist war, San Sebastian was already a preferred destination for the Madrid elites, who sought a respite from the scorching summer sun of the capital. Royals, too, would occasionally pay the city a visit, and the affluence of distinguished outsiders would only increase after 1854, when Emperor Napoleon III and his wife Eugenia chose the nearby Biarritz for their holidays.[21] However, it was not only blue-blooded aristocrats that found the treasures of the region endearing. "Guipuzcoa has highly renowned spas and seaports, which more than one hundred thousand visitors frequent during the summer season—some seeking relief from their ailments, and others looking to rest and enjoy the pleasant climate of this region, and to regain strength to resume their usual occupations."[22] An entire circuit of bathhouses dotted the hinterland of the province, and a plethora of guides for travelers, in Spanish and other languages, publicized the charms—and dangers—that awaited those pursuing the best deals. In San Sebastian, hotels and restaurants made sure to offer not the "never very palatable" local food, but the distinguished *cuisine á la Française* that suited a gentleman.[23] A French connection that the new streets of the town, crisscrossing at regular intervals the plains that stretched south of the old walled city, only reaffirmed. With its boulevards, its enormous casino, and the fantasy-like silhouette of the royal chateau on the shoreline, the dwellers of San Sebastian could feel proud when the newly arrived foreigner, baffled by the view, would exclaim that "it was not a Spanish town," for, in a sense, it was not. Instead, it was "the cheerful city of northern Spain—of industrious, commercial, and wealthy Spain, shining with beauty like its lovely Basque women; active and proud like its Basque men, with their high foreheads and direct gaze."[24] A "petit Paris," if you like—but with its feet on the sea.

Mass tourism brought activity, expenditure, and investment to the region, but it also produced, in the eyes of some, a sort of relaxation. Progress, with its straight paved avenues, its railways, its restaurants, might have opened for economically depressed fishing villages like Fuenterrabia or Zarauz the road to a new future. But what kind of future—contemporaries wondered—was this? "In the past, castles were built; more recently, temples; today, casinos. Morality is declining, while freedom moves into the open field."[25] These commentators agreed in regarding the modern world as an unstoppable force, but they were not so sure about it being a positive one. In San Sebastian, while tourists halted to admire the beauty of the new town and the spectacle of the sunrays bathing the bay of the Concha, some locals lamented the loss of "our prosaic yet healthy food" in favor of that "indigestible French *charcouterie*."[26] "Sieges, fires, and assaults . . . have been replaced by sieges and assaults on guesthouses, inns, and hotels by some 80,000 visitors who come to see us during the months of July, August, and September."[27]

Even politicians in high places, for all that they were no doubt cashing in on the development of these attractions, might occasionally display a concern for what this might mean for the country's identity. A fear that had prompted provincial authorities to sponsor the works of anthropologists, historians, and artists, so that "the memory of what we once were [could] serve as an effective incentive for us to always prove ourselves worthy of our honorable past and of our venerable traditions."[28] Back in the age of the Carlist wars, propagandists, in their intellectual struggle against the evils of modernity, had fetishized every minor detail—the law, the character, the language—of the traditional society they wished to uphold.[29] But that world was now gone. What remained was a rearguard, pessimistic attempt at preserving as much as possible of what was being lost. And this seemed, all things considered, all that could be done for the proud inheritance of Guipuzcoa.

If this was the case in what was still, despite its growing appeal, the playground of aristocratic ladies and gentlemen, well-schooled in the conduct proper to decent and cultured individuals, what could an industrial powerhouse like Bilbao expect? There, too, one could encounter posh restaurants and ample avenues, but their targets were not necessarily the scions of distinguished families, but rather those most favored by their city's enrichment. For the rest—the mass of workers, cooks, servants, plumbers, and stevedores, among others—conditions were much, much harsher. Crammed in insalubrious ghettos and covered by the debilitating mantle of a perennial smog, migrants from nearby regions—Guipuzcoa and Rioja, Burgos and Santander—led an existence that could only be described as appalling by even the lowest of standards. So deplorable were these slums, in fact, that all throughout Europe only in Saint Petersburg, in distant Russia, could comparably awful mortality rates be found.[30] The city, lively though it certainly had grown to be, had paid for this a high price indeed. That of becoming, for thousands and thousands of newcomers looking for a chance at improvement, a hellhole.

And a hellhole which, in the early 1890s, some—among them Sabino Arana—believed was about to engulf the rest of Biscay. "With that . . . invasion, . . . you are corrupting Biscayne society. For it is a comet that brings nothing but filth in its wake and foretells only calamities: impiety, all kinds of immorality, blasphemy, crime, free thought, unbelief, socialism, anarchism . . . all of that is its doing."[31] This was perhaps a predictable response. The young man from Abando, after all, had been raised in a tradition—Carlism—that put a premium on keeping things the way these had always been. This, by definition, could not but oppose the scale of the social and demographic transformation now taking place around the Nervion. Arana's opinions mirrored the views, not of the mythical heroes of *fuerist* imagination that populated the pages of Navarro Villoslada's "Amaya," but those of their rivals. It was the pagan Amagoya's obdurate stubbornness that appeared dearest to his heart. Strolling along the shoreline, leaving behind barbed wire fences, mounds of coal, and piles of rusted machinery, Sabino must have weighed heavily the options available, if any remained, to turn back the clock—and he must have despaired. To believe that anything could go back to what it had been before 1876 was a utopia. Not even the restoration of the liberties to which lifelong advocates of the *fueros* clung so dearly could hope to reverse the pollution, moral and otherwise, that now suffocated Bilbao. Each new worker admitted to toiling for a foreign mining company, every newly arrived girl made to serve as a maiden for a wealthy family: These were only nails in the already lifeless body of Biscay all the same. And not necessarily because these people were migrants. Not even because most of them were poor. It was because—most damningly, perhaps—they were overwhelmingly Spaniards.

To pour venom upon outsiders and their customs had been a mainstay of *foral* rhetoric that dated back, at least, to the times of Larramendi. And yet, in the years that had followed the abolition of the traditional laws of the provinces, such scornful comparisons had grown increasingly more frequent and intense. Especially among the most radical *fuerist* factions, the idea that Guipuzcoa, Biscay, Alava, and Navarre were an "Euskarian family" wronged by a succession of Spanish governments was one that found more support each passing day. For this "fundamentalist" clique—whose members used to meet from 1878 onward in the *Sociedad Euskalerria* of Bilbao—"there [was] only one way to be a *fuerist* and that way [came] down to being uncompromising": uncompromising about the restoration of the *foral* order, and uncompromising about the brotherhood of all Basque provinces.[32] Two objectives that, for one reason or another, were simultaneously hindered by the action of Spanish parties and institutions and their pernicious influence on the local population. "Castilian politics, then, must keep us perpetually divided under the labels of liberals, Carlists, and democrats; only Basque-Navarrese politics can unite us all under the common name of *fuerists*."[33]

A call for consensus that echoed the soon-to-be King García's attempts in "Amaya" at carving out a Christian identity out of the divisions between Goths and Basques. But one which, on special junctures like the anniversary of the *foral* abolition, could veer perilously toward a contemptuous view of the opponent. At times, these outbursts of frustration might take the shape of tendentious comparisons between the peoples of Madrid—ignorant, "incapable of spiritual life" and, most repulsively, prone to "concubinage, venal love, and illegitimate children"—and the education and morality of these Western Pyreneans—a result, of course, of the "*foral* regime [they] lost."[34] On other occasions the complaint was directed instead to Spanish peoples in general. "For it was a golden dream for all Spaniards, especially since the beginning of this century, to strip these sister provinces of their wise liberties and of their own institutions."[35] Articles such as these, which imagined Spanish politicians and audiences alike partaking in a concerted effort to deprive the Basque provinces of their ancient system of government, must have sown the seeds of a deep-rooted animosity in those who read them. The reasoning behind them, however, was pretty simple. After all, for members of a group that had thrived under the wing of the *foral* system, the new landscape, marked as it was by mass migration of foreign voters, the electoral domination of Spanish parties, and the agreement of local politicians with their counterparts in Madrid, could not help but appear a most hostile environment to prosper in—and one, therefore, that had to be rejected in earnest. "Spanish-style elections!"—these die-hard *fuerists* would lament,

> Well, now we're happy. Never mind that we drag the chains of slavery; that every day the whip of arbitrariness strikes our face; that our *fueros* are dead—those blessed *fueros* that made the Basque people the greatest, freest, and happiest in the world. Never mind that our homeland is fading, and that in its convulsions it draws ever closer to the abyss, into which it will tumble at last.[36]

At times, the contrast between Castile and the Basque provinces was painted in tones that only tangentially touched on the political. Landscape comparisons, for instance, were a favorite of Romantic sensibilities. That was the case of Arturo Campión, a radical *fuerist* from Pamplona, who would address the Pyrenees as follows: "Holy mountains that raise your misty peaks to the sky, never under your shadow were faint-hearted spirits born! The iron from your core passed into souls and shone in history."[37] Compared to these sentiments, sprouting as they did from a view that inflamed the sublime instincts of the poet, how different was the impact of the Castilian countryside! Confronted with "the barren mountains, the yellowish fields . . . , or the thirsty and scorched land whose every ugliness is brought into relief by the sun's relentless fire," any elevated soul shrank and withered.[38] Castile was the herald of a destitute wasteland; the Western Pyrenees, on the other hand, was the dwelling of awe-inspiring wonders. The parallels with the unfavorable portrayal of Castilians penned by Chaho were unmistakable: "serfs under the Visigoths, slaves under the Moors . . . ; you are only a herd of men, penned in on uncultivated lands."[39]

And if it was sometimes the task of the artist to prove this point, it was on other occasions the scientist's turn to step in. Campión, a cultured and erudite individual attuned to the most up-to-date intellectual currents of Europe, might have had the heart of a bard, but he was equally at home in bringing in defense of his beliefs arguments taken from archaeology, philology, or even phrenology. In his opinion, and in that of many of his most fervent colleagues, the size of a cranium reinforced conclusions extracted from the analysis of a word.[40] And so, when he—an inhabitant not of the industrialized surroundings of Bilbao but of the somewhat peripheral Pamplona—complained about Spanish migrants saying that they brought "blasphemy, switchblades, indecent dances, and vulgar examples" to Navarre, he was only contributing to a wider debate about the debasement of a pristine world of virtue.[41] "The Euskarian type is losing ground. The tide is rising; the corrupting waters of assimilation push their silt up to the peaks of the high mountains . . . the decline of the Euskarian type in Navarre represents a tremendous fall in the level of social, family, and individual morality among our popular classes."[42]

No *fuerist* author, however,—with the exception, perhaps, of the *sui generis* Chaho—had ever dared to venture as far as did Sabino Arana. Whereas previous polemicists had charged against what they perceived as the Castilianization of the provinces, now the man from Abando identified the source of the Biscayne malady with the unrestrained advent of Spaniards of any kind. These *maketos*—as Arana, employing a derogatory slang, called them—were in his eyes the spearhead of a carefully crafted project aimed at stamping out the Lordship's liberties. And not only them. For if Larramendi had once, more than a century earlier, denounced the great local families, with their powdered wigs and their scientific gatherings, as the necessary vehicles for the spreading pollution to extend, so too now Sabino pointed toward those "treacherous Biscaynes" that had, in accepting the compromise of 1876, put the future of their country in jeopardy. In Navarro Villoslada's epic, Amagoya had once proclaimed that she hated Goths less than she did "the wicked Basques."[43] Now, the most radical of Basque thinkers would espouse the verdict of the matriarch. "There has been Spanishness among our rulers; Spanishness among our historians; Spanishness among our jurists; and the Biscayne people, in general, have been inadvertently infected with Spanishness, as they drew their knowledge from these sources."[44] The "virus" was, in fact, so contagious, that already Bilbao, that most populous metropole, belonged "no longer to the Biscaynes, but to the *maketos*."[45]

Had this been all, little would have singled Sabino out from his various fundamentalist counterparts. And yet, a massive mental gap separated what men like Larramendi had espoused and the messages penned by Arana in his articles and editorials. After all, the old Jesuit, its irate complaints about the Castilians notwithstanding, had not ever once doubted that "every Guipuzcoan would rather have an arm cut off than suffer this separation from Castile."[46] Similarly, in their articles published after 1876, affiliates of *Euskalerria* defended their goal of patriotic regeneration as a means of contributing "most effectively to the peace and well-being of Spain."[47] No such words would ever come out of Arana's lips. In fact, he most likely would have regarded them as proof of how deep the course of the infection truly ran. "Biscay"—he would defiantly proclaim—"has never been Spanish—not by race, nor by customs, nor by language, not even by territory. . . . The Spaniards, the Spanishized liberal Biscaynes, and the liberals: these are the enemies of my Homeland."[48]

Herein lay, in all its red-hot nakedness, the molten core of his message. Because if, admittedly, Sabino had been raised to be a Carlist just like his father, he had shortly after returning to Bilbao embraced a much more radical path: separatism. As he would much later relate, this had not come to the seventeen-year-old as a rejection of his erstwhile devotion, but rather as the culmination of an existential crisis triggered by an intellectual dispute between him and his older brother Luis.

> He presented me with so many historical and political arguments to convince me that Biscay was not Spain, and he made such an effort to show me that Carlism—even as a means to achieve not total isolation and a complete break from Spain, but simply the return to the traditional lordship—was not only unnecessary but inconvenient and harmful, that my mind, recognizing that my brother knew more history than I and was not one to deceive me, entered a phase of doubt.[49]

And what a phase it was. Coming back to Abando in the summer of 1888 after a stay of almost six years in Barcelona—during which he had tried unsuccessfully to graduate in Law—Sabino had made sure to let everyone know that he had not wasted his time. He might have proven to be a subpar university student, but he had at least vindicated himself in the study of all things Biscayne, from its customs and its language to its history and its laws. Coming as he did from an affluent family—which, as was usual among members of their class, were Spanish-speakers—Sabino had had to learn *Euskera* from scratch. It was during these years that he had come to acknowledge that Biscay was not, and had never been, a part of Spain. Submitting articles to various newspapers, Arana started to make his radical stance known in radical *fuerist* circles and then, in 1892, he made his grand entrance to the political arena. First, he published a polemic booklet called *Biscay for its independence*; then, some months later, in a meeting with other sympathizers of the cause, Arana presented his separatist ideology to his peers. On June 8, 1893, he set in motion *Bizkaitarra*—"Biscayne"—a newspaper he founded, owned, and directed, and which would quickly become the preferred outlet for all separatist opinions.[50] By 1895, he had already created his own political party.

One might define Arana's approach to Basque identity as an ideology of moral animadversion, and the way he conceived of a "Biscayne race" played a key role in that claim. Unlike the Navarrese Campión, whose ideas of race bore the indelible perfume of that cutting-edge Social Darwinism that was making inroads in Europe and elsewhere, Arana's conceptualization of the term was instead founded upon concepts that reeked of half-updated Tubalism.[51] "Our race remains a virgin jungle for scientific investigation, a true island in the midst of humanity. The Spanish race, on the other hand, is a Latin-Gothic-Arabic product with faint traces of Phoenician, Greek, and Carthaginian, which retains not a trace of the peninsula's original race—which was ours."[52] It was impossible not to see in this a trace of Humboldt and Chaho. The racial purity of the Basques stood, in his imagination, as the direct opposite to the debilitating mixture of the Spanish race: "A great number of them seem to be irrefutable proof of Darwin's theory, for more than men they resemble apes, little less beastly than the gorilla: do not look in their faces for any expression of human intelligence or of any virtue; their gaze reveals only idiocy and brutality."[53]

To prevent this corruption of the body and the mind from spreading across Biscay had been the guiding drive of the young Arana ever since his fateful conversation with his brother. Unfortunately, the battle against the Spanish disease was more than half-lost. Everywhere he looked, Sabino saw the mass of the proletariat, trapped in their insalubrious ghettos; he grinned at the spectacle of Spanish parties bribing their way into local and provincial institutions; he despaired at the submissiveness of Biscaynes, rich and humble, who sacrificed their ancient uprightness for the chance of assimilating with the "vilest and most despicable race in Europe."[54] In this he mirrored that ancient seer who, in contact with foreign customs, had "at times wanted to fly, as if crossing a plague-stricken land, and at others stopped suddenly, as if afraid to walk among vipers."[55]

Uprooting so entrenched a malady from the social body would require an equally radical treatment. And yet, before any such remedy could be prescribed, the causes that had brought the erstwhile Lordship to this deplorable condition had to be identified and eradicated. This meant, for starters, cutting off relations with Spain in every sense—political, linguistic, cultural. But so too were any disease vectors within the local tradition, precisely because they allowed the contagion to take hold in the first place, next on the chopping block. After all, never—or so Sabino Arana believed—would the Spanish have triumphed in penetrating Biscay's immune system had locals not surrendered their own right to self-defense. This, in turn, made the task of inculcating this message back into their minds an even more urgent one. "Biscaynes"—Sabino, taking the role of the stern doctor, would warn—"Biscay is perishing . . . and you are the ones killing her!"[56]

A handful of radical *fuerists*, it was true, had already toyed with the notion of Castilians having co-opted certain native institutions to use them as spearheads to introduce their pernicious influence in the Western Pyrenees. One such proponent had been that well-known polymath, Arturo Campión, who had explained that an all-too-ready tendency of Pamplonese and Navarrese monarchs to import foreign models of kingship had massively contributed to the alienation of the Western Pyrenean peoples.[57] But in all, it remained an article of faith shared by most associates of *Euskalerria* and more moderate wings of the *fuerist* clique alike that the true watershed in Basque history had been the abolition of the *foral* order after the end of the last war in 1876.[58] A self-evident date, of course, and one which required little justification. Was it so weird, after all, that members of *fuerist* families, who had dictated the destinies of the provinces during most of the century and had handsomely benefited from it, would have identified the end of their dominion with the source of all problems?

Sabino Arana, on the other hand, and for all that he might have inherited many tropes from these fundamentalists, remained at heart the son of his father—and for this reason an outsider. This, which on many occasions had—and would—work to his disadvantage, placed him in an enviable position when it came to diagnosing the faults of the previous regime. And his diagnosis was, in fact, damning. To say that Spaniards had only managed to corrupt Biscay since 1876 onward was to exhibit an awful short-sightedness, since "what is historically and legally accurate and precise is that Spain has conquered and subjugated the Basque people in this century."[59] If anything, 1839, when the first amendments had been made to the *foral* system, had a much stronger case going for it as the first demonstration of Spanish meddling in the Western Pyrenees.[60] But Arana did not stop there. Since Larramendi had already, a century prior to the Carlist wars, denounced the importation of foreign customs into the region, the origin of the poison had to predate it. And at long last, after long research, Sabino had uncovered its source. The Lordship first established by Jaun Zuria—just like the monarchy in Navarre—had marked the first bout of Spanishness in Biscay. The selfish interests of these lords in Castilian politics had contaminated their character and that of their people. Once the title of King of Castile and that of Lord of Biscay had befallen the same dynasty, the idea of the two territories as part of a single nation, ruled by a single monarch, had put down roots among Biscaynes. So had begun "a circle of decadence of ten centuries" culminating "in this cursed century of slavery and darkness."[61] Amagoya, once again, thundered on top of its mountain.

By furnishing a history of an ideal Biscay perennially embattled with its Spanish enemy, Sabino Arana bathed the main constituents of the *foral* discourse in the waters of a subversive stream. The myth of a race of unconquered warriors, perched upon the heights of their rugged homeland and fending off the advance of the foe, came no longer to provide a point of origin for the Spanish Reconquista or to the distinctiveness of

Western Pyreneans. The kind of complacent ideology for the Basque origins of Spain that the tale of "Amaya" had gilded with a legendary patina was, in fact, turned entirely on its head. Sabino now reframed these battles as primordial events of resistance against the corruption of the Biscayne soul. While generations of provincial historians had taken for granted that the region was the shield that guarded the peninsula and its dwellers, as the first and most ancient among the Spaniards, now these verdicts were proven wrong. Nothing—not race, not government, not language—tied the northerners to the rest. Rather, what stood revealed was an almost eternal aversion. "And I am not referring to a specific class of *maketos*, but to all of them in general: all the *maketos*, aristocrats and commoners, bourgeois and proletarians, wise and ignorant, good and bad—all are enemies of our Homeland, more or less covert, but always bitter."[62]

Hatred of such a kind, because it elevated what might have otherwise been little skirmishes to the stature of clashes of transcendental significance, could paradoxically lend also a certain mystique to those it targeted. The Biscaynes—pure, religious, freeborn—and the Spanish—mixed, impious, servile—were for Sabino Arana the two sides of a single coin. And, for that very reason, the creation of an eternal *Euzkadi*—as he would baptize the Basque homeland in 1896—necessitated, for it to make sense, an equally eternal Spain. The glow of self-identification, as so frequently had done in the Western Pyrenees, could not help but occasionally bring outsiders too into more definite light.

But did this belief in the rights of an independent Biscay—or an independent *Euzkadi*, even—make Sabino Arana a nationalist? There were certainly grounds for such a claim. Dotted throughout his production, one could encounter occasional references to his project of reformation as "Biscayne nationalism."[63] Talk of nations, of peoples, of rights, and liberties was a mainstay of his abrasive rhetoric. Not that this should surprise anyone. A child of his own age, as Arana certainly was, trained in Barcelona and living in a bustling port buzzing with the sound of new and exciting ideas at that, it would have been astonishing not to encounter these popular terms scattered across his prolific writings. These were times, after all, of nationalist effervescence. A century on from the cataclysmic impact—mental and otherwise—of the French Revolution, societies in Europe and beyond were still trying to restrain the forces that this event had set loose. Statesmen and agitators across the globe were dealing with the consequences of having to adapt—just as Arana seemed to be doing—their previous patterns of identification to a new set of criteria.[64] Trust in chosen peoples, in supernatural lawgivers, in pristine, irrecoverable golden ages was giving way to an intellectual framework that divided the world into a set of homogeneous, natural communities, each one endowed with the right to rule itself in a land over which it possessed an allegedly eternal and indisputable claim.[65] These were communities, too, that resembled living organisms, for they were said to grow and develop, and to do so according to their own temperament and personality. As Katharine Coman and Elizabeth Kendall would summarize in the preface to an account of English history in 1894:

> The national traits inherited from ancestral races and the tendencies impressed by the physical features of the country give to a people its peculiar character. A nation's

> history, the sum of its achievements, is the essential expression of its individuality. Circumstance may modify its development. Propitious events may further, or hostile interference may thwart, the accomplishment of its destiny. But at no time in the history of a nation is the effect of physical environment and race inheritance wholly obscured.[66]

Arana would probably have agreed with that assertion. First off, as his historical articles showcased, he was ready to imagine the world as partitioned in watertight compartments, each one belonging to one—and only one—national group. He even confessed that "if the Spaniard would stay in his own land, we would have no reason to resent him."[67] Moreover, like many nationalist activists around the world, he also underscored the importance of popular education, especially history, as a tool for Biscaynes to gain back consciousness of their natural rights.[68] However, and owing to Biscay's "racial" makeup, his methods to determine who was a member of this community were a hard fit in the nationalist worldview. The difficulty did not reside, of course, in racism itself: for by the late nineteenth century, this kind of approach to human diversity was everywhere to be found. Instead, the problem was the overbearing significance that Sabino put upon the racial union of all Biscaynes as the main foundation of their community—and which, in his arguments much more than in those of other nationalists, came at the expense of everything else. In this, too, he was following in the footsteps of an imagined ancestor. For Amagoya, that mouthpiece of Basque intransigence, had likewise "renounce[d] the children of Aitor who do not preserve the purity of their lineage."[69]

Language, for starters, was less significant to him than race because "language—provided there is a good grammar and a good dictionary—can be restored even if no one speaks it, whereas race, on the other hand, cannot be resurrected once lost." But if this sounded perhaps like sensible pragmatism, the extent to which the survival of *Euskera* proved an afterthought in the preservation of the Biscayne race was apparent elsewhere. "If our invaders were to learn *Euskera*"—Sabino would hypothesize—"we would have to abandon it . . . and devote ourselves to speaking Russian, Norwegian, or any other language unknown to them, for as long as we remained under their rule."[70] Actually, any stark interest he might have in the preservation and spread of *Euskera*—a question which he, in fact, considered pivotal to Biscay's salvation—owed primarily to his realization that it was a tongue that almost no Spaniard had bothered to learn. Mirroring the argument made by anti-liberal factions in the early nineteenth century, Sabino thus defended that difference in language was the best means to prevent cross-contamination with foreigners. It was for this reason, and no other, that it was imperative for Biscaynes to learn and use *Euskera*, and to never—under no circumstance—teach it to the *maketos*.[71]

Sabino Arana proved, in simultaneously disdaining *Euskera* as a source of communal identity and in instrumentalizing it to serve loftier goals, an heir to the most revered traditions of the early modern provincial order. But if it was true that Western Pyrenean grandees had long been in the business of putting off the hopes of Basque speakers, it was nonetheless more unusual that they might be ready to give up their privileges too. After all, it was the unique laws of the Lordship that had allowed Biscaynes to gain an enviable position in the heyday of the empire. And it was these *fueros*, after 1876, that had come to be worshipped as embodiments of the true soul of the land.

But if these were limits no *fuerist* would ever dare to trespass, these were for Arana, again, only means to a nobler end. He had already denounced the lord's position as a source of alienation, but there were other institutions—like the charters and franchises that had governed urban life in Biscay since the Middle Ages—that he considered just as pernicious.[72] Only in the rural countryside, in that primordial, idealized landscape so praised by provincial authorities to defend the *Hidalguía*, had the corruption brought by foreigners been contained. But, yet again, even the virtuous codes and rulings penned by this community of freedom-lovers would be rendered meaningless if the preservation of the Biscayne race was not attained. "If we were given the choice between, on one hand, the total and absolute death of Biscay . . . and on the other hand, a *maketo* Biscay, independent and governed by the laws of our forefathers, possessing our language and inheriting our history, we would choose the former."[73]

If there was one aspect, however, that distanced Arana decisively from nationalist ideologues around the world this was the way in which his notions of race interplayed with the territory itself. Whereas a main tenet of nationalism as an ideology preached the conundrum formed by one community, one government, and one land, the last of these elements was for Arana wholly insignificant in comparison to the first. In this, Sabino was a prisoner of his own ideological background. Essayists, back in the late sixteenth century, had once defended the nobility of all Biscaynes "not because the estate itself grants nobility, but because the ancient and well-known nobility of its time-honored owners has imprinted that quality upon it."[74] Now, more than three centuries on, a similar reasoning filled in the pages of *Bizkaitarra*:

> What does it matter to us to have a free Biscay here among these mountains, as opposed to having it elsewhere? It would only matter to us as much as it matters to someone who, when moving house, is forced to leave the home where they were born and raised; and it would matter to us just as little as that person cares about their move. . . . On the contrary: if there were a Biscay, yes, free, but made up of the Spanish race, would it truly be Biscay? Only on maps . . . So, in that case, only the name 'Biscay' would remain, simply because the territory once occupied by the Biscayne nation would still be there. It would, in truth, be better for an earthquake to sink that territory, so that the name would also disappear.[75]

The racial community of Arana, then, shared no necessary ties with the land it inhabited, beyond the incidental one of its mountains having rendered the whole task of its defense a more manageable one to undertake. Biscay was for Sabino not a place in space, but rather a community of peoples bound together by their descent from a mysterious and primordial seed and therefore capable of keeping a purity of heart unattainable to the fallen races that surrounded them. That he was able to imagine the Basques—and more specifically, the Biscaynes—in this manner owed less to the aftereffects of any revolutionary process than to the accounts of early modern authors that had for centuries publicized the provincials as the children of Tubal.

See them from this angle, and Sabino's works then cast a very different shadow. Rather than a nationalist, it appeared instead as one of the last religious reformers, a Moses—following a common comparison between the Basques and the Israelites after 1876—leading a chosen people out of their Spanish slavery to restore them to their primordial cleanliness, for "otherwise, here, in this land we tread, it is not possible to work for the glory of God."[76] Everything—language, laws, independence even—was to be sacrificed to this task. And if, as a consequence of his labor, he was to suffer censorship, or disdain, or even imprisonment—then so be it. At times, in fact, Sabino seemed to have delighted in wearing, with calculated stoicism, the shroud of the martyr. In the months of his imprisonment in 1902, for example, he would make a show of his abnegation. "I do not resist—nor will I resist—the mistreatment I have faced or may yet face, because, for now, we nationalists must lower our heads and suffer."[77] He knew, after all, that it was a prophet's destiny to face contempt in his own country, and among his own kind, and in his own house. A thought that did not prevent his followers from worshipping him as "a Basque Jesus" and, looking up to his creed, address him as their "Teacher."[78]

An exaggeration, perhaps, for Arana's preaching owed much, not only to his talents but also to an enormous organizational effort. In addition to *Bizkaitarra* and other separatist journals, the message of his *Partido Nacionalista Vasco* (PNV, "Basque Nationalist Party") was supplied to the population through a variety of means. These ranged from private clubs which only admitted racially Basque members to dance and theater courses—Arana himself wrote two plays—in which "true" Basque customs and traditions were first purified and then exhibited for the education of fellow countrymen.[79] Not for nothing, nationalist activists considered music a favorite means of broadcasting their doctrines for, as they believed, "before reasonings reach the heart, the sounds of a *txistu* do."[80] Articles in Spanish and *Euskera* on the most varied of topics were routinely penned by Arana's closest collaborators to "honor the Fatherland, foster nationalism, and serve God."[81] Even mountain hiking, a favorite pastime in the rural countryside, was taken advantage of as a vehicle of proselytization.[82]

In all of this, just as in many other aspects, the "Teacher" himself had proven to be the leading light for his disciples. In July 1894, mere months after having set his first journal in motion, Arana had already planned out a recreational society in which the many Basque speakers residing in Bilbao and its surroundings could "gather and establish close bonds of friendship among themselves."[83] Directly inspired by the beliefs of his main promoter, the statutes of this club aimed at creating a virtuous community of patriots. So virtuous, in fact, that it only took partaking in a *fuerist* demonstration, or otherwise conducting oneself without regard to the appropriate moral standards, to merit expulsion.[84] Centers shaped on the example of this first *Euskaldunen Batzokija*—in *Euskera*, "meeting-place of the Basque-speakers"—would soon come to dot the entire length of Biscay.[85]

This apparent obsession with creating networks of socialization owed much to the fact the endeavor Arana attempted to set in motion was not—unlike that gloomy *fuerism* always sobbing over on the rags of a lost Arcadia—a backward-looking project. Instead, it was a decisively progressive one. In this, more than in anything else, the young man from Abando proved a revolutionary. Generations of provincial ideologues had attempted, from the times of the first Carlist war and even before, to conduct a rearguard action against the chipping onslaughts of a succession of Spanish governments. Following the example of Amagoya, who sang ancient hymns while remaining cloistered in her deep valley, they too had made a habit out of preserving what could be salvaged of their tradition. Only such a fetish for doomed resistance could explain their fixation with historical episodes, ancient songs, and the restoration of the *foral* order.

Arana's projects for *Euzkadi*, on the other hand, went much further than mere lamentations. While he might have inherited much from *fuerist* politicians and writers, he differed from the latter mostly in his starting point. In his view, the men that populated *fuerist* clubs like the *Euskalerria* society in Bilbao had wrongly identified their fellow Basques as a race of virtue, unjustly undergoing a process of acculturation. The truth was, instead, that *Euzkadi* was almost lost for good: unconscious of the danger and invaded by the *maketos*. The patriotic regeneration that *fuerist* journals ceaselessly thundered about, rather than a political affair to be carried out in the corridors of ministries or in the parliament in Madrid, had to begin in the provinces themselves. It had to be undertaken inside the house of the peasant and in the mind of the worker "in order to shake off the yoke of slavery and vigorously and with dignity restore the Fatherland."[86] It was, for lack of a better word, a movement. And just like any movement, its success rested, ultimately, on its ability to never come to a halt.

Not even the most devoted of Messiahs, though, was free from the occasional test of his faith. Amagoya, at the conclusion of her story, had herself despaired about the state of the world. Defeated, she had recognized the dominion of the new Christian dynasty founded by García and Amaya and, in a vain gesture of hopeless heroism, had strolled up the highest mountain of the land, there to die frozen and forgotten. Sabino, too, upon finally getting out of prison, seemed to have embraced a similar defeatism. "When I start to think"—he had some months earlier confessed to one of his confidents—"about language as well as about race, I clearly understand that they are both vanishing; everything will be gone before the century that has just begun comes to an end. The only remedy lies in money, and that is nowhere to be found."[87] Money, certainly, had been a recurrent problem for Arana and his party. This might seem paradoxical, given that Bilbao was a great metropolis and an industrial powerhouse, but the truth is that enriched magnates, who had made their fortunes in the city and abroad, were little interested in a chauvinist ideology that promised only to massively reduce the size of their internal market.[88] Only a handful of individuals from the upper middle classes, for the most part erstwhile members of the most radical wing of the *fuerist Euskalerria* society and led by the industrial magnate Ramón de la Sota, bought into the ideas of *Bizkaitarra*. Perhaps—Arana must have thought—were the most intransigent aspects of the separatist message were tuned down, such difficulties might be overcome. In 1902, therefore, he started to suggest a new idea: the creation of a political organization which would attempt to gain from the Spanish government, not outright independence, but a large measure of autonomy instead.

As it was bound to happen, the sudden change of course immediately raised eyebrows in the ranks of the PNV. Was the "Teacher" now not falling into the same kind of Spanish trap that he had so vehemently criticized in his opponents? Disagreeing voices began to rise in the separatist circles, and the risk of an internal breakout in the movement grew more real by the day. Luckily for the party's future, Arana's timely death in November 1903 put an end to this "Spanish drift." In the absence of the leader's authoritative opinion, everyone was left to believe whatever he or she found dearest in his message. Those most intransigent of separatists staunchly enshrined the memory of the undeterred and fierce Sabino of the first period. The moderates, on the other hand, adopted a less overtly confrontational approach to independence through autonomy, which they saw vindicated in the final writings of their late founder. In all, pragmatism triumphed: While the radicals could not do without the resources of the moderates, the latter knew well that their way into power depended on the people's emotional response to the irate and heated rhetoric of their most die-hard colleagues.[89] In addition, the slogan Sabino had coined for his party, *Jaungoikoa eta Lagi Zarra*—"God and the Ancient Law"—proved so fuzzy that it could very well promise to keep the various tendencies within Basque separatism under its wings. For who knew, in the wake of more than half a century of discussions about the true origins and meanings of the legal order of the ancient Basques, what exactly the "restoration of the old *fueros*" truly meant? Were these the incorruptible, untranslatable traditions of an oppressed race, contaminated by centuries of foreign intrusion? Or did they instead represent the flexible set of rulings that had allowed Western Pyreneans to adapt to the various political regimes that had surrounded them and which were abolished in 1876? The "essence of the fact," as Pedro Novia de Salcedo had put it, remained completely detached from any surface-level particulars.

And yet, some particulars proved harder to sideline than others. The question of who—and under which conditions—merited recognition as a member of the nation was too pivotal an issue to leave out in ambiguity. Arana, in carving out his ideology, had been exceedingly vague in this regard. At times, he was at home with the idea that the seven historical territories populated by Basque speakers—Biscay, Guipuzcoa, Alava, Navarre, Labourd, *Ultrapuertos*, and Soule—were part of a single "national family," whose members were "related by their race and their language, and similar in their faith, their character, and their customs."[90] His verdict resembled the views of older defenders of the *foral* world like Navarro Villoslada or Chaho, who had already imagined all Western Pyreneans as descendants from a primitive confederation founded by the patriarch Aitor.[91] More frequently, though, this kind of pan-Euskarism was tempered by more pragmatic slogans—also commonplace in *fuerist* intellectual circles—that limited true belonging in the Basque nationality to the four provinces under Spanish rule.[92] Because he imagined *Euzkadi* not in geographical, but rather in racial terms, such alternative reverence for the *Laurak bat* ("The four are one") or the *Zazpiak bat* ("The seven are one") mottos did not necessarily collide with nor require altering the rest of his views.

And yet, despite these utterances, Arana had been, first and foremost, a *Biscayne* patriot. It was for this territory that he had created a flag in 1893 and also a renewed coat of arms—appropriately "purified" with the erasure of the two wolves representing the Haro lineage.[93] The entire historical underpinning of his separatist ideology, with his condemnation of foreign lords and his rejection of the king of Spain as king of Biscay, was tailored to fit the particular circumstances of the Lordship. Even his first major publication had borne the telling—and transparent—name of "Biscay for its independence." He might have looked fondly upon the reclamations and protests of other regions, and might occasionally dream of a united country in the Western Pyrenees. But he likewise seems to have painfully accepted that the problems he faced in Biscay were vastly different in other parts of *Euskal Herria*. Racial brotherhood might perhaps unite all Basques, and yet, history seemed poised to divide them. Amagoya, on top of her mountain, had never failed to think of converted Christians like García as her blood and kin, but this had not prevented her from taking pride in being the only Basque who still clung to her illustrious father's inheritance. By the same token, Arana too believed that only in Biscay, owing to a record of victories against invaders and its status as a lordship, had such a thing as the true preservation of the ancient Basque tradition been attained. The purification of the rest of the Western Pyrenees, if it was ever to take place, would thus need to begin with the restoration of Biscay's independence, and from there to expand, little by little, to the rest.

While this might be the overall position of the "Teacher," most of his followers proved to be less maximalist in this than the late Sabino. Marinated in the undercurrents of radical *fuerism* as they were, they had come to frame the struggle of the Basques as one that pitted the degenerate Castilians, on the one hand, and the united provinces, on the other. Once again, mentions of the inhabitants of *Iparralde*, who had rarely shared in the enthusiasm their southern counterparts felt for their *foral* order, amounted to little more than lip service. Which was, of course, rather unsurprising. The PNV was, after all, a Spanish party; or, better put, it was a party whose ideological coordinates made sense within political and cultural traditions that only existed within the Spanish state. It was all about supporting or rejecting the old *foral* order, about embracing or pushing away Cantabrian or Tubalian myths, and about the need to square—or not to square—the pristine customs of an unconquered race of mysterious mountaineers with the modern necessities of a constitutional style nation-state. In none of these discussions did *Iparralde* factor in at all, just as it had hardly factored in back in the seventeenth century when its intellectuals had complained about the disinterest of their southern brethren. The northerners remained, for the leading luminaries of the PNV, what they had always been for generations and generations of Spanish-oriented provincials: the little cousin, inconsequential in its own debility, that could always be rallied but who hardly ever received any compensation for his trouble.

If this was the case with *Iparralde*, things were different regarding the other provinces. Here, Arana's successors at the head of the separatist project made sure to tread with more caution. In doing so, they proved to be the true creators, at least when it came to Guipuzcoa, Navarre, Biscay, and Alava, of Basque nationalism. It was they, after all, that transplanted Arana's aspatial notions of race and tied them indissociably to a particular and definite territory: that of the provinces themselves. Arguments and reclamations that pertained only to Biscay were slowly cast aside. Others, like the reformed laws of October 25, 1839, because they could be framed as an episode affecting all Basque territories—or those that mattered the most, at any rate—became the focus of ever-increasing adoration. *Euskera*, too, saw its status improved after the lukewarm role it had played in Arana's separatist schemes. Following on the trail of contemporary *fuerist* radicals like Antonio Campión, who had once lamented that "with the Basque language departs the Basque people, because to change one's language is to change one's soul," an assembly of nationalists proclaimed in 1908 *Euskera* "the only language of *Euzkadi*."[94] These attempts at broadening the horizons of the "Teacher's" Biscayanism seemed to have paid off quickly. In the spring of 1908, the party would extend its activities to Guipuzcoa. Three years later, in 1911, new branches were founded in Alava and Navarre. The spread of the organization in *Iparralde*, as befitted the region's marginal status, would have to wait for almost an entire century.

On May 4, 1917, Ramón de la Sota y Aburto, namesake and son of the lifelong *fuerist*-turned-nationalist, took up the charge of president of the Deputation of Biscay. As a leading figure within the moderate faction of the PNV, the party's electoral triumph appeared to vindicate that middle ground that Sabino Arana, in the final months of his life, had so polemically embraced. The new president summarized this position masterfully in his inaugural speech. "The full collective development of the race cannot be achieved within the political regime by which Biscay is governed today. It is therefore necessary that we work to radically alter it, so that in Basque affairs we may be governed by a Basque government, entirely Basque." This, of course, was nothing if not a message meticulously crafted to appeal both to the most radical separatists as well as those who still dreamed of the restoration of the ancient *fueros*. That consensus was in fact going to be a priority for the new executive was also demonstrated in his willingness to lend a hand to his opponents and together to guide "our Biscay along the path that shall lead the Basque people to the place that God has reserved for those peoples who knew how to create their own personality and their own culture."[95]

And yet, despite these most beautiful intentions, Ramón de la Sota had been inaugurated in a half-emptied room. His opponents, rather than putting up with the spectacle of a separatist becoming the highest representative of the Spanish state in the former Lordship, had simply refused to attend the ceremony. Nothing better than their boycott could illustrate the extent to which the events and developments of the previous three decades had come to define the politics of the Basque provinces. Only two years later, the writer Pío Baroja would provide a demolishing critique of the entire project of rebirth the new governing party had sought to undertake. "We want *fueros*, say the Basque nationalists, laws different from the rest of Spain. For what? What is it that you must defend? I see nothing more than that you want there to be more religious intolerance, more friars, more processions, more enthronements, and more clerical ostentation with a Judaic air."[96] In his opinion, as traditional as the invented legends so cherished by the *fuerists* or the rural society so revered by Arana were the encyclopedic horizons of illustrious men like Peñaflorida. Moreover, even within the ranks of the PNV, some now were beginning to doubt the sacrosanct authority of the motto *Jaungoikoa eta*

Lagi Zarra. Party leaders themselves were conscious of this drift away from the fervent Catholicism of its founder.

> If there were another Basque nationalist party . . . one—more liberal, for example, or less traditionalist—it is certain that the non-*Jelist* [*Jaungoikoa eta Lagi Zarra*] nationalists would go to it, as being more in tune with their feelings and ideas. If they are with us, it is because they have nowhere else to go, because [this] is today the only organized nationalist force, and because they truly are patriots, even if their patriotism is of a different kind than ours.[97]

A split, indeed, was not far in the future.

The internal divisions of the PNV, as well as the looming tensions that existed between the party and other forces within the Basque political landscape, were demonstrative of two things. The first one was Arana's and his heirs' genius in creating a powerful and multifaceted organization from scratch, capable of sheltering individuals ranging from former Carlists to radical democrats, and of rallying them, albeit uneasily, behind the flag of Basque independence—or, at the least, Basque autonomy. The second, on the other hand, evidenced the extent to which this success owed to traditions and debates inherited from the past. A surprising conclusion, perhaps. Not for nothing, Arana, in cutting the Gordian knot that for centuries had tied together the defense of the *foral* order to a staunch loyalty toward Spain, seemed to his contemporaries to have let loose vicious energies that had previously been kept under strict control. Discussions about the Basque origins of the ancient Cantabrians, or about the precise circumstances of Jaun Zuria's accession, because they only made sense within the bounds of such a discursive framework, became obsolete overnight and quickly disappeared. Gone for good alongside them, simultaneously assaulted by the Spanish parties on one side and the separatists on the other, was *fuerism* itself.

But while this was true of some traditions, other debates lingered on. Baroja, in his attack, had not made the nationalist zeal to restoring a long-lost past the target of his reproach, but rather the Christian superstition such a project entailed. In doing so, he was self-consciously opposing that precious notion—ultimately stemming from the Tubalian story—which saw the Basques as early worshippers of the Christian God. The problem, in other words, was not that the recovery of the *foral* order could not restore the Basques to their primitive traditions, but that these might not be the ones that nationalists believed them to be. "If the Basque race, instead of receiving into its innermost being a ruinous, outdated, and dead doctrine such as Catholicism, had breathed an atmosphere of freedom and thought, it might perhaps have borne ripe fruits for civilization."[98]

Herein lay a direct rejection of Sabino Arana's theocratic image of the Biscayne nation but also a criticism that went much further than that. After all, Navarro Villoslada, almost half a century earlier, had made religion the central topic of his most famous epic. Now, the totemic nature of the characters he had invented seemed to have been conjured up to life yet again. García, the virtuous king of yesterday, could pass in the new world as either for the sensible autonomist or for the vehicle of religious denigration. Amagoya, on the other hand, who he had depicted as an irredeemable and deplorable pagan, could as easily play the part of the uncompromising independentist or that of warden of the true virtues of the race. And, in the midst of these two forces, tilting toward each one of them at frequent yet unpredictable intervals, there stood Amaya, by blood a Basque and a Goth by upbringing: the perfect image of a Basque society torn between the equally terrifying prospects of a future of assimilation or a slumber in a gilded stasis.

Notes

1 Novia de Salcedo, *Defensa Histórica del Señorío de Vizcaya y Provincias de Álava y Guipúzcoa* (1851). Quoted in Juaristi, *El linaje de Aitor*, 58.

2 Yoeli-Rimmer, "Jewish Villains and Basque Heroes: Ethnic Identities and National Narratives in Francisco Navarro Villoslada's *Amaya,o los vascos del siglo VIII*," 796.

3 Navarro, *Amaya*, I, 85.

4 Navarro, 7.

5 Navarro, 58.

6 *El Nervión, Periódico independente*, September 2, 1902.

7 "Letter from Sabino Arana to Nicolasa Atxika-allende," August 30, 1902. In Agirresazkuenaga, *Barne-muinetako Sabin Arana Goiri. Gutunak I (1876–1903)*, 156–7.

8 Juaristi, *El linaje de Aitor*, 200.

9 "Letter from Sabino Arana to Nicolasa Atxika-allende," September 30, 1899. In Agirresazkuenaga, *Barne-muinetako Sabin Arana Goiri*, 53.

10 "Letter from Sabino Arana to Nicolasa Atxika-allende," October 9, 1899. In Agirresazkuenaga, *Barne-muinetako Sabin Arana Goiri*, 61.

11 "Letter from Sabino Arana to Nicolasa Atxika-allende," November 5, 1899. In Agirresazkuenaga, *Barne-muinetako Sabin Arana Goiri*, 84.

12 Bramsen, *Remarks on the North of Spain*, 54.

13 Serrano, "Paisaje e industria en el Bilbao del despegue (1860–1930)," 224–33.

14 Borges, *Vizcaya*, VII.

15 Borges, 79.

16 Urgell, "Primer Vasco Moderno," 594; Mees, *The Basque Contention*, 43.

17 Serrano, "Paisaje e industria," 238.

18 Pérez de Laborda, "La inmigración en Bilbao, 1860–1910," 150.

19 Pérez de Laborda, 151.

20 Pérez de Laborda, 161.

21 Larrinaga, "A century of Tourism in Northern Spain: The Development of High-quality Provision between 1815 and 1914," 93.

22 Lancis y Buch, *Guía general de Guipúzcoa histórico-geográfico-descriptiva, comercial é industrial*, 26.

23 Borges, *Vizcaya*, 133.

24 Planté, *San Sebastian. Notes de Voyage*, 30.

25 Laffite, *Tierra Euskara. Excursiones, cuadros, y notas de Guipúzcoa*, 61.

26 Laffite, 115.

27 Laffite, 195.

28 Rubio, *La identidad vasca en el siglo XIX*, 221–2.

29 Aller, "El Fuero como retórica. De reliquia positiva a canon identitario," 55–80.

30 Zabaltza, *Mater Vasconia*, 182.

31 *Bizkaitarra*, January 20, 1895. In Arana, *Obras Completas de Arana-Goiri'tar Sabin*, 441.

32 Fidel de Sagarnímaga, *Memorias históricas de Vizcaya* (1880). Quoted in Rubio, "Prensa política regionalista en el siglo XIX: El diario fuerista la Unión Vasco-Navarra (1880–1894)," 382.

33 *La Unión Vasco-Navarra*, July 13, 1880. Quoted in Rubio, "Prensa política regionalista," 387–8.

34 *La Unión Vasco-Navarra*, July 21, 1883. Quoted in Rubio, "Prensa política regionalista," 389.

35 *La Unión Vasco-Navarra* July 21, 1888. Quoted in Rubio, "Prensa política regionalista," 388–9.

36 *La Unión Vasco-Navarra*, August 21, 1881. Quoted in Rubio, "Prensa política regionalista," 397.

37 Campión, *El genio de Nabarra*, 20–1. For further information, see Majuelo, *La idea de la historia en Arturo Campión*.

38 Campión, 16.

39 Chaho, *Voyage en Navarre*, 420–1.

40 Juaristi, *El linaje de Aitor*, 169. Also, Zabaltza, *Mater Vasconia*, 254–5.

41 Wulff, "Nacionalismo, Historia, Historia Antigua: Sabino Arana (1865–1903), la fundación del nacionalismo vasco y el uso del modelo historiográfico español," 196–7.

42 Campión, *El genio de Nabarra*, 101–2.

43 Navarro, *Amaya*, II, 192.

44 *Bizkaitarra*, July 21, 1894. In Arana, *Obras Completas*, 317–18.

45 *Bizkaitarra*, March 31, 1894. In Arana, *Obras Completas*, 261.

46 Larramendi, *Sobre los fueros de Guipúzcoa*, 47–8.

47 *La Unión Vasco-Navarra*, July 13, 1880. Quoted in Rubio, "Prensa política regionalista," 387–8.

48 "Letter from Sabino Arana to D. Lorenzo de A. Mascarua," November 26, 1890. In Agirresazkuenaga, *Barne-muinetako Sabin Arana Goiri*, 376.

49 "Discurso de Larrazabal" (1892). In Arana, *Obras Completas*, 157–8.

50 De la Granja, "Cronología de Sabino Arana (1865–1903)," 287–8.

51 See, for example, Aguirresarobe, *Nation and the Writing of History in China and Britain (1880–1930)*, 107–11; 115–16.

52 *Bizkaitarra*, December 17, 1893. In Arana, *Obras Completas*, 182.

53 *Bizkaitarra*, May 31, 1895. In Arana, *Obras Completas*, 594–5.

54 *Bizkaitarra*, September 30, 1894. In Arana, *Obras Completas*, 364–5.

55 Navarro, *Amaya*, II, 165.

56 *Bizkaitarra*, September 30, 1894. In Arana, *Obras Completas*, 364–5.

57 Campión, *El genio de Nabarra*, 112.

58 Zabaltza, *Mater Vasconia*, 162–3.

59 Quoted in Zabaltza, *Mater Vasconia*, 167–8.

60 Wulff, "Nacionalismo, Historia, Historia Antigua," 199–200. Also, Zabaltza, *Mater Vasconia*, 162–3.

61 "Bizcaya por su independencia" (1892). In Arana, *Obras Completas*, 122–3.

62 *Bizkaitarra*, December 17, 1893. In Arana, *Obras Completas*, 196.

63 *Bizkaitarra*, June 29, 1894. In Arana, *Obras Completas*, 312.

64 Aguirresarobe, *Nation and the Writing of History*, 195.

65 Aguirresarobe, 31.

66 Coman and Kendall, *The Growth of the English Nation*, 9.

67 *Bizkaitarra*, December 17, 1893. In Arana, *Obras Completas*, 196.

68 *Bizkaitarra*, May 31, 1895. In Arana, *Obras Completas*, 596. This utterance is strikingly similar, for example, to that made by the Chinese nationalist activist Liang Qichao in 1902: "The study of history, as a discipline, is the broadest and most vital. It is the brilliant mirror of a nation. It is the origin of patriotism."

69 Navarro, *Amaya*, III, 333.

70 *Bizkaitarra*, October 31, 1894. In Arana, *Obras Completas*, 404.

71 *Bizkaitarra*, October 31, 1894. In Arana, *Obras Completas*, 404.

72 *Bizkaitarra*, June 29, 1894. In Arana, *Obras Completas*, 308–9.

73 *Bizkaitarra*, October 31, 1894. In Arana, *Obras Completas*, 404.

74 Poza, *Fuero de hidalguía Ad pragmaticas de Toro & Tordesillas*, V, 111.

75 *Bizkaitarra*, March 31, 1895. In Arana, *Obras Completas*, 546.

76 *Bizkaitarra*, January 20, 1895. In Arana, *Obras Completas*, 448. Also, Juaristi, *El linaje de Aitor*, 84. This idea echoes notions of choseness masterfully described in Smith, *Chosen Peoples. Sacred Sources of National Identity*.

77 "Letter from Sabino Arana to Nicolasa Atxika-allende," October 8, 1902. In Agirresazkuenaga, *Barne-muinetako Sabin Arana Goiri*, 164.

78 "Letter from José Arriandiaga to Engracio Aranzadi," December 7, 1903. In De la Granja, *Ángel o demonio: Sabino Arana. El patriarca del nacionalismo vasco*, 254. Also, Zabaltza, *Mater Vasconia*, 295–6.

79 Juaristi, *El linaje de Aitor*, 205.

80 *Euzkadi*, July 2, 1935. In Sánchez, "'Antes que los razonamientos llegan al corazón los sonidos': El folclore como medio de propaganda del primer nacionalismo vasco (1895–1939)," 190. This phrase, albeit uttered much later, embodies the approach of many early nationalists.

81 "Letter from Sabino Arana to Angel Zabala," June 4, 1901. In Agirresazkuenaga, *Barne-muinetako Sabin Arana Goiri*, 212.

82 Mees, *The Basque Contention*, 56–7. Also, Sánchez, "Antes que los razonamientos," 183–4.

83 *Bizkaitarra*, May 24, 1894. In Arana, *Obras Completas*, 279.

84 De la Granja, *Ángel o demonio*, 117–18.

85 Mees, *The Basque Contention*, 57.

86 "Discurso de Larrazabal" (1892). In Arana, *Obras Completas*, 158. Also, Mees, *The Basque Contention*, 56–7.

87 "Letter from Sabino Arana to Engracio Aranzadi," January 5, 1901. In Zabaltza, *Mater Vasconia*, 293.

88 Zabaltza, *Mater Vasconia*, 184.

89 Mees, *The Basque Contention*, 61–2.

90 *Bizkaitarra*, April 27, 1894. In Arana, *Obras Completas*, 277.

91 Chaho, *Voyage en Navarre*, 89. Also, Navarro, *Amaya*, I, 92.

92 Rubio, "Prensa política regionalista," 374.

93 After Sabino's death, in fact, his brother Luis attempted to create a national flag for the whole of *Euskal Herria*, but his efforts would crash against the already-massive notoriety of the previous *ikurriña*. See Zabaltza, *Mater Vasconia*, 190–1; 266. Also, Rubio, *La identidad vasca en el siglo XIX*, 84.

94 Campión, *El genio de Nabarra*, 28–9. Also, Zabaltza, *Mater Vasconia*, 120–1.

95 Lobera, "Discurso de Ramón de la Sota y Aburto en su designación como presidente de la Diputación foral de Bizkaia, el día 4 de mayo de 1917."

96 Baroja, *Momentum Catastrophicum* (1919). In Juaristi, *El linaje de Aitor*, 283.

97 Eleizalde, "Prosigue el mismo tema: *Puritanismo* y *confusionismo*," *Euzkadi*, July 13, 1921. In Antxustegi, *El debate nacionalista. Sabino Arana y sus herederos*, 257–8.

98 Baroja, *Nuevo Tablado de Arlequín* (1917). In Juaristi, *El linaje de Aitor*, 271.

EPILOGUE

> The framing of a national case from a historical point of view—as has been done with the Basque case—is misleading. The Basques do not have the right to independence because they had it in past centuries, but because they constitute an ethnic group. Thus, to base the right to Basque independence on a previous "status" in which they enjoyed the ability to legislate autonomously entails a serious mistake: it reduces the Basque national case to a mere Spanish or French issue.[1]

So wrote in 1962 Frederico Krutwig, the greatest theorist of Basque nationalism of the second half of the twentieth century. To Krutwig, who was himself the son of German and Basque parents, the notions of racial purity that Arana had once defended had come to seem, six decades from the latter's death, a hard principle to ratify. On the contrary—and no doubt influenced by his own familiar circumstances—his views on who was or was not entitled to rank as a Basque had less to do with lineage than with language. "There is no doubt that a person with all Castilian, Gascon, or French surnames who regularly uses the Basque language is more Basque than someone with fully Basque surnames who speaks at length—and poorly—about oppressive states but never learns or uses the Basque language in daily life."[2] Krutwig's motto, in other words, was one that echoed the dreams of Echepare and Leizarraga more than it did those of Arana. For it was clear to him that "the essence of . . . Basque identity lies, almost exclusively, in *Euskera*."[3]

A conclusion that many others shared. Much had changed, after all, in the fateful decades that separated Krutwig from the "Teacher." In 1936, thanks to an agreement with the Spanish Republic, an autonomous region had been established in the provinces of Biscay, Guipuzcoa, and Alava. Promising though this newfound status might have seemed to members of the Basque Nationalist Party at the time, their hopes would be thwarted almost immediately. The following year, war struck the land. The forces of Francisco Franco, assisted by those of Nazi Germany and Fascist Italy, overran the defenses put in place to contain them and conquered Guipuzcoa and Biscay. Some Western Pyreneans, it is true, rather than siding with the recently appointed autonomous government, had looked fondly upon Franco's advance.[4] Tradition, national unity, and the defense of the Catholic faith—the ideas under which Franco's side had revolted against the Spanish Republic—still held a powerful grip over the heirs of those who had once rallied behind the standards of Carlism. The defeated, in turn, were made an example to those opposed to the unity of the Spanish nation. The autonomous institutions were immediately dismantled, nationalist leaders were forced into exile, and *Euskera*—tainted by its association with the separatist cause—was completely eradicated from place names, branding, advertisement, and predication. The sense of trauma, felt by many in the aftermath of the conflict, was predictably overwhelming. But for the new regime's supporters, these were wonderful developments. "The days of *Gora Euskadi* are over; we are in times of *Long Live Spain*."[5]

The dictatorial administration put in place by Franco and his followers in the wake of the Spanish Civil War of 1936–9 would persist for almost forty years. It would be, for many in the Western Pyrenees, an age of repression of their customs and assimilation into foreign ones.[6] What it was not, at any rate, was an age of stagnation. A second industrial revolution—not unlike the one which had once transformed Biscay—now engulfed Guipuzcoa, Alava, and Navarre. This time, too, crowds of migrants, looking for opportunities to improve their lives and seeking a future for themselves and their families, accompanied it. The arrival of new peoples was seen by the self-appointed guardians of tradition as a threat to their own survival. They denounced the newcomers, their behavior, their immorality, and their language, and explained—in terms reminiscent of Campión and Arana—that "this change in the way of life has brought about a transformation of mentality."[7] They did not mean it as a compliment.

Under such circumstances, resistance did not take long in crystallizing. Krutwig's writings, for example, were composed in exile, smuggled into the Western Pyrenees, and then passed from hand to hand under cover. So too were other equally subversive pamphlets. Paradoxically, the thundering voice of a dictatorship roaring about the homogeneity of the Spanish people had allowed southern Western Pyreneans to understand their northern counterparts better. If, in the wake of the French Revolution, the inhabitants of Labourd, *Ultrapuertos*, and Soule had once instinctively turned to language to highlight their particularities, the dwellers of Guipuzcoa and Biscay now found in *Euskera* the lingering symbol of their lost uniqueness. *Euskal Herria*, as a whisper uttered in back alleys and foreign halls, endured. And for many Western Pyreneans, discontented with what they perceived to be the trampled rights of their homeland, it became an idea to die—and to kill—for.

It was the self-proclaimed goal of this book to trace the origins and evolution of the Basque exception. Throughout its pages, I have sought to demonstrate that this notion, far from originating in some "natural" and radical distinction, stemmed instead from historically traceable circumstances. The story of the Basque exception is one of underdogs aspiring to the top but also of the mighty coming to terms with the limits imposed by man and nature upon their ambitions. The Western Pyrenees, peripheral and poor throughout most of their history, were hardly an enviable seat of empire, but they were not an unimportant backwater either. Happenstance—the destruction brought by the *Bacaudae*, the limits of the Arab invasion, the disinterest of high-ranking lineages tempted by the riches of Al-Andalus—might have cut the region from its neighbors, but at the same time left it incapable of standing on its own feet. A land untamed yet unruly, placed at the hinge between the Iberian Peninsula and the rest of Europe, constituted the perfect breeding ground for a sense of exclusivity to emerge. And so, in the shadows cast by the towering silhouettes of mighty empires and kingdoms, the Basque exception was nurtured and given shape.

Some readers might find it weird, then, that I have chosen to leave the history of the twentieth and twenty-first centuries out of this tale. The events sketched at the beginning of this section—and many unmentioned ones—all affected the ways in which Western Pyrenean peoples looked—and still look—at themselves and others. In fact, had the scope of this book been slightly different, each and every one of these would have merited a sizable part of the resulting text.

Why, then, am I confident in glossing them over? There are, I think, two main reasons that justify this choice. The first one is professional humility. The study of this latter period—including the evolution of all kinds of identifications, institutions, and narratives of belonging—has constituted the lifework of a plethora of scholars whose talents and erudition I can never aspire to emulate. Their works offer a window into these seismic societal transformations to which my own words would add preciously little.

But the second—and most important—argument concerns scope. It is my firm conviction that the dramatic episodes that dot the century and more that spans from the death of Arana to our own times, traumatic and distressing though they have often been, have rarely shaken the well-established idea that constitutes this book's subject: the exceptionality of the Basque peoples. Both Franco's regime, in pursuing the main symbols of Basque nationalism, and individuals like Krutwig, who tailored contemporary Marxist and anti-colonial discourses to match the situation of Western Pyreneans, assumed that these peoples had something special about them. Their arguments, be they to show how Basques were nothing but a branch of the Spanish and French nations or how little they had in common with them, all were indebted to debates and positions that were already in place by the early 1900s. These, in turn, displayed traces of disputes that had once pestered early modern partisans, members of the *Bascongada*, or *fuerist* writers. The story of Basque exceptionalism, in other words, did not conclude with the late nineteenth-century invention of Basque nationalism. But it is my firm belief that the latter provided a framework—imaginary and symbolic—that is still widely shared by the majority of those talking about Basque society today.

Not everything, of course, remained the same. The antagonism between Franco's regime and Basque nationalism, for example, is preserved in the self-image of Basque independence. While Arana had once presumed that the most important aspect of the motto *Jaungoikoa eta Lagi Zarra* was, in fact, not independence but the service owed to God, the new generation—born under a dictatorship which dressed his authoritarianism in the garb of Catholicism—found such overtones much less appealing. Confronted with the overt right-wing politics of the regime and inspired by anti-colonial forces in Algeria and elsewhere, these young nationalists crafted for themselves an alternative identity as freedom fighters. And so—in a process aided no doubt by the high-profile actions of the violent group ETA—an image of the Basques as paradigms of antiauthoritarian resistance and minority rights began to set in.

As ever, external factors also played a role. While the idea of *Euskal Herria*—that is, a community whose roots lie in language rather than in descent—dated back, at least, to the sixteenth century, its major surge in Biscay, Guipuzcoa, Alava, and Navarre from the 1960s onward owed much to the censorial measures against *Euskera* put in place by Franco's government. Much, but not everything. Rather, to an international society schooled in the macabre example of the Holocaust, notions of blood superiority as the ones encouraged by individuals like Arana or Campión could not help but appear not only outdated but positively calamitous. Against the pretended objectivity of biology, a new generation opposed the subjectivity of culture. Through song and poem, in the dance rehearsed in secret and the book intimately devoured, they modeled what men like Echepare or Abbadie had once dreamed of: a sense of Basque exceptionality that put knowledge of Basque at its center. An identity that, following the spirit of the age, could be performed by the native and the migrant alike; which could be learned and passed down freely; and which might hope—in presenting *Euskera* not as the fulcrum of miraculous virtues but as a minority language maltreated by an oppressive government—to mobilize large swathes of Western Pyrenean society discontented with the regime. A people aspiring to be free, after all, could only benefit from casting their speech as the language of freedom.

But just as a lot of things were transformed, many more still were not. Take the case of Athletic Club football team. Created in Bilbao in 1898, from the get-go it was the institution's declared principle to only hire individuals born in the Basque Country—that is, in the seven provinces of *Euskal Herria*. However, over time, those in charge of Athletic's recruitment policies began to loosen these ethnic biases. First, in the 1970s, the team opened to players who, although not born in the region, had grown up within it. Then, from the 1990s onward, it became sufficient for the selected individual to have been trained in the youth academy of any "Basque" team.[8] In all, the move followed the main currents of Basque ascription in the region: from putting blood and lineage in its center to focusing, instead, on a more broad—and vague—sense of cultural belonging. And just as the identity of Athletic Club remains to this day tied indissolubly to the team's self-declared "Basqueness," so too endures the article of faith at its core. That there is something different—hard to pinpoint exactly, but important and valuable nonetheless—that singles Western Pyrenean society from the rest.

A belief sustained not only by locals. In early September 2025, the *Vuelta a España*, one of the world's greatest cycling competitions, was forced to a standstill near Bilbao by crowds of protesters opposed to the participation of an Israeli team. Given the importance of the event, Spanish social media outlets quickly became flooded with opinions and commentaries about it. Those ideologically opposed to the actions of the Israeli government in Palestine voiced their support for the demonstrators in Bilbao. Others regarded the episode as an unnecessary interruption of a sporting event that tainted the Spanish brand abroad. The terms of the debate, however, soon shifted to a different question: what the episode told about the Basques themselves. Were these freedom fighters, allies to the oppressed peoples of the world? Or were they instead exemplars of a narcissistic and self-centered society, easily manipulable by political elites bent on gaining independence from Spain? Were they *good* or *bad* Spaniards? Were they Spaniards at all? Once again, and for all that the dispute was not precisely a display of erudition nor understanding, the incident demonstrated the extent to which Western Pyrenean exceptionalism retains its power in the contemporary world.

But for how long? Once, marginality—geographical, economic, political, linguistical—underpinned the efforts of Western Pyreneans to present themselves as a distinct piece in the mosaic of monarchies and states that surrounded them. In the twenty-first century, however, circumstances are vastly different than they were, say, in the sixteenth. Great tunnels and viaducts, feats of engineering beyond the wildest dreams of the early modern monarchs, had wounded the landscape of the region. Industrial enclaves and cities brimming with tourist attractions had enriched their population. The provinces of Biscay, Guipuzcoa, and Alava, it is true, brought the dream of an autonomous Basque government within Spain to completion in 1978, three years after Franco's death, and *Euskera*, once a language toying with extinction, has been the object of an unparalleled effort of recovery.[9] However, in all, doubts about the future of the Basque exception persist. In a globalized world, in which fluxes of people, information, and goods travel at a speed unequaled in history, the arguments and ideologies developed for a slower age risk being cast aside as useless. How can a society which consumes similar media, similar products, and similar entertainment as its neighbors still defend its entitlement to being taken as different from the rest? It is hard to predict what the future holds in store. And yet, for the time being at any rate, *Euskera* appears to be playing the role of the central pillar that carries the weight of the Basque sense of uniqueness.[10]

This might seem unsurprising. Classical works dealing with the origins of national identity have often emphasized the role played in it by communities of language.[11] Speakers of a tongue, pushed by the circumstances of modernity to interact within new settings dominated by speakers of a different one, would rapidly—according to these accounts—come to realize their own uniqueness, and a sense of common identity would follow. Many, among them nationalist authors themselves, have similarly argued that this was precisely what happened to the Basques within the Spanish and French states.

And yet, as this book has attempted to demonstrate, this framing obscures the crucial significance of another element: the sense of self-importance that many Western Pyreneans already possessed long before the coming of nationalism. The Basques, in the eyes of these men and women, were not special *because* they spoke a different language from that of their neighbors or their lords. Rather, they were already a special and primordially virtuous community and *therefore*, as a projection of this extraordinary standing, they spoke a distinct speech. Many arguments—historical, religious, and otherwise—compounded this conclusion. It was precisely the fact that this discourse did not rely on any single one of its components to survive that had granted it such a long lifespan. This factor, too, had allowed politicians and scholars in the Spanish Western Pyrenean territories, the cradle of Basque nationalism, to regard *Euskera*, simultaneously, as a sacred language and as an unworthy means of communication. A language, indecipherable to strangers and unrelated to any other, might have proved a perfect embodiment of the exceptionality these provincials claimed to enjoy, but it was far from the only one. Many other ingredients had contributed to baking the Basque exception. It was therefore this conviction in the superiority of their compatriots, and not any linguistic solidarity, that Sabino Arana and many others had inherited, and which would lead them, in time, to successfully advocate the rights of a distinct community called the Basques. Only once all the remaining historical and religious underpinnings of such a discourse were slowly eroded or abandoned over time would *Euskera* endure, alone, to carry the torch of what had once been a widespread belief: that the Basques were, indeed, not only different, but better than the rest.

The history of the Western Pyrenean exception, in other words, vastly predated that of the Basque people. And if the story of the Vascones, the provincials, or the *vascongados* can be taken as a precedent, it might—one day—outlast it too.

Notes

1 Sarrailh, *Vasconia*, 33.

2 Sarrailh, 91.

3 Sarrailh, 27.

4 Zabaltza, *Mater Vasconia*, 73–4. Also, Mees, *The Basque Contention*, 94–5.

5 Quoted in Sánchez, "Antes que los razonamientos," 187.

6 Mees, *The Basque Contention*, 95–6.

7 "Anonymous letter to *Jon*," September 20, 1955. Quoted in Mees, *The Basque Contention*, 98–9.

8 Gutiérrez, "Entre Asensios y Diarras. El Athletic Bilbao y la construcción de identidades," 160–71.

9 Baztarrika, "El Euskera: un caso de revitalización," 83–146.

10 Aguirresarobe, "Hand in Hand: Consuming symbols, language and identity in post-ETA Basque society," 575–88.

11 See, for example, Gellner, *Nations and Nationalism*; Hobsbawm, *Nations and nationalism since 1780. Programme, Myth, Reality*; Anderson, *Imagined Communities. Reflections on the Origin and Spread of Nationalism*.

BIBLIOGRAPHY

Achón, Jose Ángel. "Los parientes mayores." *Iura Vasconiae* 3 (2006): 221–47.

Aernouts, Nadine. "Presencia vasca en Brabante en el siglo XVI: ¿Licenciado Poza Antwerpensis?" In *El licenciado Poza en Flandes*, edited by Natalia Bausela and Itxaso Erroteta. Diputación Foral de Bizkaia, 1996.

Agirresazkuenaga, Joseba, ed. *Barne-muinetako Sabin Arana Goiri. Gutunak I (1876-1903).* Vasconiae, 2010.

Aguirre, Sabino, ed. *Las dos primeras crónicas de Vizcaya.* Caja de Ahorros Vizcaína, 1986.

Aguirre, Sabino. *Lope García de Salazar. El primer historiador de Bizkaia (1399-1476).* Diputación Foral de Bizkaia, 1994.

Aguirresarobe, Asier H. "Hand in Hand: Consuming Symbols, Language and Identity in post-ETA Basque Society." *Nations and Nationalism* 31, no. 3 (2025): 575–88.

Aguirresarobe, Asier H. *Nation and the Writing of History in China and Britain (1880-1930).* Routledge, 2022.

Alberdi, Xabier. "Reforma de la administración de los recursos navales de Gipuzkoa a principios del siglo XVIII. La búsqueda de un nuevo equilibrio entre la política naval y económica de la Monarquía y las actividades de los principales hombres de negocios de la provincia." In *Una década prodigiosa. Beligerancia y negociación entre la corona y las provincias vascas (1717-1728)*, edited by Álvaro Aragón and Alberto Angulo. Universidad del País Vasco, 2019.

Aldekoa, Iñaki. "El Renacimiento en la literatura vasca: Juan Pérez de Lazarraga." *Revista de Filología Románica* 29, no. 1 (2012): 145–61.

Aller, David. "El Fuero como retórica. De reliquia positiva a canon identitario." *Sancho el Sabio* 31 (2009): 55–80.

Almagor, Eran. "Who is a barbarian? The barbarians in the ethnological and cultural taxonomies of Strabo." In *Strabo's Cultural Geography*, edited by Daniela Dueck, Hugh Lindsay, and Sarah Pothecary. Cambridge University Press, 2005.

Álvarez, José, and Gregorio De la Fuente. *El relato nacional. Historia de la historia de España.* Taurus, 2017.

Anderson, Benedict. *Imagined Communities. Reflections on the Origin and Spread of Nationalism.* Verso, 2006.

Andreu, Javier. "Regere imperio populos pacique imponere morem: sobre la alteridad, la etnicidad y la identidad en Roma." *Espacio Tiempo y Forma, Serie II, Historia Antigua* 22 (2009): 213–25.

Andreu, Javier, and Ángel Jordán. "Nuevas reflexiones en torno a las fuentes literarias sobre los Vascones en la Antigüedad." *Lvcentvm* XXVI (2007): 233–52.

Anelier de Tolosa, Guilhem. *La Guerra de Navarra. Edición trilingüe: occitano, castellano, vasco.* Edited by Maurice Berthe. Gobierno de Navarra, 1995.

Angulo, Alberto. "Una década peligrosa (1717-1727). Los provincianos en Madrid y la negociación del traslado aduanero." In *Una década prodigiosa. Beligerancia y negociación entre la corona y las provincias vascas (1717-1728)*, edited by Álvaro Aragón and Alberto Angulo. Universidad del País Vasco, 2019.

Angulo, Alberto, and Iñaki Reguera. "Los valores de la sociedad vasca en la Edad Moderna." In *Historia del País Vasco. Edad Moderna (siglos XVI-XVIII)*, edited by Alberto Angulo, Rosario Porres and Iñaki Reguera. Hiria, 2004.

Antxustegi, Esteban. *El debate nacionalista. Sabino Arana y sus herederos.* Universidad de Murcia, 2007.
Aragón, Álvaro. "Linajes urbanos y Parientes Mayores en Guipúzcoa a finales de la Edad Media (1450-1520)." *En la España Medieval* 35 (2012): 249–83.
Aragón, Álvaro, and Xabier Alberdi. "El control de la producción histórica sobre Gipuzkoa en el siglo XVII. Un instrumento de defensa del régimen foral." *Vasconia* 25 (1998): 37–52.
Arana, Sabino. *Obras Completas de Arana-Goiri'tar Sabin.* Sabindiar-batza, 1965.
Aranzadi, Juan. *Milenarismo Vasco. Edad de Oro, etnia y nativismo.* Taurus, 2000.
Araquistain, Juan Venancio. *Tradiciones vasco-cántabras.* Tolosa, 1866.
Arce, Javier. "Vascones y romanos: las deformaciones de la historiografía antigua." *Bitarte* 20 (2000): 81–94.
Arias de Saavedra, Inmaculada. "Educación y economía. Las Sociedades Económicas de Amigos del País en el reformismo de la Ilustración." In *Las Reales Sociedades Económicas de Amigos del País: Nuevas aproximaciones (siglos XVIII-XXI)*, edited by Jorge Martínez. Ediciones Trea, 2024.
Arnoldsson, Sverker. *La Leyenda Negra. Estudios sobre sus orígenes.* Elanders Boktryckery Aktiebolag, 1960.
Arregui, Pilar. "El trasfondo político de las recopilaciones del Reino de Navarra." *AHDE* XC (2020): 189–233.
Arrieta, Jon. "Nobles, libres e iguales, pero mercaderes, ferrones... y frailes. En torno a la historiografía sobre la hidalguía universal." *AHDH* LXXXIV (2014): 799–842.
Arriolabengoa, Julen. "Ibarguen-Cachopín Kronika. Edizioa eta Azterketa." PhD Diss., Universidad del País Vasco, 2006.
Artola, Andoni. "La antimodernidad en el País Vasco: prácticas sociales y discursos (1765-1833)." *Cuadernos dieciochistas* 10 (2009): 121–47.
Arzáns, Bartolomé. *Historia de la villa imperial de Potosí.* Edited by Lewis Hanke and Gunnar Mendoza. Brown University Press, 1965.
Astigarraga, Jesús. *Los ilustrados vascos. Ideas, instituciones y reformas económicas en España.* Crítica, 2003.
Axular, Pedro. *Gero.* Bordeaux, 1643.
Ayerbe, María Rosa. "Defensa de las regalías y beneficio de la causa pública, de Don Joseph de Zabala y Miranda (Vizcaya, 1746)." In *La diadema del rey. Vizcaya, Navarra, Aragón y Cerdeña en la Monarquía de España (siglos XVI-XVIII)*, edited by Jon Arrieta, Xavier Gil and Jesús Morales. Universidad del País Vasco, 2017.
Ayerbe, María Rosa. *Documentación medieval del Archivo Municipal de Azkoitia (m.s. XIII-1500).* Eusko Ikaskuntza, 1993.
Ayerbe, María Rosa. "El señorío guipuzcoano de la casa de Lazcano. De Parientes mayores a grandes de España de segunda clase (s.XIII-XXI)." *Boletín de Estudios Históricos sobre San Sebastián* 44 (2011): 15–75.
Ayerbe, María Rosa. *Historia del condado de Oñate y Señorío de los Guevara (s.XI-XVI).* Diputación Foral de Guipúzcoa, 1985.
Azkarate, Agustín, and Ismael García. "Las casas-torre bajomedievales. Análisis sistémico de un proceso de reestructuración espacial/territorial." *Arqueología de la Arquitectura* 3 (2004): 7–37.
Azurmendi, Mikel. *Nombrar, embrujar. Para una historia del sometimiento de la cultura oral en el País Vasco.* Alberdania, 1993.
Azurmendi, Mikel. *Y se limpie aquella tierra. Limpieza étnica y de sangre en el País Vasco (siglos XVI-XVIII).* Taurus, 2000.

Bacon, John. *Six years in Biscay. A personal narrative of the sieges of Bilbao in June 1835 and October 1836 and of the principal events which occurred in that city and the Basque provinces during the years 1830 to 1837.* London, 1838.
Baury, Ghislain. "Los ricoshombres y el rey en Castilla: el linaje Haro (1076-1322)." *Territorio, Sociedad y Poder* 6 (2011): 53–72.
Bazán, Iñaki. (1999). "El crimen de lesa majestad divina: brujería y superstición vasco-navarra (s. XIII-c.1530)." *Heresis* 29 (1999): 83–108.
Baztarrika, Patxi. "El Euskera: un caso de revitalización." In *La normalización social de las lenguas minoritarias*, edited by Javier Giralt and Francho Nagore. Universidad de Zaragoza, 2019.
Becerro Galicano Digital. Available in: www.ehu.eus/galicano (accessed September 24, 2025).
Bermejo, Daniel. "La caída de una clase política - Los reformistas vascos en la crisis del Antiguo Régimen." PhD Diss., Universidad del País Vasco, 2019.
Besga, Armando. *Astures et Vascones*. Librería Astarloa, 2003.
Bilbao, Gidor, et al., eds. *Lazarraga eskuizkribua: edizioa eta azterketa*. Universidad del País Vasco: 2011. Available in: http://lazarraga.com (accessed September 24, 2025).
Blázquez, José María. "Los vascones en las fuentes literarias de la Antigüedad y en la historiografía actual." *Trabajos de arqueología Navarra* 20 (2007): 103–50.
Borges, Ellen. *Vizcaya or, life in the land of the Carlists at the Outbreack of the insurrection 1872-73.* London, 1884.
Bramsen, John. *Remarks on the North of Spain*. London, 1823.
Burgess, R. W. *The Chronicle of Hydatius and the Consularia Constantinopolitana: Two Contemporary Accounts of the Final Years of the Roman Empire*. Clarendon Press, 1993.
Campión, Arturo. *El genio de Nabarra*. Beñat Idaztiak, 1936.
Castellanos, Santiago. "Astures, Cantabri, and Vascones: The Peoples of the Spanish North during the Late and Post-Roman Period." In *Curta, Florin, Neglected Barbarians*, edited by Florin Curta. Brepols, 2010.
Castellanos, Santiago. *The Visigothic Kingdom in Iberia: Construction and Invention*. University of Pennsylvania Press, 2020.
Castillo, Janire. "'¡Quemaré todo Aramayona!' Mujeres, conflicto y guerra feudal en el País Vasco a finales de la Edad Media." *Arenal* 28, no. 2 (2021): 335–59.
Celaya, Adrián. *Los Fueros de Bizkaia. I. Como nacieron. II. El licenciado Poza y la defensa de la hidalguía*. Academia Vasca de Derecho, 2009.
Cerdá y Rico, Francisco, ed. *Cronica de Alfonso el Onceno de este nombre de los Reyes que reynaron en Castilla y en Leon: parte I*. Madrid, 1787.
Chaho, Joseph Augustin. *Voyage en Navarre pendant l'insurrection des Basques (1830-1833)*. Paris, 1836.
Cieza de León, Pedro. *Parte primera de la chronica del Peru. Que tracta la demarcación de sus provincias, la descripción dellas. Las fundaciones de las nuevas ciudades. Los ritos y costumbres de los indios, y otras cosas estrañas dignas de ser sabidas*. Sevilla, 1553.
Ciriquain, Mariano. *Los vascos y la pesca de la ballena*. Txertoa, 2005.
Coman, Katharine and Elizabeth Kendall. *The Growth of the English Nation*. New York, 1894.
Conde, José Antonio. *Censura crítica de la pretendida excelencia y antigüedad del vascuence*. Madrid, 1804.
Crespo, Miguel Ángel, José Ramón Cruz, José Manuel Gómez and José Ángel Lema, eds. *Colección documental del Archivo Municipal de Mondragón (1260-1400)*. Sociedad de Estudios Vascos, 1992.
Dacosta, Arsenio. *Los linajes de Bizkaia en la Baja Edad Media: Poder, parentesco y conflicto*. Universidad del País Vasco, 2003.

De Brestian, Scott. "Vascones and Visigoths: Creation and Transformation of Identity in Northern Spain in Late Antiquity." In *Romans, Barbarians, and the Transformation of the Roman World: Cultural Interaction and the Creation of Identity in Late Antiquity*, edited by Ralph W. Mathisen and Danuta Shanzer. Ashgate, 2011.

De la Campa, Mariano, ed. *La Estoria de España de Alfonso X: Estudio y Edición de la Versión Crítica desde Fruela II hasta la muerte de Fernando II*. Universidad de Málaga, 2009.

De la Granja, José Luis. 2015. *Ángel o demonio: Sabino Arana. El patriarca del nacionalismo vasco.* Tecnos, 2015.

De Lancre, Pierre. *Tableau de l'inconstance des mauvais anges et demons*. Paris, 1613.

De Uriarte, Luis. *El Fuero de Ayala*. Diputación Foral de Álava, 1974.

Dechepare, Bernard. *Linguae Vasconum Primitiae*. Real Academia de la Lengua Vasca Euskaltzaindia, 1995.

Dedieu, Jean-Pierre. "La Nueva Planta en su contexto. Las reformas del aparato del Estado en el reinado de Felipe V." *Manuscrits* 18 (2000): 113–39.

Delgado, Josep. "Construir el Estado, destruir la nación. Las reformas fiscales de los primeros borbones. El colapso del sistema de equilibrios en el imperio español (1714-1796)." *Illes i imperis* 13 (2010): 63–86.

Díaz de Durana, José Ramón. "La hidalguía universal en el País Vasco. Tópicos sobre sus orígenes y causas de su desigual generalización." *Cuadernos de Alzate* 31 (2004): 49–64.

Díaz de Durana, José Ramón. *La otra nobleza: escuderos e hidalgos sin nombre y sin historia. Hidalgos e hidalguía universal en el País Vasco al final de la Edad Media (1250-1525)*. Universidad del País Vasco, 2004.

Díaz de Durana, José Ramón. "La reforma municipal de los Reyes Católicos y la consolidación de las oligarquías urbanas: el capitulado vitoriano de 1476 y su extensión por el nordeste de la Corona de Castilla." In *La formación de Álava: 650 aniversario del pacto de Arriaga (1332-1982)*, 1985.

Díaz de Durana, José Ramón, and Arsenio Dacosta. "La dimensión social del liderazgo del linaje: solidaridad, poder y violencia (País Vasco, siglo XV)." *Studia Zamorensia* XII (2013): 87–106.

Díaz de Durana, José Ramón, and Jon Andoni Fernández de Larrea. "La frontera de los malhechores: Bandidos, linajes y villas entre Álava, Guipúzcoa y Navarra durante la Baja Edad Media." *Studia Historica, Historia Medieval* 23 (2005): 171–205.

Díaz de Durana, José Ramón, and Jon Andoni Fernández de Larrea. "Las relaciones contractuales de la nobleza y las élites urbanas en el País Vasco al final de la Edad Media (c.1300-1500)." In *El contrato político en la Corona de Castilla - Cultura y sociedad políticas entre los siglos X al XVI*, edited by François Foronda and Ana Isabel Carrasco. Dykinson, 2008.

Dümmler, Ernest, ed. *Poetae Latini Aevi Carolini, II*. Berlin, 1884.

Eguía, Joaquín María. "Elogio de Don Xavier Maria de Munive Idiaquez, Conde de Peñaflorida." In *Extractos de las Juntas Generales celebradas por la Real Sociedad Bascongada de los Amigos del País en la villa de Vergara por julio de 1785*. Madrid, 1786.

El Duende Crítico de Madrid. Obra histórico política del siglo pasado, adornada con más de 160 grabado en madera, varias vistas y retratos de los personajes que figuran en ella. Publicada por una sociedad de artistas. Madrid, 1844.

Enríquez, Javier, ed. *Colección Documental del Archivo Municipal de Marquina (1355-1516)*. Eusko Ikaskuntza, 1989.

Escalona, Julio. "Los nobles contra su rey. Argumentos y motivaciones de la insubordinación nobiliaria de 1272-1273." *Cahiers de linguistique hispanique médiévale* 25 (2002): 131–62.

Escalona, Julio. "Unidades territoriales supralocales: una propuesta sobre los orígenes del señorío de behetría." In *Los señoríos de behetría*, edited by Carlos Estepa and Cristina Jular. Consejo Superior de Investigaciones Científicas, 2001.

Estatutos aprobados por S. M. para gobierno de la Real Sociedad Bascongada de los Amigos del País (1774-1765). Caja de Ahorros Municipal de San Sebastián, 1985.
Etxeberria, Ekaitz. "Guerras privadas y linajes urbanos: violencia banderiza en el Bilbao bajomedieval." *Roda da Fortuna* 1-1 (2015): 78–97.
Etxezarraga, Iosu. "La organización del territorio de San Sebastián y su entorno durante la Alta Edad Media: Una visión panorámica de su evolución." In *Los fueros de Estella y San Sebastián*, edited by Xabier Irujo and Amaia Álvarez. Fundación Iura Vasconiae, 2020.
Evelyn White, Hugh, trans. *Ausonius, I*. William Heinemann and G.P. Putnam, 1919.
Fagel, Raymond. "Los hombres de la lana y del hierro: mercaderes vascos en los Países Bajos Siglos XVI." In *El licenciado Poza en Flandes*, edited by Natalia Bausela and Itxaso Erroteta. Diputación Foral de Bizkaia, 1996.
Falque, Emma, ed. *Lucae Tudensis Chronicon Mundi*. Brepols, 2003.
Fear, Andrew, and Jamie Wood, eds. *Isidore of Seville and his Reception in the Early Middle Ages: Transmitting and Transforming Knowledge*. Amsterdam University Press, 2006.
Fernández de Larrea, Jon Andoni. *Guerra y sociedad en Navarra durante la Edad Media*. Universidad del País Vasco, 1992.
Fernández de Larrea, Jon Andoni, and José Ramón Díaz de Durana. "El discurso político de los protagonistas de las luchas sociales en el País Vasco al final de la Edad Media." *Annexes des Cahiers de linguistique et de civilisation hispaniques médiévales* 16 (2004): 313–36.
Fernández de Larrea, Jon Andoni, and José Ramón Díaz de Durana. "La construcción de la memoria: de los linajes a las corporaciones provinciales en Álava, Guipúzcoa y Vizcaya." In *Memoria e Historia. Utilización política en la Corona de Castilla al final de la Edad Media*, edited by Jon Andoni Fernández de Larrea and José Ramón Díaz de Durana. Sílex, 2010.
Fernández, Francisco María. "El 'Chronicon' de Juan de Bíclaro. La crónica del rey Leovigildo y del III Concilio de Toledo. Estudio y traducción." *Toletana* 16 (2007): 29–66.
Flórez, Enrique. *La Cantabria. Disertación sobre el sitio, y extensión que en tiempo de los romanos tuvo la región de los cántabros*. Madrid, 1768.
Floristán, Alfredo. "Conquista e incorporación del Reino de Navarra a la Monarquía de España." In *La diadema del rey. Vizcaya, Navarra, Aragón y Cerdeña en la Monarquía de España (siglos XVI-XVIII)*, edited by Jon Arrieta, Xavier Gil and Jesús Morales. Universidad del País Vasco, 2017.
Fonseca, Luis. *Relación summaria del auto de la fe que los señores Doctor Alonso Bezerra Holguin, del Abito de Alcantara, Licenciado Ioan de Valle Albarado, Licenciado Alonso de Salaçar Frias, Inquisidores Apostolicos en el Reyno de Navarra y su destricto, celebraron en la Ciudad de Logroño, en siete y ocho dias del mes de Noviembre, de mil y seyscientos y diez años*. Burgos, 1611.
Fortún, Luis Javier. "La quiebra de la soberanía navarra en Álava, Guipúzcoa y el Duranguesado (1199-1200)." *Revista Internacional de Estudios Vascos* 45, no. 2 (2000): 439–94.
Fortunatus, Venantius. *Venantii Fortunati opera poetica*. Edited by Friedrich Leo. Berlin, 1881.
Fortunatus, Venantius. *Venantius Fortunatus: Personal and Political Poems*. Translated and edited by Judith George. Liverpool University Press, 1995.
Fredegarius. *Fredegarii et aliorum chronica. Vitae Sanctorum*. Edited by Bruno Krusch. Hannover, 1888.
Gaminde, Víctor Luis. *Impugnación al arreglo de los fueros de las Provincias Bascongadas por la Comisión de Gobierno de las mismas Provincias*. Bilbao, 1852.
Garate, Justo. *Viajeros extranjeros en Vasconia*. Editorial Vasca Ekin, 1989.
Garate, Montserrat. *La Real Compañía Guipuzcoana de Caracas*. Sociedad Guipuzcoana de Ediciones y Publicaciones, 1990.
García, Ernesto. "El linaje Avendaño: causas y consecuencias de su ascenso social en la baja Edad Media." *Anuario de Estudios Medievales* 37, no. 2 (2007): 527–61.

García, Ernesto. *Gobernar la ciudad en la Edad Media: Oligarquías y élites urbanas en el País Vasco*. Diputación Foral de Álava, 2004.
García de Cortázar, José Ángel. "Álava, Guipúzcoa y Vizcaya en los siglos XIII a XV: de los valles a las provincias." *Revista Internacional de Estudios Vascos* 45, no. 1 (2000): 197–234.
García de Cortázar, José Ángel. "La sociedad guipuzcoana antes del Fuero de San Sebastián." *Donostiako Forua eta bere Garaia* (1982): 89–111.
García de Salazar, Lope. *Libro de las Buenas Andanças e Fortunas que fizo Lope García de Salazar*. Edited by María Consuelo Villacorta. Universidad del País Vasco, 2015.
Gari, Ángel. "La brujería en los Pirineos (siglos XIII al XVII): Aproximación a su historia." *Cuadernos de Etnología y Etnografía de Navarra* 85 (2010): 317–54.
Garibay, Esteban. *Los siete libros de la progenie y parentela de los hijos de Estevan de Garibay*. Edited by José Ángel Achón. Arrasateko Udala, 2000.
Garibay, Esteban. *Los XL libros del Compendio Historial de las Chronicas y universal Historia de todos los reynos de España*. Antwerp, 1571.
Garmendia, Vicente. *Jaungoicoa eta foruac. El carlismo vasconavarro frente a la democracia española (1868-1872)*. Universidad del País Vasco, 1999.
Garriga, Carlos. "Orden jurídico y poder político en el Antiguo Régimen." *Istor: revista de historia internacional* 16 (2004): 1–21.
Gaudemet, Jean, and Brigitte Basdevant. *Les Canons des Conciles Mérovingiens (VIe-VIIe siècles)*. Les Éditions du Cerf, 1989.
Gellner, Ernest. *Nations and Nationalism*. Cornell University Press, 1983.
Giucciardini, Francesco. *Scritti Autobiografici e rari*. Edited by Roberto Palmarocchi. Laterza, 1936.
Glaber, Rodulfus. *Rodvlfi Glabri Historiarum libri quinque*. Edited by John France. Clarendon Press, 1989.
Goizueta, José María. *Leyendas Vascongadas*. Madrid, 1851.
González, Manuel, ed. *Crónica de Alfonso X*. Academia Alfonso X el Sabio, 1999.
Gorrochategui, Joaquín. "Onomástica vascónica y aquitana: elementos para el conocimiento de la historia antigua de Navarra." In *Navarra en la Antigüedad: Propuesta de Actualización*, edited by Javier Andreu. Departamento de Cultura y Turismo Gobierno de Navarra, 2006.
Goyheneche, Eugène. *Bayonne et la région Bayonnaise du XIIe au XVe siècle*. Universidad del País Vasco, 1990.
Goyheneche, Eugène. *Le Pays Basque*. Société nouvelle d'editions regionales et de diffusion, 1979.
Goyhenetche, Manex. *Histoire Générale du Pays Basque. Tome IV: La Révolution de 1789*. Elkar, 2002.
Grassotti, Hilda. "Homenaje de García Ramírez a Alfonso VII." *Príncipe de Viana* 94–95 (1964): 57–66.
Gregory of Tours. *History of the Franks*. Translated by Lewis Thorpe. Penguin Books, 1974.
Guerrero, Rafael. "Familias en la encrucijada. Redes sociales, lealtades y resistencias durante la Guerra de Sucesión (País Vasco y Navarra, 1680-1715)." *Estudios De Historia De España* 23, no. 2 (2021): 121–39.
Guerrero, Rafael. *Las elites vascas y navarras en el gobierno de la monarquía borbónica. Redes sociales, carreras y hegemonía en el siglo XVIII (1700-1746)*. Universidad del País Vasco, 2012.
Gutiérrez, Fernando. "Entre Asensios y Diarras. El Athletic Bilbao y la construcción de identidades." *Revista Latina de Sociología* 8, no. 3 (2018): 160–71.
Harper, Kyle. *Plagues Upon the Earth. Disease and the Course of Human History*. Princeton University Press, 2021.
Hausberger, Bernd. "La guerra de los vicuñas contra los vascongados en Potosí y la etnicización de los vascos a principios de la edad moderna." In *Excluir para ser. Procesos identitarios y*

fronteras sociales en la América Hispánica (siglos XVII-XVIII), edited by Christian Büschges and Frédérique Langue. Ahila, Iberoamericana and Vervuert, 2005.
Henningsen, Gustav. *The Witches' Advocate: Basque witchcraft and the Spanish Inquisition (1609-1614)*. University of Nevada Press, 1980.
Herbers, Klaus, and Manuel Santos, eds. *Liber Sancti Jacobi Codex Calixtinus*. Xunta de Galicia, 1999.
Hershkowitz, Paula. *Prudentius, Spain and Late Antique Christianity: Poetry, visual culture, and the cult of the martyrs*. Cambridge University Press, 2017.
Hirschi, Caspar. *The Origins of Nationalism: An Alternative History from Ancient Rome to Early Modern Germany*. Cambridge University Press, 2012.
Hobsbawm, Eric. *Nations and Nationalism since 1780. Programme, Myth, Reality*. Cambridge University Press, 1990.
Hoepffner, Ernest, ed. *Oeuvres de Guillaume de Machaut*. Paris, 1821.
Ibáñez, José Agustín. *Manifiesto histórico de los servicios que ha hecho el muy noble y muy leal señorío de Vizcaya en la última guerra con la Francia*. Bilbao, 1798.
Iglesias, José Manuel. "Estudio preliminar." In Gerónimo Zurita, *Cantabria. Descripción de sus verdaderos límites*. Universidad de Cantabria, 2000.
Ilacqua, Talitha. "Territory and the Politics of Identity in the Basque Country during the French Revolution." *French History* 31, no. 3 (2017): 329–50.
Imizcoz, José María. "Costumbres en tensión. El proceso de la civilización en las tierras vascas, de las costumbres compartidas a la fractura de la comunidad (1700-1833)." In *Procesos de Civilización: Culturas de élites, culturas populares. Una historia de contrastes y tensiones (siglos XVI-XIX)*, edited by ImízcozJosé María, Máximo García and Javier Ochoa. Universidad del País Vasco, 2019.
Imízcoz, José María. "La clase política del reformismo borbónico: las redes sociales del cambio." *Magallánica, Revista de Historia Moderna* 4, no. 7 (2017): 10–62.
Imízcoz, José María. "Las élites vasco-navarras y la monarquía hispánica: construcciones sociales, políticas y culturales en la edad moderna." *Cuadernos de Historia Moderna* 33 (2008): 89–119.
Iñarra, Xabier. "La razón de la sinrazón. Actitudes hacia las ideas ilustradas en las provincias vascas (1748-1839)." *Vasconia* 45 (2021): 29–78.
Iñarra, Xabier. "Las luces en penumbra: Proyectos ilustrados y conflicto comunitario en las provincias vascas (1748-1833)." *Revista de Historia Moderna* 40 (2022): 274–305.
Intxaustegi, Nere Jone. "Las instituciones territoriales y locales en el Señorío de Vizcaya durante la Edad Moderna: Convergencias y divergencias." *Revista de Empresa, Derecho y Sociedad* 12 (2018): 166–78.
Irijoa, Iago. "Gobierno urbano en San Sebastián a fines de la Edad Media: Crisis de linaje, conflictos y reestructuración política." *Boletín de Estudios Históricos sobre San Sebastián* 49 (2016): 15–205.
Isidore of Seville. *Etymologies*. Translated by Stephen A. Barney, W. J. Lewis, J. A. Beach and Oliver Berghof. Cambridge University Press, 2006.
Isidore of Seville. *History of the Goths, Vandals, and Suevi*. Translated by Guido Donini and Gordon B. Ford. Brill, 1970.
Jiménez de Rada, Rodrigo. *Historia de los hechos de España*. Translated by Juan Fernández. Alianza Editorial, 1989.
Jimeno, Roldán. "La Contrarreforma en la Navarra incorporada a la Corona castellana: las instituciones educativas (1515-1630)." In *La diadema del rey. Vizcaya, Navarra, Aragón y Cerdeña en la Monarquía de España (siglos XVI-XVIII)*, edited by Jon Arrieta, Xavier Gil and Jesús Morales. Universidad del País Vasco, 2017.
Jimeno, Roldán. *Los Fueros de Navarra*. Agencia Estatal Boletín Oficial del Estado, 2016.

Jimeno, Roldán. *Orígenes del Cristianismo en la tierra de los vascones.* Pamiela, 2003.
Jimeno, Roldán, and Aitor Pescador. *Colección documental de Sancho Garcés III, el Mayor, rey de Pamplona (1004-1035).* Pamiela, 2003.
Juaristi, Jon. *El linaje de Aitor: La invención de la tradición vasca.* Taurus, 1998.
Kramer, Heinrich, and Jacob Sprenger. *Malleus Maleficarum.* Translated by Montague Summers. John Rodker, 1928.
Kulikowsky, Michael. "Cities and Government in Late Antique Hispania: Recent Advances and Future Research." In *Hispania in Late Antiquity: Current Perspectives*, edited by Kim Bowes and Michael Kulikowski. Brill, 2005.
Laborda, Juan José. *El Señorío de Vizcaya. Nobles y fueros (c.1452 -1727).* Marcial Pons Historia, 2012.
Lacarra, José María, ed. *Colección Diplomática de Irache. Vol. 1. (958-1222).* Consejo Superior de Investigaciones Científicas, 1965.
Lacarra, José María. "El Señorío de Vizcaya y el Reino de Navarra en el siglo XII." In *Edad Media y Señoríos: El Señorío de Vizcaya.* Imprenta Provincial de Vizcaya, 1972.
Lacarra, José María. "Las villas navarras y la colonización urbana." In *Las formas del poblamiento en el Señorío de Vizcaya durante la Edad Media.* Real Sociedad Vascongada de los Amigos del País and Junta de Cultura de Vizcaya, 1975.
Laffite, Alfredo. *Tierra Euskara. Excursiones, cuadros, y notas de Guipúzcoa.* Tolosa, 1886.
Lafourcade, Maïté. "L'autonomie administrative du Pays Basque de France sous l'Ancien Regime." *JADO* 19 (2010): 111–39.
Lakarra, Joseba. "La Prehistoria de la Lengua Vasca." In *Historia de la Lengua Vasca*, edited by Joaquín Gorrochategui, Iván Igartua and Joseba Lakarra. Eusko Jaurlaritza, 2018.
Laliena, Carlos. *Siervos medievales de Aragón y Navarra en los siglos XI-XIII.* Universidad de Zaragoza, 2012.
Lamikiz, Xabier. "La matxinada de 1718 y su trasfondo socioeconómico." In *Una década prodigiosa. Beligerancia y negociación entre la corona y las provincias vascas (1717-1728)*, edited by Álvaro Aragón and Alberto Angulo. Universidad del País Vasco, 2019.
Lancis y Buch, Lamberto. *Guía general de Guipúzcoa histórico-geográfico-descriptiva, comercial é industrial.* Donostia-San Sebastián, 1896.
Landazuri, Joaquín José. *Suplemento a los Quatro Tomos de la Historia de la M.N. y M. L. Provincia de Alava.* Vitoria-Gasteiz, 1799.
Larramendi, Manuel. *Corografía o descripción general de la muy noble y muy leal Provincia de Guipúzcoa.* Barcelona, 1882.
Larramendi, Manuel. *El imposible vencido. Arte de la lengua bascongada.* Pio Zuazua, 1853.
Larramendi, Manuel. *Sobre los fueros de Guipuzcoa. Conferencias curiosas, políticas, legales y morales sobre los fueros de la M.N. y M.L. Provincia de Guipuzcoa.* Edited by José Tellechea. Donostiako Aurrezki Kutxa Munizipalaren Kultur Ekintza, 1983.
Larrañaga, Koldo. *El Hecho Colonial Romano en el Área Circumpirenaica Occidental.* Universidad del País Vasco, 2007.
Larrañaga, Koldo. "Proceso cristianizador y pervivencia de rituales paganos en el País Vasco en la Tarda antigüedad y Alta Edad Media." *Hispania Sacra* 51, no. 104 (1999): 613–21.
Larrañaga, Miguel. *Campesinado y conflictividad social en la Navarra bajomedieval.* Universidad SEK, 2005.
Larrea, Juan José. "El reinado de García de Nájera, entre el viejo y el nuevo orden: rey, barones e infanzones entre la monarquía isidoriana y la feudal." In *García Sánchez III 'el de Nájera' un rey y un reino en la Europa del siglo XI*, edited by José Ignacio de la Iglesia. Instituto de Estudios Riojanos, 2005.
Larrea, Juan José. "La herencia vasca: acción política y arquitectura social en Vizcaya y Álava antes de su incorporación al reino de Alfonso VI." In *Alfonso VI y su época. Los precedentes del reinado (966-1065)*, edited by E. Fernández and J. Pérez. Universidad de León, 2007.

Larrea, Juan José. *La Navarre du IVe au XIIe siècle: Peuplement et sociète*. De Boeck Université, 1998.
Larrinaga, Carlos. "A century of Tourism in Northern Spain: The Development of High-quality Provision between 1815 and 1914." In *Histories of Tourism*, edited by John Walton. Clevedon, 2005.
Ledesma, María Luisa, ed. *Cartulario de San Millán de la Cogolla (1076-1200)*. Anubar, 1989.
Leizarraga, Joanes. *Iesus Christ Gure Iaunaren Testamentu Berria*. La Rochelle, 1571.
Lema, José Ángel. "'Por los procuradores de los escuderos hijosdalgo': de la Hermandad general a la formación de las juntas de la provincia de Guipúzcoa (siglos XIV-XVI)." In *El triunfo de las élites urbanas guipuzcoanas. Nuevos textos para el estudio del gobierno de las villas y de la Provincia (1412-1539)*, edited by José Ángel Lema et al. Diputación Foral de Guipúzcoa, 2002.
Lema, José Ángel. "Un obscuro pasado: Gipuzkoa y Navarra (siglos X-XII)." In *Los fueros de Estella y San Sebastián*, edited by Xabier Irujo and Amaia Álvarez. Fundación Iura Vasconiae, 2020.
Letteron, Maëlys. "Échanges transpyrénnéens dans les textes navarrais du Codex de Roda (VIIIe - Xe siècles)." In *Las fronteras pirenaicas en la Edad Media (siglos VI-XV) - Les frontières pyrénéennes au Moyen Âge (VIe-XVe siècles)*, edited by Gasc, Sébastien, Philippe Sénac, Clément Venco and Carlos Laliena. Universidad de Zaragoza, 2018.
Llorente, Juan Antonio. *Noticias históricas de las tres provincias vascongadas*. Madrid, 1807.
Lobera, Gotzon, ed. "Discurso de Ramón de la Sota y Aburto en su designación como presidente de la Diputación foral de Bizkaia, el día 4 de mayo de 1917." Available in: https://dialnet.unirioja.es/descarga/articulo/6361327.pdf (accessed August 20, 2025).
López, José Eduardo. *Crónica Mozárabe de 754. Edición Crítica y traducción*. Anubar, 1980.
López, Santiago. "'Non placet Hispania'. Los orígenes de la leyenda negra." In *España ante sus críticos: las claves de la leyenda negra*, edited by Yolanda Rodríguez, Antonio Sánchez, Harm den Boer and Santiago López. Iberoamericana, 2015.
López de Ayala, Pedro. *Crónicas de los Reyes de Castilla Don Pedro, Don Enrique II, Don Juan I, Don Enrique III con las enmiendas del Secretario Geronimo Zurita y las correcciones y notas añadidas por Don Eugenio de Llaguno Amirola*. Madrid, 1779.
Lorenzo, Jesús. *La Dawla de los Banu Qasi. Origen, auge y caída de una dinastía muladí en la frontera superior de Al-Andalus*. Consejo Superior de Investigaciones Científicas, 2010.
Lorenzo, Jesús. *La Vasconia peninsular en las fuentes árabes (años 711-929)*. Euskaltzaindia, 2018.
Lorenzo, Jesús, and Ernesto Pastor. "Al-Andalus ¿en la periferia de Vasconia?: Sistemas de dominación de bilad Banbaluna y de Alaba wa-l-Qila en la octava centuria." In *Vasconia en la Alta Edad Media 450-1000: Poderes y comunidades rurales en el Norte Peninsular*, edited by Juan Antonio Quirós. Universidad del País Vasco, 2011.
Luengo, Félix, and Ander Delgado, "El árbol de Gernika. Vicisitudes del símbolo foral de los vascos." *Historia y Política: Ideas, procesos y movimientos sociales* 15 (2006): 23–44.
Madariaga, Juan. *Anthology of Apologists and Detractors of the Basque Language*. University of Nevada, 2006.
Majuelo, Emilio. *La idea de la historia en Arturo Campión*. Txalaparta, 2015.
Mañaricua, Andrés. *Historiografía de Vizcaya. Desde Lope García de Salazar a Labayru*. Universidad de Deusto, 2012.
Mañaricua, Andrés. *Polémica sobre Vizcaya en el siglo XVII: El búho gallego y El tordo vizcaíno*. La Gran Enciclopedia Vasca, 1976.
Mañaricua, Andrés. *Vizcaya, siglos VIII al XI: los orígenes del Señorío*. Caja de Ahorros Vizcaína, 1984.
Marín, José Antonio. *"Semejante Pariente Mayor". Parentesco, solar, comunidad y linaje en la institución de un pariente Mayor en Gipuzkoa: los señores del solar de Oñaz y Loyola (siglos XIV-XVI)*. Diputación Foral de Gipuzkoa, 1998.

Marín, José Antonio. "¿Qué es un Pariente Mayor? El ejemplo de los señores de Oñaz y Loyola." In *La lucha de bandos en el País Vasco: de los Parientes Mayores a la Hidalguía Universal. Guipúzcoa, de los bandos a la Provincia (siglos XIV a XVI)*, edited by José Ramón Díaz de Durana. Universidad del País Vasco, 1998.

Martín, Ángel, ed. *Documentación medieval de Leire (siglos IX a XII)*. Diputación Foral de Navarra, 1983.

Martín, Ángel. *Sancho III el Mayor de Pamplona. El rey y su reino (1004-1035)*. Gobierno de Navarra, 2007.

Martín, Ángel. "Vasconia en la Alta Edad Media. Somera aproximación histórica." *Revista Internacional de Estudios Vascos* 44 (1999): 871–908.

Martínez, Antxoka, Mikel Argandoña, and Pedro Argandoña. "El campamento romano (castra aestiva) de Gazólaz (Navarra)." *Munibe* 70 (2014): 251–70.

Martínez, Carlos. *Casa, Provincia, Rey. Para una historia de la cultura del poder en el País Vasco*. Alberdania, 1993.

Martínez, Gonzalo. *El condado de Castilla (711-1038). La historia frente a la leyenda*. Junta de Castilla y León and Marcial Pons Historia, 2005.

Martínez, Gonzalo. "Poblamiento y Ordenamiento Jurídico en el País Vasco. El Estatuto Jurídico de la población rural y urbana." In *Las formas del poblamiento en el Señorío de Vizcaya durante la Edad Media*. Real Sociedad Vascongada de los Amigos del País and Junta de Cultura de Vizcaya, 1975.

Martínez, Gonzalo. *Sancho III el Mayor. Rey de Pamplona, Rex Ibericus*. Marcial Pons, 2007.

Martínez, Joaquín, ed. *The Story of Wamba: Julian of Toledo's* Historia Wambae regis. The Catholic University of America Press, 2005.

Martínez de Isasti, Lope. *Compendio Historial de Guipúzcoa*. La Gran Enciclopedia Vasca, 1972.

Martínez de Zaldibia, Juan. *Suma de las cosas cantábricas y guipuzcoanas*. Diputación de Gipuzkoa, 1945.

Mees, Ludger. *The Basque Contention: ethnicity, politics, violence*. Routledge, 2020.

Méndez, Ricardo. "El fraude en la Casa de Moneda de Potosí. Otro episodio de la lucha entre vicuñas y vascongados por la preeminencia local." *Red Sociales, Revista del Departamento de Ciencias Sociales* 8, no. 1 (2021): 89–107.

Minguito, Ana. "Los Guevara (siglo VIII-siglo XVI). Morir antes que ser deshonrado: proceso de consolidación de un linaje en su paso de la Edad Media a la Edad Moderna." *Hidalguía* 386 (2021): 13–40.

Miranda, Fermín. "Sacralización de la guerra en el siglo X. La perspectiva pamplonesa." *Anales de la Universidad de Alicante. Historia medieval* 17 (2011): 225–43.

Molina, Fernando. "Delenda est Carthago? La nación española y los fueros vascos (1868-1898)." In *El País Vasco y España: Identidades, nacionalismos y Estado (Siglos XIX y XX)*, edited by Luis Castells, Arturo Cajal, and Fernando Molina. Universidad del País Vasco, 2007.

Monreal, Gregorio. *Fuentes del Derecho Histórico de Bizkaia*. Agencia Estatal Boletín Oficial del Estado, 2021.

Monreal, Gregorio. "La ley abolitoria de fueros de 21 de julio de 1876 (antecedentes y paso por el congreso)." *Iura Vasconiae* 10 (2013): 39–192.

Monreal, Gregorio. *The Old Law of Bizkaia (1452). Introductory study and critical edition*. Center for Basque Studies, 2005.

Monreal, Gregorio, and Roldán Jimeno, eds. *Textos Histórico-Jurídicos Navarros I: Historia Antigua y Medieval*. Gobierno de Navarra, 2008.

Monteano, Peio. *La ira de Dios. Los navarros en la Era de la Peste (1348-1723)*. Pamiela, 2002.

Morales, Ambrosio. *Coronica General de España*. Madrid, 1791.

Moret, José. *Annales del Reyno de Navarra*. Pamplona, 1766.

Mounole, Céline, and Joseba Lakarra, "El Euskera arcaico." In *Historia de la Lengua Vasca*, edited by Joaquín Gorrochategui, Iván Igartua and Joseba Lakarra. Eusko Jaurlaritza, 2018.
Munibe, Xabier María. "Discurso preliminar. Leído en la primera Junta General Preparatoria de la Sociedad, celebrada en Vergara el día 7 de febrero de 1765." In *Ensayo de la Sociedad Bascongada de los Amigos del Pais. Año 1766. Dedicado al Rey N. Señor*. Vitoria-Gasteiz, 1768.
Navarro, Francisco. *Amaya o los vascos en el siglo VIII*, I-III. Administración el apostolado de la prensa, 1914.
Noble, Thomas, ed. *Charlemagne and Louis the Pious: the lives of Einhard, Notker, Ermoldus, Thegan, and the Astronomer*. Pennsylvania State University Press, 2009.
Observaciones sobre la necesidad de examinar el régimen administrativo de las Provincias Vascongadas para fallar con acierto en esta materia. Madrid, 1834.
Oihenart, Arnauld. *Notitia utriusque Vasconiae tum Ibericae, tum Aquitanicae*. Paris, 1688.
Ojeda, Juan de la Cruz. "El Señorío de Ayala durante el reinado de Alfonso XI." PhD Diss., Pontificia Universidad Católica Argentina, 2007.
Orella, José Luis. "El control de los judíos, conversos y extranjeros en Guipúzcoa durante el siglo XIV y la afirmación de la hidalguía vasca." *Sancho el Sabio* 4 (1994): 105–48.
Orella, José Luis. "La gasconización medieval occidental del Reino de Navarra." *Lurralde* 33 (2010): 177–208.
Orella, José Luis. "Relaciones medievales entre Gascuña y Guipúzcoa: la diócesis de Pamplona y de Bayona." *Azkoaga* 11 (2001): 93–212.
Orella, José Luis. "Territorio y sociedad en la Gipuzkoa medieval: Los parientes mayores." *Lurralde* 36 (2013): 67–119.
Orosius, Paulus. *Seven Books of History against the Pagans*. Translated by A.T. Fear. Liverpool University Press, 2010.
Ortiz de Urbina, Carlos. *La génesis de la identidad histórica alavesa*. Círculo Vitoriano, 2007.
Otazu, Alfonso. *La burguesía revolucionaria vasca a fines del siglo XVIII*. Txertoa, 1982.
Pavón, Julia. *Poblamiento altomedieval navarro. Base socioeconómica del espacio monárquico*. Universidad de Navarra, 2001.
Pavón, Julia. "Pompaelo y su distrito durante la etapa hispano-goda (siglos V-VII)." *Anuario de Estudios Medievales* 30, no. 1 (2000): 3–17.
Pelat, Mathieu. "Les identifications ethniques en Novempopulanie, Wasconie et Aquitaine dans l'Antiquité tardive et au haut Moyen Age (IIIe-IXe siècle)." *Travaux & documents: Journées de l'Antiquité et des temps anciens* 51 (2017): 191–212.
Pelat, Mathieu. "Les identités ethniques en Novempopulanie, Wasconie et Aquitaine dans l'Antiquité tardive et haut Moyen âge (IIIe-IXe siècle)." Master's Thesis, Université de Pau et des Pays de l'Adour, 2016.
Pérez, Fernando. "El ejemplar regio de un libro real." In *Joanes Leizarraga. Vida y Obra*. Caja de Ahorros y Monte de Piedad de Navarra, 2007.
Pérez de Laborda, Alberto. "La inmigración en Bilbao, 1860-1910." *Bidebarrieta* 13 (2003): 149–68.
Pescador, Aitor. "Tenentes y tenencias del Reino de Pamplona en Álava, Vizcaya, Guipúzcoa, La Rioja y Castilla (1004-1076)." *Vasconia* 29 (1999): 107–44.
Pina, Francisco. "Sertorio, Pompeyo y el supuesto alineamiento de los Vascones con Roma." In *Los Vascones de las fuentes antiguas: en torno a una etnia de la Antigüedad peninsular*, edited by Javier Andreu. Universitat de Barcelona, 2009.
Placer, Félix. *La religión en Euskal Herria*. Txalaparta, 2010.
Planté, Adrien. *San Sebastian. Notes de Voyage*. Pau, 1886.
Poetae Saxonis Annalium de Gestis Caroli Magni Imperatoris Libri Quinque. Hannover, 1826.
Polverel, M. *Tableau de la Constitution du Royaume de Navarre et des ses rapports avec la France*. Paris, 1789.

Pontet, Josette. *Histoire de Bayonne.* Toulouse: Privat, 1991.
Porres, Rosario. "Las contribuciones vascas a la hacienda real en la Edad Moderna: algunos contrastes provinciales." *Obradoiro de Historia Moderna* 19 (2010): 87–124.
Porres, Rosario. "Los medios y miedos humanos." In *Historia del País Vasco. Edad Moderna (siglos XVI-XVIII)*, edited by Alberto Angulo, Rosario Porres and Iñaki Reguera. Hiria, 2004.
Poza, Andrés. *De la Antigua lengua, poblaciones y comarcas de las Españas, en que de paso se tocan algunas cosas de la Cantabria.* Bilbao, 1587.
Poza, Andrés. *Fuero de hidalguía Ad pragmaticas de Toro & Tordesillas.* Edited by Carmen Muñoz. Universidad del País Vasco, 1997.
Pozo, Mikel. "Vasconia y los vascones de la crisis del imperio romano a la llegada del Islam (siglos V-VIII): Evolución sociopolítica y génesis de la gens effera." PhD Diss., Universidad del País Vasco, 2016.
Pozo, Mikel. *Vasconia tardoantigua. Entre la evolución sociopolítica y la construcción intelectual (400-711).* Consejo Superior de Investigaciones Científicas, 2022.
Prieto, José Ramón. "Las leyendas de los Señores de Vizcaya y la tradición melusiniana." PhD Diss., Universidad Complutense de Madrid, 2002.
Real Academia de la Historia. *Diccionario Geográfico-Histórico de España. Sección I, II.* Madrid, 1802.
Reguera, Iñaki. "El mundo del ocio." In *Historia del País Vasco. Edad Moderna (siglos XVI-XVIII)*, edited by Alberto Angulo, Rosario Porres and Iñaki Reguera. Hiria, 2004.
Rezusta, Benigno. *Apuntes sobre la historia de la revolución en Guipúzcoa.* Tolosa, 1872.
Risco, Manuel, ed. *España sagrada. Tomo XL: antigüedades de la ciudad y Sta. Iglesia de Lugo.* Madrid, 1796.
Ritter, Raymond. "Jeanne d'Albret et la Réforme chez les Basques." In *VIIème Congrès d'Etudes Basques (7. 1948. Biarritz).* Eusko Ikaskuntza, 2003.
Roldán, José María, ed. *Colección Diplomática el Archivo Municipal de Tolosa (1256-1407).* Eusko Ikaskuntza, 1991.
Rosell, Cayetano. *Crónicas de los reyes de Castilla, vol. 3.* Madrid, 1878.
Rubio, Coro. *La identidad vasca en el siglo XIX. Discursos y agentes sociales.* Biblioteca Nueva, 2003.
Rubio, Coro. "Prensa política regionalista en el siglo XIX: El diario fuerista la Unión Vasco-Navarra (1880-1894)." *Memoria y Civilización* 27, no.2 (2024): 371–403.
Salaberri, Patxi. "El Euskera en la Edad Media." In *Historia de la Lengua Vasca*, edited by Joaquín Gorrochategui, Iván Igartua and Joseba Lakarra. Eusko Jaurlaritza, 2018.
Sanadon, Barthélemy. *Essai sur la noblesse des Basques, pour servir d'Introduction à l'Histoire générale de ces Peuples. Rédigé sur les Mémoires d'un Militaire Basque, par un Ami de la Nation.* Pau, 1785.
Sánchez, Ana. *La casa de Mendoza hasta el tercer duque del infantado (1350-1531). El ejercicio y alcance del poder señorial en la Castilla bajomedieval.* Palafox & Pezuela, 2001.
Sánchez, Karlos. "'Antes que los razonamientos llegan al corazón los sonidos': El folclore como medio de propaganda del primer nacionalismo vasco (1895-1939)." In *Discursos y prácticas musicales nacionalistas (1900-1970)*, edited by Pilar Ramos. Universidad de La Rioja, 2012.
Sánchez-Prieto, Juan María. "Constitución, fueros y democracia. Motivaciones, discursos y actitudes políticas con relación a la permanencia o abolición de los fueros vasco-navarros." *Iura Vasconiae* 9: 101–57.
Sarasti, Ignacio. *Memoria de la Revolución Francesa y de la Guerra de España por la parte de Navarra y Gipuzkoa en los años de 1793, 1794 y 1795.* Edited by José Ramón Cruz. Diputación Foral de Gipuzkoa, 1993.
Sarrailh, Fernando. *Vasconia.* Ediciones Norbait, 1962.

Sayas, Juan José. "Algunas consideraciones sobre la cristianización de los vascones." *Príncipe de Viana* 46, no. 174 (1985): 35–56.
Scholz, Bernard Walter, and Barbara Rogers, trans. *Carolingian Chronicles: Royal Frankish Annals and Nithard's Histories*. The University of Michigan Press, 1970.
Segura, Santiago. *Mil años de historia vasca a través de la literatura greco-latina: De Aníbal a Carlomagno*. Universidad de Deusto, 1997.
Serrano, Susana. "Paisaje e industria en el Bilbao del despegue (1860-1930)." *Historia Contemporánea* 24 (2002): 223–43.
Silvan, Leandro. *La vida y obra del Conde de Peñaflorida, fundador de la Real Sociedad Bascongada de Amigos del País*. Izarra, 1971.
Smith, Anthony. *Chosen Peoples. Sacred Sources of National Identity*. Oxford University Press, 2003.
Smith, Anthony. *The Ethnic Origin of Nations*. Blackwell, 1986.
Smith, Anthony. *Ethno-Symbolism and Nationalism: A Cultural Approach*. Routledge, 2009.
Soria, Lourdes. "La Hidalguía Universal." *Iura Vasconiae* 3 (2006): 283–316.
Storm, Eric. *Nationalism. A World History*. Princeton University Press, 2024.
Tellechea, José, ed. *La ilustración vasca. Cartas de Xavier María de Munibe, conde de Peñaflorida, a Pedro Jacinto de Álava*. Eusko Legebiltzarra, 1987.
Tena, Soledad. *La sociedad urbana en la Guipúzcoa costera medieval: San Sebastián, Rentería y Fuenterrabía (1200-1500)*. Instituto Dr. Camino, 1997.
Thompson, Henry John, trans. *Prudentius, II*. William Heinemann and Harvard University Press, 1953.
Ubieto, Antonio, ed. *Cartulario de San Juan de la Peña*. Anubar, 1962.
Ubieto, Antonio, ed. *Crónica de Alfonso III*. Anubar, 1971.
Ubieto, Antonio, ed. *Crónica Najerense*. Anubar, 1985.
Urgell, Blanca. "Primer Vasco Moderno." In *Historia de la Lengua Vasca*, edited by Joaquín Gorrochategui, Iván Igartua and Joseba Lakarra. Eusko Jaurlaritza, 2018.
Urteaga, Mertxe. "El puerto romano de Irun (Gipuzkoa)." *Mar exterior: el Occidente atlántico en época romana* (2003): 87–103.
Vázquez, Iñaki. "La cultura política aranista. Génesis y definición del nacionalismo vasco." *Revista Internacional de Ciencias Sociales y Humanidades SOCIOTAM* 19, no. 1 (2009): 197–223.
Villanueva, Jesús. "Francisco Calça y el mito de la libertad originaria de Cataluña." *Zurita* 69–70 (1994): 75–87.
Wade, Margaret. *Gascony, England's first colony, 1204-1453*. Hamish Hamilton, 1980.
Wood, Ian. *The Merovingian Kingdoms, 450-751*. Longman, 1994.
Woolf, Greg. *Tales of the Barbarians. Ethnography and Empire in the Roman West*. Wiley-Blackwell, 2011.
Wulff, Fernando. "Nacionalismo, Historia, Historia Antigua: Sabino Arana (1865-1903), la fundación del nacionalismo vasco y el uso del modelo historiográfico español." *Dialogues d'histoire ancienne* 26, no.-2 (2000): 183–211.
Wulff, Fernando. "Vascones, autoctonía, continuidad, lengua. Entre la historia y la historiografía." In *Los Vascones de las fuentes antiguas: en torno a una etnia de la Antigüedad peninsular*, edited by Javier Andreu. Universitat de Barcelona, 2009.
Yanguas y Miranda, ed. *Historia de la Conquista del Reino de Navarra por el Duque de Alba*. Pamplona, 1843.
Yoeli-Rimmer, Nettah. "Jewish Villains and Basque Heroes: Ethnic Identities and National Narratives in Francisco Navarro Villoslada's *Amaya, o Los Vascos Del Siglo VIII*." *Bulletin of Spanish Studies* 95, no. 7 (2018): 795–813.

Zabala, Mikel. “Las Juntas Generales de Bizkaia a principios de la Edad Moderna: desequilibrios y enfrentamientos anteriores a la concordia.” *Cuadernos de Historia Moderna* 30 (2005): 85–124.
Zabalo, Javier. “Una encuesta de 1349 sobre bandoleros navarros y guipuzcoanos.” *Príncipe de Viana* 232 (2004): 477–510.
Zabaltza, Xabier. *Mater Vasconia. Lenguas, fueros y discursos nacionales en los países vascos.* Hiria, 2005.
Zaragoza, Justo. *Castellanos y vascongados. Tratado breve de una disputa y diferencia que hubo entre dos amigos el uno castellano de Burgos y el otro vascongado en la villa de Potosí, reino del Perú.* Madrid, 1876.
Zurita, Gerónimo. *Cantabria. Descripción de sus verdaderos límites.* Universidad de Cantabria, 2000.

INDEX

Abando 285, 287–8, 295
Aitor (patriarch) 266, 269, 279, 292, 296
Alaba, see Alava
Al-Andalus 57, 63–5, 69, 72, 74–5, 78–80, 92, 98, 100, 128, 136, 306
Alani 29–30
Alaric, Gothic chief 35–9, 41, 46, 48
Alava xiii, xix, 110–11, 114, 117–18, 121–3, 129–30, 133, 149, 161–2, 186, 196, 206–7, 209, 217–18, 223, 232–3, 236, 238, 241, 245–6, 255, 261–3, 265, 267–70, 286, 296–8, 305–7, 309
  abolition of the *fuero* 272–4
  and *Hidalguía Universal* 190, 246
  incorporation to Castile 105–6, 110
  and the kingdom of Navarre 80, 82–4, 89–92, 98–102, 103, 113
  and Muslims and Asturians 70, 71–4, 76, 78
  as part of ancient Cantabria 198–9
  surrendering of local governance 123–5, 128, 131
Alfonso I 'the Battler', King of Aragon and Pamplona 101–4
Alfonso I, King of Asturias 69–70
Alfonso VIII, King of Castile 106–7, 114, 265
Alfonso XI, King of Castile 123–6, 128, 131
Alfonso XIII, King of Spain 281
Amaya (literature) 279–81, 285–6, 291, 295, 300
Antwerp 208–9, 226
Aquae Tarbelli 17
Aquitaine 22–3, 25, 31, 58–60, 81, 84
Aracaeli 32–3
Aragon 82–3, 89, 92–3, 100–4, 186, 194, 209, 233, 235, 238
Arana, Sabino xiii–xv, 281–2, 284–5, 287–99, 309
  and an independent Biscay 288–91, 296–7
  and *Euskera* 292
  as a nationalist 291–4
Arana, Santiago 282–3
Aranzazu, Virgin of 206–7
Arianism 39, 41, 44–5
Arriaga (Confraternity) 121–6, 129–31, 135, 147, 153, 156, 162
Arrigorriaga 157, 198
Arzallus, Xabier xv
Asturias, kingdom of 69–71, 72–6, 78–9, 98, 113, 186
Athletic Club 308
Ausonius 23–6, 40, 46
Autrigones 13, 18–19
Azcoitia 161, 181–2, 229, 231, 243–5
Azpeitia 152, 235

Bacaudae 32–3, 36–7, 45, 56, 127, 306
bandos 142, 146–7, 149–50, 155, 158–62, 184, 201–2, 208
Banu Qasi 65–6, 72–5, 78
Baroja, Pío 298
Bascles 109, 110, 118
Basques (*Euskera*-speakers in France) 215–16, 219, 225–6, 255–6, 266–7
Basse-Navarre, *see Ultrapuertos*
Basses-Pyrénées, Département des 257
Bayonne 116, 126, 130, 162, 189, 209, 229, 234, 239, 256, 282
Bearne 210–11, 214, 216, 217–19, 256–7
Bermeo 117, 149, 160, 235
Berones 9, 18–19
Biarritz 116, 189, 284
Bilbao 149, 155, 159–60, 200, 218–19, 226, 234–5, 243, 246, 260, 262–3, 270–72, 281–2, 285–8, 294–5, 308
  industrialization 282–5
Biscay xiii, xv, xix, 73, 78, 80, 82–4, 90–3, 98–102, 104–6, 110–11, 117–19, 133–4, 138, 142, 147–50, 158–60, 161–2, 183, 193, 200, 206, 208–9, 213, 218, 235–6, 241, 258, 260, 269, 281, 286–8, 298–9, 305–7, 309
  abolition of the *fuero* 272–4
  as different from Spain 288–91, 296–7
  dynastic union with Castile, 121–6, 128, 130–1
  fuero 155–8, 160, 182, 185–90, 193–8, 202, 233–4, 239, 261, 265, 267
  Hermandad 150, 155
  industrialization and population growth 283–5
  as part of ancient Cantabria 198–9
Biscay, Nation of the Coast of 208
Biscaynes, 207–8, 232, 241, *see also vascongado (identity)*
Bordeaux 57, 80, 109, 218, 222, 244
Brotherhood of the Seas 147
Brotherhood, *see Hermandad*
Butrón, Gómez González de 145–6

Index

Calagurris, *see* Calahorra
Calahorra 10, 12, 17, 21, 25, 62, 75, 91, 104
Campión, Arturo 287, 289, 290, 298, 306, 308
Cánovas del Castillo, Antonio 272
Cantabrians 8, 12, 42
  as forefathers of the Basques 198–200, 237, 239, 258, 261, 266, 268–9, 297, 299
Caracas, Guipuzcoan Company of 237–8, 249
Carlism 262–4, 265–7, 270–3, 282, 284–6, 288, 290, 295, 299, 305
Carolingians 58–61, 63–4, 66, 76, 78–80
Castile 74, 77, 80–2, 89, 91, 93, 97–8, 100–3, 110, 113–14, 117, 121–4, 126, 128, 129–31, 133, 135, 147, 151–2, 158, 160, 162, 186, 188, 194, 216, 233–4, 242, 247
  conquest of Navarre 209–13, 218
  incorporation to the kingdom of Pamplona 82–3
  incorporation of Western Pyrenean Provinces 103–6
  as opposed to Western Pyrenean provinces 241, 267, 287–8, 290
Catherine I, Queen of Navarre 210, 212
Chaho, Joseph Augustin 266–70, 273, 287, 289, 296
Charlemagne 53–5, 58–66, 83
Charles II, King of Castile and Aragon 229, 239
Charles III, King of Spain 245–6
Charles V, King of Castile and Holy Roman Emperor 211–13
Chelidonius 21–2
Christianity 19–21, 39, 44–7, 55, 58, 69, 72, 74–5, 77–84, 87, 97–9, 183, 216, 226, 279–80, 286, 295, 297
  early church in the Western Pyrenees 21–6
  in *foral* discourse 188, 259, 271, 299
  reformation 199, 213–15, 219–20
  and witchcraft 221–2, 225
Clovis, Frankish chief 35–7, 39, 41, 48, 58
Constantine III, 29–30
Cordoba 63–5, 72–6, 78–9
Covadonga 69–70, 270
cuisine xiii, 284
custom houses 234–6, 238, 259, 262, 264, 272

D'Abbadie, Antoine 269–70, 284, 308
De la Sota y Aburto, Ramón 298
De Lancre, Pierre 222–5
Díaz de Haro, María, Lady of Biscay 125, 130
Diocletian 20–1
Don Carlos, Carlist pretender 262–4, 271
Don Marcelo 100, 102
Durango 105–6, 149, 158, 205

EAJ-PNV (Basque Nationalist Party) xv, 294, 296–9
Ebro River 4–6, 10, 44, 55, 58–9, 64–6, 70, 75, 89, 91, 103–5, 110, 197
Echepare, Bernat de 216–19, 225, 256, 269, 305, 308
economic concerts 273
Edward, the Black Prince of England 128–9
Eleanor of Aquitaine 106, 109
Elorrio 135, 158
Emeterius 21–2
Enneco Arista, Pamplonese chief 64–6, 70, 72–5
Enrique II Trastámara, King of Castile 128–31, 133, 136, 139, 199
Enrique IV, King of Castile 152, 158–60
Espartero, Baldomero 264–5
Estella 112–13, 127
ETA (*Euskadi ta Askatasuna*) xii, 307
Euskadi xii, xix, 306
Euskal Herria xix, 215, 218, 226, 255, 257–8, 266, 269, 297, 306–8
Euskera xiii, xvi–xvii, 206, 208, 215–17, 219, 241, 258–9, 268–9, 306–9
  and Basque nationalism 282, 289, 292, 294, 298, 305
  diglossia 116, 201–2, 223, 225–6, 242, 248
  in *foral* discourse 196–7, 199, 256, 261
  Proto-Basque 61, 111
Euzkadi 291, 295–6, 298
exceptionalism xiv–xv, xvii, 9–11, 156, 238–40, 242, 245, 248, 257–9, 261, 264–7, 307–9

Ferdinand I, King of Castile and Leon 82–4, 89, 91–2
Ferdinand II, King of Aragon and 'Catholic King' 182, 210–12, 230
Ferdinand VI, King of Spain 232
Ferdinand VII, King of Spain 261–2
Flanders 114, 186, 189, 196, 208, 229, 231, 283
Flórez, Enrique 258–9, 261
Fortún One-eyed, Pamplonese chief 74
Fortunatus, Venantius 42–3, 46, 57
France xix, 36, 107, 114, 129, 136, 160, 162, 189, 207, 209–10, 213, 229–30, 236, 248, 259, 261, 263, 265–6, 269, 283
  reformation and witch-hunts 213, 219–20, 222–3
  revolution 255–7
Francia 35–40, 42–3, 45, 47, 54, 56–66
Francis I, King of France 213, 217
Franco, Francisco xii, 305–7, 309
Frankish bourgs 112–13, 115–17
Franks 35–44, 47–8, 53–64, 66, 69, 71–2, 75–6, 83, 109, 117
  kingdom of (*see Francia*)
Fruela, King of Asturias 70–2
Fuenterrabia 114, 134, 147, 162, 209, 257, 284
fuerism 265, 267, 269–71, 273, 281, 285–7

and Basque nationalism 287–90, 293–9
fuero (city charter) 110–15, 118, 121–3, 139–40, 148, 212
fuero of Biscay 155–8, 160, 182, 185–90, 193–8, 202, 233–4, 239, 261, 265, 267

García Ramírez, 'the Restorer', King of Pamplona 103
García, King of Pamplona 82–3, 88–92, 99, 103
Garibay, Esteban de 202
Gascon (speech) 115–16, 196, 217, 225, 256, 305
Gascony 64, 76, 109, 113, 162
Gasteiz 113
gentilitas 19, 22, 25
Godoy, Manuel 257–61
Goizueta, José María 267–9
Goths 30–1, 33, 35–7, 38, 194, 197, 279–81, 286, 288–9, 300
Gregory of Tours 43–7, 54, 57, 78
Guernica xii–xiii, 126, 128, 135, 156–7, 271
Guetaria 114, 116, 205
Guevara (family) 139–42, 145, 151, 160, 189
Guipuzcoa xiii, xv, xix, 94, 100–2, 104–5, 121–3, 131, 133–5, 139, 146, 152–3, 158–60, 162, 185–6, 189–90, 195, 197, 200, 206, 208–9, 217–19, 224, 229, 231–4, 237–9, 241–4, 245–6, 248–9, 255, 257–9, 261, 263, 267, 268–9, 288, 296–8, 305–7, 309
  abolition of the *fuero* 272–4
  first cities 113–15
  founded by God 240–1
  Hermandad 147–50, 151, 155, 161
  Hidalguía Universal 181–3, 187–8, 190, 193, 201–2, 207, 235–6
  incorporation to Castile 105–6, 110
  as part of ancient Cantabria 198–9
  tourism and its impact 284–5

Habsburgs 229–30, 233, 235, 238
Harbor of Peace 260
Haro (family) 101–2, 104, 106, 110, 114, 117, 122–3, 125–6, 128, 130–1, 135, 189, 297
Henry II, King of Navarre 211, 213, 216
Henry IV, King of Navarre and France
Hermandad 147–9, 150–2, 155, 157, 159, 161–2, 183–5, 189
Hermenegild 39–40, 44–5
Hernani 264
Hidalguía Universal 181–3, 186–7, 189–90, 193–4, 199–202, 208, 219, 235, 293
Hippocrates 7
Hispani Wascones 61
Hispania 5, 9, 12–13, 22–3, 25, 29, 30–1, 33, 35–7, 39–41, 44–6
Honorius 29–30

humanitas 8, 11, 13

Idiáquez (family) 202, 229–33, 236–8, 242–3
Idiáquez, Juan de, Duke of Granada de Ega 231, 233, 236–8, 242
ikurriña (Basque flag), xiii, 296
Inquisition 220, 223–5, 248, 260
Iparraguirre, José María 269
Iparralde ('the north') 267, 269, 297–8
iron 208–9, 247, 281, 283, 287
Isabella I, Queen of Castile 160, 230
Isabella II, Queen of Spain 262–5, 271
Isasti, Lope Martínez de 201
Isidore of Seville 45–7, 54, 57, 71, 78, 110, 195
iter XXXIV 29, 31–3, 47, 69
Izurun 113, 116

Jaun Zuria ('the White Lord') 157, 186, 265–6, 290, 299
Jaungoikoa eta Lagi Zarra (slogan) 296, 299, 307
Jeanne d'Albret, Queen of Navarre 213–15, 219
Juan II, King of Castile and Lord of Biscay 130–1
Juan III, King of Navarre 210, 212–13

Krutwig, Federico 305–7

Labourd xix, 162, 196, 215, 217–18, 222–5, 255–7, 306
Ladrón, Count of Alava 102–3
Larramendi, Manuel de 239–44, 248, 256, 260–2, 286–8, 290
Leizarraga, Joanes 215–17, 219, 225, 256, 305
Leniz, valley of 129, 133
Leon, kingdom of 77–84, 88–9, 91–2, 97–8, 100, 124, 147, 157, 186, 194, 198
Leovigild, King of the Visigoths 38–41, 44–5, 54–5, 71
Leyre, San Salvador of (monastery) 72, 74
Lizarrara 112–13
López de Haro, Diego 101–2, 104
López, Iñigo 90, 92–3, 99–101, 123
Louis the Pious, King of the Franks 63–4, 66
Louis XIV, King of France 229, 233
Louis XVI, King of France 255, 257
Loyola 193, 232, 236, 239
Lupo, Duke in Wasconia 58–60, 65

Madrid 232, 236, 238–9. 241–3, 245–6, 247–8, 259–60, 264–5, 270–2, 284, 286, 295
maketo 287–8, 291–3, 295
Margaret of Valois 213
Marquina 135, 161
mayorazgo 123, 201–2, 229, 240, 242, 243, 246, 248–9, 259–60, 262–3, 283
Mendoza (family) 129, 189, 247

Merovingians 36–7, 40–5, 47, 56–60, 82, 97
millares ('thousands') 201, 242, 248
modernism (nationalism) xvii, 309
Mondragón 133–5, 139–40, 143, 145–6, 149, 151–2, 155, 158, 160, 185
Motrico 114
Munguía 159–60
Munia of Castile 77, 80–2, 91, 94

nabarrus (or *navarrus*) 61, 109
Nájera 75, 101, 103–4
Narros, Marquis of 244–5, 249
Navarre xiii, xix, 105–7, 109–12, 118, 123, 127–8, 134–5, 149, 183, 189, 196, 206–7, 214, 217, 218, 224, 232–4, 238, 258–9, 263–4, 265, 267, 286–7, 289–90, 296, 298, 306–7
  Castilian conquest 209–13
  King of (title) 104
  medieval cities 112–13, 115
Navarreria 115
Navarro Villoslada, Francisco 280, 285, 288, 296, 299
Núñez de Lara, Juan, Lord of Biscay 126, 156

Oiasso 17
Oihenart, Arnauld 258
Olaso, Martin de 145–6
Oñate 134, 139–40, 142–3, 145, 205
Orendain, Juan Bautista de 237
Oyarzun 259

Pampilonenses 61
Pamplona 58–9, 61, 62–6, 220, 263, 287
  and Alava and Biscay 97–9
  conquest by Castile 210–11
  kingdom of 72–6, 78–84, 88–94, 103–6
  medieval bourgs 112–13, 115
  and Muslims 55–7
  in Roman times 4, 9–13, 17–18, 25
  survival in Late Antiquity 29, 33, 36–7, 40, 44
  and the Visigoths 47–8
Parientes Mayores 135–8, 145–8, 151–3, 155, 157–61, 189, 195, 224, 231
  in the *foral* era 161, 183, 185–8, 190, 199–202, 207–8, 217, 257–8
  ideology 141–3, 193, 197–8
  and their opponents 139–41, 148–51, 183–4, 189–90
Paulinus of Nola 23–6, 40, 109
Pedro I, King of Castile 128–31, 133, 142
Pedro Novia de Salcedo 280, 296
Pelayo, King of Asturias 69–70, 74, 270, 280
Peñaflorida, Count of (Xabier María de Munibe e Idiáquez) 243–6, 248–9, 258–60, 262, 298
Philip II, King of Castile and Aragon 202, 230
Philip V, King of Spain 229–33, 235–7, 240, 243, 249, 258–9
plague 127–8
Pompey the Great 4, 9–10, 13, 18, 40–1, 46, 79
possessores 31–3, 37, 56
Potosí 205–7, 226, 232
Poza, Andrés de 193
prejudice xv, xx, 7–8, 12–14, 24–6, 41–2, 46, 55, 60, 76, 111
Prudentius 21–6, 31, 40–1, 46, 91, 110

Ramiro, son of Sancho the Great 83, 89–93
Ramón, brother of Sancho of Peñalén 87–8, 93
Reccared, King of the Visigoths 44–6
Reformation (religion) 199, 213–15, 219–20
Ribagorza 80, 82–3
Rioja 75, 79, 82–3, 90, 93, 102, 104–5, 198, 208, 285
Rodrigo, King of the Visigoths 48, 54–6, 279–80
Roland, Chanson de 53, 59
romanitas 8, 12, 42
Rome xx, 20–2, 29–33, 79, 84, 111, 195, 198
  assimilation of provincial population 11–12, 17–19
  conquest of the Western Pyrenees 3–6, 9
  ethnography 7–8, 13, 24–5
  in *foral* discourse 198–9, 258
  imitators 37–8, 41–2, 43–4
Roncesvalles 53–5, 59–60, 63–4, 66, 266
Royal Congregation of Saint Ignace of Loyola 232, 236, 249

Saint Fermin 112
Saint Palais 214
Saint Saturnin (bourg) 112–13, 115
San Sebastian 105, 110–11, 113–16, 140, 209, 219–20, 234–5, 248, 257, 262–3, 270, 284
Sancho 'the Wise', King of Navarre 103–6, 110–11, 113, 209
Sancho Garcés I, King of Pamplona 74–5, 78–80, 88
Sancho Garcés III the Great, King of Pamplona 77, 80–4, 87–8, 90–1, 93–4, 98, 211
  inheritance 82–4
  titles 83
Sancho Guillaume, Duke in Wasconia 80–1
Sancho of Peñalén, King of Pamplona 87–9, 92–3, 99–100, 102
Sancho Ramírez 93–4
Sangüesa 112
Saragossa 31, 58, 101
Scott, Walter 267–8, 280
Segura 146
Seminar of Vergara 247–9, 260
Seville 181, 187, 207, 226, 231, 232, 238, 241, 246
Sobrarbe 80, 82–3
Sociedad Bascongada de Amigos del País 245–9

Sociedad Euskalerria 286, 288, 290, 295
Soule xix, 214–15, 217–20, 255–8, 266–8, 296, 306
Spain xii, xix, 222–3, 229, 231, 233, 238, 240, 249, 257, 259, 261–4, 265, 269, 272, 280
  and *Euskera* 197
  as a geographical concept 103, 138, 157, 212
  as opposed to Biscay 288–91, 296–7
  as opposed to the Basques 266, 299
  as a political concept 186, 194, 240
Strabo 8, 10, 17, 23–4, 40, 46, 109, 196, 265
Suevi 29–33, 38

Tamarón 83–4, 89, 91
Tarraconensis (Roman province) 29–31, 36
tenancy system 88–90, 92–3, 101–3, 105
Tierra Llana ('flatland') 150, 155–7, 190, 200
Toda, Queen of Pamplona 78, 80–1
Toledo 38–9, 41, 44, 48, 54–5, 62, 279
Tolosa 134, 183–4, 187, 194
Toulouse 31, 33, 35–6, 57, 112, 243
tourism 284
Tubal 195–200, 239–40, 258–9, 261, 266, 268, 294
Tubalism 195–200, 239–40, 266, 289, 297, 299
Tudela 63, 75, 104

Ultrapuertos xix, 211, 213, 216–18, 220, 225, 255–7, 296, 306
universal nobility, *see Hidalguía Universal*
urundiru ('flour money') 116

Valladolid 182, 190
Vandals 29–30
Vardulians 9, 13, 18–19
Vascones 4, 8–10, 12–14, 17–19, 55–7, 61, 71, 74, 76, 78–9, 82–4, 105, 111, 198, 216, 279, 310
  and paganism xiii, 22–4, 26
  revival of ethnonym in Late Antiquity 40–8
vascongado (identity) 196, 206–7, 215–16, 218–19, 232, 236, 238, 241–2, 245–7, 249, 256–9, 263–5, 267–71, 310
vascongado (speech), *see Euskera*
Vasconia xix, 23–4, 41, 45, 84, 271
Vela (family) 74, 81–4, 99–100, 102, 104, 110, 114, 129
Velasco, Pedro de, Count of Haro 158–60
Veleia 17, 29, 33, 69–70, 114
Vergara 246–8, 260
Vermudo III, King of Leon 81, 83–4
Vikings 73
Visigoths 37–41, 43–8, 54–7, 59, 62, 65, 69, 71, 74–5, 78–9, 82, 97, 185, 195, 198, 266, 279–80, 287
Vitoria 105–6, 110–11, 114, 121, 123–4, 130, 147, 152, 160, 162, 246, 262–3, 270
Vouillé 35–8, 48

Wasconia, duchy of 57–1, 63–6, 73, 76, 80–1, 83, 92, 94
Western Pyrenees xix–xx
witchcraft 220–5
Wordsworth, William xiii

Zaldibia, Juan Martínez de 198
Zugarramurdi 223, 225

www.ingramcontent.com/pod-product-compliance
Ingram Content Group UK Ltd.
Pitfield, Milton Keynes, MK11 3LW, UK
UKHW021921051026
476330UK00001B/76

9 781350 446175